Hellenistic Philosophy

Hellenistic Philosophy
Introductory Readings

Second Edition

Translated,
with Introduction and Notes,
by

Brad Inwood

and

L. P. Gerson

Hackett Publishing Company
Indianapolis/Cambridge

First edition copyright © 1988
by Brad Inwood and L. P. Gerson

Second edition copyright © 1997
by Brad Inwood and L. P. Gerson

Printed in the United States of America

21 20 19 18   5 6 7 8 9

For further information, please address

Hackett Publishing Company, Inc.
P.O. Box 44937
Indianapolis, Indiana 46244-0937

Cover design by Listenberger Design & Associates
Text design by Dan Kirklin

Library of Congress Cataloging-in-Publication Data

Hellenistic philosophy: introductory readings/translated, with
introduction and notes, by Brad Inwood and L. P. Gerson.—2d ed.
   p.   cm.
Includes bibliographical references and index.
ISBN 0-87220-379-4.   ISBN 0-87220-378-6 (pbk.)
1. Philosophy, Ancient.   I. Inwood, Brad.   II. Gerson, Lloyd P.
B505.H45   1997
180—dc21   97-26796
                                                                CIP
   ISBN-13: 978-0-87220-379-2 (cloth)
   ISBN-13: 978-0-87220-378-5 (pbk.)

To Our Students

Contents

Preface to the Second Edition

This revised and expanded edition gives us the opportunity to provide a more generous selection of texts than we were able to include in the first edition. The expansion and consolidation of Epicurean material in part I corresponds to the selections in *The Epicurus Reader*. The additional material in part II includes the first English translation of the doxography of Stoic ethics attributed to Arius Didymus which is preserved in the works of John Stobaeus; substantial additional material from Plutarch, Galen, and Seneca is also found in part II. Part III contains a comparably expanded selection of texts. The addition of this material and some slight rearrangements have necessitated a complete renumbering of the selections. We are grateful to Rodney Ast for his careful work on the adaptation of the General Index.

We would like to thank Oxford University Press for their permission to include here several translations first published in Brad Inwood's *Ethics and Human Action* (Oxford 1985).

Preface to the
First Edition

This work began as a series of texts produced for use in undergraduate survey courses in Greek philosophy at the University of Toronto. The authors had for many years been keenly aware of the limitations of existing translations of the works of the Hellenistic philosophers. We began with limited and sporadic efforts to remedy the situation by producing bits and pieces of translation. It gradually became clear that a more permanent and comprehensive solution was required. Hence the present work, which consists of completely new translations of much more material. We feel that the additional material will make the book useful to more advanced students, as well as to its original audience. We have aimed throughout to provide sufficient material to enable the reader at whatever level to acquire a good grasp of the main lines of thought in Hellenistic philosophy. We have also attempted to provide a bridge to the growing mass of excellent secondary literature. A student acquainted with the material in this book should be able to appreciate some of the first-rate contemporary philosophy being done by scholars working on Stoicism, Epicureanism, and Scepticism.

In deciding what material to include we have been especially concerned to convey a sense of ongoing discussion among the Hellenistic philosophers, a sense which will be most strongly felt with the Stoics and Sceptics. In addition, we have made a special effort to provide longer passages of unexcerpted original sources, rather than short and more thematically focussed texts. We hope that extended texts will be more readable, will give a clearer sense of the major philosophical movements in this period, and will provide the student with an appreciation for the nature of the evidence for what is, after all, a relatively badly documented period of Greek philosophy.

There is at once too much and too little in this book. There is too much in the sense that we have sometimes allowed our authors to speak beyond the minimum necessary to make a point. We have also not been very scrupulous about avoiding repetition of arguments, especially when this makes an entire passage clearer. An instructor using this book as a textbook will no doubt wish to make judicious selections of material. It is of course very likely that not everyone's favorite texts are included. We are, however, confident that there is enough material to meet the needs of most courses.

There is too little in this book in the sense that we have excluded authors, such as Panaetius and Posidonius, who certainly deserve serious attention. If the label 'Hellenistic philosophy' is to be of much use it should refer primarily to an historical period, in which case, Theophrastus, some later Peripatetics, and many others might have been included. In a sense there is also too much material from a later period which is, strictly speaking, post-Hellenistic; Sextus Empiricus (the main spokesman for Pyrrhonian scepticism) should not be as fully represented as he is, since he represents a philosophical movement which began just as the Hellenistic period proper was drawing to a close and in many respects bears the imprint of the rather different approach taken to philosophy in the Imperial period. But Sextus's importance to later philosophy is so great, and his connection to earlier, strictly Hellenistic, philosophy so close, that to curtail his role in this book was unthinkable.

In translating the fragments and reports of the teachings of the Hellenistic philosophers we were faced with some especially vexing problems. First, although there is a common conceptual ground for most of the argumentation in the texts, they were written over a period of some eight hundred years and in two languages, Greek and Latin. Languages change and the meanings of words change as well. This fact makes consistent translation a somewhat delicate matter. The highly technical nature of much of the vocabulary of Hellenistic philosophy also presents problems for the translator; we face neither the literary and therefore relatively straightforward language of Plato, nor the familiar jargon of the Aristotelian school, but rather, we face new and unfamiliar terminology at every turn; it was the genius of the Greek language that it lent itself to creative neologism, and so facilitated the kind of linguistic innovation to which philosophers have always been prone. But this very flexibility produced turns of phrase which are sometimes bizarre and rebarbative in Greek and which have had to remain so in English.

Second, precisely because the common conceptual ground of Hellenistic philosophy is so frequently charged with hostility, one author may well interpret the argument of his opponent according to a legitimate, although altered, sense of a term. We have made an effort to be consistent in translation in the three main sections of the book where this is crucial. Where it is not, we have tried to be true to the immediate context.

We have used what we judge to be the best available editions of the texts and have not troubled the reader with textual minutiae except where this is essential or where we[1] propose new solutions to long-standing problems. Material added by editors to the text of the ancient authors in order to restore it to its original state is placed inside pointed brackets. Square brackets are used for short explanatory notes, and to make explicit what is only implicit in the actual text, and to indicate interpretive material which goes beyond the bounds of a normally literal translation. This device is employed in part for the convenience of the reader and in part as a compensation for the limitations of the translators. Rounded brackets are used as ordinary punctuation devices.

We have included notes only where necessary to explain an otherwise unintelligible allusion or reference. The glossary is intended to supply quick access to definitions of key technical terms. In keeping with the introductory nature of this text, we have provided no commentary on the philosophical meaning of the material we translate and, in the introduction, only the briefest overview of the period. Students will of course need more help with the problems raised. The best source of this is, we believe, A. A. Long's excellent overview of the period, *Hellenistic Philosophy: Stoics, Epicureans, Sceptics* (second edition, University of California Press, 1986), which contains an up-to-date bibliography of further readings.

It remains for us to acknowledge the considerable help given to us by a number of our friends and colleagues. Arthur Madigan S.J., John Rist, Gary Rubinstein and others have all made valuable suggestions regarding appropriate material and the translations. As reader for the Press, Michael Frede examined with great care a longer version of this book; we are grateful for his thoroughness and efficiency, which have contributed immeasurably to the accuracy and readability of our translations. A great debt is also owed to our colleague Doug Hutchinson, who not only read an entire draft and made many acute suggestions, but undertook to scour the back alleys of antiquity in search of relevant and illuminating texts. He is also responsible for the index, an awe-inspiring task, which he voluntarily and vigorously accepted. In closing, we should note that even such generous help from so many hands has not saved us from the inevitable errors, omissions and inelegant phrasing which remain.

---

1. Or just as often, Hackett's reader, Michael Frede. We are grateful for his generous assistance with several very difficult texts.

Introduction

The challenge of Hellenistic philosophy, which is at the same time its principal attraction, is the balance in it between continuity and change. The accomplishments of the Pre-Socratic period of Greek thought and the towering achievements of the fourth century (as seen in the work of Plato and Aristotle) were never far from the concerns of the main Hellenistic thinkers. Time after time we find inescapable evidence that Epicurus, Zeno, and others worked on problems set by their predecessors, and found their conceptual tools in the ideas of earlier philosophers. Yet the novelty of the period is undeniable. After the eloquent explorations of idealism by Plato and the exacting revision of his thought by Aristotle, the Hellenistic thinkers struck out on a new path. The most efficient way of outlining this balance between continuity and change is perhaps to resort to that traditional crutch for the history of philosophy, -isms.

It is always dangerous to systemize philosophical ideas by grouping them under general and therefore misleading headings. It tells us little about the richness of Plato's thought, for example, to describe it as a form of idealism; it is certainly no substitute for close study of the living argument that makes his theory of Forms what it is. But such generalizations do have a role to play in orienting the student to new material. Taking our lead, then, from the systematic tendencies of the Hellenistic period itself, let us suggest that three -isms best define the continuity and novelty of the period: materialism, empiricism and naturalism.

These headings correspond to the three divisions of philosophy that became standard in the Hellenistic world, physics, logic and ethics. It was the Academic Xenocrates who first claimed that this tripartite division best described the structure of philosophy; the traditional grouping of Aristotle's works into the Organon, Physical works, Metaphysics and Ethical/Political philosophy (with practical subjects such as poetics and rhetoric as a kind of appendix) owes as much to the systematic thrust of his own work as it does to the tendencies of the Hellenistic Peripatetics who organized the corpus as we now have it. The Stoics followed the Xenocratean division exactly. The Epicureans eliminated logic in favour of something they called 'canonic' (the study of sense-perception and scientific method), which they subordinated to physics; but later tradition forced their breakdown into the standard threefold division, as it did

Aristotle's. The sceptics, both Academic and Pyrrhonian, did not, of course, advance their own doctrines, so a division of philosophy does not play a positive role in their work; but in criticizing nonsceptics, whom they called 'dogmatists' (which means something like 'those who hold definite beliefs'), they naturally followed the organizational scheme of their opponents. The result, then, is that virtually all of Hellenistic philosophy can be usefully broken down into logic (including epistemology and the study of investigative method), physics (including what Aristotelians called metaphysics), and ethics (a grouping broad enough to include all of the so-called 'practical sciences', especially politics).

To return to the three -isms. The most evident general tendency in Hellenistic physics is materialism, the rejection in one form or another of the belief in incorporeal entities. This rejection is, of course, not absolute; Epicureans maintained the existence of void; the Stoics found that they needed four kinds of incorporeal entity: void, place, time and 'things said' or *lekta*[2] (singular *lekton*), a novel kind of incorporeal indispensable for their philosophy of mind, their theory of language and their analysis of causality. This proliferation of incorporeals might seem to make 'materialism' a poor catch-phrase for orienting the student to Hellenistic physics and metaphysics, but that impression is misleading, if only because the Stoics were always careful to stipulate that only corporeal things *exist*, and that incorporeals, although they 'subsist', are not 'existent' things in the strict sense of the word.

Moreover, on the crucial issues both the Stoics and the Epicureans set themselves deliberately and consciously against what they took to be the views of Plato and Aristotle. The prime candidates for incorporeal status in the fourth century were forms (in Plato's and perhaps in Aristotle's theory), Aristotle's Unmoved Mover(s), and the soul (or mind); it is primarily because they reject the immateriality of these entities that the Hellenistic schools earn the label 'materialists'.

Aristotle's commitment to 'dualism' is highly controversial; both authors of the present work hold that there is a sense in which for Aristotle the form of an individual thing and, therefore, soul too are incorporeal, although not separately existing entities.[3] And no matter what one's view of the character of soul in general, it is clear that in a human soul the active intellect is incorporeal in the clearest sense. Moreover, the paradigm instance of a substance for Aristotle was the Unmoved Mover, i.e., a

---

2. Traditionally but misleadingly translated as 'meanings' or something similar. Long and Sedley have recently coined the term 'sayable' for this difficult bit of Stoic jargon.

3. Some scholars doubt this; but for present purposes it need only be accepted that this view of Aristotle as a kind of deviant Platonist was plausible in the Hellenistic period.

being which is pure form, by which he meant a form with no admixture of matter whatsoever. Because substance in the sense of form was central to Aristotle's theory of causal explanation (in that all four causes are focussed on form) and to his metaphysics (in that the primary sense of being was held to be a separate immaterial form, i.e., god or the Unmoved Mover), a rejection of his doctrine of substance would entail the complete abandonment of Aristotelian theoretical philosophy. The Epicureans and Stoics clearly believed that a refutation of Aristotle's doctrines of causal explanation and substance was inescapable.

The Epicureans and Stoics firmly and hard-headedly rejected incorporeal status for forms and for the soul. Direct evidence for rejection of the Unmoved Mover is less abundant, but this is almost certainly a result of the general rejection of the theory even among Aristotle's own followers. Throughout the course of later Greek philosophy a philosopher's stance on the incorporeality of forms and the soul served as a doctrinal litmus test. Hence the thorough-going rejection of the incorporeal soul and non-material forms by these schools is a clear mark of their 'materialism' in the present sense.

This much, then, is novel with respect to Plato and Aristotle, though the Epicureans and Stoics certainly had many predecessors who were materialists in some sense. What distinguishes them from their predecessors is, we think, the care with which they seem to have defended the position against the anti-materialist arguments of Plato and Aristotle.

The empiricism of the Hellenistic schools is more complex. Certainly it stands in sharp contrast to the epistemological stance of Plato; but equally clearly it is a development of Aristotle's own rather tentative empiricism. Aristotle believed, in the words of the scholastic tag, that there was nothing in the mind which was not previously in the senses; but he also held that his empiricist account of concept formation was incomplete without a final stage required to render inductively derived concepts sufficiently certain that they could serve as the basic principles of the sciences. This reasonable belief, which shows a keen awareness of the limitations of empirical procedures in grounding stable and irrefutable knowledge, was rejected by the Hellenistic schools. Their empiricism, consequently, is more thorough-going and also more vulnerable to sceptical attack. It is tempting to see one stimulus for the rise of scepticism in the rigour of Hellenistic empiricism.

In ethics the continuity of Hellenistic thought with Plato and Aristotle is even more impressive. For here the key word is 'naturalism', which represents the belief that a true conception of the good life for man must be based on a clear and accurate conception of the nature of man. This belief we take to have been the implicit position of pre-philosophical

Greek ethics; it was given clear expression by Plato and Aristotle. There is always a close correlation in Greek thought between the view taken of the human soul and its natural function and the excellence of that soul's activity. Both the Epicureans and the Stoics retained this belief, and indeed supported it with much more explicit argument and theorizing.

The views of the Hellenistic philosophical schools on the nature of the human soul mark one more very important point of contrast to those of Plato and Aristotle. And if we may dare one more -ism, let us label this belief the Socraticism of Epicurus and the Stoics. In the earliest dialogues of Plato, those in which we conventionally assume that Socrates' own views are expressed most clearly, there is, fairly obviously, an assumption that the human soul is fundamentally and exclusively a rational entity. For ethical purposes, it is assumed throughout the early dialogues that reason dominates the life of the soul to such a degree that rational decisions about the best life fully determine the behaviour of the human being. That view was eventually rejected by Plato and Aristotle, both of whom argued for the existence in the soul of fundamentally non-rational desiderative powers, which were, to be sure, amenable to control by reason, but which nevertheless were quasi-autonomous in their function. The struggle for the good life, then, was no longer simply a matter of rational decision about the best way for a man to behave and live, but depended for its success on the subordination or training of the non-rational parts of the soul; if they were not made obedient to man's reason they would interfere with his rational plans and decisions. The prospect of what Plato called 'civil war in the soul' always loomed.

The Epicureans and the orthodox Stoics returned to the view of Socrates, that the entire human soul was dominated by reason, that all of its desiderative states and powers were in some way expressions of a man's beliefs and decisions. It followed that weakness of will, 'civil war in the soul' was impossible. Moral errors were, consequently, just that; mistakes about the good life for man. This is, in a way, a much more optimistic view of the nature of human life. Reason and reason alone was responsible for our happiness or misery. This fundamentally Socratic belief may not be correct; but it unmistakably defines the general character of Hellenistic ethics. It is often held that the Epicureans and Stoic pursued human happiness through a blind denial of the importance of external circumstances and conditions, out of a sort of despair concerning the power of the individual in the new social conditions of the Hellenistic age. It is, we think, more likely that the uncompromising and perhaps implausible emphasis on the autonomy of human reason for happiness is a result of a carefully considered Socraticism in their understanding of the nature of the human soul.

Hellenistic sceptics rejected attempts to explain what is evident by what is non-evident, which is a generalization of the rejection of the attempt to explain the material by the immaterial. The two forms of scepticism in our period, Academic and Pyrrhonist, focussed their attacks on the leading dogmatic schools of their day, and this meant first and foremost the Stoics; the Epicureans were also attacked, and Sextus certainly found room in his capacious works for attacks on Plato, Aristotle and other earlier thinkers as well. But the very success of the Hellenistic dogmatists in displacing the giants of fourth-century thought from centre-stage led sceptics of both persuasions to focus their efforts on the theories of their contemporaries.

Despite the strong similarity between the two sceptical schools represented in this book, they should be carefully distinguished. The Academics, who turned to scepticism under the leadership of Arcesilaus in the early third century B.C., looked to Socrates for their main inspiration. The spirit of Socraticism, for Arcesilaus and his most important successor Carneades, lay in his refutative activity. The endeavour to subject every positive belief held by his interlocutors to cross-examination and refutation inspired them to pursue a rigorous intellectual purity by arguing against the principal dogmas of the philosophers of their own day. The dialectical power of Arcesilaus and Carneades manifested itself exclusively in oral debate; like Socrates, neither committed his work to writing—as though the very act of fixing live debate in written form would betray its dialectical character. This activity was practiced for its own sake; those who report on them by and large give the impression that they believed that the Academics were unconcerned with any goal beyond the activity of dialectic. Whether the Academics in fact concealed some arcane ethical or metaphysical goal behind their acute refutative activity is not clear; certainly they presented to the outside world only the enigmatic face of dialecticians ready to argue for or against any given thesis. In so doing, they helped to uncover latent weaknesses in the dogmatism of the other Hellenistic schools and stimulated them to buttress their theories with more acute arguments and more careful formulations. The subtle interplay between dogmatic theorizing and dialectical examination which first emerged at the very beginning of Greek philosophical activity is alive and well in the Hellenistic period.

With Pyrrhonian scepticism the situation is significantly different. Pyrrhonism as we know it seems to have originated in the first century B.C. with Aenesidemus, an Academic who reacted against the growing dogmatism of his own school, which was embodied first and foremost by Antiochus of Ascalon. To underline the renewed scepticism of their own thought, Pyrrhonists looked outside the Socratic/Academic tradition for the early 'founder' which every school wished to have to legitimate its intellectual stance. In this case, the founder selected was Pyrrho of Elis, an otherwise shadowy figure of the mid-fourth century. Pyrrho's life and thought are a mystery to us today; since he wrote nothing, our only sources for his activity are the later Pyrrhonists, who had a strong revisionist motivation, and a younger contemporary, the intellectual satirist Timon of Phlius, whose poetic works are preserved in very fragmentary form. That Pyrrho was a sceptic is clear enough, but the exact character and motivation of his scepticism are virtually impossible to determine. What is clear though is that later Pyrrhonists differed markedly from Academic sceptics in having a clear notion of the ethical goal of their sceptical activity. Sextus Empiricus, the long-winded medical man who is our chief extant source of Pyrrhonism of all periods, makes it very clear that freedom from disturbance is the purpose of scepticism. Thus the motivation for preserving one's freedom from dogmatic intellectual commitments became much clearer than it was for the Academics. And, perhaps as a result of this, the epistemic stance of Pyrrhonian scepticism is also significantly different from that of the Academics. It is no longer just freedom from assent, but the careful balancing of the sceptic's mind between equally plausible but opposing views which is the key to the Pyrrhonian sceptic's intellectual tranquillity.

✴✴✴✴✴

The development of Greek philosophy in the Hellenistic period is a matter of great historical importance. Ultimately, however, one must also form an opinion about its philosophical significance; this will inevitably be closely bound up with the judgement one forms of the relationship between Hellenistic and classical Greek philosophy and the merits of both its continuity and its innovations. It is fitting to leave the reader to form his or her own view of the originality and permanent value of Hellenistic thought; we hope that this book will provide a useful starting point for this task.

Abbreviations

A:	Arrighetti, *Epicuro Opere*
CIAG:	*Commentaria in Aristotelem Graeca*
D.K.:	*Fragmente der Vorsokratiker*, edd. H. Diels and W. Kranz
D.L.:	Diogenes Laertius
Dox. Gr.:	*Doxographi Graeci*, ed. H. Diels
M:	Sextus Empiricus, *Adversus Mathematicos*
PH:	Sextus Empiricus, *Outlines of Pyrrhonism*
Prep. Ev.:	Eusebius, *Preparatio Evangelica*
SVF:	*Stoicorum Veterum Fragmenta*, ed. H. von Arnim
U:	Usener, *Epicurea*
W-H:	Wachsmuth-Hense

Hellenistic Philosophy

I: Epicureanism

The ancient biography of Epicurus

The Life of Epicurus: **Diogenes Laertius** [I-1]
10.1–16 (selections)

1. Epicurus, son of Neocles and Chairestrate, was an Athenian citizen of the deme Gargettus and of the clan Philaidae, according to Metrodorus in his *On Noble Birth.* It is said, especially by Heracleides in his summary of Sotion, that he was raised on Samos after the Athenians sent colonists there; that at eighteen years of age he went to Athens, when Xenocrates was in [charge of] the Academy and Aristotle was spending time in Chalcis; that he went to join his father in Colophon when Alexander of Macedon had died and Perdiccas expelled the Athenians [from Samos]; 2. that he spent some time there and gathered students around him, then returned to Athens again in the archonship of Anaxicrates [307–306 B.C.]; and that up to a certain time he philosophized in conjunction with the others, but later developed the system which bears his name and taught his own distinctive views.

He himself says that he began to practice philosophy when he was fourteen years old. Apollodorus the Epicurean says, in book one of his *Life of Epicurus*, that he turned to philosophy because he was contemptuous of the school-teachers for not being able to interpret for him the [lines about] chaos in Hesiod. Hermippus says that he had been a grammar teacher, but then came across Democritus' treatises and threw himself headlong into philosophy.... 9. .... There is abundant evidence of the fellow's unsurpassed kindness to all men: his country honoured him with bronze statues; his friends were so numerous that they could not be counted by entire cities; all his followers were transfixed by the siren-song of his teachings, except Metrodorus of Stratonicea, who went over to Carneades, overburdened perhaps by his unsurpassed acts of goodness; though nearly all the others have died out, his succession has always persisted, one student following another in a numberless sequence of leaders; 10. and [there is] his gratitude to his parents, kindness to his brothers, and gentleness to his servants, as is clear both from the

3

provisions of his will and from the fact that they joined him in philosophizing, the most notable being the aforementioned Mus; in a word, he was
a friend to all mankind. His piety to the gods and love for his country
were too great for words. So gentlemanly was he that he did not even
participate in political life. And despite the severely troubled times then
afflicting Greece, he lived out his life there, travelling through Ionia two
or three times to see friends. And friends came to him from all over,
and lived with him in the Garden (as Apollodorus too says); and he
bought it for eighty minas.

11. Diocles says in book three of his summary that they lived very
simply and frugally. "At any rate," he says, "they were content with a
half-pint serving of weak wine and generally their drink was water." And
that Epicurus did not think it right to put one's possessions into a common
fund, as did Pythagoras who said "friends' possessions are common";
for that sort of thing is a mark of mistrust; and if there is mistrust there
is no friendship. In his letters he himself says that he is content with
just water and simple bread. And he says, "Send me a little pot of cheese
so that I can indulge in extravagance when I wish." This was the character
of the man who taught that pleasure is the goal. . . .

12. . . . According to Diocles he was most impressed by Anaxagoras
among earlier philosophers, although he opposed him on some points,
and by Archelaus, Socrates' teacher. He used to train his followers,
[Diocles] says, even to memorize his treatises.

13. Apollodorus in his *Chronology* says that he studied under Nausi-
phanes and Praxiphanes. He himself denies it, and says in the letter to
Eurylochus that he is self-taught. He denies that there ever was a philo-
sopher named Leucippus, and so does Hermarchus; some, including
Apollodorus the Epicurean, say that Leucippus was Democritus' teacher.
Demetrius of Magnesia says that he studied under Xenocrates too. . . .

14. . . . Ariston says in his life of Epicurus that he copied the *Canon*
straight out of the *Tripod* of Nausiphanes, under whom he also says he
studied, in addition to Pamphilus the Platonist in Samos. And that he
began to philosophize at the age of twelve and founded his school at the
age of 32.

He was born, according to Apollodorus in his *Chronology*, in the third
year of the 109th Olympiad, in the archonship of Sosigenes [341 B.C.]
on the seventh day of the month of Gamelion, seven years after Plato's
death. 15. When he was 32 he first founded a school in Mytilene and
Lampsacus [and stayed] for five years. Then he moved to Athens and
died there in the second year of the 127th Olympiad in the archonship
of Pytharatus [271–270 B.C.], at the age of 72. Hermarchus, son of Agem-
ortus, of Mytilene, took over the school.

He died of kidney stones, as Hermarchus too says in his letters, after an illness of fourteen days. At that point, as Hermippus also says, he got into a bronze bathtub filled with warm water, asked for unmixed wine, and tossed it back. 16. He then bade his friends to remember his teachings and died thus.

The Extant Letters

The following three letters are preserved because Diogenes Laertius included them in his biography. They are the most important surviving evidence for the philosophy of Epicurus. The *Letter to Herodotus* (I-2) is a summary of physical doctrine; the *Letter to Menoeceus* (I-4) is an even briefer summary of ethics; the authenticity of the summary of meteorology in I-3 (*Letter to Pythocles*) has been questioned, but we regard it as probably genuine.

Letter to Herodotus: Diogenes Laertius [I-2] 10.34–83

34. Epicurus to Herodotus, greetings:

35. For the sake of those, Herodotus, who are unable to work out with precision each and every detail of what we have written on nature and who lack the ability to work through the longer books I have composed, I have myself prepared an adequate summary of the entire system, to facilitate the firm memorization of the most general doctrines, in order that at each and every opportunity they may be able to help themselves in the most important issues, to the degree that they retain their grasp on the study of nature. Even those well advanced in the examination of the universe must recall the outline of the entire system; and this outline is structured according to basic principles. For we frequently need the overall application [of the intellect], but not so often the detailed application.

36. We must, then, approach those [general points] continually, and get into our memory an amount [of doctrine] sufficient to permit the most vital application [of the intellect] to the facts; moreover, complete precision on detailed points will be discovered if the general outlines are comprehensively grasped and remembered. For even the fully expert [student of physics] gets as the most vital benefit of complete precision the ability to make nimble use of his applications, and ⟨this would happen if every point⟩ were united in [a set of] simple principles and maxims. For it is not possible to know the concentrated result of our continuous

overview of the universe unless one can have in oneself a comprehensive grasp by means of brief maxims of all that might also be worked out in detail with precision.

37. Since this kind of method is useful to *all* those who are concerned with the study of nature, I recommend constant activity in the study of nature; and with this sort of activity more than any other I bring calm to my life. That is why I have composed for you this type of summary statement of the basic principles of the entire set of doctrines.

First, Herodotus, we need to have grasped what is denoted by our words, [1] so that by referring to what they denote we can make decisions about the objects of opinion, investigation, or puzzlement and [2] so that all of these things will not remain undecided, [as they would] if we tried to give an infinitely long demonstration, and [3] so that our words will not be empty. **38.** For it is necessary that we look to the primary conception corresponding to each word and that it stand in no need of demonstration, if, that is, we are going to have something to which we can refer the object of search or puzzlement and opinion. Again, it is also necessary to observe all things in accordance with one's sense-perceptions, i.e., simply according to the present applications, whether of the intellect or of any other of the criteria, and similarly [to observe everything] in accordance with our actual feelings, so that we can have some sign by which we may make inferences both about what awaits confirmation and about the non-evident.

After distinguishing these points we must next arrive at a general view about the things which are non-evident. The first point is that nothing comes into being from what is not; for [in that case] everything would be coming into being from everything, with no need of seeds. **39.** And if that which disappears were destroyed into what is not, all things would have been destroyed, since that into which they were dissolved does not exist. Further, the totality [of things] has always been just like it is now and always will be. For there is nothing for it to change into. For there exists nothing in addition to the totality, which could enter into it and produce the change.

Moreover,[1] the totality is [made up of] ⟨bodies and void⟩; for in all cases sense-perception itself testifies that bodies exist, and it is by sense-perception that we must infer by reasoning what is non-evident, as I already said. **40.** And if there did not exist that which we call void and space and intangible nature, bodies would not have any place to be in or move through, as they obviously do move. Beyond these two things

---

1. A scholiast in antiquity added: "He makes this point in the *Major Summary* at the beginning and in book one of the *On Nature*."

[viz. bodies and void] nothing can be conceived, either by a comprehensive grasp or analogously to things so grasped, [at least not if we mean] grasped as complete natures rather than as what are termed properties or accidents of these [two] things.

Further, among[2] bodies, some are compounds, and some are those things from which compounds have been made. **41.** And these are atomic and unchangeable, if indeed they are not all going to be destroyed into not being but will remain firmly during the dissolutions of compounds, being full by nature and not being subject to dissolution in any way or fashion. Consequently the principles of bodies must be atomic natures.

Moreover, the totality is unlimited. For what is limited has an extreme; but an extreme is seen in contrast to something else, so that since it has no extreme it has no limit. But since it has no limit it would be unlimited and not limited.

Further, the totality is unlimited in respect of the number of bodies and the magnitude of the void. **42.** For if the void were unlimited and bodies limited, bodies would not come to a standstill anywhere but would move in scattered fashion throughout the unlimited void, since they would lack anything to support them or check them by collision. But if the void were limited, the unlimited bodies would not have a place to be in.

In addition, the bodies which are atomic and full, from which compounds both come to be and into which they are dissolved, are ungraspable when it comes to the differences among their shapes. For it is not possible that so many differences [in things] should come to be from the same shapes having been comprehensively grasped. And for each type of shape there is, quite simply, an unlimited number of similar [atoms], but with respect to the differences they are not quite simply unlimited but only ungraspable.

43.[3] And the atoms move continuously[4] for all time, some recoiling far apart from one another [upon collision], and others, by contrast, maintaining a [constant] vibration when they are locked into a compound or enclosed by the surrounding [atoms of a compound]. **44.** This is the result of the nature of the void which separates each of them and is not

---

2. The scholiast adds: "This is also in book one of the *On Nature* and in books fourteen and fifteen, as well as in the *Major Summary*."

3. Scholiast: "A bit later he also says that division does not go on indefinitely; and he says since the qualities change, unless one intends simply to extend them indefinitely with respect to their magnitudes too." This scholion is probably corrupt, and the sense is unclear.

4. Scholiast: "and he says a bit later that they also move with equal speed since the void gives an equal yielding [i.e., lack of resistance] to the lightest and to the heaviest."

able to provide any resistance; and their actual solidity causes their rebound vibration to extend, during the collision, as far as the distance which the entanglement [of the compound] permits after the collision.

There is no principle for these [entities], since the atoms and the void are eternal.[5] **45.** If all these points are remembered, a maxim as brief as this will provide an adequate outline for [developing] our conceptions about the nature of what exists.

Moreover, there is an unlimited number of cosmoi, and some are similar to this one and some are dissimilar. For the atoms, which are unlimited (as was shown just now), are also carried away to very remote distances. For atoms of the sort from which a world might come to be or by which it might be made are not exhausted [in the production] of one world or any finite number of them, neither worlds like this one nor worlds unlike them. Consequently, there is no obstacle to the unlimited-ness of worlds.

46. Further, there exist outlines [i.e., images, *eidola*] which are similar in shape to solids, only much finer than observed objects. For it is not impossible for such compounds to come into being in the surrounding environment, nor that there should be favourable opportunities for the production of hollow and thin [films], nor that effluences should retain the relative position and standing [i.e., order] that they had in the solid objects. These outlines we call 'images'. Further, since their movement through the void occurs with no conflict from [atoms which] could resist them, it can cover any comprehensively graspable distance in an inconceivably [short] time. For the presence and absence of resistance take on a similarity to slowness and speed.

47. The moving body itself, however, cannot reach several places at the same time, speaking in terms of time contemplated by reason; for that is unthinkable. Yet when considered as arriving in perceptible time from any point at all in the unlimited, it will not be departing from the place from which we comprehensively grasp its motion as having come from. For it will be like resistance even if to this point we leave the speed of the movement free from resistance. The retention of this basic principle too is useful.

Next, none of the appearances testifies against [the theory] that the images have an unsurpassed fineness; and that is why they have unsur-passed speed too, since they find every passage suitably sized for there

---

5. Scholiast: "He says a bit later that there are not even any qualities in atoms, except shape and size and weight; in the *Twelve Basic Principles* he says that their colour changes according to the arrangement of the atoms; and that they cannot have every magnitude—at any rate an atom has never been seen with sense-perception."

being no or few [bodies] to resist their flow, whereas there is some [body] to resist a large or infinite number of atoms.

48. In addition, [none of the facts testifies against the claim] that the production of images occurs as fast as thought. For there is a continuous flow from the surface of bodies, though it is not obvious from any reduction in bulk because the [objects are] refilled [by other atoms]; [and this flow] preserves for quite some time the position and order of the atoms which it had in the solid, even if it is sometimes disrupted; and [two-dimensional] compounds are quickly produced in the surrounding environment, since they do not need to be filled out with depth—and there are certain other ways in which such natures [i.e., compound images] can be produced. None of these [claims] is testified against by the senses, providing one considers the clear facts in a certain way; one will also refer to [the senses] the [fact that] harmonious sets [of qualities] come to us from external objects.

49. One must also believe that it is when something from the external objects enters into us that we see and think about their shapes. For external objects would not stamp into us the nature of their own colour and shape via the air which is between us and them, nor via the rays or any kind of flows which move from us to them, as well as [they would] by means of certain outlines which share the colour and shape of the objects and enter into us from them, entering the vision or the intellect according to the size and fit [of the effluences] and moving very quickly;

50. then, for this reason, they give the presentation of a single, continuous thing, and preserve the harmonious set [of qualities] generated by the external object, as a result of the coordinate impact from that object [on us], which [in turn] originates in the vibration of the atoms deep inside the solid object. And whatever presentation we receive by a form of application, whether by the intellect or by the sense organs, and whether of a shape or of accidents, this *is* the shape of the solid object, produced by the continuous compacting or residue of the image. Falsehood or error *always* resides in the added opinion ⟨in the case of something which awaits⟩ testimony for or against it but in the event receives neither supporting testimony ⟨nor opposing testimony⟩.[6]

51. For the similarity of appearances (which are like what are grasped in a representational picture and occur either in dreams or in some other applications of the intellect or the other criteria) to what are called real and true things would never occur if some such thing were not added [to the basic experience]. And error would not occur if we did not have

6. Scholiast: "According to a certain motion in ourselves which is linked to the application to presentations but is distinct, according to which falsehood occurs."

some other motion too in ourselves which is linked ‹to the application to presentations› but is distinct; falsehood occurs because of this, if it is not testified for or is testified against; but if it is testified for or is not testified against, truth occurs.

52. One must, then, keep this doctrine too quite firmly in mind, in order to avoid destroying the criteria of clear facts and to avoid having error placed on an equal basis with that which has been established, which would confound everything.

Moreover, hearing too occurs when a flow moves from that object which makes an utterance or produces a sound or makes a noise or in any other way causes the auditory experience. This flow is broken into small masses which are homogeneous with the whole which at the same time preserve an harmonious set [of qualities] relative to each other and also a unique kind of unity which extends back to the originating source and, usually, produces the perceptual experience occasioned by the flow; and if not, it only makes the external object apparent. 53. For without some harmonious set [of qualities] coming from there, this sort of perceptual experience could not occur. So one must not think that the air itself is shaped by the emitted voice or even by things of like character—for it is far from being the case that it [i.e., air] is affected in this way by that [i.e., voice]—but rather when we emit voice the blow which occurs inside us precipitates the expulsion of certain masses which produce a flow similar to breath, and which causes in us the auditory experience.

Further, one must also believe that the [sense of] smell, like hearing too, would never have produced any experience if there were not certain masses moving from the object and being commensurate for the stimulation of this sense organ, some of them of one sort, i.e., disturbing and uncongenial, and some of another, i.e., non-disturbing and congenial [to the organ of smell].

54. Further, one must believe that the atoms bring with them none of the qualities of things which appear except shape, weight, and size and the [properties] which necessarily accompany shape. For every quality changes, while the atoms do not change in any respect; for it is necessary that during the dissolution of compounds something should remain solid and undissolved, which will guarantee that the changes are not into what is not nor from what is not, but come about by rearrangements in many cases, and in some cases too by additions and subtractions [of atoms from the compound]. That is why it is necessary that the things which are rearranged should be indestructible and not have the nature of what changes, but rather their own masses and configurations. For it is also necessary that these things should remain [unchanged].

55. For even with things in our experience which change their shapes

by the removal [of matter], the shape is grasped as inhering in the object which changes, while its qualities do not so inhere. The shape remains, but the qualities are eliminated from the entire body. So these features which are left behind [after a change] are sufficient to produce the differences in compounds, since it *is* necessary that some things be left behind and that there not be a destruction into what is not.

Moreover, one should not believe that atoms have every [possible] magnitude, so that one may avoid being testified against by the appearances. But one should believe that there are some differences in magnitude. For if this [doctrine] is added, then it will be easier to account for what, according to our feelings and sense-perceptions, actually happens. **56.** But [to suppose] that *every* magnitude exists is not useful for [accounting for] the differences of qualities, and at the same time it would be necessary that some atoms reach the point of being visible to us—which is not seen to occur nor can one conceive how an atom could become visible.

In addition to these points, one must not believe that there can be an unlimited number of masses—no matter how small—in any finite body. Consequently, not only must one eliminate unlimited division into smaller pieces (to avoid making everything weak and being forced in our comprehensive grasps of compound things to exhaust the things which exist by reducing them to non-existence), but one must also not believe that within finite bodies there is an unlimited movement, not even by smaller and smaller stages.

57. For as soon as one says that there is in some thing an unlimited number of masses, no matter how small, then one cannot think how this magnitude could any longer be limited. For obviously these unlimited masses must be of some size or other; and no matter how small they might be, the magnitude [of the whole object] would for all that be unlimited. And since the limited has an extreme which can be distinguished even if it cannot be observed on its own, it is impossible not to conceive that the thing next to it is of the same character and that by moving forward from one point to the next in this fashion it turns out that one will in this fashion reach the unlimited conceptually.

58. And we must conceive that the minimal perceptible [part] is neither such as to be traversible nor is it totally and altogether unlike this. It has something in common with things which permit of being traversed, but [unlike them] it does not permit the distinguishing of parts [within it]; but whenever, because of the resemblance created by what they have in common, we think that we are going to distinguish some [part] of it— one part here, another over there—it must be that we encounter something of equal size. We observe these one after another, starting from the first, and not [as being] in the same place nor as touching each other's parts with their own, but rather we [see] them measuring out magnitudes in their own unique way, more of them measuring out a larger magnitude and fewer of them a smaller.

One must believe that the minimal part in the atom also stands in this relation. **59.** It is obvious that it is only in its smallness that it differs from what is observed in the case of perception, but it does stand in the same relation. For indeed it is because of this relation that we have already asserted that the atom has magnitude, and have merely extended it far beyond [perceptible things] in smallness. And again we must believe that the minimal and indivisible parts are limits which provide from themselves as primary [units] a standard of measurement for the lengths of larger and smaller [atoms], when we contemplate invisible things with reason. For what they have in common with things which do not permit of movement [across themselves] is enough to get us this far; but it is not possible for these [minimal parts] to possess motion and so move together [into compounds].

60. Further, one must not assert that the unlimited has an up and a down in the sense of an [absolutely] highest and lowest point. We know, however, that what is over our heads from wherever we stand, or what is below any point which we think of—it being possible to project both indefinitely—will never appear to us as being at the same time and in the same respect both up and down. For it is impossible to conceive of this. Consequently, it is possible to grasp as one motion the one conceived of as indefinitely [extended] upwards and the one conceived of as indefinitely [extended] downwards, even if a thousand times over a thing moving from us towards the places over our heads should arrive at the feet of those above us or a thing moving from us downwards should arrive at the head of those below us.

61. Furthermore, it is necessary that the atoms move at equal speed, when they move through the void and nothing resists them. For heavy things will not move faster than small and light ones, *when*, that is, nothing stands in their way; nor do small things move faster than large ones, since they all have a passage commensurate to them, when, that is, nothing resists these atoms either; nor is upward [movement] faster; neither is the sideways [movement] produced by collisions faster; nor is the downward [movement] caused by their own weight faster either. For as long as either ⟨of them⟩ prevails, the motion will continue as fast as thought, until it meets with resistance, either from an external source or from its own weight counteracting the force of a colliding body.

62. Moreover, with respect to compounds, some will move faster than others, though the atoms [by themselves] move at equal speed, because the atoms in aggregates are moving towards one place [i.e., in the same direction] in the shortest continuous time, even if they do not do so in the [units of] time which reason can contemplate; but they frequently collide, until the continuity of the motion becomes perceptible. For the added opinion concerning the invisible—i.e., that the [units of] time which reason can contemplate will allow for continuous motion—is not true in such cases. For everything that is observed or grasped by the intellect in an [act of] application is true.

63. Next, one must see, by making reference to our sense-perceptions and feelings (for these will provide the most secure conviction), that the soul is a body [made up of] fine parts distributed throughout the entire aggregate, and most closely resembling breath with a certain admixture of heat, in one way resembling breath and in another resembling heat. There is also the ⟨third⟩ part which is much finer than even these [components] and because of this is more closely in harmony with the rest of the aggregate too. All of this is revealed by the abilities of the soul, its feelings, its ease of motion, its thought processes, and the things whose removal leads to our death.

Further, one must hold firmly that the soul is most responsible for sense-perception. **64.** But [the soul] would not have acquired this [power] if it were not somehow enclosed by the rest of the aggregate. But the rest of the aggregate, though it provides for the soul this cause [of sense-perception], itself has a share in this property because of the soul; still it does not share in all the features [of sense-perception] which the soul has. That is why, when the soul has departed, it does not have sense-perception. For it could not have acquired this power all by itself, but something else which came into being with it provided body [with this power]; and this other thing, through the power actualized in itself by its motion, immediately produced for itself a property of sense-perception and then gave it (because of their close proximity and harmonious relationship) to the body too, as I said.

65. That is why the soul, as long as it is in [the body], will never lack sense-perception even if some other part has departed; but no matter what [parts] of it are destroyed along with the container's dissolution (whether entire or partial), *if* the soul survives it will be able to perceive. But the rest of the aggregate—whole or part—is not able to perceive even if it survives, when the number of atoms, however small it be, which makes up the nature of the soul, has departed.

Furthermore, when the entire aggregate is destroyed, the soul is scattered and no longer has the same powers, nor can it move; consequently, it does not then [in fact] have [the power of] sense-perception. **66.** For it is not possible to conceive of it as perceiving if it is not in this complex and not executing these movements, [i.e.,] when the containing and surrounding [parts] are not such as now contain it and make possible these motions.[7]

67. Moreover, one must also think of this, that we apply the term 'incorporeal', in the most common meaning of the term, to what could be conceived of as independently existing. But the incorporeal cannot be thought of as independently existing, except for the void. And the void can neither act nor be acted upon but merely provides [the possibility of] motion through itself for bodies. Consequently, those who say that the soul is incorporeal are speaking to no point. For if it were of that character, it could neither act nor be acted upon at all. But in fact both of these properties are clearly distinguished as belonging to the soul.

68. So, if one refers all of these calculations concerning the soul to the feelings and sense-perceptions, and remembers what was said at the outset, one will see the points comprehended in the outline with sufficient clarity to be able to work out the details from this basis with precision and certainty.

Further, the shapes and colours and sizes and weights and all the other things which are predicated of body as accidents, either of all [bodies] or of visible ones, and are known by sense-perception itself, these things must not be thought of as independent natures (for that is inconceivable). **69.** Nor [must it be thought] that they are altogether non-existent, nor that they are distinct incorporeal entities inhering in [the body], nor that they are parts of it. But [one should think] that the whole body throughout derives its own permanent nature from all of these [properties]—though not in such a way as to be a compound [of them], just as when a larger aggregate is produced from the masses themselves, whether the primary ones or magnitudes smaller than the whole object in question—but only, as I say, deriving its own permanent nature from all of these. But all of these [are known by] their own peculiar forms of application and comprehension, always in close accompaniment with the aggregate and in no way separated from it, which is given the predicate 'body' by reference to the aggregate conception.

70. Further, it often happens that some impermanent properties, which are neither invisible nor incorporeal, accompany bodies. Consequently,

---

7. Scholion: "Elsewhere he says that it is also composed of very smooth and very round atoms, differing quite a bit from those of fire. And that part of it is irrational, and is distributed throughout the rest of the body, while the rational part is in the chest, as is evident from [feelings of] fear and joy. And that sleep occurs when the parts of the soul which are distributed through the whole compound are fixed in place or spread apart and then collide because of the impacts. And semen comes from the entire body."

using this term in the commonest sense, we make it clear that the[se] properties neither have the nature of an entire thing, which we call a body when we grasp it in aggregate, nor the nature of the permanent accompaniments without which it is not possible to conceive of a body. They would all be referred to according to certain applications of the aggregate which accompanies [them]—**71.** but [only] when they are observed to inhere [in bodies], since the properties are not *permanent* accompaniments [of those bodies]. And we should not eliminate this clear evidence from what exists just because [the properties] do not have the nature of an entire thing which happens to be what we also call a body, nor the nature of the permanent accompaniments; but neither are they to be regarded as independent entities, since this is not conceivable either in their case or in the case of permanent accidents; but one must think that they are all, just as they appear [to be], properties somehow ⟨related to⟩ the bodies and not permanent accompaniments nor things which have the status of an independent nature. But they are observed just as sense-perception itself presents their peculiar traits.

72. Moreover, one must also think of this very carefully: one should not investigate time as we do the other things which we investigate in an object, [i.e.,] by referring to the basic grasps which are observed within ourselves, but we must reason [on the basis of] the clear experience according to which we utter [the phrases] "for a long time" or "for a short time" interpreting it in a manner closely connected [to our experience]. Nor must we alter the terms we use in order to 'improve' them, but we must apply the current terms to [time]; nor must one predicate anything else of it, as though it had the same substance as this peculiar thing—for there are people who do this. But the best policy is to reason solely by means of that which we associate with this peculiar thing and by which we measure it. **73.** For this needs no demonstration, but [only] reasoning, because we associate it with days and nights and their parts, and similarly with the feelings too and with the absence of them, and with motions and states of rest, again, having in mind in connection with them precisely and only this peculiar property according to which we apply the term "time."[8]

On top of what has been said, one must believe that the cosmoi, and every finite compound which is similar in form to those which are frequently seen, have come into being from the unlimited, all these things having been separated off from particular conglomerations [of matter], both larger and smaller; and that they are all dissolved again, some more

---

8. Scholiast: "He also says this in book two of the *On Nature* and in the *Major Summary*."

quickly and some more slowly, and some undergoing this because of one kind of cause, some because of others.[9]

74. Again, one must not believe that the cosmoi necessarily have one kind of shape. . . .[10] For no one could demonstrate that a cosmos of one sort would not have included the sort of seeds from which animals, plants, and the rest of the observable things are formed as compounds, or that a [cosmos of a] different sort *could* not have [included the same things].[11]

75. Further, one must suppose that [human] nature was taught a large number of different lessons just by the facts themselves, and compelled [by them]; and that reasoning later made more precise what was handed over to it [by nature] and made additional discoveries—more quickly among some peoples, and more slowly among others and in some periods of time ⟨making greater advances⟩ and in others smaller ones.

Hence, names too did not originally come into being by convention, but the very natures of men, which undergo particular feelings and receive particular presentations according to the tribes they live in, expelled air in particular ways as determined by each of their feelings and presentations, in accordance too with the various local differences among their tribes. 76. And later [the names] were established by a general convention in each tribe, in order that their meanings might be less ambiguous for each other and might be expressed more succinctly. And those who were aware of certain previously unobserved things introduced them [to their tribes] and with them handed over certain words [for the things], some being forced to utter them, others choosing them by reasoning, following the commonest [mode of causation],[12] and communicated [their meaning] in this fashion.

Moreover, when it comes to meteorological phenomena, one must believe that movements, turnings, eclipses, risings, settings, and related phenomena occur without any [god] helping out and ordaining or being about to ordain [things] and at the same time having complete blessedness

---

9. Scholiast: "It is clear, then, that he says that the cosmoi are destructible, [this happening] when the parts undergo change. And elsewhere he says that the earth is supported by the air."

10. There is a lacuna at this point in the text. A scholiast adds: "But he himself says in book 12 of the *On Nature* that they are different: some are spherical, some egg-shaped, and others have different sorts of shapes; but they do not have every [possible] shape. Nor are they animals separated off from the unlimited."

11. Scholiast: "Similarly they are nourished in it. One must believe that it happens in the same way on earth too."

12. The text may be corrupt here; the sense should be that the inventors or discoverers followed an analogy with words already used in their own societies when deliberately coining new terms.

and indestructibility; **77.** for troubles and concerns and anger and gratitude are not consistent with blessedness, but these things involve weakness and fear and dependence on one's neighbours. Nor again can they be in possession of blessedness if they [the heavenly bodies] are at the same time balls of fire and adopt these movements by deliberate choice; rather, we must preserve the complete solemnity implied in all the terms applied to such conceptions, so that we do not generate from these terms opinions inconsistent with their solemnity; otherwise, the inconsistency itself will produce the greatest disturbance in our souls. Hence, one must hold the opinion that it is owing to the original inclusion of these compounds in the generation of the cosmos that this regularly recurring cycle too is produced.

78. Moreover, one must believe that it is the job of physics to work out precisely the cause of the most important things, and that blessedness lies in this part of meteorological knowledge and in knowing what the natures are which are observed in these meteorological phenomena, and all matters related to precision on this topic.

And again, [one must accept] that in such matters there is no room for things occurring in several ways and things which might occur otherwise, but that anything which suggests conflict or disturbance simply cannot occur in the indestructible and divine nature. And it is possible to grasp with the intellect that this is unqualifiedly so.

79. And what falls within the ambit of investigation into settings and risings and turnings, and eclipses and matters related to these, makes no further contribution to the blessedness which comes from knowledge; but people who know about these things, if they are ignorant of what the natures [in question] are and what the most important causes are, have fears just the same as if they did not have this special knowledge— and perhaps even more fears, since the wonderment which comes from the prior consideration of these phenomena cannot discover a resolution or the orderly management of the most important factors.

That is why even if we discover several causes for turnings and settings and risings and eclipses and things of this sort (as was also the case in [the investigation] of detailed occurrences) **80.** we must not believe that our study of these matters has failed to achieve a degree of accuracy which contributes to our undisturbed and blessed state. Consequently, we should account for the causes of meteorological phenomena and everything which is non-evident, observing in how many different ways similar phenomena occur in our experience; and [we should] disdain those who fail to recognize what exists or comes to be in a single manner and what occurs in many different ways, because they overlook the [fact that the] presentation [comes] from great distances and are, moreover, ignorant

of the circumstances in which one cannot achieve freedom from disturbance and those, similarly, in which one can achieve freedom from disturbance. So if we think that [a phenomenon] might also occur in some
particular way and recognize the very fact that it [might] happen in many
different ways, we shall be as free from disturbance as if we *knew* that
it occurred in some particular way.

81. In addition to all these points in general, one must also conceive
that the worst disturbance occurs in human souls [1] because of the
opinion that these things [the heavenly phenomena] are blessed and
indestructible and that they have wishes and undertake actions and exert
causality in a manner inconsistent with those attributes, and [2] because
of the eternal expectation and suspicion that something dreadful [might
happen] such as the myths tell about, or [3] even because they fear that
very lack of sense-perception which occurs in death, as though it were
relevant to them, and [4] because they are not in this state as a result of
their opinions but because of some irrational condition; hence, not setting
a limit on their dread, they suffer a disturbance equal to or even greater
than what they would suffer if they actually held these opinions. 82. And
freedom from disturbance is a release from all of this and involves a
continuous recollection of the general and most important points [of
the system].

Hence, one must attend to one's present feelings and sense-perceptions,
to the common sense-perceptions for common properties and to the
individual sense-perceptions for individual properties, and to every immediately clear fact as revealed by each of the criteria. For, if we attend to
these things, we will give a correct and complete causal account of the
source of our disturbance and fear, and [so] dissolve them, by accounting
for the causes of meteorological and other phenomena which we are
constantly exposed to and which terrify other men most severely.

Here, Herodotus, in summary form are the most important points
about the nature of the universe; 83. consequently, I think that this
account, if mastered with precision, would be able to make a man incom-
parably stronger than other men, even if he does not go on to all of the
precise details of individual doctrines. For he will also be able to clarify,
by his own efforts, many of the precise details of individual doctrines in
our entire system, and these points themselves, when lodged in memory,
will be a constant aid.

For [these doctrines] are such that even those who have already worked
out the details of individual doctrines sufficiently well or even completely,
can, by analysing them into [intellectual] applications of this sort, acquire
most of the [elements of the] survey of nature as a whole. But those who
are not among the completely accomplished [students of nature] can, on

the basis of these points and following the method which does not involve verbal expression, with the speed of thought achieve an overview of the doctrines most important for [achieving] tranquillity.

Letter to Pythocles: Diogenes Laertius   [I-3]
10.83–116

83. Epicurus to Pythocles, greetings:

84. Cleon delivered to me your letter, in which you continued to display a good will to us worthy of our concern for you and tried, not unconvincingly, to recall the lines of reasoning which contribute to a blessed life; and you requested that I send you a brief and concise [statement of our] reasoning concerning meteorological phenomena in order to facilitate your recollections. For our other writings on the topic are hard to recall, even though, as you said, you have them constantly in hand. We were pleased to receive this request from you and were seized by pleasant expectations. 85. Therefore, having written all the rest, we shall produce what you requested, since these lines of reasoning will be useful to many others too, and especially to those who have just begun to sample true physics and those who are entangled in preoccupations more profound than some of the general studies. So grasp them well and, holding them keenly in your memory, survey them in conjunction with the rest [of my summary of physics], which I sent to Herodotus as the Smaller Summary.

First of all, do not believe that there is any other goal to be achieved by the knowledge of meteorological phenomena, whether they are discussed in conjunction with [physics in general] or on their own, than freedom from disturbance and a secure conviction, just as with the rest [of physics]. 86. [Our aim is] neither to achieve the impossible, even by force, nor to maintain a theory which is in all respects similar either to our discussions on the ways of life or to our clarifications of other questions in physics, such as the thesis that the totality [of things] consists of bodies and intangible nature, and that the elements are atomic, and all such things as are consistent with the phenomena in only one way. This is not the case with meteorological phenomena, but rather these phenomena admit of several different explanations for their coming to be and several different accounts of their existence which are consistent with our sense-perceptions.

For we should not do physics by following groundless postulates and stipulations, but in the manner called for by the phenomena; 87. for our life does not now need irrationality and groundless opinion, but rather for us to live without tumult. And everything happens smoothly and (providing everything is clarified by the method of several different explanations) consistently with the phenomena, when one accepts appropriately what is plausibly said about them. But when one accepts one theory and rejects another which is equally consistent with the phenomenon in question, it is clear that one has thereby blundered out of any sort of proper physics and fallen into mythology. Some of the phenomena which are within our [experience] and are observed just as they really are do provide signs applicable to what comes to pass in meteorology, but we cannot observe meteorological phenomena; for they can occur in several different ways. 88. We must, however, observe the appearance of each thing and, with regard to the things connected with it, we must distinguish those whose coming to pass in several different ways is not testified against by what happens within our experience.

A cosmos is a circumscribed portion of the heavens which contains stars and an earth and all the phenomena, whose dissolution will involve the destruction of everything within it; it is separated off from the unlimited and terminates at a boundary which is either rare or dense; it is either revolving or stationary; it has an outline which is either round or triangular, or some shape or other. For all of these are possibilities. For none of the phenomena in this cosmos testifies against [these possibilities], since here it is not possible to grasp a limit [of our cosmos].

89. It is possible to grasp that there is an unlimited number of such cosmoi; and that such a cosmos can come into existence both within a[nother] cosmos and in an intercosmos, which is what we call the interval between cosmoi, in a place containing much void and not in an extensive area which is completely void, as some people say; [this happens] when certain seeds of the right sort rush in from one cosmos or intercosmos— or even from several—[thereby] gradually causing conjunctions and articulations and movements to another place (if it so happen) and influxes from [atoms] which are in the right condition, until [the cosmos] is completed and achieves stability, [i.e.,] for as long as the foundations laid can accept additional material. 90. For one does not need just to have an aggregate come into being, or a rotation in the void in which a cosmos comes to be by necessity, as opinion holds, and [then] grows until it collides with another [cosmos], as one of the so-called physicists says. For this is in conflict with the phenomena.

The sun and the moon and the other heavenly bodies did not come into being on their own and then get included by the cosmos, but they immediately began to take shape and grow (and similarly for the earth and sea) by means of infusions and rotations of certain natures with fine parts, either breath-like or fiery or both. For sense-perception suggests that they [come into being] thus.

91. The size of the sun and the other heavenly bodies relative to us is just as big as it appears.[13] But relative to itself it is either bigger or a bit smaller than it is seen as being, or just the same size.[14] For in our experience too fire-signals, when seen from a distance, are observed in this way by our sense-perception. And every objection directed at this portion [of our theory] will be easily dissolved if only one pays attention to the clear facts, which we set out in our book *On Nature*. **92.** The risings and settings of the sun and the moon and the other heavenly bodies could occur by kindling and extinguishing, as long as the circumstances in both locales [i.e., east and west] are such as to produce the aforementioned events; for none of the appearances testifies against this. ⟨And⟩ they could also be produced by the appearance [of these bodies] above the earth and a subsequent blocking [by it]; for none of the appearances testifies against this either. And it is not impossible that their motions come to pass because of the rotation of the entire cosmos, or by its rest and their rotation, produced by the necessity generated when they [first] rose, at the beginning when the cosmos was [first] coming into being. [There is probably a lacuna in the text here.] **93.** . . . by extreme heat produced by a certain kind of distribution of the fire which constantly impinges on the adjoining places.

The turnings of the sun and moon could come to pass because of the obliquity of the heaven, which is compelled in this way at [certain] times; similarly, it could also be because of the resistance in the air, or because the fuel which regularly fits their requirements is burned up or is insufficient in quantity; or even because these heavenly bodies had forced on them from the very beginning the sort of rotation which causes them to have a kind of spiral motion. For all such possibilities and those like them are in no way inconsistent with any of the clear facts, providing one always in such detailed enquiries keeps a firm hold on what is possible and can refer each of them to what is consistent with the phenomena, not fearing the slavish technicalities of the astronomers.

94. The waning of the moon and its subsequent waxing could come to pass by means of the turning of this body and just as well by means of the changing shapes of the air, and again, also because of the interposition [of other bodies], and in all the ways which the phenomena in our experience suggest for the explanation of this kind of thing—as long as one is not so enamoured of the method of unique explanations as to

---

13. Scholiast: "This is also in book 11 of the *On Nature*; for, he says, if its size had been reduced because of the distance, its brightness would have been even more reduced; for there is no other distance more symmetrical with this [degree of brightness]."

14. Scholiast: "But not at the same time."

groundlessly reject the others, because of a failure to understand what it is possible for a man to understand and what is not, for this reason desiring to understand what cannot be understood. And again, it is possible that the moon produces its own light, and also possible that it receives it from the sun. 95. For in our own experience we see many things which produce their own light, and many which receive it from other things. And none of the meteorological phenomena is a hindrance [to these possibilities], as long as one always remembers the method of several different explanations, considers together the hypotheses and explanations compatible with these, and does not, by looking to things which are not compatible, give them a pointless importance and so slide, in different ways on different occasions, into the method of unique explanations. And the appearance of a face in [the moon] could occur because of the variation among its parts, and because [some parts] are blocked, and by all the methods one might consider which are consistent with the phenomena. 96. For in the case of all the meteorological phenomena one must not give up tracking down such [possibilities]. For if one is in conflict with the clear facts, one will never be able to partake of genuine freedom from disturbance.

The eclipse of the sun and the moon could also come to pass by extinguishing, as is also observed to occur in our experience; and also by being blocked by certain other bodies, either the earth or the heavens or some other such thing. And one should in this way consider the methods [of explanation] which are consistent with each other, and that it is not impossible that some of them may occur together.[15]

97. And again, we should grasp the orderliness of the cyclical periods [of the heavenly bodies] [as happening] in the same way that some of the things which also happen in our experience [occur]; and let the nature of the divine not be brought to bear on this at all, but let it go on being thought of as free from burdensome service and as [living] in complete blessedness. For if this is not done, the entire study of the explanations for meteorological phenomena will be pointless, as it has already been for some who did not pursue the method of possible explanations and so were reduced to pointlessness because they thought that [the phenomena] only occurred in one manner and rejected all the other explanations which were also possible, and so were swept off into an unintelligible

---

15. Scholiast: "He says the same in book 12 of *On Nature*, and in addition that the sun is eclipsed by the fact that the moon darkens it, and the moon by the shadow of the earth, but also by its own retreat. This is also said by Diogenes the Epicurean in book 1 of his *Selections*."

position and were unable to consider together the phenomena which one must accept as signs.

98. The varying lengths of nights and days [could occur] as a result of the alternate swift and slow motions of the sun over the earth, ⟨or even⟩ as a result of covering the varying distances between places and certain places either faster or slower, as is also observed [to happen] with some things in our experience; and we must speak in a manner consistent with these when we speak of meteorological phenomena. But those who accept one explanation are in conflict with the phenomena and have lost track of what it is possible for a man to understand.

Predictive weather signs could occur as a result of coincidental conjunctions of events, as in the case of animals which are evident in our experience, and also as a result of alterations and changes in the air. For both of these are not in conflict with the phenomena; 99. but it is not possible to see in what sort of cases the explanation is given by reference to this or that cause.

Clouds could come to be and to be formed both as a result of thickenings of air caused by the pressure of the winds, and as a result of the entanglements of atoms which grip one another and are suitable for producing this effect, and as a result of a collection of effluences from both earth and bodies of water; and it is not impossible that the formation of such compounds is also produced in several other ways. So rains [lit. waters] could be produced from the clouds, sometimes when they are compressed and sometimes when they undergo change; 100. and again, winds, by their egress from suitable places and motion through the air, [can cause rain] when there is a relatively forceful influx from certain aggregates which are suitable for such discharges.

Thunder can occur as a result of the confinement of wind in the hollows of the clouds, as happens in closed vessels [in] our [experience], and as a result of the booming of fire combined with wind inside the clouds, and as a result of the rupture and separation of clouds, and by the friction between clouds and their fragmentation when they have taken on an ice-like solidity. And the phenomena invite us to say that the entire topic as well as this part of it are subject to several different explanations.

101. And lightning flashes similarly occur in several different ways; for the [atomic] configuration which produces fire is squeezed out by the friction and collision of clouds and so generates a lightning flash; [it could] also [occur] as a result of the wind making the sort of bodies which cause this luminiscence flash forth from the clouds; and by the squeezing of clouds when they are compressed, either by each other or by the winds; and by the inclusion [in them] of the light scattered from

the heavenly bodies, which is then driven together by the motion of the clouds and winds and is expelled by the clouds; or as a result of the filtering of the finest form of light through the clouds[16] and as a result of its movement; and by the conflagration of the wind which occurs because of the vigour of its movement and its extreme compression; 102. and because the clouds are broken by the winds and the atoms which produce fire are then expelled and so produce the presentation of the lightning flash. And it will be easy to see [that it could happen] in a great many other ways, for him who clings always to the phenomena and who is able to contemplate together what is similar to the phenomena.

The lightning flash precedes the thunder in this sort of arrangement of clouds because the configuration which produces the lightning flash is expelled at the same time as the wind strikes [the cloud] and subsequently the wind, being confined, produces this booming noise; and because although both strike together, the lightning flash moves with a more vigorous speed towards us, 103. while the thunder comes later, just as happens with some things which strike blows and are observed from a distance.

Thunder bolts can occur as a result of repeated gatherings of winds, and their compression and powerful conflagration, and the fracture of one part and its very powerful expulsion towards the areas below, the breakage occurring because the places adjacent to it are more dense owing to the thickening of the clouds; and [it may occur] just as thunder too can occur, simply because of the expulsion of the fire, when a great deal of it is confined and very powerfully struck by the wind and has broken the cloud because it cannot escape to the adjacent areas since they are always compacting together.[17] 104. And thunderbolts can be produced in several different ways—just be sure that myths are kept out of it! And they will be kept out of it if one follows rightly the appearances and takes them as signs of what is unobservable.

Whirlwinds can occur as a result of a cloud being forced in the form of a column downwards to regions below, being pushed by a mass of wind and driven by the power of the wind, while at the same time the wind outside pushes the cloud to one side; and by the formation of the wind into a circle when some air presses down on it from above; and as a result of the compacting of the air around it, when a great flow of winds takes place and is not able to flow off to the side. 105. And when the whirlwind is forced down to the earth, tornadoes are produced, in

16. Scholiast: "Or clouds were incinerated by the fire and the thunder is produced."
17. Scholiast: "It generally [strikes] on a high mountain, on which thunderbolts most often fall."

whatever way their production might take place owing to the movement of the wind; and when it [is forced down] on the sea, waterspouts are produced.

It is possible that earthquakes occur as a result of the enclosure of wind in the earth and the juxtaposition of small masses [of wind?] with the earth and its constant movement, all of which produce the shaking in the earth. And [the earth] either takes this wind into itself from the outside or because solid blocks of earth fall inwards into cavernous places in the earth and turn the enclosed air into wind. ⟨And⟩ earthquakes may also be produced as a result of the mere transmission of the movement produced by the falling of many solid blocks of earth and the transmission [of this shock] back again when it collides with some more densely compressed parts of the earth. **106.** And these movements of the earth may also occur in many other ways. [There may be a lacuna in our text here.]

And the winds happen to occur from time to time when on any occasion some foreign matter gradually enters in, and as a result of the collection of a tremendous amount of water; and the rest of the winds occur when even just a few fall into the many hollow spaces, if there occurs a transmission of their force.

Hail is produced by a quite powerful solidification, [a result of] a circular movement and [subsequent] division of certain breathlike particles; and also ⟨because of⟩ a more moderate solidification of certain watery particles ⟨and⟩ their simultaneous fracture, which at the same time condenses them and breaks them up, so that the solidified material forms compounds both within the distinct parts and in the aggregation. **107.** It is not impossible that their circular shape is produced both because the extremities on all sides melt off and because, at the formation of the compound, [particles] (either watery or breathlike) surround it evenly, part by part on all sides, as is said.

Snow could be produced by the outpouring of fine [drops of] water from the clouds owing to the symmetry of the pores and to the constant and powerful friction on the right sort of clouds by the wind, followed by the solidification of this [water] during its movement as a result of some powerful conditions of coldness in the lower regions of the clouds. And as a result of a solidification in the clouds which have a uniform rareness this sort of outflow can also occur when the watery clouds rub against each other and lie side by side; and these cause a kind of compression and so produce hail—something which happens mostly in the spring. **108.** And this aggregation of snow could also vibrate off when the clouds which have undergone solidification rub against each other. And it is also possible that snow is produced in other ways.

Dew is produced by the assembling from the air of [particles] which become productive of this sort of moisture; and also by an exhalation either from wet areas or areas which have bodies of water (which is the sort of place where dew is most likely to be produced) followed by their assembling in the same place and their production of moisture and finally by its movement to lower regions, exactly as certain such things in our own experience ⟨are observed being produced. And frost⟩ 109. is produced ⟨no differently⟩ from dew, when certain such things are solidified in a certain way because of a certain condition of cold air.

Ice is produced both by the expulsion of the round configuration from the water and by the compression of the scalene and acute-angled [particles] which exist in the water; and also by the addition from the outside of such [particles], which are driven together and so produce solidification in the water by expelling a certain number of round [particles].

The rainbow occurs as a result of the sun shining on water-laden air; or as a result of some peculiar coalescence of light and air which will produce the peculiar properties of these colours, either all [together] or one type at a time; and again, as a result of the reflection of this light the neighbouring regions of the air will take on the sort of coloration which we see because the sun shines on its parts. 110. This presentation of roundness occurs because the vision observes the distance as [being] equal from all directions, or [possibly] because the atoms in the air (or those in the clouds which are derived from the same air) are compressed in such a way that this compound gives off [the appearance of] roundness.

The halo around the moon is produced because air from all sides moves towards the moon; or when it evenly restricts [the movement of] the effluences sent off from it to such an extent that this cloudlike phenomenon forms around it in a circle and is not interrupted in the slightest extent; or it restricts [the movement of] the air around it symmetrically on all sides so that what is around it takes on a round and dense formation. 111. And this happens in certain parts either because a certain effluence forces its way in from outside or because heat occupies passages suitable for the production of this effect.

Comets occur when, under suitable circumstances, fire is collected in certain places in the meteorological region at certain intervals of time; or when from time to time the heavens above us adopt a particular kind of movement, so that such heavenly bodies make their appearance; or the [comets] just rush in by themselves at certain times because of some circumstances and approach the regions where we happen to be and become prominently visible; and they disappear owing to opposite causes. 112. Certain heavenly bodies rotate in place [i.e., those near the pole, which never set], which occurs not only because that part of the cosmos around which the rest rotates is stationary, as some people say, but also because there is a circular rotation of air around it which prevents them from wandering around, as the other heavenly bodies do; or also because they do not have any appropriate fuel in adjacent regions, while there is [a supply of fuel] in the area where they are observed. And this [phenomenon] could also be produced in several other ways, provided one can reason out what is consistent with the appearances.

The wandering of some of the heavenly bodies, if they really do happen to have this kind of movement, 113. and the regular motion of others could be a result of them starting out with circular movement and [then] having been forced in such a way that some of them move in the same uniform rotation while others move with a rotation which at the same time has certain irregularities; and it could also be that, according to the regions over which they move, in one place there are uniform regions of air which push them on continuously in the same direction and which burn uniformly, while elsewhere there are irregular [regions of air] of such a nature that the observed differences are produced. But to supply one cause for these facts, when the phenomena suggest that there are several different explanations, is the lunatic and inappropriate behaviour of those who are obsessed with a pointless [brand of] astronomy and of certain [others] who supply vain explanations, since they do not in any way liberate the divine nature from burdensome service. 114. That some heavenly bodies are observed being left behind by others occurs because although they move around in the same orbit they do so more slowly; and because they also move in the opposite direction being drawn backwards by the same rotation; and also because some rotate through a larger area and some through a smaller, though they turn with the same rotation. But to pronounce unqualifiedly on these matters is appropriate to those who wish [only] to make a display of wonders for the masses.

So-called falling stars could be produced in part by their own friction, and also because they fall wherever there is a massive outburst of wind, just as we said [occurred] in the case of lightning flashes; 115. also by a collection of atoms capable of producing fire, when similar material [congregates] to produce this result and also a motion where the surge produced by the original collection occurs; and also because wind is concentrated in certain dense and misty places and this ignites as a result of its confinement, then breaks through the surrounding environment and is borne to the place to which the movement makes its surge; and there are other non-mythical ways in which this phenomenon could be produced.

The predictive weather signs which occur in certain animals occur by a coincidental conjunction of events; for the animals do not bring any necessity to bear on the production of winter, nor does any divine nature sit around waiting for these animals to come out [of hibernation] and [only] then fulfils these signs. 116. For such foolishness would not afflict any ordinary animal, even if it were a little more sophisticated, let alone one who possessed complete happiness.

Commit all of this to memory, Pythocles; for you will leave myth far behind you and will be able to see [the causes of phenomena] similar to these. Most important, devote yourself to the contemplation of the basic principles [i.e., atoms] and the unlimited [i.e., void] and things related to them, and again [the contemplation] of the criteria and the feelings and the [goal] for sake of which we reason these things out. For if these things above all are contemplated together, they will make it easy for you to see the explanations of the detailed phenomena. For those who have not accepted these [ideas] with complete contentment could not do a good job of contemplating these things themselves, nor could they acquire the [goal] for the sake of which these things should be contemplated.

Letter to Menoeceus: Diogenes Laertius   [I-4]
10.121–135

121. Epicurus to Menoeceus, greetings:

122. Let no one delay the study of philosophy while young nor weary of it when old. For no one is either too young or too old for the health of the soul. He who says either that the time for philosophy has not yet come or that it has passed is like someone who says that the time for happiness has not yet come or that it has passed. Therefore, both young and old must philosophize, the latter so that although old he may stay young in good things owing to gratitude for what has occurred, the former so that although young he too may be like an old man owing to his lack of fear of what is to come. Therefore, one must practise the things which produce happiness, since if that is present we have everything and if it is absent we do everything in order to have it.

123. Do and practise what I constantly told you to do, believing these to be the elements of living well. First, believe that god is an indestructible and blessed animal, in accordance with the general conception of god commonly held, and do not ascribe to god anything foreign to his indestructibility or repugnant to his blessedness. Believe of him everything which is able to preserve his blessedness and indestructibility. For gods do exist, since we have clear knowledge of them. But they are not such as the many believe them to be. For they do not adhere to their own

views about the gods. The man who denies the gods of the many is not impious, but rather he who ascribes to the gods the opinions of the many. **124.** For the pronouncements of the many about the gods are not basic grasps but false suppositions. Hence come the greatest harm from the gods to bad men and the greatest benefits [to the good]. For the gods always welcome men who are like themselves, being congenial to their own virtues and considering that whatever is not such is uncongenial.

Get used to believing that death is nothing to us. For all good and bad consists in sense-experience, and death is the privation of sense-experience. Hence, a correct knowledge of the fact that death is nothing to us makes the mortality of life a matter for contentment, not by adding a limitless time [to life] but by removing the longing for immortality. **125.** For there is nothing fearful in life for one who has grasped that there is nothing fearful in the absence of life. Thus, he is a fool who says that he fears death not because it will be painful when present but because it is painful when it is still to come. For that which while present causes no distress causes unnecessary pain when merely anticipated. So death, the most frightening of bad things, is nothing to us; since when we exist, death is not yet present, and when death is present, then we do not exist. Therefore, it is relevant neither to the living nor to the dead, since it does not affect the former, and the latter do not exist. But the many sometimes flee death as the greatest of bad things and sometimes choose it as a relief from the bad things in life. **126.** But the wise man neither rejects life nor fears death. For living does not offend him, nor does he believe not living to be something bad. And just as he does not unconditionally choose the largest amount of food but the most pleasant food, so he savours not the longest time but the most pleasant. He who advises the young man to live well and the old man to die well is simple-minded, not just because of the pleasing aspects of life but because the same kind of practice produces a good life and a good death. Much worse is he who says that it is good not to be born, "but when born to pass through the gates of Hades as quickly as possible."[18] **127.** For if he really believes what he says, why doesn't he leave life? For it is easy for him to do, if he has firmly decided on it. But if he is joking, he is wasting his time among men who don't welcome it. We must remember that what will happen is neither unconditionally within our power nor unconditionally outside our power, so that we will not unconditionally expect that it will occur nor despair of it as unconditionally not going to occur.

One must reckon that of desires some are natural, some groundless;

18. Theognis 425, 427.

and of the natural desires some are necessary and some merely natural; and of the necessary, some are necessary for happiness and some for freeing the body from troubles and some for life itself. **128.** The unwavering contemplation of these enables one to refer every choice and avoidance to the health of the body and the freedom of the soul from disturbance, since this is the goal of a blessed life. For we do everything for the sake of being neither in pain nor in terror. As soon as we achieve this state every storm in the soul is dispelled, since the animal is not in a position to go after some need nor to seek something else to complete the good of the body and the soul. For we are in need of pleasure only when we are in pain because of the absence of pleasure, and when we are not in pain, then we no longer need pleasure.

And this is why we say that pleasure is the starting-point and goal of living blessedly. **129.** For we recognized this as our first innate good, and this is our starting point for every choice and avoidance and we come to this by judging every good by the criterion of feeling. And it is just because this is the first innate good that we do not choose every pleasure; but sometimes we pass up many pleasures when we get a larger amount of what is uncongenial from them. And we believe many pains to be better than pleasures when a greater pleasure follows for a long while if we endure the pains. So every pleasure is a good thing, since it has a nature congenial [to us], but not every one is to be chosen. Just as every pain too is a bad thing, but not every one is such as to be always avoided. **130.** It is, however, appropriate to make all these decisions by comparative measurement and an examination of the advantages and disadvantages. For at some times we treat the good thing as bad and, conversely, the bad thing as good.

And we believe that self-sufficiency is a great good, not in order that we might make do with few things under all circumstances, but so that if we do not have a lot we can make do with few, being genuinely convinced that those who least need extravagance enjoy it most; and that everything natural is easy to obtain and whatever is groundless is hard to obtain; and that simple flavours provide a pleasure equal to that of an extravagant life-style when all pain from want is removed, **131.** and barley cakes and water provide the highest pleasure when someone in want takes them. Therefore, becoming accustomed to simple, not extravagant, ways of life makes one completely healthy, makes man unhesitant in the face of life's necessary duties, puts us in a better condition for the times of extravagance which occasionally come along, and makes us fearless in the face of chance. So when we say that pleasure is the goal we do not mean the pleasures of the profligate or the pleasures of consumption, as some believe, either from ignorance and disagreement or from deliberate misinterpretation, but rather the lack of pain in the body and disturbance in the soul. **132.** For it is not drinking bouts and continuous partying and enjoying boys and women, or consuming fish and the other dainties of an extravagant table, which produce the pleasant life, but sober calculation which searches out the reasons for every choice and avoidance and drives out the opinions which are the source of the greatest turmoil for men's souls.

Prudence is the principle of all these things and is the greatest good. That is why prudence is a more valuable thing than philosophy. For prudence is the source of all the other virtues, teaching that it is impossible to live pleasantly without living prudently, honourably, and justly, and impossible to live prudently, honourably, and justly without living pleasantly. For the virtues are natural adjuncts of the pleasant life and the pleasant life is inseparable from them.

133. For who do you believe is better than a man who has pious opinions about the gods, is always fearless about death, has reasoned out the natural goal of life and understands that the limit of good things is easy to achieve completely and easy to provide, and that the limit of bad things either has a short duration or causes little trouble?

As to [Fate], introduced by some as the mistress of all, ⟨he is scornful, saying rather that some things happen of necessity,⟩ others by chance, and others by our own agency, and that he sees that necessity is not answerable [to anyone], that chance is unstable, while what occurs by our own agency is autonomous, and that it is to this that praise and blame are attached. **134.** For it would be better to follow the stories told about the gods than to be a slave to the fate of the natural philosophers. For the former suggests a hope of escaping bad things by honouring the gods, but the latter involves an inescapable and merciless necessity. And he [the wise man] believes that chance is not a god, as the many think, for nothing is done in a disorderly way by god; nor that it is an uncertain cause. For he does not think that anything good or bad with respect to living blessedly is given by chance to men, although it does provide the starting points of great good and bad things. And he thinks it better to be unlucky in a rational way than lucky in a senseless way; **135.** for it is better for a good decision not to turn out right in action than for a bad decision to turn out right because of chance.

Practise these and the related precepts day and night, by yourself and with a like-minded friend, and you will never be disturbed either when awake or in sleep, and you will live as a god among men. For a man who lives among immortal goods is in no respect like a mere mortal animal.

Ancient Collections of Maxims

The Principal Doctrines: Diogenes Laertius   [I-5]
10.139–154

I What is blessed and indestructible has no troubles itself, nor does it give trouble to anyone else, so that it is not affected by feelings of anger or gratitude. For all such things are a sign of weakness.[19]

II Death is nothing to us. For what has been dissolved has no sense-experience, and what has no sense-experience is nothing to us.

III The removal of all feeling of pain is the limit of the magnitude of pleasures. Wherever a pleasurable feeling is present, for as long as it is present, there is neither a feeling of pain nor a feeling of distress, nor both together.

IV The feeling of pain does not linger continuously in the flesh; rather, the sharpest is present for the shortest time, while what merely exceeds the feeling of pleasure in the flesh lasts only a few days. And diseases which last a long time involve feelings of pleasure which exceed feelings of pain.

V It is impossible to live pleasantly without living prudently, honourably, and justly and impossible to live prudently, honourably, and justly without living pleasantly. And whoever lacks this cannot live pleasantly.

VI The natural good of public office and kingship is for the sake of getting confidence from [other] men, [at least] from those from whom one *is* able to provide this.

VII Some men want to become famous and respected, believing that this is the way to acquire security against [other] men. Thus if the life of such men is secure, they acquire the natural good; but if it is not secure, they do not have that for the sake of which they strove from the beginning according to what is naturally congenial.

VIII No pleasure is a bad thing in itself. But the things which produce certain pleasures bring troubles many times greater than the pleasures.

IX If every pleasure were condensed and were present, both in time and in the whole compound [body and soul] or in the most important parts of our nature, then pleasures would never differ from one another.

X If the things which produce the pleasures of profligate men dissolved the intellect's fears about the phenomena of the heavens and about death

---

19. Scholiast: "Elsewhere he says that the gods are contemplated by reason, and that some exist 'numerically' [i.e., are numerically distinct, each being unique in kind] while others are similar in form, because of a continuous flow of similar images to the same place; and that they are anthropomorphic."

and pains and, moreover, if they taught us the limit of our desires, then we would not have reason to criticize them, since they would be filled with pleasures from every source and would contain no feeling of pain or distress from any source—and that is what is bad.

XI If our suspicions about heavenly phenomena and about death did not trouble us at all and were never anything to us, and, moreover, if not knowing the limits of pains and desires did not trouble us, then we would have no need of natural science.

XII It is impossible for someone ignorant about the nature of the universe but still suspicious about the subjects of the myths to dissolve his feelings of fear about the most important matters. So it is impossible to receive unmixed pleasures without knowing natural science.

XIII It is useless to obtain security from men while the things above and below the earth and, generally, the things in the unbounded remained as objects of suspicion.

XIV The purest security is that which comes from a quiet life and withdrawal from the many, although a certain degree of security from other men does come by means of the power to repel [attacks] and by means of prosperity.

XV Natural wealth is both limited and easy to acquire. But wealth [as defined by] groundless opinions extends without limit.

XVI Chance has a small impact on the wise man, while reasoning has arranged for, is arranging for, and will arrange for the greatest and most important matters throughout the whole of his life.

XVII The just life is most free from disturbance, but the unjust life is full of the greatest disturbance.

XVIII As soon as the feeling of pain produced by want is removed, pleasure in the flesh will not increase but is only varied. But the limit of mental pleasures is produced by a reasoning out of these very pleasures [of the flesh] and of the things related to these, which used to cause the greatest fears in the intellect.

XIX Unlimited time and limited time contain equal [amounts of] pleasure, if one measures its limits by reasoning.

XX The flesh took the limits of pleasure to be unlimited, and [only] an unlimited time would have provided it. But the intellect, reasoning out the goal and limit of the flesh and dissolving the fears of eternity, provided us with the perfect way of life and had no further need of unlimited time. But it [the intellect] did not flee pleasure, and even when circumstances caused an exit from life it did not die as though it were lacking any aspect of the best life.

XXI He who has learned the limits of life knows that it is easy to provide that which removes the feeling of pain owing to want and make one's whole life perfect. So there is no need for things which involve struggle.

XXII One must reason about the real goal and every clear fact, to which we refer mere opinions. If not, everything will be full of indecision and disturbance.

XXIII If you quarrel with all your sense-perceptions you will have nothing to refer to in judging even those sense-perceptions which you claim are false.

XXIV If you reject unqualifiedly any sense-perception and do not distinguish the opinion about what awaits confirmation, and what is already present in the sense-perception, and the feelings, and every application of the intellect to presentations, you will also disturb the rest of your sense-perceptions with your pointless opinion; as a result you will reject every criterion. If, on the other hand, in your conceptions formed by opinion, you affirm everything that awaits confirmation as well as what does not, you will not avoid falsehood, so that you will be in the position of maintaining every disputable point in every decision about what is and is not correct.

XXV If you do not, on every occasion, refer each of your actions to the goal of nature, but instead turn prematurely to some other [criterion] in avoiding or pursuing [things], your actions will not be consistent with your reasoning.

XXVI The desires which do not bring a feeling of pain when not fulfilled are not necessary; but the desire for them is easy to dispel when they seem to be hard to achieve or to produce harm.

XXVII Of the things which wisdom provides for the blessedness of one's whole life, by far the greatest is the possession of friendship.

XXVIII The same understanding produces confidence about there being nothing terrible which is eternal or [even] long-lasting and has also realized that security amid even these limited [bad things] is most easily achieved through friendship.

XXIX Of desires, some are natural and necessary, some natural and not necessary, and some neither natural nor necessary but occurring as a result of a groundless opinion.[20]

XXX Among natural desires, those which do not lead to a feeling of pain if not fulfilled and about which there is an intense effort, these are

---

20. Scholiast: "Epicurus thinks that those which liberate us from pains are natural and necessary, for example drinking in the case of thirst; natural and not necessary are those which merely provide variations of pleasure but do not remove the feeling of pain, for example expensive foods; neither natural nor necessary are, for example, crowns and the erection of statues."

produced by a groundless opinion and they fail to be dissolved not because of their own nature but because of the groundless opinions of mankind.

XXXI The justice of nature is a pledge of reciprocal usefulness, [i.e.,] neither to harm one another nor be harmed.

XXXII There was no justice or injustice with respect to all those animals which were unable to make pacts about neither harming one another nor being harmed. Similarly, [there was no justice or injustice] for all those nations which were unable or unwilling to make pacts about neither harming one another nor being harmed.

XXXIII Justice was not a thing in its own right, but [exists] in mutual dealings in whatever places there [is] a pact about neither harming one another nor being harmed.

XXXIV Injustice is not a bad thing in its own right, but [only] because of the fear produced by the suspicion that one will not escape the notice of those assigned to punish such actions.

XXXV It is impossible for someone who secretly does something which men agreed [not to do] in order to avoid harming one another or being harmed to be confident that he will escape detection, even if in current circumstances he escapes detection ten thousand times. For until his death it will be uncertain whether he will continue to escape detection.

XXXVI In general outline justice is the same for everyone; for it was something useful in mutual associations. But with respect to the peculiarities of a region or of other [relevant] causes, it does not follow that the same thing is just for everyone.

XXXVII Of actions believed to be just, that whose usefulness in circumstances of mutual associations is supported by the testimony [of experience] has the attribute of serving as just whether it is the same for everyone or not. And if someone passes a law and it does not turn out to be in accord with what is useful in mutual associations, this no longer possesses the nature of justice. And if what is useful in the sense of being just changes, but for a while fits our basic grasp [of justice], nevertheless it was just for that length of time, [at least] for those who do not disturb themselves with empty words but simply look to the facts.

XXXVIII If objective circumstances have not changed and things believed to be just have been shown in actual practice not to be in accord with our basic grasp [of justice], then those things were not just. And if objective circumstances do change and the same things which had been just turn out to be no longer useful, then those things were just as long as they were useful for the mutual associations of fellow citizens; but later, when they were not useful, they were no longer just.

XXXIX The man who has made the best arrangements for confidence about external threats is he who has made the manageable things akin to himself, and has at least made the unmanageable things not alien to himself. But he avoided all contact with things for which not even this could be managed and he drove out of his life everything which it profited him to drive out.

XL All those who had the power to acquire the greatest confidence from [the threats posed by] their neighbours also thereby lived together most pleasantly with the surest guarantee; and since they enjoyed the fullest sense of belonging they did not grieve the early death of the departed, as though it called for pity.

The Vatican Collection of Epicurean Sayings[21]   [I-6]

4. Every pain is easy to despise. For [pains] which produce great distress are short in duration; and those which last for a long time in the flesh cause only mild distress.

7. It is hard to commit injustice and escape detection, but to be confident of escaping detection is impossible.

9. Necessity is a bad thing, but there is no necessity to live with necessity.

11. In most men, what is at peace is numbed and what is active is raging madly.

14. We are born only once, and we cannot be born twice; and one must for all eternity exist no more. You are not in control of tomorrow and yet you delay your [opportunity to] rejoice. Life is ruined by delay and each and every one of us dies without enjoying leisure.

15. We value our characters as our own personal possessions, whether they are good and envied by men or not. We must regard our neighbours' characters thus too, if they are respectable.

16. No one who sees what is bad chooses it, but being lured [by it] as being good compared to what is even worse than it he is caught in the snare.

17. It is not the young man who is to be congratulated for his blessedness, but the old man who has lived well. For the young man at the full peak of his powers wanders senselessly, owing to chance. But the old man has let down anchor in old age as though in a harbour, since he has

---

21. Some of the maxims in this collection are identical to some Principal Doctrines; some are attributed to Epicurus' followers rather than to the master himself. The Sayings selected by Arrighetti (in *Epicuro: Opere*) are translated here and his text is used.

secured the goods about which he was previously not confident by means of his secure sense of gratitude.

18. If you take away the chance to see and talk and spend time with [the beloved], then the passion of sexual love is dissolved.

19. He who forgets the good which he previously had, has today become an old man.

21. One must not force nature but persuade her. And we will persuade her by fulfilling the necessary desires, and the natural ones too if they do not harm [us], but sharply rejecting the harmful ones.

23. Every friendship is worth choosing[22] for its own sake, though it takes its origin from the benefits [it confers on us].

24. Dreams have neither a divine nature, nor prophetic power, but they are produced by the impact of images.

25. Poverty, if measured by the goal of nature, is great wealth; and wealth, if limits are not set for it, is great poverty.

26. One must grasp clearly that both long and short discourses contribute to the same [end].

27. In other activities, the rewards come only when people have become, with great difficulty, complete [masters of the activity]; but in philosophy the pleasure accompanies the knowledge. For the enjoyment does not come after the learning but the learning and the enjoyment are simultaneous.

28. One must not approve of those who are excessively eager for friendship, nor those who are reluctant. But one must be willing to run some risks for the sake of friendship.

29. Employing frankness in my study of natural philosophy, I would prefer to proclaim in oracular fashion what is beneficial to men, even if no one is going to understand, rather than to assent to [common] opinions and so enjoy the constant praise which comes from the many.

31. (= Metrodorus fr. 51) One can attain security against other things, but when it comes to death all men live in a city without walls.

32. To show reverence for a wise man is itself a great good for him who reveres [the wise man].

33. The cry of the flesh: not to be hungry, not to be thirsty, not to be cold. For if someone has these things and is confident of having them in the future, he might contend even with ⟨Zeus⟩ for happiness.

34. We do not need utility from our friends so much as we need confidence concerning that utility.

---

22. This is an emendation for the mss' 'a virtue'; we regard the emendation as virtually certain, though the transmitted text has been defended.

35. One should not spoil what is present by desiring what is absent, but rather reason out that these things too [i.e., what we have] were among those we might have prayed for.

37. Nature is weak in the face of the bad, not the good; for it is preserved by pleasures and dissolved by pains.

38. He is utterly small-minded for whom there are many plausible reasons for committing suicide.

39. The constant friend is neither he who always searches for utility, nor he who never links [friendship to utility]. For the former makes gratitude a matter for commercial transaction, while the latter kills off good hope for the future.

40. He who claims that everything occurs by necessity has no complaint against him who claims that everything does not occur by necessity. For he makes the very claim [in question] by necessity.

41. One must philosophize and at the same time laugh and take care of one's household and use the rest of our personal goods, and never stop proclaiming the utterances of correct philosophy.

42. In the same period of time both the greatest good and the dissolution ⟨of bad⟩ are produced.

43. It is impious to love money unjustly, and shameful to do so justly; for it is unfitting to be sordidly stingy even if one is just.

44. When the wise man is brought face to face with the necessities of life, he knows how to give rather than receive—such a treasury of self-sufficiency has he found.

45. Natural philosophy does not create boastful men nor chatterboxes nor men who show off the 'culture' which the many quarrel over, but rather strong and self-sufficient men, who pride themselves on their own personal goods, not those of external circumstances.

46. We utterly eliminate bad habits like wicked men who have been doing great harm to us for a long time.

48. [We should] try to make the later stretch of the road more important than the earlier one, as long as we are on the road; and when we get to the end [of the road], [we should] feel a smooth contentment.

52. Friendship dances around the world announcing to all of us that we must wake up to blessedness.

53. One should envy no one. For the good are not worthy of envy, and the more good fortune the wicked have, the more they spoil it for themselves.

54. One must not pretend to philosophize, but philosophize in reality. For we do not need the semblance of health but true health.

55. Misfortunes must be cured by a sense of gratitude for what has been and the knowledge that what is past cannot be undone.

56–57. The wise man feels no more pain when he is tortured ⟨than when his friend is tortured, and will die on his behalf; for if he betrays⟩ his friend, his entire life will be confounded and utterly upset because of a lack of confidence.

58. They must free themselves from the prison of general education and politics.

59. The stomach is not insatiable, as the many say, but rather the opinion that the stomach requires an unlimited amount of filling is false.

60. Everyone leaves life as though he had just been born.

61. The sight of one's neighbours is most beautiful if the first meeting brings concord or [at least] produces a serious commitment to this.

62. For if parents are justifiably angered at their children, it is surely pointless to resist and not ask to be forgiven; but if [their anger] is not justifiable but somewhat irrational, it is ridiculous for someone with irrationality in his heart to appeal to someone set against appeals and not to seek in a spirit of good will to win him over by other means.

63. There is also a proper measure for parsimony, and he who does not reason it out is just as badly off as he who goes wrong by total neglect of limits.

64. Praise from other men must come of its own accord; and we must be concerned with healing ourselves.

65. It is pointless to ask from the gods what one is fully able to supply for oneself.

66. Let us share our friends' suffering not with laments but with thoughtful concern.

67. A free life cannot acquire great wealth, because the task is not easy without slavery to the mob or those in power; rather, it already possesses everything in constant abundance. And if it does somehow achieve great wealth, one could easily share this out in order to obtain the good will of one's neighbours.

68. Nothing is enough to someone for whom enough is little.

69. The ingratitude of the soul makes an animal greedy for unlimited variation in its life-style.

70. Let nothing be done in your life which will cause you to fear if it is discovered by your neighbour.

71. One should bring this question to bear on all one's desires: what will happen to me if what is sought by desire is achieved, and what will happen if it is not?

73. Even some bodily pains are worthwhile for fending off others like them.

74. In a joint philosophical investigation he who is defeated comes out ahead in so far as he has learned something new.

75. This utterance is ungrateful for past goods: look to the end of a long life.

76. As you grow old, you are such as I would praise, and you have seen the difference between what it means to philosophize for yourself and what it means to do so for Greece. I rejoice with you.

77. The greatest fruit of self-sufficiency is freedom.

78. The noble man is most involved with wisdom and friendship, of which one is a mortal good, the other immortal.

79. He who is free from disturbance within himself also causes no trouble for another.

80. A young man's share in salvation comes from attending to his age and guarding against what will defile everything through maddening desires.

81. The disturbance of the soul will not be dissolved nor will considerable joy be produced by the presence of the greatest wealth, nor by honour and admiration among the many, nor by anything which is a result of indefinite causes.

Doxographical Reports

Introductory report of Epicurus' views: [I-7]
Diogenes Laertius 10.29–34

29. . . . So philosophy is divided into three parts: canonic, physics, ethics. 30. Canonic provides procedures for use in the system and it is contained in one work entitled *The Canon*. Physics comprises the entire study of nature and it is contained in the 37 books of the *On Nature* and in outline form in the letters. Ethics comprises the discussion of choice and avoidance and it is contained in the book *On Ways of Life* and in the letters and in *On the Goal of Life*. They are accustomed, however, to set out canonic together with physics and they describe it as dealing with the criterion and with the basic principle, and as being fundamental. And physics is about generation and destruction, and about nature. And ethics is about things worth choosing and avoiding and about ways of life and about the goal of life.

31. They reject dialectic as being irrelevant. For it is sufficient for natural philosophers to proceed according to the utterances made by the facts. So, in *The Canon* Epicurus is found saying that sense-perceptions, basic grasps, and feelings are the criteria of truth, and the Epicureans add the applications of the intellect to presentations. He says this also

in the epitome addressed to Herodotus and in the *Principal Doctrines.* "For," he says, "every sense-perception is unreasoning and incapable of remembering. For neither is it moved by itself nor can it add or subtract anything when moved by something else. Nor is there anything which can refute sense-perceptions. 32. For a perception from one sense cannot refute another of the same type, because they are of equal strength; nor can a perception from one sense refute one from a different sense, because they do not judge the same objects. Nor indeed can reasoning [refute them]; for all reasoning depends on the sense-perceptions. Nor can one sense-perception refute another, since we attend to them all. And the fact of our awareness of sense-perceptions confirms the truth of the sense-perceptions. And it is just as much a fact that we see and hear as that we feel pain; hence, it is from the apparent that we must infer about the non-evident. Moreover, all ideas are formed from sense-perceptions by direct experience or by analogy or by similarity or by compounding, with reasoning also making a contribution. And the appearances which madmen have and those in dreams are true, for they cause motion [in minds], and what does not exist does not move anything."

33. They say that the basic grasp is like an act of grasping or a correct opinion or a conception or a universal idea stored [up in the mind], i.e., a memory of what has often appeared in the external world. For example, this sort of thing is "man". For as soon as "man" is uttered, immediately one has an idea of the general outline of man, according to our basic grasp, following the lead of our senses. Therefore, what is primarily denoted by every word is something clear; and we could never have inquired into an object if we had not first been aware of it. For example, "is what is standing far off a horse or a cow?" For one must at some time have been aware of the shape of horse and cow according to a basic grasp.

Nor would we have given a name to something if we had not first learned its general outline according to a basic grasp. Therefore, our basic grasps are clear. And an object of opinion depends on something prior and clear, by referring to which we speak [of it], for example, "On what basis do we know if this is a man?"

34. And they also say that opinion is a supposition, and that it can be true or false. For if it is testified for or not testified against, it is true. But if it is not testified for or is testified against, it turns out false. Hence they introduced the idea of "what awaits confirmation." For example, one awaits confirmation of and comes nearer to a tower, to learn how it appears close up.

They say there are two feelings, pleasure and pain, which occur in every animal; and the one is congenial to us, the other uncongenial. By means of them we judge what to choose and what to avoid. Of inquiries, some deal with objective facts, others with mere words.

This, then, is an elementary account of the division of philosophy and the criterion.

Report of Epicurus' Ethical Views: [I-8]
Diogenes Laertius 10.117–121

117. . . . . He writes as follows on matters related to living and how we should choose some things and avoid others. But first let us relate the opinions of Epicurus and his followers about the wise man.

Harm from other men comes either as a result of hate or envy or contempt, which the wise man overcomes by reasoning. Moreover, once a man has become wise he can no longer take on the opposite disposition nor feign it willingly. But he will be more affected by feelings—for they would not hinder his progress towards wisdom. Nor indeed could people with every bodily condition become wise, nor can people from every race. 118. And even if the wise man is tortured on the rack, he is happy. Only the wise man will be grateful and he will persist in speaking well of friends equally whether they are present or absent. But when he is tortured on the rack he will moan and groan. The wise man will not have intercourse with a woman in a manner forbidden by the laws, according to Diogenes in his summary of Epicurus' ethical doctrines. Nor will he punish his servants, but rather will pity them and forgive one who is virtuous. They do not believe that the wise man will fall in love, nor that he will worry about his burial, nor that love is sent by the gods, according to Diogenes in his . . . [There is a lacuna here.] . . . Nor will he be a good public speaker. "Sexual intercourse", they say, "never helped anyone, and one must be satisfied if it has not harmed."

119. And indeed the wise man will marry and father children, as Epicurus says in his *Problems* and in the *On Nature*. But he will marry [only] when it is indicated by the circumstances of his life at a given time. And some will be diverted from this. Nor indeed will he rant and rave while under the influence of drink, as Epicurus says in his *Symposium*. Nor will he participate in civic life, as he says in book one of *On Ways of Life*. Neither will he be a tyrant or a Cynic, as he says in book two of *On Ways of Life*; nor will he be a beggar. But if he were to be blinded he would go on living, as he says in the same book. And the wise man will feel pain, as Diogenes says in book five of his *Selections*. 120a. And he will serve as a juror, and leave written treatises, though he will not deliver panegyrics. And he will take thought for his possessions and for

the future. He will like the countryside. He will resist fate, and will betray none of his friends. He will take thought for good reputation only so far as [to ensure] that he is not held in contempt. He will take more delight in contemplation than other men.

121b. He will erect statues. If he is ‹well› off, he will be indifferent to it. Only the wise man could converse properly on music and poetry, but he will not actually write poems. One [wise man] is no wiser than another. He will earn money when in dire straits, but only by [exploiting] his wisdom. And he will serve a monarch, when the occasion is appropriate. He will be grateful to someone for being corrected. And he will set up a school, but not so as to draw a crowd. And he will give a public reading, but not unless pressed. He will hold firm opinions and will not be at a loss. And he will be of the same character while asleep. And he will sometimes die for a friend.

120b. They believe that [moral] errors are not equal. And that health is for some a good thing and for others an indifferent. Courage does not come to be by nature, but by a reasoning out of what is advantageous. And friendship comes to be because of its utility; but one must nevertheless make a preliminary sacrifice [for a friend] (for one must also sow the ground), and it is [then] formed by a sharing among those who are fulfilled by their pleasures.

121a. Happiness is conceived of in two ways: the highest happiness, which is that of god and does not admit of further intensification, and that which ‹is determined by› the addition and subtraction of pleasures.

Diogenes Laertius 10.136–138 [I-9]

136. He disagrees with the Cyrenaics on the question of pleasure. For they do not admit katastematic pleasure, but only kinetic pleasure, and he admits both types in both the body and the soul, as he says in *On Choice and Avoidance* and in *On the Goal* and in book one of *On Ways of Life* and in the *Letter to His Friends in Mytilene*. Similarly, Diogenes too in book seventeen of his *Selections* and Metrodorus in the *Timocrates* take the same position: both kinetic and katastematic pleasures are conceived of as pleasure. And Epicurus, in his *On Choices*, says this: "For freedom from disturbance and freedom from suffering are katastematic pleasures; and joy and delight are viewed as kinetic and active."

137. Further, he disagrees with the Cyrenaics [thus]. For they think that bodily pains are worse than those of the soul, since people who err are punished with bodily [pain], while he thinks that pains of the soul are worse, since the flesh is only troubled by the present, but the soul is troubled by the past and the present and the future. In the same way, then, the soul also has greater pleasures. And he uses as a proof that the goal is pleasure the fact that animals, as soon as they are born are satisfied with it but are in conflict with suffering by nature and apart from reason. So it is by our experience all on its own that we avoid pain. . . .

138. The virtues too are chosen because of pleasure, and not for their own sakes, just as medicine is chosen because of health, as Diogenes too says in book twenty of the *Selections*; he also says that basic education is a [form of] pastime. And Epicurus says that only virtue is inseparable from pleasure, and that the other things, such as food, may be separated [from pleasure].

Diogenes Laertius 2.88–90 (an account of Cyrenaic hedonism) [I-10]

88. Particular pleasure is worth choosing for its own sake; happiness, however, is not worth choosing for its own sake but because of the particular pleasures. A confirmation that the goal is pleasure is found in the fact that from childhood on we involuntarily find it [i.e., pleasure] congenial and that when we get it we seek nothing more and that we flee nothing so much as its opposite, pain. And pleasure is good even if it comes from the most indecorous sources, as Hippobotus says in his *On Choices*. For even if the deed is out of place, the pleasure at any rate is worth choosing for its own sake and good.

89. They hold that the removal of the feeling of pain is not pleasure, as Epicurus said it was, and that absence of pleasure is not pain. For both are kinetic, while neither absence of pain nor absence of pleasure is a motion, since absence of pain is like the condition [*katastasis*] of somebody who is asleep. They say that it is possible that some people do not choose pleasure, because they are corrupted. However, not all pleasures and pains of the soul occur as a result of bodily pleasures and pains; for joy results from the simple prosperity of one's fatherland, just as it does from one's own. But further, they say, pleasure is not produced by the recollection or expectation of good things, as Epicurus thought. For the soul's movement is dissolved by the passage of time. 90. They say that pleasures are not produced by the simple act of vision or hearing. At any rate we enjoy hearing those who imitate lamentations and do not enjoy hearing genuine lamentations. [They held that] absence of pleasure and absence of pain are intermediate conditions [*katastaseis*], and moreover that bodily pleasures are much better than those of the soul, and that bodily disturbances are worse. And that is why wrong-doers are punished with these instead [of those]. For they supposed that being in pain is more difficult and that enjoying pleasure is more congenial. . . .

Clement of Alexandria *Stromates:* 2.21,127.2   [I-11]
p. 182 Stählin (450 U)

For the Cyrenaics and Epicurus belong to the class of those who take their starting point from pleasure; for they say expressly that living pleasantly is the goal and that only pleasure is the perfect good, but Epicurus says that the removal of pain is also pleasure; and he says that that which first and by itself draws [us] to itself is worth choosing, and obviously this thing is certainly kinetic.

Ibid.: 2.21,128.1, p. 182 Stählin (509 U)   [I-12]

Epicurus and the Cyrenaics say that what is primarily [or: at first] congenial to us is pleasure; for virtue comes along for the sake of pleasure and produces pleasure.

Ibid. 2.21,130.8–9 pp. 184–5 Stählin (451 U)   [I-13]

. . . These Cyrenaics reject Epicurus' definition of pleasure, i.e., the removal of what causes pain, stigmatizing it as the condition of a corpse; for we rejoice not only over pleasures, but also over conversations and ambitions. But Epicurus thinks that all joy of the soul supervenes on the prior experiences of the body.

The Testimony of Cicero

The Roman statesman and philosophical writer, Cicero (active in the first century B.C.), was a lively critic of Epicureanism. He is sometimes unfair and dismissive, but even his polemic yields information of value to the student of Epicureanism.

On Goals 1.18–20   [I-14]

18. Epicurus generally does not go far wrong when he follows Democritus . . . but these are the catastrophes which belong to Epicurus alone. He thinks that these same indivisible and solid bodies move down in a straight line by their own weight and that this is the natural motion of all bodies. 19. Then this clever fellow, when it occurred to him that if they all moved directly down and, as I said, in a straight line, it would never come about that one atom could make contact with another and so . . . he introduced a fictitious notion: he said that an atom swerves by

a very little bit, indeed a minimal distance, and that in this way are produced the mutual entanglements, linkages, and cohesions of the atoms as a result of which the world and all the parts of the world and everything in it are produced. . . . The swerve itself is made up to suit his pleasure— for he says that the atom swerves without a cause . . . —and without a cause he tore from the atoms that straight downward motion which is natural to all heavy objects (as he himself declared); and by so doing he did not even achieve the goal he intended when he made up this fiction. 20. For if all the atoms swerve, none will ever cohere in a compound; but if some swerve and some move properly by their own impetus, this will amount, first of all, to assigning different spheres of influence, so to speak, to the atoms, some to move straight, others to move crookedly; and second, that very same confused concourse of atoms (and this is the point which Democritus too had trouble with) will not be able to produce the orderly beauty of this world.

On Fate 18–48 (selections)   [I-15]

18. If it were stated thus, "Scipio will die by violence at night in his room", that would be a true statement. For it would be a statement that what was going to occur actually was going to occur; and one ought to know that it was going to occur from the fact that it did happen. And "Scipio will die" was no more true than "he will die in that manner", nor was it any more necessary that he die than that he die in that manner; nor was [the statement that] "Scipio was killed" any more immune from a change from truth to falsehood than [the statement that] "Scipio will be killed".

And the fact that these things are so does not mean that Epicurus has any reason to fear fate and seek aid from the atoms by making them swerve from their paths, and so at one time to burden himself with two unsolvable difficulties: first, that something should occur without a cause, which means that something comes to be from nothing (and neither he nor any other physicist believes that); second, that when two atoms move through the void one goes in a straight line and the other swerves.

19. Epicurus can concede that every proposition is either true or false and still not fear that it is necessary that everything occur by fate. For it is not in virtue of eternal causes derived from a necessity of nature that the following proposition is true: "Carneades will go down to the Academy"; but neither is it uncaused. Rather, there is a difference between causes which just happen to precede [the event] and causes which contain in themselves a natural efficacy. So it always was true that "Epicurus

will die at the age of seventy-two in the archonship of Pytharatus", but there were not any fated causes why it should occur like this; rather, what happened certainly was going to happen as it [indeed did] happen. 20. And those who say that what is going to occur is immutable and that a true future statement cannot be converted into a false one are not in fact asserting the necessity of fate, but merely indicating what our words mean. But those who introduce an eternal series of causes are the ones who strip the human mind of free will and bind it by the necessity of fate.

But so much for this; let us move on. Chrysippus reasons thus. "If there is a motion without a cause, not every proposition, which the dialecticians call an *axioma*, will be either true or false. For what will not have effective causes will be neither true nor false. But every proposition is either true or false. Therefore, there is no motion without a cause. 21. And if this is so, everything which happens happens in virtue of prior causes; and if this is so, all things happen by fate. So it is shown that whatever happens happens by fate."

First of all, if I here chose to agree with Epicurus and deny that every proposition is either true or false, I would rather accept that blow than approve of the claim that all things happen by fate. For that claim is at least subject to debate, but this latter is intolerable. And so Chrysippus exerts all his efforts to persuade us that every *axioma* is either true or false. Just as Epicurus fears that if he should concede this, he must concede that whatever happens happens by fate (for if one of the two is true from eternity, it is also certain, and if certain, then necessary too: that is how he thinks that necessity and fate are confirmed), so Chrysippus feared that, if he did not maintain that every proposition was either true or false, he could not maintain that everything happened by fate and as a result of eternal causes of future events.

22. But Epicurus thinks that the necessity of fate can be avoided by the swerve of an atom. And so a third kind of motion appears, in addition to weight and collision, when an atom swerves by a minimal interval (he calls it an *elachiston* [smallest]); and he is forced to concede, in fact if not in his words, that this swerve is uncaused. For an atom does not swerve because it is struck by another atom. For how can one be struck by another if the atomic bodies are moving, owing to their weight, downward in straight lines, as Epicurus thinks? It follows that, if one atom is never displaced by another, then one atom cannot even contact another. 23. From which it is also concluded that if an atom exists and it does swerve, it does so without cause. Epicurus introduced this line of reasoning because he was afraid that if an atom always moved by its natural and necessary heaviness, we would have no freedom, since our

mind would be moved in such a way that it would be compelled by the motion of atoms. Democritus, the founder of atomism, preferred to accept that all things happened by necessity than to tear from the atomic bodies their natural motions.

Carneades was even more acute and showed that the Epicureans could defend their case without this fictitious swerve. For since they taught that there could be a voluntary motion of the mind, it was better to defend that claim than to introduce the swerve, especially since they could not find a cause for it. And if they defended this [the possibility of a voluntary motion of the mind] they could easily resist Chrysippus' attack. For although they conceded that there was no motion without a cause, they did not concede that everything which occurred occurred by antecedent causes. For there are no external and antecedent causes for our will. **24.** Thus we [merely] exploit the common linguistic convention when we say that someone wills or does not will something without cause. For we say "without cause" in order to indicate "without external and antecedent cause," not "without any cause at all"; just as when we refer to an "empty jar" we do not speak as the physicists do, who do not believe that there is a genuinely empty space, but to indicate that the jar is without water or wine or oil, for example. Thus when we say that the mind is moved without cause, we say that it is moved without an external and antecedent cause, not without any cause at all. It can even be said of the atom itself that it moves without a cause when it moves through the void because of weight and heaviness, since there is no external cause.

25. But again, to avoid being mocked by the physicists if we say that anything occurs without a cause, one must make a distinction and say that the nature of the atom itself is such that it moves because of weight and heaviness and that exactly this is the cause of its moving the way it does. Similarly, no external cause is needed for the voluntary motions of the mind; for voluntary motion itself contains within it a nature such that it is in our power and obeys us, but not without a cause. Its very nature is the cause of this fact.

37. . . . But from all eternity this proposition was true: "Philoctetes will be abandoned on the island", and this was not able to change from being true to being false. For it is necessary, when you have two contradictories—and here I call contradictories statements one of which affirms something and the other of which denies it—of these, then, it is necessary that one be true and the other false, though Epicurus disagrees. For example, "Philoctetes will be wounded" was true during all previous ages, and "he will not be wounded" was false. Unless, perhaps, we want to accept the view of the Epicureans, who say that such propositions are neither true nor false, or, since they are ashamed of that, say what is [in fact] even more outrageous: that disjunctions of such contradictories are true, but that neither of the propositions contained in them is true. 38. What an amazing audacity and what a wretched ignorance of logic! For if in speech there is something which is neither true nor false, certainly it is not true. But how can what is not true not be false? Or how can what is not false not be true? So the principle defended by Chrysippus will be retained, that every proposition is either true or false. Reason itself will require that certain things be true from all eternity, that they not have been bound by eternal causes, and that they be free from the necessity of fate. . . .

46. This is how this matter should be discussed, rather than seeking help from wandering atoms which swerve from their [natural] course. He says, "an atom swerves." First of all, why? Democritus had already given them another kind of force, that of collision, which he called a "blow"; and you, Epicurus, had given them the force of heaviness and weight. What new cause, then, is there in nature which would make the atom swerve? Or surely you don't mean that they draw lots with each other to see which ones will swerve and which not? Or why do they swerve by the minimal interval, and not by a larger amount? Or why do they swerve by one minimal interval, and not by two or three? This is wishful thinking, not argument. 47. For you do not say that the atom moves from its place and swerves because it is struck from outside, nor that there is in the void through which the atom moves any trace of a cause for it not to move in a straight line, nor is there any change in the atom itself which would cause it not to maintain the natural motion of its weight. So, although he adduced no cause to produce that swerve, he still thinks that he is making sense when he makes the claim which everyone's mind rejects and recoils from. 48. And I do not think that there is anyone who does more to confirm, not just fate, but even a powerful necessity governing all things, or who has more effectively abolished voluntary motions of the mind, than [Epicurus], who concedes that he could not have resisted fate in any other way than by taking refuge in these fictitious swerves. For even supposing that there were atoms, which can in no way be proven to my satisfaction, nevertheless, those swerves will remain unexplained. For if it is by natural necessity that atoms move [downwards] owing to their weight, since it is necessary that every heavy body should move and be carried along when there is nothing to prevent it, then it is also necessary for certain atoms (or, if they prefer, all atoms) to swerve, . . . naturally . . .

On the Nature of the Gods 1.43–56   [I-16]

43. . . . For he [Epicurus] is the only one who saw, first, that the gods exist, because nature herself has impressed a conception of them on the souls of everyone. For what people or race of men is there which does not have, even without being taught, a basic grasp of the gods, which is what Epicurus calls a *prolepsis*, i.e., a kind of outline of the thing [in question], which is antecedently grasped by the mind, and without which nothing can be either understood or investigated or debated? We have learned the force and utility of this line of inference from that divine book of Epicurus on the canon or standard [of truth]. **44.** You see, then, that the point which is the foundation of this investigation has been laid very well indeed. For since the opinion is established not on the basis of some convention or custom or law, but is and remains a solid and harmonious consensus of all men, it is necessary to understand that there are gods, because we have implanted, or rather innate, conceptions of them. For what all men by nature agree about must necessarily be true. So one must concede that the gods exist. Since this point is accepted by virtually everyone, philosophers and laymen alike, let us admit that the following point too is established, that we have this basic grasp, as I said before, or preconception about the gods—for new names must be assigned to new things, just as Epicurus himself referred to a *prolepsis*, which no one had previously designated by this term—**45.** we have, then, this basic grasp, that we consider the gods to be blessed and immortal. And the same nature which gave us an outline of the gods themselves has also inscribed in our minds the notion that they are eternal and blessed. And if this is so, that was a true maxim expounded by Epicurus, that what is blessed and eternal neither has any troubles of its own nor provides them to others, and so is subject to neither anger nor gratitude, since everything of this nature is weak.[23]

Enough would have been said already, if all we were looking for were pious worship of the gods and freedom from superstition; for the excellent nature of the gods would be worshipped by pious men because of that nature's blessedness and eternity (for whatever is excellent is justifiably the object of reverence), and all fears of the anger or power of the gods would have been expelled (for it is understood that anger and gratitude are banned from a blessed and immortal nature, and when these are removed no fears about the beings above hang over us). But in order to confirm this opinion, the mind enquires into the form of god, the kind

23. Principal Doctrine I.

of activity which characterizes his life, and the mode of operation of his intellect.

46. Nature tells us part of what we need to know about the form of the gods, and the rest is the instruction of reason. For by nature all of us, men of all races, have no other view of the gods but that they have human form; for what other form ever appears to anyone either waking or sleeping? But so that every point will not be referred to the primary notions, reason herself reveals the same thing. **47.** For it seems appropriate that the most excellent nature, excellent either for its blessedness or for its eternity, should also be the most beautiful. So what configuration of the limbs, what arrangement of features, what shape, what general appearance can be more beautiful than the human? . . . **48.** But if the human shape is superior to the form of all living things, and a god is a living thing, then certainly he has that shape which is most beautiful of all. And since it is agreed that the gods are most blessed, but no one can be blessed without virtue, nor can virtue exist without reason, nor can reason exist except in a human form, one must concede that the gods have human appearance. **49.** But that appearance is not [really] a body, but a quasi-body, nor does a god have blood, but quasi-blood.

Although Epicurus was so acute in the discovery of these truths and expounded them so subtly that not just anyone could grasp them, still I can rely on your intelligence and expound them more briefly than the subject matter actually demands. Epicurus, then, who not only has a mental vision of hidden and deeply abstruse matters but even manipulates them as though they were tangible, teaches us that the force and nature of the gods is as follows. First, they are perceived not by the senses but by the intellect, and not in virtue of some solidity or numerical identity (like those things which because of their resistance he calls 'solids' [*steremnia*]), but rather because the images [of the gods] are perceived by virtue of similarity and transference; and since an unlimited series of very similar images arises from innumerable atoms and flows to[24] the gods, our intellect attends to those images and our intelligence is fixed on them with the greatest possible pleasure, and so it grasps the blessed and eternal nature [of the gods]. **50.** It is most worthwhile to reflect long and hard on the tremendous power of infinity, which we must understand is such as to make it possible that all [classes of] things have an exact and equal correspondence with all other [classes of] things. Epicurus calls this *isonomia*, i.e., equal distribution. In virtue of this it comes about that if

---

24. This is the reading of the manuscripts. Many editors accept the simple and attractive emendation "from the gods."

there is such and such a number of mortal beings, there is no less a number of immortal beings, and if there is an innumerable set of forces which destroy, there ought also to be an infinite set of forces which preserve.

Balbus, you [Stoics] often ask us what the life of the gods is like and how they pass their time. **51.** Well, they spend their time in such a manner that nothing can be conceived which is more blessed or better supplied with all kinds of good things. For a god is idle, is entangled with no serious preoccupations, undertakes no toilsome labour, but simply rejoices in his own wisdom and virtue, being certain that he will always be in the midst of pleasures which are both supreme and eternal. **52.** This god we could properly call blessed, but your [i.e., the Stoic] god is assigned to very hard labour. For if god is the world itself, what can be less restful than to be revolving around the heaven's axis at amazing speed, with not even a moment of rest? But nothing is blessed if it is not at rest. But if there is some god *in* the world to rule and guide it, to maintain the orbits of the heavenly bodies, the changes of the seasons and the ordered variations of [natural] events, to oversee land and sea to ensure that men have lives full of advantages, then surely that god is entangled with burdensome and laborious obligations. **53.** But we claim that happiness is a matter of freedom from disturbance in the mind and leisure from all duties. For the same person who taught us the rest [of this theory] also taught us that the world was produced by nature and that there was no need for someone to make it, and that the task which you say cannot be carried out without divine wisdom is so easy that nature has produced, is producing and will produce an unlimited number of worlds. Since you do not see how nature can do so without [the use of] intelligence, you take refuge like tragedians in [the agency of] god when you cannot work out the conclusion of the plot. **54.** You would certainly not need the assistance of god if you realized the unlimited magnitude of space which is unbounded in all directions; the intellect casts itself into and contemplates this [infinity] and travels so far and wide that it can see no final boundary at which it might stop. So, in this immense length, breadth, and height there flies about an infinite quantity of innumerable atoms, which (despite the interspersal of void) cling to each other and are linked together by their mutual contacts. From this are produced those forms and shapes which you think cannot be produced without the use of a veritable blacksmith's shop! And so you have burdened us with the yoke of an eternal master whom we are to fear by day and by night; for who would not fear an inquisitive and busy god who foresees everything, thinks about and notices everything, and supposes that everything is his own business? **55.** This is the origin of that fated necessity which you call *heimarmene*, and which leads you to say that whatever happens has flowed from an eternal [set of] truth[s] and a continuous chain of causes. But how much is your philosophy worth, if it thinks, like old women—and uneducated ones at that—that everything occurs by fate. Your *mantike* follows too, which is called 'divination' in Latin, because of which we would be drenched in such superstition (if we were prepared to listen to you [Stoics]) that we would have to worship the soothsayers and augurs, the oracular priests and the prophets, and even the diviners! **56.** We are freed from these terrifying fears by Epicurus; we are liberated from them! We do not fear [gods] whom we know do not create trouble for themselves nor for anyone else, and we worship in piety and holiness their excellent and supreme nature.

On the Nature of the Gods 1.69–76 excerpts [I-17]

69. You [Epicureans] do this all the time. You say something implausible and want to avoid criticism, so you adduce something which is absolutely impossible to support it! It would be better to give up the point under attack than to defend it in such a brazen manner. For example, when Epicurus saw that, if the atoms moved by their own weight straight down, nothing would be in our power, since the atoms' movements would be certain and necessitated, he found a way to avoid necessity—a point which had escaped Democritus' notice. He says that an atom, although it moves downward in a straight line because of its weight and heaviness, swerves a little bit. **70.** This claim is more shameful than the inability to defend the point he is trying to support. He does the same thing in his debate with the dialecticians. They have an accepted teaching to the effect that, in all disjunctions which have the form "either this or not this," one of the two disjuncts must be true; but Epicurus was afraid that if a statement such as "Epicurus will either be alive tomorrow or he will not" were admitted, then one of the two disjuncts would be necessary. So he denied that all statements of the form "either this or not this" were necessary. What could be more stupid than this?

Arcesilaus attacked Zeno because, while he himself said that all sense-perceptions were false, Zeno said that some were false, but not all. Epicurus was afraid that, if one sense-perception were false, none would be true; so he said that all sense-perceptions were messengers of the truth. None of these cases shows great cleverness; in order to ward off a minor blow, he opened himself up to a more serious one.

71. He does the same thing with the nature of the gods. While trying to avoid saying that [the gods are] a dense compound of atoms, so that he will not have to admit that they perish and dissipate, he says that the

gods do not have a body, but only a quasi-body, and that they do not
have blood, but only quasi-blood. It is taken to be remarkable if one
soothsayer can see another without laughing, but it is even more remarkable, that you [Epicureans] can restrain your laughter when you are by
yourselves. "This is not a body, but a quasi-body"; I could understand
what this would be like if we were talking about waxen images and
earthenware figurines. But I cannot understand what quasi-body and
quasi-blood are supposed to be in the case of a god. And neither can
you, Velleius, but you don't want to admit it. . . .

. . . 73. Now, what do you understand by that quasi-body and quasi-
blood? 74. Not only do I concede that you understand them better than
I, but I am even happy about it. But when the idea is expressed in words,
what reason is there that Velleius should be able to understand it and
Cotta should not? So I know what body is and what blood is; but in no
way do I understand what quasi-body is or what quasi-blood is. Yet you
do not hide [your view] from me, as Pythagoras used to hide his views
from outsiders, nor do you deliberately speak in riddles like Heraclitus;
rather, to speak frankly between ourselves, you yourself do not understand. 75. I am aware that you contend that there is a kind of image of
the gods which has nothing solid or dense about it, no definite shape,
no depth, but is refined, light, and translucent. So we will speak of it as
we do of the Venus on Cos: it is not a body but like a body, and the
blush blended with pallor which suffuses [her skin] is not blood but a
sort of semblance of blood. In the same way Epicurean gods are not real
things but semblances of real things.

But suppose that I believe in things which I cannot even understand.
Now show me the outlines and shapes of those shadowy gods of yours!
76. Here you suffer from no lack of arguments designed to show that
the gods have human form. First [is the argument that] our minds contain
an outline and basic grasp of such a nature that when a man thinks about
a god, a human form appears to him; second, that since the divine nature
is better than everything else, it ought also to have the most beautiful
form, and none is more beautiful than the human form; the third argument
you adduce is that no other shape can house an intellect.

On the Nature of the Gods 1.103–110   [I-18]

103. Let us suppose it true, then, as you wish, that god is an image
and semblance of man: what home, what dwelling, what place does he
have? what, indeed, are his activities? in virtue of what is he, as you
claim, happy? For he who is going to be happy ought to both use and
enjoy his own goods. And even inanimate natures have each their own

proper place; for example, earth occupies the lowest place, water floods the earth, air is above it, and the highest reaches [of the cosmos] are set aside for the fires of the heavens. Some animals are terrestrial, some aquatic, some are 'double', as it were, living in both environments; there are even some which are thought to be born in fire and which often appear flying about in blazing furnaces! **104.** So I ask, first, where does this god of yours live? next, what cause motivates him to move spatially— if, that is, he ever does move? then, since it is characteristic of animals that they pursue what is adapted to their nature, what does god pursue? to what, pray tell, does he apply his mind and reason? finally, *how* is he happy, *how* is he eternal?

Whichever of these issues you touch on, it is a weak spot. A theory with such a bad foundation cannot come to a successful conclusion. **105.** You claimed that the appearance of god is perceived by thought, not the senses; that it has no solidity and is not numerically identical over time; that the visual image of it is such that it is discerned by similarity and transference; that there is an unfailing supply of similar [images] from the infinite atoms; and that this is why our mind, when directed at these things, believes that their nature is blessed and eternal. Now, in the name of the very gods we are talking about, what sort of a claim is this? For if they are only valid for thought and have no solidity or depth, then what difference does it make whether we think about a centaur or a god? The rest of the philosophers call that sort of mental condition an 'empty motion [of the mind]', but you claim that it is the approach and entry of images into the mind. **106.** So when I seem to see Tiberius Gracchus making a speech on the Capitol and bringing out the voting-urn for the verdict on Marcus Octavius, I say that is an empty motion of the mind; but you say that the images of Gracchus and Octavius, which arrived at the Capitol and came to my mind, persist[25]—and that the same thing happens in the case of god (by whose image our minds are frequently struck) and that this is why the gods are thought of as blessed and eternal.

107. Suppose that there are images which strike our minds; it is still only a certain appearance put before us and not also a reason for it to be happy and eternal. What are these images of yours, and where do they come from? Of course, this free-wheeling idea came from Democritus. But

---

25. Many translators and editors emend the text of this very difficult sentence. Cicero's hasty composition makes certainty impossible, but the sense seems to be this: images of Gracchus and Octavius travel to the Capitol hill, where their famous confrontation took place in 133 B.C.—almost sixty years before the dramatic date of the dialogue! These images meet at the Capitol and then travel on to Cotta's mind, where together they present him with a visual impression of the event as occurring at the Capitol. The absurdity of such a theory, which Cotta claims the Epicureans are committed to, is evident.

he has been criticized by many, and you [Epicureans] cannot find a way out. The whole theory wobbles and limps. For what could be less plausible than that my mind is struck by images of Homer, Archilochus, Romulus, Numa, Pythagoras, and Plato, let alone by images faithful to the original people! So how do those people [come to my mind]? And whose images are these? Aristotle holds that the poet Orpheus never existed and the Pythagoreans claim that the surviving Orphic poem was written by a certain Cercon. But Orpheus, i.e., on your theory his image, often comes into my mind. 108. And what about the fact that your mind and mine receive different images of the same man? What about the fact that we get images of things which never existed at all and never could have, like Scylla and Charybdis? What about the fact that we get images of people, places, and cities which we have never seen? What about the fact that an image is instantly available as soon as I feel like it? What about the fact that images come unbidden, even to those who are asleep. Velleius' whole theory is nonsense! But you [Epicureans] impose these images not just on our eyes, but on our minds too—that's how recklessly you blather on! 109. And how careless it is. 'There is a steady succession of flowing visual images so that the many produce the appearance of one.' I would be ashamed to admit that I don't understand this, if you yourselves, who defend this stuff, really understood it. For how do you prove that the images move continuously, or if they do move continuously, how are they eternal? 'The infinity of atoms keeps the supply up,' he says. So does the same 'infinity of atoms' make everything eternal? You take refuge in 'equal distribution' (let us use this term for *isonomia*, if you will) and say that, since there exists a mortal nature, there must also exist an immortal nature. By that reasoning, since men are mortal, there should be some immortal men too, and since they are born on land, they should also be born in water. 'And because there are forces of destruction, there must also be forces of preservation.' Of course there are. But they preserve things which exist; but I don't think those gods exist. 110. Anyway, how do all your images of things arise from the atomic bodies? Even if they existed, which they don't, they might perhaps bump into each other and be shaken up by their collisions; but they could not impart form, shape, colour, and life. Therefore you [Epicureans] utterly fail to show that there is an immortal god.

Tusculan Disputations 3.41–42   [I-19]

41. . . . Are these your words, [Epicurus,] or not? In the book which sums up your entire teaching you say this (and here I merely translate, so that no one will think that I am making this up): "Nor do I know

what I could understand that good to be, if I set aside the pleasures we get from sex, from listening to songs, from looking at [beautiful] shapes, from smooth motions, or any other pleasures which affect any of man's senses. Nor, indeed, can it be said that only mental rejoicing is [to be counted] among the goods; for this is my understanding of mental rejoicing: it lies in the expectation that our nature will avoid pain while acquiring all those things I just mentioned." **42.** That is exactly what he said, so that anyone can grasp what kind of pleasure Epicurus recognizes. Then a bit later: "I have often asked," he says, "those who are called wise, what they would have left [to put] in the category of goods if they removed those things—unless they were willing to emit empty sounds. I was able to learn nothing from them. And if they wish to burble about virtues and wisdom, they will be referring to nothing except the means by which those pleasures which I mentioned above are produced."

Tusculan Disputations 3.47 [I-20]

The same man says that pleasure does not increase once pain is removed, but that the greatest pleasure lies in not being in pain. . . .

On Goals 1.29–33 [I-21]

29. . . . First, then, he said, I will handle the subject in the manner approved of by the founder of this school: I will settle what it is that we are talking about and what qualities it has, not because I think that you do not know, but so that my discourse might proceed in an orderly and systematic fashion. So, we are asking what is the final and ultimate good, which according to the view of all philosophers ought to be what everything should be referred to, but which should itself be referred to nothing else. Epicurus places this in pleasure, which he claims is the highest good and that pain is the greatest bad thing. And the beginning of his teaching about this is as follows.

30. As soon as each animal is born, it seeks pleasure and rejoices in it as the highest good, and rejects pain as the greatest bad thing, driving it away from itself as effectively as it can; and it does this while it is still not corrupted, while the judgement of nature herself is unperverted and sound. Therefore, he says that there is no need of reason or debate about why pleasure is to be pursued and pain to be avoided. He thinks that these things are perceived, as we perceive that fire is hot, that snow is white, that honey is sweet. None of these things requires confirmation by sophisticated argumentation; it is enough just to have them pointed out. For there is a difference between the rational conclusion of an argument and simply pointing something out; for the former reveals certain hidden and, as it were, arcane facts, while the latter indicates things which are evident and out in the open. Moreover, since there is nothing left if you deprive man of his sense-perception, it is necessary that nature herself judge what is natural and what is unnatural. And what does nature perceive or judge, with reference to what does she decide to pursue or avoid something, except pleasure and pain?

31. There are, however, some members of our school [Epicureans] who want to teach a more subtle form of this doctrine, and they say that it is not sufficient to let sense-perception judge what is good and what is bad, but that the intellect and reason can also understand that pleasure by itself is worth pursuing for its own sake and that pain by itself is to be avoided for its own sake. And so they say that we have this conception, which is, as it were, naturally implanted in our souls, and that as a result of this we perceive that the one is to be pursued and the other to be rejected. But there are other Epicureans too, men with whom I agree, who do not think it right for us to be too sure of our case, since so many philosophers say so much about why pleasure ought not to be counted as a good thing and pain ought not to be counted as a bad thing; they think that one must argue and debate with great care, and employ well researched lines of argument in the dispute about pleasure and pain.

32. But so that you will see the origin of the mistake made by those who attack pleasure and praise pain, I shall open up the whole theory and explain exactly what was said by that discoverer of the truth [Epicurus], who was a kind of architect of the happy life. No one rejects or dislikes or avoids pleasure itself just because it is pleasure, but rather because those who do not know how to pursue pleasure rationally meet with great pains as a result. Nor again is there anyone who loves, pursues, and wants to acquire pain just because it is pain, but rather because sometimes circumstances of such a nature occur that he can pursue some great pleasure by means of effort and pain. To cite a minor instance: who among us undertakes any demanding regimen of physical training except in order to get some sort of benefit from it? Who, moreover, could justifiably criticize either a man who wished to have the sort of pleasure which is followed by no pains or a man who avoids a pain which serves to produce no pleasure?

33. But we do attack and indeed find most worthy of justified hatred those who are seduced and corrupted by the allures of present pleasures and, being blinded by desire, do not foresee the pains and troubles which they are bound to incur; similarly to blame are those who abandon their duties because of moral weakness, i.e., a tendency to avoid efforts and pains. The distinction here is simple and clear enough. For at a moment of free time, when we have an unrestricted opportunity to select and

there is no hindrance to our doing what will be most pleasing to us, [in such circumstances] every pleasure is to be accepted and every pain rejected. But at certain other times, because of the press of responsibilities or the obligations imposed by circumstances it will often happen that pleasures are to be turned down and pains are not to be rejected. And so the wise man sticks with this [principle of] of choosing, that he either acquires greater pleasures by rejecting some of them, or that he avoids worse pains by enduring some of them.

On Goals 1.37–38 [I-22]

37. . . . Now I will explain what pleasure is and what it is like, to remove any misunderstandings which inexperienced people may have and to help them to understand how serious, self-controlled, and stern our doctrine is, though it is commonly held to be hedonistic, slack and soft. For we do not just pursue the kind [of pleasure] which stimulates our nature itself with a kind of smoothness and is perceived by the senses with a sort of sweetness, but rather we hold that the greatest pleasure is that which is perceived when all pain is removed. For since when we are freed from pain we rejoice in this very liberation from and absence of annoyance, and since everything in which we rejoice is a pleasure (just as everything which irritates us is a pain), then it is right to call the absence of all pain pleasure. Just as when hunger and thirst are driven out by food and drink, the very removal of annoyance brings with it a resulting pleasure, so in every case too the removal of pain brings with it a consequent pleasure. 38. So Epicurus did not think that there was some intermediate state between pleasure and pain; for that state which some people think is an intermediate state, viz. the absence of all pain, is not only pleasure but it is even the greatest pleasure. For whoever perceives the state which he is in must in fact be in pleasure or in pain. But Epicurus thinks that the limit for the greatest pleasure is set by the absence of all pain; and though later [i.e., after all pain has been eliminated] pleasure can be varied and adorned, it cannot be increased or augmented.

On Goals 1.55–57 [I-23]

55. I shall give a brief account of what follows from this firm and well established view. There is no possibility of mistake about the limits of good and bad themselves, that is about pleasure and pain; but people do make mistakes in these matters when they are ignorant of the means by which they are produced. Moreover, we say that the pleasures and pains of the mind take their origin from the pleasures and pains of the body (and so I concede the point which you were making recently, that any

Epicurean who disagrees is abandoning his case—and I know that there are many who do so, but they are inexperienced); moreover, although mental pleasure and pain do produce good and bad feelings, nevertheless both of them have their origins in the body and take the body as their point of reference; nevertheless, the pleasures and pains of the mind are much greater than those of the body. For with the body we can perceive nothing except what immediately affects it in the present, but with the mind we can also perceive past and future. Even granted that when we feel pain in the body our pain is equal [to what we feel in the mind], still there can be a very large increase [in this pain] if we think that there is some eternal and unlimited bad thing hanging over us. And you may transfer the point to pleasure, so that it is greater if we are not afraid of some such thing. 56. But this point, at any rate, is already clear, that the greatest pleasure or annoyance in the mind makes much more difference to the production of a blessed or wretched life than either one of them would if they lasted an equally long time in the body. But we do not think that pain immediately follows as soon as pleasure is removed, unless by chance a pain should move into the place of the pleasure; on the other hand we are delighted when pains are eliminated even if no pleasure of the kind which stimulates the senses moves into their place; and from this one can understand just how great a pleasure it is to be free of pain.

57. But just as we are thrilled by the expectation of good things, so too we are pleased by the recollection of good things. But fools are tortured by the recollection of bad things, while wise men enjoy past goods kept fresh by a grateful recollection. For it is a deeply rooted part of human nature to bury in virtually eternal oblivion things which go badly and to recall with satisfaction and contentment things which go well. But when we contemplate past events with a keen and attentive mind, then we feel distress if what we recall was bad, and joy if it was good.

On Goals 2.98   [I-24]

You have often said that no one rejoices or feels pain except because of the body . . . you deny that there is any joy in the mind which is not referred to the body.

Tusculan Disputations 5.93–96   [I-25]

93. You realize, I believe, how Epicurus divided the kinds of desires, perhaps not in a very sophisticated fashion, but usefully at any rate. Some are natural and necessary, some natural and not necessary, some neither [natural nor necessary]. The necessary can be satisfied with next to nothing; for nature's riches are easily acquired. He holds that the

second type of desires is not difficult, either to acquire or to do without. The third type he thought should be utterly rejected, since they are clearly vain and not only unnecessary but also unnatural. **94.** At this point the Epicureans make a number of arguments and make excuses one by one for the pleasures of the types which they do not condemn, but which they ⟨do not⟩ seek an abundance of. For they say that even obscene pleasures, which they spend quite a bit of time talking about, are easy, common, and readily available; and that if nature does require them they must be evaluated not with reference to family background, social station, or rank, but only with respect to beauty, age, and figure; and it is not at all difficult to refrain from them, if that is required by poor health, duty, or concern for one's reputation; and in general, that this type of pleasure is to be chosen, if it does not do any harm, but that it never actually benefits anyone. **95.** The upshot of his entire discussion of pleasure is this. He holds that pleasure itself should always be wished for and pursued for its own sake because it is pleasure, and that by the same reasoning pain should always be avoided, just because it *is* pain; and so the wise man will employ a principle of compensation, and will avoid pleasure if it will produce a greater pain and will endure pain if it produces a greater pleasure; and that all pleasing feelings are to be referred to the mind, although they are actually judged by bodily senses. **96.** As a result the body is pleased for only so long as it perceives a present pleasure, while the mind perceives a present pleasure just as much as the body does, but also foresees a pleasure which is coming in the future and does not let a past pleasure slip from its grasp. So the wise man will always have a continuous and interconnected [set of] pleasures, since the expectation of hoped-for pleasures is linked to the memory of pleasures already perceived.

On Goals 1.65–70 [I-26]

65. There remains a topic which is especially important for our present debate, that is friendship. You [the critics] claim that if pleasure is the greatest good there will be no friendship at all. Epicurus indeed says this on the topic:[26] that of all the things which wisdom has contrived which contribute to a blessed life none is more important, more fruitful, or more pleasing than friendship. And he proved this not just in his discourse, but much more clearly by his life and deeds and character. The fictitious tales told by the ancients make it clear how important it is; but in all those stories, so many and so varied and drawn from the most remote

26. Principal Doctrine XXVII.

periods of antiquity, you could hardly find three pairs of [true] friends, starting with Theseus and finishing up with Orestes. But in just one household—and a small one at that—Epicurus assembled such large congregations of friends which were bound together by a shared feeling of the deepest love. And even now the Epicureans do the same thing.

But let us get back to the point; we do not need to speak of individuals. **66.** I see that the question of friendship has been dealt with in three ways by our school. Some say that our friends' pleasures are not in themselves as worthy of pursuit as are our own (a doctrine which some think undermines the stability of a friendship), but nevertheless they do defend this claim and easily, as I think, get themselves out of their difficulties. Just as we said about the virtues somewhat earlier, so for friendship: they deny that it can be separated from pleasure. For since a solitary life without friends is full of dangerous traps and fear, reason herself advises us to get some friends; and when we do so our mind is reassured and becomes indissolubly linked to the expectation that pleasures will thereby be acquired. **67.** And just as hatred, envy, and contempt are inimical to pleasures, so friendships are not only the most trustworthy supports for our pleasures, but they also produce them, as much for our friends as for ourselves. We enjoy friends not only while they are present with us, but we are also elated by our expectations for the immediate and for the more distant future. Because we cannot possibly secure a stable and long-lasting pleasantness in our life without friendship, and cannot maintain friendship itself unless we cherish our friends just as much as we do ourselves, it follows both that this kind of thing does occur in friendship and that friendship is linked with pleasure. For we rejoice at our friends' joys just as much as at our own, and grieve just as much for their anguish. **68.** That is why a wise man will have the same feelings for his friend as for himself and will undertake the same labours for the sake of a friend's pleasure as he would undertake for the sake of his own.

What we said about the way the virtues are always found to be essentially connected to pleasures must also be said about friendship. For Epicurus made a splendid declaration, in almost exactly these words:[27] One and the same doctrine has reassured our minds that there is no eternal or even long-lasting bad thing to fear and has also seen that in this present span of life the most reliable source of protection lies in friendship.

69. There are, however, some Epicureans who are more timid in the face of your abusive criticisms, but are nevertheless pretty sharp-witted;

27. Principal Doctrine XXVIII.

they are afraid that if we believe that friendship is to be pursued for the sake of our own pleasure, all of friendship might seem to be crippled. So they say that people first meet, pair up, and desire to form associations for the sake of pleasure, but that when increasing experience [of each other] has produced the sense of a personal bond, then love flowers to such a degree that even if there is no utility to be gained from the friendship the friends themselves are still loved for their own sake. Indeed, if we typically come to love certain locations, temples, cities, gymnasia, playing fields, dogs, horses, public games (whether with gladiators or animals) just because of familiarity, how much easier and more fitting is it for this to happen in the case of human familiarity?

70. There are also those who say that there is a kind of agreement between wise men, to the effect that they will not cherish their friends less than themselves. We know that this can happen, and that it often does happen; and it is obvious that nothing can be discovered which would be more effective for the production of a pleasant life than this sort of association.

From all of these considerations one can draw the conclusion that not only is the case of friendship not undermined if the highest good is located in pleasure, but also that without this no firm basis for friendship could possibly be discovered.

The Testimony of Lucretius

The Epicurean Lucretius (first century B.C.) wrote an epic poem *On the Nature of Things* in six books. It should be read in its entirety as crucial evidence for Epicureanism. But two extracts are of particular importance and so are included here.

On the Nature of Things: 4.469–499 [I-27]

Moreover, if someone thinks that he knows nothing, he also does not know whether this can be known, since he admits that he knows nothing. So I shall not bother to argue with him, since he is standing on his head already. But nevertheless, conceding that he does know this, I would also ask the following question: since he has never before seen anything true in the world, how does he know what it is to know and what it is not to know? What could have created the conceptions of truth and falsity, and what could have proven that the doubtful is distinct from what is certain? You will discover that the conception of truth was originally created by the senses, and that the senses cannot be refuted. For one must find something with greater authority which could all on its own refute what is false by means of what is true. But what should be given greater authority than the senses? Will reason, which derives from a false sense-perception, be able to contradict them, when it is completely derived from the senses? And if they are not true, all of reason becomes false as well. Will the ears be able to criticize the eyes, or the eyes the touch? Furthermore, will the taste organs of the mouth quarrel with the touch, or will the nose confute it, or the eyes disprove it? In my view, this is not so. For each sense has been allotted its own separate jurisdiction, its own distinct power. And so it is necessary that we separately perceive what is soft and cold or hot and separately perceive the various colours and see the features which accompany colour. Similarly the mouth's taste is separate, and odours come to be separately, and sounds too are separate. And so it is necessary that one set of senses not be able to refute another. Nor, moreover, will they be able to criticize themselves, since they will at all times have to command equal confidence.

On the Nature of Things: 2.216–293 excerpts   [I-28]

216. On this topic I want you to learn this too, that when the atoms move straight down through the void by their own weight, they deflect a bit in space at a quite uncertain time and in uncertain places, just enough that you could say that their motion had changed. But if they were not in the habit of swerving, they would all fall straight down through the depths of the void, like drops of rain, and no collision would occur, nor would any blow be produced among the atoms. In that case, nature would never have produced anything.

225. And if by chance someone thinks that heavier atoms, in virtue of their more rapid motion straight through the void, could fall from above on the lighter atoms, and that in this way the blows which generate the productive motions could be produced, he has strayed very far from the true account. For everything which falls through water or light air must fall at a speed proportional to their weights, simply because the bulk of the water and the fine nature of the air can hardly delay each thing equally, but yield more quickly to the heavier bodies, being overwhelmed by them. But by contrast, at no time and in no place can the empty void resist any thing, but it must, as its nature demands, go on yielding to it. Therefore, everything must move at equal speed through the inactive void, though they are not driven by equal weights. Therefore, heavier atoms can never fall upon lighter atoms from above, nor can they by themselves generate blows which will produce change in the motions through which nature produces things. Again and again, that is why it

is necessary that the atoms swerve slightly—but not more than the minimum; otherwise, we would seem to be inventing oblique motions and then the plain facts would refute us. For we see this obviously and apparently, that heavy bodies, insofar as they are heavy bodies, cannot move obliquely, when they fall from above, at least not enough that you could observe it. But who could claim to perceive that none of them swerves at all from a perfectly straight path?

251. Finally, if every motion is always linked to another, and new motions always arise from the old in definite order, and the atoms do not produce by swerving a starting point for motion which can break the bonds of fate and prevent one cause from following another from infinity, where does this free will which living things throughout the world have, where, I say, does this will torn from the grasp of the fates come from? Through this we all go where each one's pleasure[28] leads and swerve from our paths at undetermined times and places, just as our minds incline to do. For it is far from doubtful that everyone's own will provides the starting point for these things and that this is the source of motion in our limbs. . . .

284. That is why it is necessary to admit the same thing for the atoms, namely, that there is another cause of motion besides blows [from collisions] and weight, which is the source of our inborn capability [to act freely], since we see that nothing can come from nothing. For the weight of the atoms prevents it from being the case that everything happens as a result of the blows [of collisions], which are like an external force. But that the mind itself does not have an internal necessity in all its actions, and that it is not forced, as though in chains, to suffer and endure, that is what this tiny swerve of the atoms, occurring at no fixed time or place, accomplishes.

The Polemic of Plutarch

The later Platonist Plutarch (first to second century A.D.) wrote a polemical treatise *Against Colotes* which contains a wide range of useful information about Epicureanism, as one might expect in a sustained criticism of one of Epicurus' early followers. What follow are excerpts dealing in particular with epistemology and physics.

---

28. 'Will' just above and 'pleasure' here appear in the opposite order in the manuscripts. We follow most editors in reversing them, although some editors defend the transmitted text. In Latin, the two words differ by one letter.

Plutarch *Against Colotes* 1109a–1121e,   [I-29]
excerpts

(1109a) . . . Anyway, he [Colotes] who even held that nothing is any more like this than like that, is using Epicurus' doctrine that all presentations received through the senses are true. (1109b) For if when two people speak and one person says that the wine is dry and the other says that it is sweet, and neither is wrong about his sense-perception, how can the wine be dry rather than sweet? And again, you can see that some people treat a bath as though it were hot and that others treat the same bath as though it were cold. For some ask for cold water to be poured in and others ask for hot. They say that a lady from Sparta came to see Berenike, the wife of Deiotaurus, and when they got close to each other they both turned away, the one nauseated by the [smell of] perfume, the other by the [smell of] butter. So if the one sense-perception is no more true than the other, it is likely both that the water is no more cold than hot and (1109c) that the perfume and the butter are no more sweet-smelling than foul-smelling. For if someone says that the same object of presentation is different for different people, he has missed the fact that he is saying that [the object] is both [at once].

And the much discussed symmetries and harmonies of the pores in the sense organs and the compound mixtures of seeds which they say produce different sense-perceptions of quality in different people by being distributed in all flavours and odours and colours, do these not immediately force things into being 'no more [this than that]' for them? For they reassure those who think that sense-perception deceives on the grounds that they see the same things having opposite effects on perceivers, and instruct them [as follows]: (1109d) since everything is combined and blended together and since different things are designed by nature to fit into different [pores], it is not possible for everyone to touch and grasp the same quality; nor does the object [of sense-perception] affect everyone the same way with all of its parts, but all of them only experience those parts [of an object] with which their sense-organs are symmetrical; so they are wrong to quarrel about whether the object is good or bad or white or not white, supposing that they are supporting their own sense-perceptions by undermining those of other people; but one must not quarrel with even one sense-perception, since all sense-perceptions make contact with something, (1109e) each drawing what is compatible and suitable to itself from the compound mixture as though from a spring; and must not assert [things] about the whole when one is in contact with [mere] parts, nor think that everyone has the same experience, but that different people have different experiences according to the differing qualities and powers of it.

So is it time to consider which men do more to inflict 'no more [this than that]' on things than those who proclaim that every sensible object is a blend of all sorts of qualities—'mixed like new wine in the filter'[29]— and who agree that their canons [of truth] would perish and their criterion would completely vanish if they left any object of perception whatsoever pure [and simple] and they did not leave each and every one of them a plurality?

Notice, then, what Epicurus has had Polyaenus (in the *Symposium*) say to him about the heating power of wine. **(1109f)** For when he said, "Epicurus, do you deny that there are heating properties in wine?" he answered, "What need is there to show that wine has heating properties?" And a bit further on: "For wine seems in general not to have heating properties, but a given quantity could be said to have a heating effect on this individual person."

And again, suggesting the cause [for this], he attributed it to **(1110a)** compactions and dispersions of atoms and to commixtures of and linkages with other atoms in the mixture of wine with the body; and then he adds: "that is why one must not say that wine has heating properties in general, but that a given quantity has a heating effect on a nature of this type which is in this sort of condition, or that a given amount could have a cooling effect on this [other] nature. For in such an aggregate [as wine] there are also the sort of natures from which coolness might be produced, or which being linked appropriately with other natures, would produce the nature of coolness. Hence, people are deceived, some into saying that wine in general has cooling properties, others that it has heating properties."

But he who says that the majority are deceived when they suppose that what heats things has heating properties, or that what cools things has cooling properties, is himself deceived, **(1110b)** unless he believes that it follows from what he says that each thing is no more like this than like that. And he adds that wine often does not enter the body with heating or cooling properties, but that when the mass has been set in motion and the rearrangement of bodies has occurred, sometimes the atoms which produce heat assemble in one place and by their numbers produce heat and fever in the body, and sometimes they are expelled and [so] chill it.

It is obvious that these arguments can be used against everything which is generally said or believed to be bitter, sweet, purgative, soporific, or

---

29. A fragment from an unknown Greek tragedy, 420 Nauck.

bright, on the grounds that nothing (1110c) has its own independent quality or power when it is in bodies, nor is it active rather than passive, but rather takes on different features and mixtures in various bodies.

For Epicurus himself, in book two of his *Against Theophrastus*, says that colours are not natural properties of bodies, but are produced by certain orderings and positions [of the atoms] relative to our vision; yet he says that, by this argument, body is no more colourless than it is coloured. And earlier he had written this, word for word: "but even without this part [of my theory] I do not know how one can say that those things which are in the dark have colour. And yet, when there is a dark cloud of air [i.e., fog] evenly wrapped around things, (1110d) it is often the case that some men perceive differences in colours while others do not because of the dullness of their vision; again, when we go into a dark house we do not see colours, but after we have stayed for a while we do." Therefore, no body will be said to have colour rather than not to have it.

And if colour is relative, so too will white and blue be relative, and if these, so too sweet and bitter; consequently it will be true to predicate of every quality that it no more exists than does not exist: for the object will be like this for people in one condition, but not for those who are not. (1110e) So Colotes ends up pouring over himself and his master the very mud and confusion in which he says those people wallow who assert that things are 'no more this than that'.

So is this the only place where this fine fellow shows that he "teems with sores though he tries to heal others"?[30] Not at all. In his second accusation [Colotes] fails even more miserably to notice how he drives Epicurus, along with Democritus, outside the pale of normal life. For he claims that Democritus' dicta, "colour is by convention and sweet is by convention" and compounds are by convention and so forth, but "in truth there are void and atoms," are opposed to sense perception; and that anyone who clings to and uses this theory could not even think of himself as human or as alive.

I have no criticism to make of this argument, and I claim that these [Democritean] views are as inseparable from Epicurus' opinions as they themselves say the shape and weight are from the atom. For what does Democritus say? that substances infinite in number, indivisible and indestructible and, moreover, qualitiless and impassible, are scattered about and move in the void; (1111a) and when they approach one another or collide or get tangled up with each other they appear, because they are

30. Euripides fr. 1086 Nauck.

aggregated, as water, fire, a plant, or a man; and that everything is what he calls atomic 'forms' and is nothing else. For there is no coming-into-being from what-is-not, and from what-is nothing could come to be since atoms can neither suffer nor change due to their solidity. Hence colour does not exist, [for it would have to be] made up of colourless things, nor do nature and soul exist, [for they would have to be] made up of qualitiless and impassive things.

So Democritus is to be criticized not for conceding what follows from his principles, but for assuming principles from which these conclusions follow. (1111b) For he ought not to have posited that the primary entities were unchangeable, but having made this postulate he ought to have seen that he has eliminated the genesis of all qualities. The most brazen position of all is to see the absurdity and to deny it. So Epicurus makes the most brazen claim, saying that he posits the same principles but does not say that "colour is by convention" and [so too] sweet and bitter and the qualities. If "does not say" means "does not admit," then he is up to his old tricks. For while destroying divine providence he says that he leaves piety intact, and while choosing friendship for the sake of pleasure he says that he would suffer the greatest pains for the sake of his friends, and he says that he postulates that the totality is unlimited but that he does not eliminate up and down. This sort of behaviour is not right even when one is joking over a drink: (1111c) to take a cup and drink as much as one wants and then to give back what is left. In argument one must recall this wise maxim: the beginnings may not be necessitated, but the consequences are. So it was not necessary to postulate—or rather to steal [the doctrine] from Democritus—that the principles of the universe are atoms; but when once he postulated the doctrine and prided himself on its superficial plausibility, then he ought to have drained its difficulties to the last drop too, or showed us how bodies which have no qualities produced most varied qualities just by coming together in a compound. For example, where did you get what is called hot and how did it come to be an attribute of your atoms, (1111d) which neither came [into the compound] already having heat, nor did they become hot by their conjunction? For the former is characteristic of something which has a quality, and the latter of something which is naturally prone to be affected; but you say that neither of these is appropriate for your atoms because they are indestructible.

. . . (1112e) . . . When Epicurus says, "the nature of existing things is bodies and place," should we interpret him as meaning that nature is something distinct from and in addition to the existing things, (1112f) or as referring just to the existent things and to nothing else? just as, for instance, he is in the habit of calling the void itself 'the nature of void' and, by Zeus, the totality [of things] the 'nature of the totality'.

. . . (1114a) Yet by saying that the totality is one he somehow prevented us from living. For when Epicurus says that the totality is unlimited and ungenerated and indestructible and neither grows nor shrinks, he discourses about the totality as though it were some one thing. In the beginning of his treatise [*On Nature*] he suggests that the nature of existing things is bodies and void, and though it is one nature, he yet divided it into two. One of these is really nothing, but you call it intangible and void and incorporeal.

. . . (1118d) . . . For if, as they think, a man is the product of both, a body of this sort and a soul, then he who investigates the nature of soul is investigating the nature of man by way of its more important principle. And let us not learn from Socrates, that sophistical boaster, that the soul is hard to understand by reason and ungraspable by sense-perception, but rather let us learn it from these wise men who get only as far as the corporeal powers of the soul, by virtue of which it provides the body with warmth and softness and tension, (1118e) when they cobble together its substance out of something hot and something breathlike and something airy, and they do not get to the most important part, but give up. For that in virtue of which it judges and remembers and loves and hates and in general the intelligent and reasoning part, this they say comes to be from a kind of 'nameless' quality.

. . (1119f) . . . Who makes worse mistakes in dialectic than you [Epicureans], who completely abolish the class of things said [*lekta*], which give substance to discourse and leave only [mere] utterances and the external things, saying that the intermediate class of 'signified things' (by means of which learning, (1120a) teaching, basic grasps, conceptions, impulses, and assents all occur) does not exist at all?

. . . (1121a) For he [i.e., Colotes] is satisfied with and welcomes arguments when they are used in Epicurus' writings, but does not understand or recognize them when they are used by others. For those who say that when a round image strikes us, or another which is bent, the sense receives a true imprint, and who do not allow the further claim that the tower is round and that the oar is bent—these men affirm their own experiences and impressions but are unwilling to agree that external objects are like this. But just as that group must refer to 'being affected horsewise or wallwise' but not to a horse or a wall, (1121b) in the same way they must say that the visual organ is 'affected roundly or anglewise' but not that the oar is bent or that the tower is round. For the image by which the visual organ is affected is bent, but the oar from which the image came is not bent. So since the [internal] experience is different from the external object, either our conviction must limit itself to the experience or, if it makes the further claim that 'it is' in addition to 'it appears', it must be refuted. And their vociferous and indignant claim about sense-perception, that it does not say that the external object is warm but that the experience in [the perception] is like that—(1121c) is this not the same as what is said about taste, viz. that he denies that the external object is sweet but says that an experience and motion in the [organ of] taste is of this character? And he who says that he receives a presentation in the shape of a man, but that he does not perceive whether there is a man, now where did he get the inspiration [for such an idea]? Was it not from those who say that they receive a curved presentation, but that the visual organ does not make the additional pronouncement that it is curved, nor even that it is round, but that a certain round impression and imprint has occurred in it?

'Yes, by Zeus,' someone will say, 'but when I approach the tower and when I take hold of the oar, I will pronounce the one to be straight and the other to be polygonal, but the other [philosopher] will agree to seeming and appearance, but nothing more, even if he does get close [to the object].' Yes, by Zeus, (1121d) because, dear sir, he [Epicurus] sees what follows [from his position] better than you do, and he sticks with it: viz. that every presentation on its own account is equally trustworthy and that no presentation is preferable to another, but that all are of equal value. But you are giving up the principle that all [perceptions] are true and that none is unreliable or false if you think that based on these one ought to further pronounce regarding external objects, but did not trust them for anything beyond the experience itself. For if they are equally trustworthy when they appear close up and when they are distant, either it is right to allow judgement to pronounce further, based on all of them or not to allow this for even these. But if there is a difference in the experience according as we are standing at a distance or close by, then it is false to say that one presentation or sense-perception (1121e) is not clearer than another; similarly, the testimony for and testimony against about which they speak have nothing to do with sense-perception, but rather with opinion. So, if they urge us to follow these and to pronounce on external objects, they make opinion judge what is the case and make sense-perception experience the appearances, and they transfer the deciding power from what is in all circumstances true to what is often mistaken.

Short Fragments and Testimonia from Known Works

From *On Nature*

See I-29, 1114a and 1112ef above.

Sextus *M* 9.333 (75 U)   [I-30]

Epicurus was in the habit of calling the nature of bodies and of the void [the] universe and [the] totality indifferently. For at one point he says, "The nature of the universe is bodies and void."

Vatican Scholiast on Dionysius Thrax,   [I-31]
Grammatici Graeci 1.3, p. 116.7–12
(Hilgard) (92 U)

And although Epicurus always made use of general outlines [of the senses of words], he showed that definitions are more worthy of respect by using definitions instead of general outlines in the treatise on physics; for he used definitions when he divided the totality into the atomic and the void, saying that "the atomic is a solid body which has no share of void included in it; ⟨and⟩ void is an intangible nature", i.e., not subject to touch.

From books 12 and 13 of *On Nature*   [I-32]
(Arrighetti 27 and 28, 84, 87, 88 U =
Philodemus *On Piety*)

And in book 12 of the *On Nature* he says that the first men got conceptions of indestructible natures. . . .

As in book 12 he also criticizes Prodicus and Diagoras and Critias and others, saying that they are madmen and lunatics, and he compares them to bacchic revellers. . . .

In book 13 [he mentions] the congeniality which god feels for some and the alienation [for others].

From book 32. An unknown author.   [I-33]
Arrighetti 32.

In book 32 he offers a brief and summary definition of what was explained at great length elsewhere: "For," he says, "the soul could be said to be a certain nature."

From book 25.[31]   [I-34]

From the very beginning we have seeds which lead us, some to these things, some to those things, and some to both; they are always [the seeds of] actions, and thoughts and dispositions, and are greater or fewer in number. Consequently, what we develop—such or such [actions, thoughts, and dispositions]—is, right from the first, quite simply a result of us; and the influences which by necessity flow from the environment through our passages are at some point up to us and to the opinions which come from within us . . . [here there is a long lacuna].

. . . the natural imprint similarly to the empty pores . . . of the same peculiarities . . . in every case [lacuna of about 12 words] of which the experiences do not cease to occur . . . to admonish and quarrel with each other and try to change each other's character, as though they had in themselves the responsibility for [their characters] and [such responsibility lay] not just in the original [condition of] the compound, and in the necessity which comes mechanically from the environment and the influx [of atoms]. For if one were to attribute to admonishing and being admonished the mechanical necessity of what always on any occasion [happens to] affect oneself, one would never in this way come to an understanding [lacuna of a few words] by blaming or praising.

But if one were to do this, one would be leaving the very action which, being in our power, creates the basic grasp of responsibility, and thereby in some respect having changed his doctrine [long lacuna, of 45 or 50 words] of such error. For this sort of argument is upside-down and can never prove that all things are like what are called 'necessitated events'. But he quarrels about this very topic on the assumption that his opponent is responsible for being foolish. And if he [goes on] indefinitely saying again [and again], always on the basis of arguments, that he does *this* by necessity, he is not reasoning it out [properly] as long as he attributes to himself responsibility for reasoning well and to his opponent responsibility for reasoning badly. But if he were not to stop [attributing responsibility] for what he does to himself and [rather] to assign it to necessity, he would not . . . [lacuna of about 30 words]

[But] if he is only changing the word when he refers to what we call "through our own [agency]" by the name of necessity and will not show that it is in virtue of a basic grasp of a sort which produces deficient outlines that we talk about responsibility through our own [agency], he

---

31. Formerly thought to be from book 35. This discussion on determinism should be compared with the discussions of the swerve above. We translate the text prepared by David Sedley and published in his article 'Epicurus' Refutation of Determinism' in *Syzetesis* (Naples 1983) 11–51.

would neither [lacuna of about 25 words] to occur, but to call even
necessity empty, from what you people say. And if someone does not
say this and has no auxiliary [cause] in us and no inclination to dissuade
us from things which we do, while calling the responsibility for them
'through our own agency', but giving everything which we now assert
that we do while naming the responsibility for it as being 'through our
own agency' the name of 'foolish necessity', then he will merely be
altering the name. And he will not change any of our actions, in the way
in which in some cases he who sees what sort of things are necessitated
usually dissuades those who are eager to act in defiance of force. And
the intellect will endeavour to find out which sort of thing one is to think
an action is, which we do somehow from within ourselves, but which
we are not eager to do.

For he has no choice but to say that what sort [of action] is necessitated
[and what not] [lacuna of about 40 words] . . . among the most senseless.
If someone does not forcibly insist on this or again set out what he is
refuting and what he is introducing, only the wording is changed, as I
have been going on about for a while now.

But those who first gave a sufficient causal account and were not only
superior to their predecessors but also many times over superior to their
successors, failed to notice—despite the fact that they removed serious
difficulties in many areas—that they gave causal accounts for everything
by referring to necessity and mechanistic explanation. And the very
argument which explains this doctrine disintegrated, and the fellow did
not notice that it brought his actions into conflict with his opinions; and
that if a kind of distraction did not possess him while he acted, he would
be constantly disturbing himself; and that insofar as his opinion held
sway, he got into the worst sort of problems, but insofar as it did not
hold sway he was filled with internal strife because of the contradiction
between his actions and his opinion. . . .

From the *Puzzles*

Plutarch *Against Colotes* 1127d (18 U,   [I-35]
12 [1] A)

. . . For in the *Puzzles* Epicurus asks himself whether the wise man
will do some things which the laws forbid, if he knows that he will escape
detection. And he answers: "the plain statement [of the answer] is not
easy", i.e., I will do it but I do not wish to admit it.

From *On the Goal*

Plutarch *A Pleasant Life* 1089d (68 U, 22 [3] A) [I-36]

. . . "For the stable condition (*katastema*) of the flesh and the reliable expectation concerning this contains the highest and most secure joy, for those who are able to reason it out."

Athenaeus *Deipnosophists* 12, 546ef (67 U, 22 [1, 4] A) [I-37]

Not only Aristippus and his followers, but also Epicurus and his welcomed kinetic pleasure; and I will mention what follows, to avoid speaking of the "storms" [of passion] and the "delicacies" which Epicurus often cites, and the "titillations" and the "stimuli" which he mentions in his *On the Goal*. For he says: "For I at least do not even know what I should conceive the good to be, if I eliminate the pleasures of taste, and eliminate the pleasures of sex, and eliminate the pleasures of listening, and eliminate the pleasant motions caused in our vision by a visible form." . . . And in his *On the Goal* he again [says]: "One must honour the noble, and the virtues and things like that, *if* they produce pleasure. But if they do not, one must bid them goodbye."

From the *Symposium*:

See I-29, 1109e–1110b above.

From *Against Theophrastus*:

See I-29, 1110cd above.

Fragments of Epicurus' Letters

Plutarch *On Living the Inconspicuous Life* 1128f–1129a (106-7 U, 98 A) [I-38]

(1128f) Moreover, if you advise good men to be inconspicuous and to be unknown . . . give yourself [Epicurus] the same advice first. Don't write to your friends in Asia, don't address the visitors from Egypt, (1129a) don't keep watch over the youths in Lampsacus, don't send

books to all, male and female alike, showing off your wisdom, and don't
give written instructions for your burial.

Plutarch *Against Colotes* 1117a (116 U, 42 A)   [I-39]

(1117a) . . . In the letter to Anaxarchus he wrote as follows: "I summon
you to constant pleasures, and not to virtues, which provide [only] empty,
pointless, and disturbing expectations of rewards."

Plutarch *A Pleasant Life* 1101ab (120 U)   [I-40]

(1101a) . . . They argue with those who eliminate pains and tears and
lamentations for the deaths of friends, and they say that the kind of
freedom from pain which amounts to insensitivity[32] is the result of another
and greater bad thing, savagery or an unadulterated lust for fame and
madness, and that this is the reason why it is better to suffer something
and experience pain, and by Zeus even to weep copiously, swoon and
[experience] all the sentiment which they indulge in and [even] write
about, and so come to seem tender and given to friendship. (1101b) For
Epicurus said this in lots of other places and he also [said it] about the
death of Hegesianax when he wrote to his father Dositheus and to Pyrson,
the brother of the deceased. For recently I chanced to go through his
letters.

Letter to Idomeneus: Diogenes Laertius 10.22   [I-41]
(138 U, 52 A)

"I write this to you while experiencing a blessedly happy day, and at
the same time the last day of my life. Urinary blockages and dysenteric
discomforts afflict me which could not be surpassed for their intensity.
But against all these things are ranged the joy in my soul produced by
the recollection of the discussions we have had. Please take care of the
children of Metrodorus in a manner worthy of the good disposition you
have had since adolescence towards me and towards philosophy."

Seneca *Letters on Ethics* 22.5–6 (133 U, 56 A)   [I-42]

Read . . . the letter of Epicurus which is entitled "To Idomeneus"; he
requests Idomeneus that he flee and hurry as much as he can, before
some greater force has a chance to intervene and take away his freedom
to 'retreat'. 6. The same man also adds that nothing should be undertaken
except when it can be undertaken fittingly and on a good occasion. But

---

32. The term used is *apathes*, the Stoic word for freedom from destructive passions.

when that long-awaited moment comes, he says one must make one's exit. He instructs the man considering escape not to be negligent, and expresses the hope that there is a salutary escape, even from the most difficult situations, providing we neither hasten before the right time nor hold back when the time has come.

Plutarch *Against Colotes* 1127de (134 U)   [I-43]

(1127d) Again, I think, in writing to Idomeneus he urges him not to live as a slave to laws and opinions, as long as they do not occasion troubles caused by a blow from one's neighbour. So if those who abolish laws and political institutions abolish human life, (1127de) then this is what Epicurus and Metrodorus do; for they urge their adherents to avoid public life and express disgust for those who participate in it, abusing the earliest and wisest lawgivers and urging contempt for the laws, providing there is no fear of beatings and punishment.

A Deathbed Letter (from Philodemus,   [I-44]
Pragmateiai 31 Diano; 177 U, 78 A)

"As I write this, it is the seventh day that I have been unable to urinate and have had pains of the kind which lead to death. So, if anything should happen, take care of Metrodorus' children for four or five years, spending no more on them than you now spend on me in a year."

Stobaeus *Anthology* 3.17.23 (vol. 3 p. 495   [I-45]
W-H; 135 U, 53 A)

"If you wish to make Pythocles wealthy, do not give him more money; rather, reduce his desires."

Plutarch *Against Colotes* 1117e (130 U, 54 A)   [I-46]

"So send us some offerings for the care of our sacred body, on your own behalf and that of the children. For so it occurs to me to say to you."

Seneca *Letters on Ethics* 21.3 (132 U, 55 A)   [I-47]

"If you are affected by glory, my letters will make you more famous than all those things which you cherish and because of which you are cherished."

Stobaeus *Anthology* 3.17.13 (vol. 3 p. 492   [I-48]
W-H; 135a U, 58 A)

"We have been keen for self-sufficiency, not so that we should employ inexpensive and plain fare under all circumstances, but so that we can be of good cheer about them."

Seneca *Letters on Ethics* 18.9 (158 U, 83 A)   [I-49]

. . . He certainly says this in the letter which he wrote to Polyaenus in the archonship of Charinus; and indeed he boasts that he could be fed for less than an obol, but that Metrodorus, because he had not yet made so much [moral] progress, required an entire obol.

Athenaeus *Deipnosophists* 13, 588ab (117 U,   [I-50]
43 A)

"I congratulate you, sir, because you have come to philosophy free of any taint of culture."

Diogenes Laertius 10.6 (163 U, 89 A)   [I-51]

And in his letter to Pythocles,[33] he writes, "O blessed one, spread your sails and flee all forms of culture."

Plutarch *A Pleasant Life* 1097cd (183 U, 99 A)   [I-52]

(1097c) . . . when [Epicurus] wrote to his friends, "you took care of us in a godlike and magnificent fashion as regards the provision of food, and (1097d) you have given proofs which reach to heaven of your good will towards me."

Seneca *Letters on Ethics* 9.1 (174 U)   [I-53]

You want to know whether Epicurus is right to criticize, as he does in one letter, those who say that a wise man is self-sufficient and so does not need a friend. Epicurus makes this objection against Stilpo and those [i.e., the Stoics] who held that the highest good is a soul free of passions.

Seneca *Letters on Ethics* 9.8 (175 U)   [I-54]

. . . Although a wise man is self-sufficient, he will still want to have a friend, if for no other reason, in order to exercise his friendship, so

---

33. Not the same letter translated above.

that so great a virtue might not go to waste; not for the reason which Epicurus gave in this very letter, so that he might have someone to attend to him when sick, and to help him when he is thrown into prison or is impoverished, but so that he might have someone whom he might himself attend when that person is sick and whom he might free from imprisonment by his enemies.

Philodemus *On Piety* 126 Gomperz (387 U, 114 A) [I-55]

Again: "let us sacrifice to the gods," he says, "piously and well, as is appropriate, and let us do everything well according to the laws, but [let us do so] not disturbing them at all with our opinions on the topic of those who are best and most majestic; again, we say that it is even right [to do this] on the basis of the opinion which I was discussing. For in this way, by Zeus, it is possible for a mortal nature to live like Zeus, as it appears."

Philodemus *On Piety* 105 Gomperz (157 U, 86 A) [I-56]

Moreover, in his letter to Polyaenus he says that one should join in the celebration of the festival of the Anthesteria. For one must remember the gods as being the causes of many good things.

Philodemus *On Piety* 125 Gomperz (116 A) [I-57]

". . . for the others, and I asked them to display benevolence to other men at all times."

Diogenes Laertius 10.11 (182 U, 123 A) [I-58]

"Send me a small measure of cheese, so that when I want to have a feast I shall be able to do so."

Stobaeus *Anthology* 3.17.33 (vol. 3 p. 501 W-H; 181 U, 124 A) [I-59]

"I revel in the pleasure of my poor body, employing water and bread, and I spit upon the pleasures of extravagance, not for their own sake, but because of the difficulties which follow from them."

Seneca *Letters on Ethics* 20.9 (206 U, 125 A)   [I-60]

"Your discourse will appear more impressive, believe you me, if you are lying on a cheap bed and wearing rags. For it will not only be uttered, then, but proven."

Porphyry *To Marcella* 29 (207 U, 126 A)   [I-61]

"It is better for you to have confidence [about the future] while lying on a cheap bed than to be disturbed while possessing a golden couch and an extravagant table."

Seneca *Letters on Ethics* 7.11 (208 U, 129 A)   [I-62]

"I write this for you, not for the many; for we are for each other a sufficiently big audience."

Gnomologium Parisinum: 1168 f. 115 r. (187 U,   [I-63] 131 A)

"I never desired to please the many, for I did not learn the things which please them, and what I did learn was far removed from their perception."

Didymus Caecus *Commentary on Ecclesiastes*   [I-64] 24.8–11 (133 A)

For he writes [in his letter] to Idomeneus that the wise man uses circumstances in a way different from he who is not wise, and he adds: "Then you were not wise, but now you have been zealous to become so. So reflect on the quality of your former life and of your present life, [to see] if you bore disease then as you do now or if you were in control of wealth as you are now in control of it."

Short Fragments and Testimonia from Uncertain Works

Logic and epistemology

Philodemus *Pragmateiai* 29 Diano (212 U, 137 A)   [I-65]

". . . bringing your letter and the reasoning which you had carried out concerning men who could see neither the analogy which obtains between the phenomena and the unseen [realities] nor the consistency which exists between the senses and the unseen [realities] and again the testimony against . . ."

Seneca *Letters on Ethics* 89.11 (242 U)   [I-66]

The Epicureans held that there are two parts of philosophy, physics and ethics; they got rid of logic. Then since they were forced by the very facts to distinguish what was ambiguous and to refute falsities lying hidden under the appearance of truth, they themselves also introduced that topic which they call 'on judgement and the criterion' [i.e., canonic]; it is [just] logic by another name, but they think that it is an accessory part of physics.

Sextus *M* 8.9 (244 U)   [I-67]

But Epicurus said that all sensibles were true and existing—for there was no difference between saying that something is true and that it is an existing object. And that is why, in giving an outline [definition] of the true and the false, he says, "that which is such as it is said to be is true" and "that which is not such as it is said to be is false."

Sextus *M* 7.203–16 (247 U)   [I-68]

203. Epicurus says that there are two things which are linked to each other, presentation and opinion, and that of these presentation, which he also calls 'clear fact,' is always true. For just as the primary feelings, i.e., pleasure and pain, come to be from certain productive factors and in accordance with the productive factors themselves (for example, pleasure comes to be from pleasant things and pain from painful things, and what

causes pleasure can never fail to be pleasant, nor can what produces pain
not be painful; but rather, it is necessary that what gives pleasure should
be pleasant and that what gives pain should in its nature be painful), so
[too] in the case of presentations, which are feelings in us: what causes
each of them is presented in every respect and unqualifiedly, and since
it is presented it cannot help but exist in truth just as it is presented [as
being]. . . . [There is a lacuna here.] . . . that it is productive of presentation.

204. And one must reason similarly for the individual [senses]. For
what is visible not only is presented as visible but also is such as it is
presented [as being]; and what is audible is not only presented as audible
but also is like that in truth; and similarly for the rest. Therefore, it
turns out that all presentations are true. And reasonably so. 205. For if,
the Epicureans say, a presentation is true if it comes from an existing
object and in accordance with the existing object, and [if] every presentation arises from the object presented (which is existent) and in accordance
with the presented object itself, [then] necessarily every presentation
is true.

206. Some people are deceived by the difference between the presentations which seem to come from the same perceptible, for example, a visible
thing, according to which [i.e., the difference] the object is presented as
being of varying colour or varying shape or as different in some other
way. For they supposed that one of the presentations which differ and
conflict in this way must be true and the one derived from the opposites
must be false. This is foolish and the product of men who do not have
a comprehensive view of the nature of [lit. in] things.

207. Let us make our case for visible things. For the solid object is
not seen in its entirety, but [we see only] the colour of the solid. And
of the colour some is on the solid itself, as in things seen from close by
and things seen from a moderate distance, and some lies outside the solid
and in the adjacent places, as in things observed from a great distance.
And since this [colour] changes in the intermediate [space] and takes on
its own shape it produces the sort of presentation which is just like what
it [i.e., the colour] itself is really like. 208. So, just as the sound which
is heard is not that in the bronze instrument being struck nor that in
the mouth of the man shouting, but rather is that which strikes our sense
[organ]; and as no one says that he who hears a faint voice from a distance
hears it falsely since when he comes closer he grasps it as being louder;
so I would not say that the vision speaks falsely because it sees the tower
as small and round from a distance but from close up sees it as larger
and square. 209. But rather [I would say] that [the vision] tells the truth,
since when the object of perception appears to it [as] small and of such

a shape it is genuinely small and of such a shape (for the edges of the images are broken off by the movement through the air), and when it again appears big and of a different shape, again it is in a similar manner big and has that different shape—the object being, however, now not the same in the two cases. For it remains for distorted opinion to think that the same object of presentation was observed from close up and from a distance.

210. It is a property of sense-perception to grasp only that which is present and stimulating it, such as colour, but not to decide that the object here and the object over there are different. So for these reasons all presentations are true ⟨though not all opinions are true⟩ but have some differences [among them]. For some of these [opinions] are true and some are false, since they are our judgements upon presentations and we judge some things correctly and some badly, either by adding and attaching something to the presentations or by subtracting something from them—in general terms, by falsifying the non-rational sense-perception.

211. Therefore, according to Epicurus, some opinions are true and some are false; those which are testified for and those which are not testified against by clear facts are true, while those which are testified against and those which are not testified for by clear facts are false. 212. 'Testimony for' is a grasp, by means of clear facts, that the object of opinion is such as it once was thought to be. For example, when Plato is approaching from the distance I guess and opine, because of the distance, that it is Plato; but when he approached there was further testimony that it was Plato (since the distance was reduced) and [finally] the clear facts themselves testified to it. 213. 'Lack of testimony against' is the consistency of the non-evident thing which is the object of supposition and opinion with what is apparent. For example, when Epicurus says that there is void, which is a non-evident object, he confirms this through a clear fact, i.e., motion; for if void does not exist, then motion ought not to exist, since the moving body would have no place to shift into because everything [would] be full and dense; 214. consequently, since there is motion what is apparent does not testify against the non-evident thing which is the object of opinion. 'Testimony against', however, is something in conflict with 'lack of testimony against'. For it is the joint elimination of what is apparent along with the supposed non-evident thing. For example, the Stoic says that there is no void, holding that it is something non-evident, and thus along with this supposed fact one ought to eliminate what is apparent, by which I mean motion; for if there is no void it follows necessarily that there is no motion, according to the mode [of argument] which we have already indicated. 215. Similarly

too, 'lack of testimony for' is in opposition to 'testimony for'. For it [i.e., the lack of testimony for] is the evidence through clear facts that the object of opinion is not just as it was opined to be. For example, when someone is approaching from afar we guess, because of the distance, that it is Plato; but when the distance is reduced we realize through clear facts that it is not Plato. And this sort of thing turns out to be 'lack of testimony for'. For the object of opinion was not testified for by what was apparent. **216.** Hence, testimony for and lack of testimony against are the criterion of something's being true, while lack of testimony for and testimony against are [the criterion of something's being] false. And clear facts are the foundation and cornerstone of all [four of these].

Aetius 4.9.5 = *Dox.Gr.* p. 396 (248 U)   [I-69]

Epicurus [says] that every sense-perception and every presentation is true, but that some opinions are true and some are false.

Sextus *M* 8.63–64 (253 U)   [I-70]

63. Epicurus said that all sensibles are true and that every presentation comes from something existing and is of the same sort as that which stimulates the sense-perception. He also says that those who say that some presentations are true and some are false are led astray because they are not able to distinguish opinion from clear fact. At least in the case of Orestes, when he thought he saw the Furies, his sense-perception which was stimulated by images was true (for the images did exist), whereas his mind, in thinking that the Furies were solid [objects], held a false opinion. **64.** And further, he says, the aforementioned [philosophers] who introduce a difference among presentations are not able to convince [us] that it is the case that some of them are true and some false. For they will not be able to instruct us in such a matter by means of an appearance (for appearances are just what is being investigated), nor by means of something non-evident (for that which is non-evident has to be demonstrated by means of an appearance).

Clement of Alexandria *Stromates* 2.4,16.3   [I-71]
p. 121 Stählin (255 U)

Indeed, Epicurus, who more than anyone prefers pleasure to truth, supposes that a basic grasp is the [basis] of the intellect's conviction; he defines a basic grasp as an application [of the intellect] to something clear and to the clear conception of the thing, and [holds] that no one can either investigate or puzzle over, nor even hold an opinion or even refute [someone], without a basic grasp.

Sextus *M* 11.21 (255 U)   [I-72]

According to the wise Epicurus it is not possible to investigate or [even] to be puzzled without a basic grasp.

Sextus *M* 8.258 (259 U)   [I-73]

. . . We see that there are some who have abolished the existence of 'things said' [*lekta*], not just [philosophers] from other schools, such as the Epicureans, but even Stoics such as Basilides and his followers, who thought that no incorporeal [entity] exists.

Sextus *M* 8.13 (259 U)   [I-74]

But the followers of Epicurus and Strato the natural philosopher leave [in existence] only two [such entities], the signifier and the object, and so they appear to belong to the second group and to make the true and the false a matter of the utterance [and not the things said, i.e., *lekta*].

Sextus *M* 8.177 (262 U)   [I-75]

. . . For Epicurus and the leaders of his school said that the sign was sensible, while the Stoics said that it was intelligible.

Physics and Theology

Pseudo-Plutarch *Stromates* 8 = *Dox.Gr.*   [I-76]
p. 581 (266 U)

. . . in the totality [of things] nothing unprecedented happens beyond [what has happened in] the unlimited time which has already passed.

Aetius 1.3.18 = *Dox.Gr.* p. 285–6 (267, 275 U)   [I-77]

Epicurus, the son of Neocles and an Athenian, philosophized in the manner of Democritus and said that the principles of existing things are bodies which can be contemplated by reason, which do not participate in void and are ungenerated and indestructible, since they can neither be broken nor be compounded [or: arranged] out of parts, nor be altered in their qualities. They are contemplated by reason. Anyway, they move in the void and through the void. And the void itself is infinite, and so are the bodies. Bodies have these three properties: shape, size, weight. Democritus said that there were two, size and shape, but Epicurus added weight to these as a third. For, he says, it is necessary that the bodies move by the blow of [an object with] weight, since [otherwise] they will not move. The shapes of the atoms are ungraspably many, but not unlimited. For there are none which are hooked or trident-shaped or ring-shaped; for these shapes are easily broken and the atoms are impassible. They have their own shapes which can be contemplated by reason. The atom is so called not because it is the minimal [particle], but because it cannot be divided, since it is impassible and does not participate in void.

Aetius 1.20.2 = *Dox. Gr.* p. 318 (271 U)   [I-78]

Epicurus [says that] void, place, and space differ [only] in name.

Sextus *M* 8.329 (272 U)   [I-79]

. . . Epicurus, for example, thinks that he has offered the most powerful demonstration that the void exists: "If motion exists, void exists; but motion does indeed exist; therefore void exists."

Sextus *M* 10.2 (271 U—addendum)   [I-80]

Therefore, we must understand that according to Epicurus one part of the nature which is termed intangible is called 'void', one part 'place', and one part 'space'. The names vary according to different applications [of the intellect], since the nature which is designated 'void' when it is empty of every body is called 'place' when it is occupied by a body and becomes 'space' when bodies pass through it. In Epicurus, however, it is called by the general term 'intangible nature' because it is deprived of 'touch' in the sense of resistance.

Sextus *M* 3.98 (273☆ U—addendum)   [I-81]

Then, as the Epicureans too say, the straight line in the void is indeed straight, but it does not turn because even the void itself is not receptive of motion either in whole or in part.

Sextus *M* 10.257 (275 U)   [I-82]

. . . which Epicurus too agreed with when he said that body was conceived as an aggregate of shape and size and resistance and weight.

Simplicius *Commentary on Aristotle's Physics*   [I-83]
232a23 ff. *CIAG* 10.938.17–22 (277 U)

For unless every magnitude were divisible, it would not always be possible for a slower object to move a lesser distance in an equal time than a quicker one. For slower and quicker objects cover the atomic and indivisible [distance] in the same time, since if [one] took more time, it would cover in the equal time a [distance] less than the indivisible [distance]. And that is why the Epicureans too think all [bodies] move at equal speed through indivisible [distances], so that they can avoid having their atomic [quantities] be divided and so no longer atomic.

Aetius 1.12.5 = *Dox.Gr.* p. 311 (275, 280 U)   [I-84]

Epicurus [says that] the primary and simple bodies are ungraspable, and that the compounds formed from them all have weight. Atoms sometimes move in a straight line, sometimes in a swerve, and those which move upwards do so by collision and rebound.

Aetius 1.23.4 = *Dox.Gr.* 319–320 (280 U)   [I-85]

Epicurus says there are two kinds of motion, the straight and the swerve.

Plutarch *On the Generation of the Soul in the*   [I-86]
Timaeus 1015bc (281 U)

. . . they do not concede to Epicurus that the atom can swerve the tiniest bit, on the grounds that he introduces a causeless motion coming from not being.

Simplicius *Commentary on Aristotle's De*   [I-87]
Caelo 275b29 *CIAG* 7.242.18–26 (284 U)

For they [Leucippus, Democritus, and Epicurus] said that the principles were unlimited in number, and they also thought that they were atomic and indivisible and impassible, because they were dense and did not have a share of the void; for they said that division takes place where there is something void in bodies, and also that these atoms, being separated from each other in the unlimited void and differing in shape and size and position and ordering, move in the void and that they catch up with each other and collide and that some rebound to any chance place while others get entangled with each other, in accordance with the symmetry of their shapes and sizes and positions and orderings; and in this way it comes about that the origin of compounds is produced.

Alexander of Aphrodisias *On Mixture*   [I-88]
214.28–215.8 (290 U)

Epicurus wanted to avoid what Democritus said followed for those who say that blending occurs by means of the juxtaposition of the components of the blend, and himself said that blending occurs by means of the juxtaposition of certain bodies, though not of bodies which are themselves mixed and [still] preserved in the division, (215) but rather of bodies that are broken down into elements and atoms from which each of [those bodies] is a sort of compound, one being wine, another water, another honey, another something else; and then he says that the blend occurs by a certain kind of reciprocal compounding of those bodies from which the components of the blend were constituted; and it is these which produce the blended body, not the water and the wine, but [it is] the atoms which make up the water, as one might call them, which are blended together with those which make up the wine by a destruction and generation of certain [bodies]. For the breakdown of each into its elements is a form of destruction, and the compounding produced from the elements themselves is ‹a sort of genesis›.

Sextus *M* 10.219–227 (294 U)   [I-89]

219. According to the account of Demetrius of Laconia, Epicurus says that time is a property of properties which accompanies days and nights and hours and feelings and absences of feeling and motions and states of rest. For all of these are accidental properties of certain things, and since it accompanies all of these, time would not unreasonably be called a property of properties. 220. For in general, to go back a bit in order to promote the comprehension of our argument, some existing things exist in their own right while others are observed to be dependent on things which exist in their own right. And the things which exist in their own right are things like substances (for example, body and void), while their so-called accidents are the things observed to be dependent on the things which exist in their own right. 221. Of these accidents, some are inseparable from that of which they are the accidents, and some are of such a nature as to be separated. Those which are inseparable from that of which they are the accidents, then, are, for example, resistance [as an accident] of body and yielding [as an accident] of void. 222. For a body cannot ever be thought of without resistance, nor can void be thought of without yielding; rather, resistance is a permanent accident of the one

and yielding of the other. Those which are not inseparable from that of which they are the accidents are, for example, motion and rest. **223.** For compound bodies are neither in perpetual motion without opportunity for rest, nor are they perpetually in a state of not moving; rather, they sometimes have motion as an accident and sometimes rest. By contrast, the atom, when it is on its own, is in perpetual motion. For [while moving] it must either meet up with void or with a body; but if it meets with void, it moves through it because of its yielding, and if it meets with a body, its motion is a rebound away from it as a result of its resistance. **224.** These, then, are the properties which time accompanies, I mean day and night and hours and feelings and absences of feeling and motion and rest. For day and night are properties of the surrounding air, day occurring when the sun illuminates it and night coming along when it is deprived of the sun's light. **225.** An hour is a part of either a day or a night, and so again is a property of the air, just as day and night are. And time is co-extensive with every day and every night and hour, which is why night and day are said to be long or short, our reference being to the time which is an accident of [each of] these. And the feelings and absences of feeling are either [states of] pleasure or pain, which is why they are not substances but rather properties of those who have a pleasant or painful experience; but properties are not without [reference to] time. **226.** In addition, motion too and rest as well are, as we have already established, properties of bodies and are not separable from time. For we measure by time the speed or slowness of motion, and again the greater or lesser extent of a period of rest. **227.** But from all this it is evident that Epicurus thinks that time is an incorporeal, though not in the same sense as the Stoics do. For they, as we have said, posited that time is an incorporeal which is conceived of all by itself, while Epicurus thinks that it is an accident of certain things.

Simplicius *Commentary on Aristotle's Physics* [I-90]
203b15 *CIAG* 9.466, 31–467.4 (297 U)

There is a fourth point which is hard to stare down: the fact that everything which is limited seems to be limited by something. For if everything which is limited is limited by something which is external to itself, then that external thing by which it is limited is itself either unlimited or limited. And if it is unlimited, then we immediately have [the conclusion] that the unlimited exists. And if it is limited, for example, the earth, then this too is limited by something else, and so on without limit. And if it goes on without limit, the unlimited exists. For one will never get one's hands on the final limit, if indeed this too is limited by something else. The Epicureans, according to Alexander, relied on this argument above all else when they said that the totality was unlimited, because everything which is limited by something has outside it something which is [in turn] limited. And Aristotle mentions this as a quite old argument.

Aetius 2.4.10 = *Dox.Gr.* p. 331 (305 U)   [I-91]

Epicurus [says that] the cosmos is destroyed in very many ways: for [it is destroyed] in the manner of an animal and in the manner of a plant and in lots of [other] ways.

Aetius 1.4.1-4 = *Dox.Gr.* p. 289–291 (308☆ U)   [I-92]

1. So the cosmos was compounded and endowed with its rounded [lit.: bent] shape in the following manner.

Because the atomic bodies, which move without providence and in a random manner, were constantly moving at the greatest of speeds, many bodies were assembled together in the same place for this reason, and had a variety of shapes and sizes ⟨and weights⟩. 2. When they were assembling in the same place, the larger and heavier bodies, at all events, moved towards the bottom and settled; but the small, round, smooth, and slippery ones were pushed out in the concourse of atoms and so moved into the upper regions. So when the force of the blows [of atomic collisions] stopped raising them up and the blow[s] no longer carried them into the upper regions, but they were prevented from moving downwards, they were squeezed into the places which were able to receive them. And these were the places around about, and the majority of the bodies were bent around to these places. By becoming entangled with each other during the bending they generated the sky.

3. Retaining the same nature and being varied, as was said, the atoms which were pushed out to the upper regions produced the nature of the heavenly bodies. The majority of the bodies which were evaporated upwards struck the air and expelled it. And [the air], being made wind-like during its movement and gathering together the heavenly bodies, drove them around with itself and by this twisting produced their present circular movement in the upper regions.

And then the earth was produced from the [bodies] which settled [at the bottom], and from those which were raised upwards the sky, fire, and air [were produced]. 4. Since a great deal of matter was still contained in the earth and this was packed densely by the blows of the [atomic] bodies and by those from the rays of the heavenly bodies, [the earth's] entire configuration, which was made up of small particles, was squeezed together and [so] produced the nature of fluids. And since this [nature] was disposed to flow, it moved down into the hollow places and those able to receive it and contain it; that, or the water all by itself hollowed out the existing places by settling [there].

So the most important parts of the cosmos were produced in this way.

Sextus *M* 7.267 (310 U) [I-93]

Epicurus and his followers thought they were able to indicate the conception of man ostensively, saying: "man is this sort of form together with possession of life."

Aetius 4.4.6 = *Dox. Gr.* p. 390 (312 U) [I-94]

Democritus and Epicurus say the soul has two parts, one which is rational and is situated in the chest area, and the other which is non-rational and is spread throughout the entire compound of the body.

Aetius 4.3.11 = *Dox. Gr.* p. 388–389 (315 U) [I-95]

Epicurus [says that the soul is] a blend of four things, a certain kind of fiery stuff, a certain kind of airy stuff, a certain kind of breathlike stuff and a fourth something which is nameless. (This was the power of sense-perception for him.) Of these, the breath provides motion, the air rest, the hot the apparent heat of the body, and the nameless element the [power of] sense-perception in us. For sense-perception is in none of the named elements.

Aetius 4.8.10 = *Dox. Gr.* p. 395 (317 U) [I-96]

Leucippus, Democritus, and Epicurus [say that] sense-perception and thought occur when images approach from the outside. For we apply neither [sense-perception nor thought] to anything in the absence of an image striking from the outside.

Aetius 4.13.1 = *Dox. Gr.* p. 403 (318 U) [I-97]

Leucippus, Democritus, and Epicurus thought that the visual experience occurred by means of the reception of images.

Alexander of Aphrodisias *Commentary on* [I-98]
Aristotle's De Sensu 438a5 ff. *CIAG* 3.1, 34.18–22 (319 U)

[Democritus] himself, and before him Leucippus and after him the Epicureans, think that certain images, which are of the same shape as the objects from which they flow, flow from them and strike the eyes of those who are seeing and that this is how seeing occurs. As a proof of this he offers the fact that there is always in the pupil of those who are seeing a reflection and image of what is seen, and this is exactly what the act of seeing is.

Aetius 4.19.2 = *Dox.Gr.* p. 408 (321 U)   [I-99]

Epicurus [says that] the voice is a flow sent out from those who make utterances or produce sounds or noises. This flow is broken up into particles of the same shape. ("Of the same shape" means that the round are like the round and the angular and the triangular are like those of those types.) And when these strike the organs of hearing the perception of voice is produced.

London Scholiast on Dionysius Thrax, [I-100]
Grammatici Graeci 1.3, p. 482.13–19 (Hilgard) (322 U)

Epicurus, Democritus, and the Stoics say that voice is a body. For everything which can act or be acted upon is a body. For example, iron: it is acted upon by fire and acts on men or wood. So if voice can act and be acted upon, it is a body. But it acts, since we proceed to enjoyment when we hear a voice or a lyre; and it is acted upon, as when we are speaking and the wind blows, which makes it harder to hear our voice.

Censorinus *De Die Natali* 4.9 (333 U)   [I-101]

Democritus of Abdera first held that men were created from water and mud. And Epicurus' view is not much different: for he believed that when the mud became warm, first there grew wombs of some kind or another which clung to the earth by roots, and these sent forth infants and then provided a natural supply of milky fluid for them, under the guidance of nature. When these [infants] had been brought up in this manner and reached maturity, they then propagated the human race.

Origen *Against Celsus* 1.24 (334 U) [I-102]

As to this, one should also say that a deep and arcane debate about the nature of names emerged: are names conventional, as Aristotle thinks; or natural, as the Stoics believe (for the first utterances imitate the things the utterances are applied to, and accordingly they introduce [them] as elements of a kind for etymology); or are names natural, as Epicurus teaches—in a manner different from that of the Stoics, since the first men burst forth with certain sounds which were applied to things?

Proclus *Commentary on Plato's Cratylus* 16, [I-103] 17 (pp. 6 and 8–9 Boissonade, 335 U)

16. That Pythagoras and Epicurus shared the view of Cratylus, while Democritus and Aristotle shared that of Hermogenes.

17. That [names are] natural in four senses. For either [they are natural] as the substances of animals and plants are (both their parts and the wholes), or as their activities and powers are (for example, the lightness and heat of fire), or as shadows and reflections in mirrors are, or as crafted images which resemble their own archetypes are. Epicurus, then, thought that names were natural in the first[34] sense, as being primary functions of nature: as the voice and vision and as seeing and hearing [are natural], in the same way naming [is natural]. So that names too are natural in the sense of functions of nature. But Cratylus [says that names are natural] in the second sense; that is why he says that each thing has its own proper name, since it was given specifically [to that thing] by the first name-givers in a craftsmanlike fashion based on an understanding [of that thing]. For Epicurus said that these men [the first name-givers] did not give names based on an understanding of things, but because they were moved in a natural fashion, like those who cough and sneeze and bellow and bark and lament.

Aetius 4.7.4 = *Dox. Gr.* p. 393 (336 U) [I-104]

Democritus and Epicurus [said that the soul] is mortal and perishes with the body.

Sextus *M* 9.25 (353 U) [I-105]

Epicurus thinks that men have derived the conception of god from presentations [received] while asleep. For, he says, since large anthropo-

---

34. Usener emends this to 'second'; but from the larger context it seems clear that Proclus rather sloppily groups the first two senses together as a new 'first sense', and is equally sloppy in his reference to Cratylus' use of the 'second' sense.

morphic images strike them while they sleep they supposed that some such anthropomorphic gods also existed in reality.

Aetius 1.7.34 = *Dox.Gr.* p. 306 (355 U)   [I-106]

Epicurus [says that] the gods are anthropomorphic and can be contemplated by reason as a result of the fineness of the nature of their images.

Sextus *M* 9.178 (357 U)   [I-107]

And again, if [the divine] exists, it is either vocal or non-vocal. Well, to say that god is non-vocal is completely absurd and in conflict with the common conceptions. But if [the divine] is vocal, then it uses its voice and has speech organs, like lungs and windpipe and tongue and mouth. But this is absurd and almost as bad as the myths told by Epicurus.

Aetius 1.7.7 = *Dox.Gr.* p. 300 (361 U)   [I-108]

[An Epicurean speaks]: Both [Anaxagoras and Plato] share this error, because they portrayed god as being concerned for human affairs and as making the cosmos for the sake of man. For a blessed and indestructible animal, overflowing with good things and free of any share of what is bad, is completely preoccupied with the continuance of his own happiness and indestructibility and so is not concerned with human affairs. For he would be wretched, like a workman or builder, if he undertook burdens and felt concern for the creation of the cosmos.

Lactantius *On the Anger of God* 13.20–22   [I-109]
(374 U)

20. And if this explanation [for the existence of bad things] . . . is true, then that argument of Epicurus is refuted. "God," he says, "either wants to eliminate bad things and cannot, or can but does not want to, or neither wishes to nor can, or both wants to and can. 21. If he wants to and cannot, then he is weak—and this does not apply to god. If he can but does not want to, then he is spiteful—which is equally foreign to god's nature. If he neither wants to nor can, he is both weak and spiteful and so not a god. If he wants to and can, which is the only thing fitting for a god, where then do bad things come from? Or why does he not eliminate them?" 22. I know that most of the philosophers who defend [divine] providence are commonly shaken by this argument and against their wills are almost driven to admit that god does not care, which is exactly what Epicurus is looking for.

Aetius 1.29.5 = *Dox.Gr.* p. 326 (375 U) [I-110]

Epicurus says that all things [occur] by necessity, by choice, and by chance.

Simplicius *Commentary on Aristotle's Physics* [I-111] 198b29 *CIAG* 9.371.30–372.16 (377* U)

In cases where everything happened as though it were for the sake of some goal, these [creatures] were preserved because, although they were formed by chance, they were formed as suitable compounds; but in other cases [the creatures] perished and still do perish, as Empedocles refers to "oxlike creatures with human faces". . . . The ancient natural philosophers who said that material necessity was the cause of things which come to be seem to hold this opinion, and among later thinkers so do the Epicureans. Their error comes, as Alexander says, from thinking that everything which comes to be for the sake of some goal comes to be by intention and calculation and from seeing that things which come about by nature do not come to be in this way. But this is not so.

Plutarch *On Stoic Self-Contradictions* 1050bc [I-112] (378 U)

(1050b) . . . And yet Epicurus somehow twists about and exercises his ingenuity (1050c) in contriving to free and liberate voluntary action from [the necessity of] eternal motion, in order not to leave vice immune to blame.

Aetius 1.29.6 = *Dox.Gr.* p. 326 (380 U) [I-113]

Epicurus [says that chance is] a cause which is unstable [or: uncertain] with respect to persons, times, and places.

Maximus the Abbott *Gnom.* 14 [I-114] (388 U)

If god acted in accordance with the prayers of men, all men would rather quickly be destroyed, since they constantly pray for many sufferings to befall each other.

Ethics

Plutarch *Against Colotes* 1127a (8 U) [I-115]

And when they write, they write about politics to discourage us from practicing politics, and write about rhetoric to discourage us from practicing rhetoric, and about kingship to discourage us from consorting with kings.

Ammianus Marcellinus 30.4.3 (51 U)   [I-116]

The rich genius of Plato defines this calling, i.e., forensic oratory, as an image of a part of politics; but Epicurus calls it "a vile technique." . . .

Seneca *Letters on Ethics* 8.7 (199 U)   [I-117]

"You ought to be a slave to philosophy in order to achieve true liberty."

Porphyry *To Marcella* 30 (200 U)   [I-118]

"When the flesh cries out, be assured that the [answering] cry of the soul can be explained by natural science. The cry of the flesh: not to be hungry, not to be thirsty, not to be cold. And while it is difficult for the soul to prevent these things, it is dangerous to neglect nature which daily proclaims self-sufficiency to the soul via the [flesh] which is intimately bonded to it."

Porphyry *To Marcella* 27 (202☆ U)   [I-119]

"So he who follows nature and not groundless opinions is in all things self-sufficient. For every possession is wealth when it comes to satisfying nature, while even the greatest wealth is poverty when it comes to the unlimited desires."

Porphyry *To Marcella* 29 (203 U)   [I-120]

"Insofar as you are stymied, you are stymied because you forget nature; for you burden yourself with unlimited fears and desires."

Plutarch *A Pleasant Life* 1105e (213 U)   [I-121]

"Sweet is the memory of a dead friend."

Maximus the Abbot *Gnomologium* 8 (214 U,   [I-122]
199 A)

"Do not avoid doing trivial favours, for you will seem to be like this in important matters too."

Maximus the Abbot *Gnomologium* 66 (215 U, 200 A) [I-123]

"Do not turn away the request of an enemy in need; just protect yourself, for he is no better than a dog."

Porphyry *To Marcella* 31 (221 U) [I-124]

"Empty is the argument of the philosopher by which no human disease is healed; for just as there is no benefit in medicine if it does not drive out bodily diseases, so there is no benefit in philosophy if it does not drive out the disease of the soul."

Plutarch *Against Colotes* 1117f (222 U) [I-125]

One of Epicurus' doctrines is that no one except the wise man is unshakeably persuaded of anything.

Vatican Scholiast on Dionysius Thrax, *Grammatici Graeci* 1.3, p. 108.27–29 (Hilgard) (227b U) [I-126]

This is how the Epicureans define craft: a craft is a method which effects what is advantageous for [human] life. "Effects" is used in the sense of "produces."

Plutarch *A Pleasant Life* 1093c (229a U) [I-127]

They even reject the pleasures which come from mathematics!

Sextus *PH* 3.194 (398 U) [I-128]

Hence, the Epicureans too think that they are proving that pleasure is naturally worth choosing; for they say that animals, as soon as they are born and while they are still uncorrupted, have an impulse to pleasure and avoid pains.

Alexander of Aphrodisias *De Anima CIAG* Supp. 2.1, p. 150.33–34 (398 U) [I-129]

The Epicureans held that what is first congenial to us, unqualifiedly, is pleasure, but they say that as we get older this pleasure becomes articulated.

Athenaeus *Deipnosophists* 12, 546f (409 U) [I-130]

And Epicurus says, "the principle and root of all good is the pleasure of the belly; and the sophisticated and refined [goods] are referred to this one."

Plutarch *Against Colotes* 1122e (411 U) [I-131]

All by themselves and without a teacher, these noble and smooth and agreeable motions of the flesh beckon, as they themselves say, even men who refuse to admit that they are swayed and softened by them.

Plutarch *A Pleasant Life* 1090b (413 U) [I-132]

So if the soul supposes that its good lies in the stable condition of the body and in confidence about [the condition of] the body [as Epicurus thinks it does], then it cannot live out its life free of fear and upset. For the body is not only subject to storms and squalls from outside itself, like the sea, but from within itself it generates more and greater upsets.

Damascius *Lectures on the Philebus*, 190 [I-133]
(p. 91 Westerink; 416 U)

Even Epicurus, referring to natural pleasure, says that it is katastematic.

Plutarch *A Pleasant Life* 1088c–e (417 U) [I-134]

(1088c) . . . Epicurus has assigned a common limit to [the pleasures], the removal of all that causes pain, as though nature increased pleasure up to the point where it eliminates the painful, but did not permit it to make any further increase in its size, though it admits of certain non-necessary variations once it gets free of distress. The journey [which we make] towards this goal, in the company of desire, constitutes the [full] measure of pleasure and it is certainly short and economical. (1088d) That is why when they sense their stinginess in this area, they transfer their goal from the body, which is a barren field, to the soul, in order to acquire there pastures and meadows lushly overflowing with pleasures. . .

So don't you think that these men do well, in starting from the body, which is the first place where pleasure makes its appearance, and going on to the soul as something more secure which perfects everything within itself? . . .

(1088e) . . . but if you hear them crying out and shouting that the soul by nature finds joy and tranquillity in no existing thing except the pleasures of the body, whether present or anticipated, and that this is its good, don't you think that they are using the soul as a kind of decanter for the body and that they suppose that by pouring pleasure, like wine, from a broken-down and leaky container to this [new container] and aging it [there] they are doing something more impressive and valuable?

Stobaeus *Anthology* 3.17.34 (vol. 3 p. 501 W-H; 422 U)   [I-135]

"We need pleasure when we are in pain because of its absence; but when we are not in this condition, and are in a stable state of sense-perception, then there is no need for pleasure. For it is not the needs of nature which produce injustice from without, but the desire based on groundless opinions."

Plutarch *A Pleasant Life* 1091b (423 U)   [I-136]

He says, "for unsurpassable joy is produced by comparison with a great bad thing which one has escaped; and this is the nature of the good, if one applies [one's intellect] properly and then takes a firm stand, but does not stroll around babbling emptily about the good."

Plutarch *A Pleasant Life* 1099d (436 U)   [I-137]

As they say, remembering previous goods is the most important factor contributing to a pleasant life.

Aristocles, quoted by Eusebius at *Prep. Ev.* 14.21.3 (442 U)   [I-138]

It is better to endure these particular pains, so that we might experience greater pleasures; and it is advantageous to refrain from these particular pleasures so that we might not suffer from more burdensome pains.

Porphyry *On Abstinence* 1.51 (463 U)   [I-139]

Variations in one's nourishment cannot possibly dissolve the disturbances of the soul, and indeed cannot even increase the pleasure in the flesh; for this too reaches its limit as soon as the removal of pain is achieved.

Stobaeus *Anthology* 3.17.22 (vol. 3 p. 495 W-H; 469 U)   [I-140]

"I am grateful to blessed Nature, because she made what is necessary easy to acquire and what is hard to acquire unnecessary."

Porphyry *To Marcella* 27 (471 U)   [I-141]

"It is rare to find a man who is ⟨poor⟩ with regard to the goal set by nature and rich with regard to groundless opinions. For no imprudent man is satisfied by what he has, but rather is distressed by what he does not have. So just as people with a fever are always thirsty and desire the most inconsistent things because of the malignancy of their ⟨disease⟩, so too those whose souls are in a bad condition always feel that they are totally impoverished and enmeshed in all sorts of desires as a result of their gluttony."

Aelian *Miscellaneous History* 4.13 (473 U)   [I-142]

"He for whom a little is not sufficient finds nothing sufficient."

Porphyry *To Marcella* 28 (476 U)   [I-143]

"Self-sufficiency is the greatest wealth of all."

Porphyry *To Marcella* 28 (478 U)   [I-144]

"Most men are afraid of parsimony in their life-style and because of this fear proceed to actions which are most likely to produce it."

Porphyry *To Marcella* 28 (479 U)   [I-145]

"Many men attain wealth but do not find therein an escape from their problems; rather, they exchange them for greater problems."

Porphyry *To Marcella* 29 (480 U)   [I-146]

"By hard labour fit for a beast a great quantity of wealth is heaped up; but life is made miserable."

Porphyry *To Marcella* 29 (485 U)   [I-147]

"For a man is unhappy either because of fear or because of unlimited and groundless desire; and by reining these in he can produce for himself the reasoning [which leads to] blessedness."

Seneca *Letters on Ethics* 12.10 (487 U)   [I-148]

"It is bad to live with necessity, but there is no necessity to live with necessity."

Plutarch *On Peace of Mind* 474c (490 U) [I-149]

"He who has least need of tomorrow will approach it with the greatest pleasure."

Seneca *Letters on Ethics* 24.22–23 (496–498 U) [I-150]

Epicurus reproaches those who long for death no less than those who fear it, and says: "it is absurd to pursue death because you are weary of life, when you have made death worth pursuing by your way of life." In another place he says something similar: "So great is the folly, nay madness, of men that some are driven to death by the fear of death." . . . "What is so absurd as to seek death when you have made your own life troubled by fearing death."

Athenaeus *Deipnosophists* 12, 547a (512 U) [I-151]

"I spit upon the honourable and on those who vainly admire it, whenever it produces no pleasure."

Clement of Alexandria *Stromates* 6.2,24.10 [I-152]
p. 441 Stählin (519 U)

"The greatest fruit of justice is freedom from disturbance."

Arrian, *Discourses of Epictetus* 2.20.6–7 [I-153]
(523 U)

6. So too Epicurus, when he wishes to abolish the natural community of men with one another, makes use of the very thing he is destroying. 7. For what does he say? Don't be deceived, men, or misled or mistaken: there is no natural community of rational beings with each other. Believe me: those who say otherwise are deceiving you and reasoning falsely.

Stobaeus *Anthology* 4.143 (vol. 4 p. 90 W-H; [I-154]
530 U)

"The laws exist for the sake of the wise, not so that they will not commit injustice but so that they will not suffer injustice."

Plutarch *A Pleasant Life* 1090cd (532 U) [I-155]

(1090c) . . . for they say that those who break the law and commit injustice live in fear and misery for all time, because even if they can escape detection, it is nevertheless impossible to be confident about escaping detection. **(1090d)** That is the source of the fear about the future which always weighs on them and does not permit them to rejoice or be of good cheer about the present.

Plutarch *A Pleasant Life* 1104b (534 U)   [I-156]

For Epicurus does not think that one ought to restrain [people] from injustice by any means other than the fear of punishment.

Plutarch *A Pleasant Life* 1097a (544 U)   [I-157]

And they themselves say that benefitting [others] is pleasanter than receiving benefits.

Plutarch *On How to Listen to Poets* 37a   [I-158]
(548 U)

"It is not great sums of money or a mass of possessions, nor even certain political offices and powers, which produce happiness and blessedness, but rather freedom from pain and gentleness in our feelings and a disposition of soul which measures out what is natural."

Aelian *Miscellaneous Histories* 4.13 (602 U)   [I-159]

[Epicurus] said that he was ready to rival Zeus for happiness, as long as he had a barley cake and some water.

II: Stoicism

Lives of the Stoics

Diogenes Laertius 7.1-38 (selections), 160–202 [II-1] (selections)

1. Zeno, the son of Mnaseas or Demeas, was a citizen of Citium on Cyprus, a Greek town which had Phoenician settlers. . . .

2. As was said above, he studied with Crates; then they say that he also studied with Stilpo and Xenocrates for ten years, according to Timocrates in his *Dion*; but he also [is said to have studied with] Polemo. Hecaton says (and so does Apollonius of Tyre in book one of his *On Zeno*) that when he consulted the oracle to find out what he should do to live the best life the god answered [that he would live the best life] if he were to join his flesh with that of the dead. Seeing what this meant, he read the works of the ancients.

He met with Crates as follows. On a commercial voyage from Phoenicia to sell purple dye he shipwrecked near the Piraeus. He went into Athens (he was thirty years old at the time) and sat down by a certain bookseller. The bookseller was reading the second book of Xenophon's *Memorabilia*; he enjoyed it and asked where men like that [i.e., like Socrates] spent their time. 3. Fortuitously, Crates came by and the bookseller pointed to him and said, "Follow this man". From then on he studied with Crates, being in other respects fit for and intent on philosophy but too modest for Cynic shamelessness. . . .

4. So he studied with Crates for a while; hence[1] when he wrote the *Republic* too some people said in jest that he had written it 'on the tail of the Dog'. . . . . . . In the end he left [Crates] and studied with those already mentioned for twenty years; hence, they also say that he said "I have had a good voyage this time, now that I have been shipwrecked." But some say he said this about Crates. 5. And others say that he was spending time in Athens when he heard about the shipwreck and [then] said, "Fortune does me a big favour by driving me to philosophy." Some say that he disposed of his cargo in Athens and so turned to philosophy.

---

1. We propose *hothen* for *hote*.

He used to set out his arguments while walking back and forth in the Painted Stoa which was also named for Peisianax, but [called] 'Painted' because of the painting by Polygnotus. He wanted to make sure that his space was unobstructed by bystanders; for under the Thirty Tyrants 1400 citizens had been slaughtered in it. Still, people came to listen to him and for this reason they were called Stoics; and his followers were given the same name, although they had previously been called Zenonians, as Epicurus also says in his letters. . . .

15. . . . He was devoted to enquiry and reasoned with precision on all topics . . . 16. He pursued his disputes with Philo the dialectician with great care, and studied along with him. Hence, [Philo] was admired by Zeno (who was younger than he) no less than his teacher Diodorus [Cronus].

20. When someone said that he thought that philosophers' arguments were brief, he said, "you're right; but if possible even the syllables in the arguments should be short." . . . He said that one should converse vigorously, as actors do, and that one should have a loud voice and great strength but not distort one's mouth—which is what people do who chatter about a lot of impossible things. . . .

23. He used to say that there was nothing more alien to the grasp of [various branches of] knowledge than [mere] opinion, and that we are in need of nothing so much as time. Someone asked him what a friend is; he said, "Another me." They say that he beat a slave for stealing. And when he [the slave] said, "it was fated for me to steal," [Zeno] said, "and to be flogged." . . . 24. Apollonius of Tyre says that when Crates dragged him away from Stilpo by the coat, [Zeno] said, "Crates, the sophisticated way to get a hold on philosophers is by the ears. So persuade me and drag me away by *them*; but if you use force on me, my body will be with you and my soul with Stilpo."

25. He also studied together with Diodorus, according to Hippobotus; it was in his company that [Zeno] worked his way through dialectic. When he was already making progress he came into Polemo's [lectures] (a result of his freedom from arrogance); so they say that [Polemo] said, "Zeno, I caught you sliding in by the garden gate to steal my doctrines and dress them up in Phoenician style." He asked the dialectician who showed him seven dialectical patterns in the Reaper argument how much he charged for them; when he was told [that the price was] a hundred drachmas, he gave him two hundred. So great was his love for learning. They also say that he was the first to use the term 'appropriate act' [*kathekon*] and to have developed a theory of it. . . .

27. . . . He had already become a kind of proverbial figure; anyway, it was he who inspired the line, "more temperate than Zeno the philoso-

pher" . . . 28. In fact he surpassed everyone in this form of virtue and in gravity and, Yes by Zeus! in blessedness. For he died at the age of ninety-eight, free of disease and healthy to the end. But Persaeus says in his *Ethical Studies* that he died at the age of seventy-two and that he came to Athens at the age of twenty-two. And Apollonius says that he headed his school for fifty-eight years. This is how he died: on leaving his school he stumbled and broke his toe; he struck the earth with his hand and uttered the line from the *Niobe*,[2] "I am coming. Why do you call me?" and immediately died by suffocating himself.

31. . . . Demetrius of Magnesia says in his *Men of the Same Name* that his father Mnaseas often came to Athens as a merchant and brought back many Socratic books to Zeno when he was still a boy; hence, he got a good training while still in his homeland. 32. And that is how he came to Athens and joined Crates. . . . They say that he swore by the caper, as Socrates did by the dog.

But some people, including the followers of Cassius the sceptic, criticize Zeno for many things, and first of all they say that he claimed, at the beginning of his *Republic*, that general culture was useless; and second that he said that all those who are not virtuous are hostile and enemies and slaves and alien to each other, parents to children and brothers to brothers ⟨and⟩ relatives to relatives. 33. Again, in the *Republic* he claimed that only virtuous men are citizens and friends and relatives and free men, so that, in the eyes of the Stoics, parents and children are enemies, since they are not wise. Similarly, in his *Republic* he takes the position that wives are [held] in common and at about line 200 [he holds] that they do not build temples or law courts or gymnasia in their cities. He writes as follows about coinage: "they do not think that one should produce coinage either for the sake of exchange or for the sake of foreign travel." And he orders that men and women should wear the same clothes and that no part [of the body] should be hidden. 34. In his work *On the Republic* Chrysippus says that the *Republic* is [indeed] by Zeno. And he wrote about erotic matters at the beginning of the book entitled *Art of Sexual Love*; but he also writes similar things in the *Diatribes*.

That is the sort of thing [one finds] in Cassius, and also in [the works of] the rhetor Isidor of Pergamum; he also says that the parts criticized by the Stoics were excised by Athenodorus the Stoic who was entrusted with the library in Pergamum; then they were restored when Athenodorus was exposed and put in jeopardy. So much about the passages of his work which have been marked as spurious. . . .

36. There were many students of Zeno, but the well-known ones

2. Of Timotheus, 787 Page.

include the following. Persaeus of Citium, son of Demetrius; some say he was his follower, others that he was a member of his household, one of those sent by Antigonus to help him with his library, having been a tutor to Antigonus' son Halcyoneus. Antigonus once wanted to put Persaeus to the test and so had a false message announced to him to the effect that his lands had been sacked by the enemy; when he frowned, Antigonus said, "do you see that wealth is not an indifferent thing?" . . .

37. [Another student of Zeno was] Ariston of Chios, the son of Miltiades, the one who introduced [the doctrine of] indifference. And Herillus of Carthage, the one who said that knowledge was the goal. And Dionysius the one who went over to hedonism; for because of a severe inflammation of the eye he became reluctant to say any longer that pain was an indifferent thing; he came from Heraclea. And Sphaerus from the Bosporus. And Cleanthes, son of Phanias, from Assos, the one who took over the school; Zeno compared him to writing tablets made of hard wax, which are hard to write on but which retain what is written. Sphaerus also studied under Cleanthes after Zeno's death, and we shall mention him in our discussion of Cleanthes. 38. The following too were students of Zeno, according to Hippobotus: Philonides of Thebes, Callippus of Corinth, Posidonius of Alexandria, Athenodorus of Soli and Zeno of Sidon. . . .

160. Ariston of Chios, the Bald, [also] nicknamed the Siren. He said that the goal was to live in a state of indifference with respect to what is intermediate between virtue and vice, acknowledging no distinction whatsoever in them but treating them all alike. For the wise man is like a good actor, who plays either role fittingly, whether he takes on the role of Thersites or Agamemnon. He abolished the topics of physics and logic, saying that the one was beyond our powers and that the other was nothing to us and that only ethics mattered to us.

161. [He said] that dialectical arguments were like spider webs: although they seem to indicate craftsmanlike skill, they are useless. He did not introduce many virtues, as Zeno did, nor did he say that there was one called by many names, as the Megarians did; rather, he appealed to relative dispositions. By philosophizing thus and conversing in Cynosarges he became important enough to be called the leader of a school. Thus Miltiades and Diphilus were called Aristonians. He was a persuasive fellow and just what the crowd liked to hear. . . .

162. He met Polemo and, as Diocles of Magnesia says, went over [to his school] when Zeno became afflicted with a long illness. He was most attached to the Stoic doctrine that the wise man is undogmatic. Persaeus opposed him on this point and had one of a set of twins deposit money with him and the other then get it back. Thus he perplexed and refuted

him. And he opposed Arcesilaus; when he saw a deformed bull with a womb he said, "Woe is me! Arcesilaus has been given an argument to use against [trusting] clear facts". **163.** To the Academic [sceptic] who said that he grasped nothing he said, "Do you not see the man sitting next to you?" And when the other said no, he said, "Who blinded you, who took away the brightness of your eyesight?" . . .

165. Herillus of Carthage said that knowledge was the goal, i.e., always living by referring everything to a life with knowledge and not being discredited by ignorance. And knowledge is a condition concerned with the reception of presentations, which is immune from being upset by argument. He once said that there was no goal, but that it changed in accordance with the circumstances and the facts, just as the same bronze becomes a statue of Alexander or of Socrates. The goal and the subordinate goal are different; for even men who are not wise aim at the latter, while only the wise man aims at the former. And the things between virtue and vice are indifferent. His books are short but are full of vigour and include some counter-arguments aimed at Zeno. . . .

168. Cleanthes of Assos, son of Phanias. He was a boxer at first, according to Antisthenes in his *Successions*. He arrived in Athens with four drachmas, as some say, and meeting Zeno he began to philosophize most nobly and stayed with the same doctrines. He was famous for his love of hard work; since he was a poor man he undertook to work for wages. And by night he laboured at watering gardens, while by day he exercised himself in arguments. . . .

171. . . . When someone said that Arcesilaus did not do what he ought to do, he said, "Stop it and do not blame the man; for even if he abolishes appropriate action by his argument, at least he supports it by his deeds." And Arcesilaus said, "I am not flattered." In response to which Cleanthes said, "Yes, I am flattering you by claiming that you say one thing and do another." . . .

174. . . . When someone criticized him for his old age, he said, "I too want to make my exit. But when I consider everything and see that I am completely healthy and able to write and to read, I continue to wait." . . .

. . . **175.** . . . And he died as follows. He got badly swollen gums, and on the orders of his doctors he abstained from food for two days. And somehow he got so much better that the doctors allowed him to eat his customary diet, but he would not agree to this, instead saying that the way was already prepared for him; and so he abstained for the rest of his days and died, according to some, at the same age as Zeno did; he had studied with Zeno for nineteen years. . . .

177. As we said above, Sphaerus from the Bosporus also studied with

Cleanthes after [studying with] Zeno; he had made considerable progress
in argumentation and then went off to Alexandria to the court of Ptolemy
Philopator. Once, when a discussion arose about whether the wise man
will form opinions, Sphaerus said that he did not; the king wanted to
refute him and ordered wax pomegranates to be set out; Sphaerus was
fooled and the king shouted that he had assented to a false presentation.
To which Sphaerus nimbly replied by saying that what he had assented
to was not that they were pomegranates, but that it was reasonable that
they were pomegranates, and that there was a difference between a
graspable presentation and a reasonable one. . . .

179. Chrysippus, son of Apollonius, from Soli (or from Tarsus, as
Alexander says in the *Successions*), was a student of Cleanthes. He had
previously been in training as a long-distance runner; then he studied
with Zeno, or Cleanthes according to Diocles and the majority [of authori-
ties], and left his school while he [Cleanthes] was still alive and became
a significant philosophical figure. He was a man of natural ability and so
extremely clever in all parts [of philosophy] that in most points he differed
with Zeno, and even with Cleanthes, to whom he frequently said that
he only needed to be taught the doctrines and he himself would discover
the demonstrations. Nevertheless, whenever he resisted Cleanthes he
regretted it, so that he constantly quoted this: "I was born blessed in all
else, except with respect to Cleanthes; in this I am not happy."[3]

180. So famous did he become in dialectic that most people thought
that if there were dialectic among the gods it would be none other than
Chrysippus'. He had abundant material, but he did not get his style
right. He worked harder than anyone else, as is shown by his writings;
for there are more than 705 of them. . . .

183. . . . He was so arrogant that when someone asked "To whom
should I send my son to study?" he said, "to me; for if I thought there
were anyone better than I, I would be philosophizing with him myself!"
Hence they say that it was said of him, "He alone has wits, and the
[others] rush around like shadows".[4] and, "If there were no Chrysippus,
there would be no Stoa."

In the end he philosophized with Arcesilaus and Lacydes, attending
[their meetings] in the Academy, according to Sotion in book 8. 184.
That is the reason why he argued both for and against [the reliability]
of ordinary experience and used the standard Academic technique when
discussing magnitudes and pluralities.

Hermippus says that he was holding his session in the Odeon when

3. Euripides *Orestes* 540-1, adapted.
4. Homer, *Odyssey* 10.495.

he was called to a sacrifice by his students; there he drank sweet, unmixed wine, and losing his head left the realm of men on the fifth day at the age of seventy-three, in the 143rd Olympiad [208–204 B.C.], as Apollodorus says in his *Chronology*. . . . **185.** But some say that he died after being seized with a fit of laughter; for when an ass had eaten his figs, he said to the old woman, "So give the ass some unmixed wine to swill", at which he cackled so heartily that he died. . . .

186. . . . The philosopher also used to put forth arguments of this sort: "He who tells the mysteries to the uninitiated is impious; but the high priest tells ⟨the mysteries⟩ to the uninitiated; therefore, the high priest is impious." Another one: "That which is not in the city is not in the house; but a well is not in the city, so it is not in the house." Another one: "There is a head; and you do not have it; there is indeed a head ⟨which you do not have⟩; therefore, you do not have a head." **187.** Another one: "If someone is in Megara, he is not in Athens; but a man is in Megara; therefore, there is not a man in Athens." And again: "If you say something, this comes out of your mouth; but you say wagon; therefore, a wagon comes out of your mouth." And: "If you have not lost something, then you have it; but you did not lose horns; therefore, you have horns". But others say that this argument is by Euboulides.

Some people assail Chrysippus for having written much that is shameful and indecent. For in his work *On the Ancient Natural Philosophers* he reinterprets the story about Hera and Zeus,[5] saying at line 600 or so things which no one could say without defiling his mouth. **188.** For, they say, he reinterprets this story into something extremely shameful, even if he does praise it as being a contribution to physics; still, it is more fitting for cheap hookers than gods. The story, moreover, is not recorded by the professional bibliographers; for [they say that] it is not found in Polemo or Hypsicrates and not even in Antigonus, but that it was made up by him. In the *On the Republic* he says [that one may] lie with mothers and daughters and sons, and he says the same thing right at the beginning of his *On Things Not Worth Choosing for Their own Sakes*. And around line 1000 of book three of *On the Just* he urges that [people] should eat the dead. And in book two of *On Life and the Making Money* he says that he is planning for how the wise man will make money. **189.** And yet, why must he make money? For if it is for the sake of life, life is an indifferent; if for the sake of pleasure, this too is indifferent; and if for the sake of virtue, then [virtue] is self-sufficient for happiness. And the means of making money are ridiculous, such as [receiving it] from a king—for one must yield to him; and [so too] for [making money] from

5. The deception of Zeus, *Iliad* 14.

friendship—for then friendship will be on sale for profit; and [so too] for [making money] from wisdom—for then wisdom will be put to work for wages.
These are the criticisms of his work.

On Philosophy

Diogenes Laertius 7.38–41   [II-2]

38. . . . It seemed a good idea to me to give a general account of all the Stoic doctrines in the life of Zeno, since he was the founder of the school. . . . The common doctrines are as follows. Let a summary account be given, as has been our custom in the case of the other philosophers.

39. They say that philosophical theory [*logos*] is tripartite. For one part of it concerns nature [i.e., physics], another concerns character [i.e., ethics] and another concerns rational discourse [i.e., logic]. Zeno of Citium first gave this division in his book *On Rational Discourse* [*logos*] and so did Chrysippus in book one of *On Rational Discourse* and book one of his *Physics* and so did Apollodorus and Syllos in the first books of their respective *Introductions to Doctrine*; and so too did Eudromus in his *Outline of Ethics*; and so too did Diogenes of Babylon and Posidonius. Apollodorus calls these parts 'topics'; Chrysippus and Eudromus call them 'species'; others call them 'kinds'.

40. They compare philosophy to an animal, likening logic to the bones and sinews, ethics to the fleshier parts and physics to the soul. Or again they compare it to an egg. For the outer parts [the shell] are logic, the next part [the white] is ethics and the inmost part [the yolk] is physics. Or to a productive field, of which logic is the wall surrounding it, ethics the fruit and physics is the land and trees. Or to a city which is beautifully fortified and administered according to reason. And, as some Stoics say, no part [of philosophy] is separate from another, but the parts are mixed. And they taught [the three parts] mixed together. Others put logic first, physics second and ethics third; Zeno (in his *On Rational Discourse*) and Chrysippus and Archedemus and Eudromus are in this group.

41. Diogenes of Ptolemais, though, begins with ethics and Apollodorus puts ethics second; Panaetius and Posidonius start with physics, as Phaenias the follower of Posidonius says in book one of his *Posidonian Lectures*. But Cleanthes says there are six parts: dialectic, rhetoric, ethics, politics, physics and theology. Others say that these are not the parts of [philosophical] discourse, but of philosophy itself, as for example, Zeno of Tarsus. Some say that the logical part is divided into two sciences, rhetoric and

dialectic. And some say it is also divided into the species concerned with definitions, and the one concerned with canons and criteria. Others omit the definitional part.

Logic and Theory of Knowledge

Diogenes Laertius 7.42–83 [II-3]

42. So they include the [study] of canons and criteria in order to discover the truth. For it is in this study that they straighten out the differences among presentations; and similarly [they include] the definitional part for the purpose of recognizing the truth. For objects are grasped by means of conceptions. And rhetorical knowledge is about speaking well in expository speeches, while dialectical knowledge is about conversing correctly in speeches of question and answer form. And that is why they also define it thus, as a knowledge of what is true and false and neither.

And they say that rhetoric itself is tripartite. For part of it is deliberative, part forensic, part encomiastic. **43.** It is divided into invention, diction, organization and delivery. And the rhetorical speech [is divided] into the introduction, the exposition, the counter-argument and the conclusion.

And dialectic is divided into the topic about the signified and [the topic about] the utterance. And the topic about the signified is [divided] into that about presentations and [that about] the *lekta* [things said] which subsist in dependence on them: propositions and complete [*lekta*] and predicates and the active and passive [*lekta*] similar [to them] and genera and species, and similarly arguments and modes and syllogisms and fallacies caused by [the form of] utterance or by the facts. **44.** These include the arguments about the Liar and the Truth-teller and the Denier, and sorites and arguments like these, incomplete, puzzling and conclusive, and the [ones about] the Hooded man and Nobody and the Reaper.

The aforementioned topic concerning the utterance itself is also proper to dialectic; in it they explain the [kind of] utterance which is articulated in letters and [also] what the parts of rational discourse are; it also concerns solecism and barbarism and poems and ambiguities and harmonious utterance and music; and, according to some, definitions and divisions and [the study of different forms of] speech.

45. They say that the study of syllogisms is extremely useful; for it indicates what is demonstrative, and this makes a big contribution towards correcting one's opinions; and orderliness and good memory indicate attentive comprehension. And an argument itself is a complex [made up of] premises and a conclusion; and a syllogism is a syllogistic argument [made up] of these. And demonstration is an argument which by means of things more [clearly] grasped concludes to something which is less [clearly] grasped.

A presentation is an impression in a soul, the name being appropriately transferred from the imprints in wax made by a seal-ring.

46. Of presentations, some are graspable, some non-graspable. The graspable presentation, which they say is the criterion of facts [*pragmata*], is that which comes from an existing object, and is stamped and moulded in accordance with the existing object itself. The non-graspable presentation is either not from an existing object, or from an existing object but not in accordance with it; it is neither clear nor well-stamped [i.e., distinct].

Dialectic itself is necessary and is a virtue which contains other virtues as species. And freedom from hasty judgement is knowledge of when one ought to assent and when not. And level-headedness is a strongminded rationality with respect to what is likely, so that one does not give in to it.

47. And irrefutability is strength in argument, so that one is not swept away by it to an opposite opinion. And intellectual seriousness is a disposition which refers presentations to right reason. Knowledge itself, they say, is either a secure grasp or a disposition in the reception of presentations not reversible by argument. And the wise man will not be free of error in argument without the study of dialectic. For truth and falsity are distinguished by it and persuasive and ambiguous statements are properly discerned by it. And without it methodical question and answer are impossible.

48. Hasty judgement in assertions has an impact on events, so that those who are not well exercised in handling presentations turn to unruliness and aimlessness. And there is no other way for the wise man to show himself to be sharp, quick-witted and, in general, clever in arguments. For the same man will be able to converse properly and reason things out and also take a position on issues put to him and respond to questions— these are characteristics of a man experienced in dialectic.

So, this is a summary of their doctrines in logic; and in order to give a detailed account also of those of their views which pertain to an introductory textbook, ⟨I shall report⟩ verbatim exactly ⟨what⟩ Diocles of Magnesia includes in his *Survey of Philosophers*, writing as follows.

49. The Stoics choose to put first the account of presentation and sense-perception, insofar as the criterion by which the truth of facts is known is, generically, the presentation; and insofar as the account of assent and the account of grasping and conception which is basic to other accounts cannot be given without presentation. For the presentation is first and then the intellect, which is verbally expressive, puts into rational discourse what it experiences because of presentation.

50. Presentation and phantasm are different. For a phantasm is a semblance in the intellect of the sort which occurs in sleep and presentation is an impression in the soul, i.e., an alteration, as Chrysippus supposes in book 2 of his *On Soul*. For one should not interpret "impression" as [being like] the stamped outline made by a seal-ring, since it is impossible for there to be many outlines in the same respect and on the same substance. One conceives of a presentation which is from an existing object and is moulded, outlined and stamped in accordance with the existing object, such as could not come from a non-existing object.

51. According to them, some presentations are sensible, some are non-sensible. Those received through one or more sense organs are sensible; non-sensible are those which come through the intellect, for example, presentations of incorporeals and the other things grasped by reason. Of sensible presentations, those which come from existing objects occur with yielding and assent. But [representational] images[6] which are "as if" from existing objects are also [counted] among the presentations. Again, of presentations some are rational, some are non-rational. The presentations of rational animals are rational, those of non-rational animals are non-rational. The rational, then, are thoughts and the irrational have been given no special name. And some presentations are technical, some non-technical. For an image is considered differently by a technical specialist and by a non-specialist.

52. According to the Stoics, 'sense-perception' refers to [a] the *pneuma* which extends from the leading part to the senses and [b] the "grasp" which comes through the senses and [c] the equipment of the sense organs (which some people may be impaired in). And [d] their activation is also called sense-perception. According to them the grasp occurs [a] through sense-perception (in the case of white objects, black objects, rough objects, smooth objects); and [b] through reason (in the case of conclusions drawn through demonstration, for example, that there are gods and that they are provident). For of conceptions, some are conceived on the basis of direct experience, some on the basis of similarity, some on the basis of analogy, ⟨some on the basis of transposition,⟩ some on the basis of composition and some on the basis of opposition.

6. See *M* 7.169.

53. Sensibles are conceived on the basis of direct experience; on the basis of similarity are conceived things [known] from something which is at hand—as Socrates is conceived of on the basis of his statue; on the basis of analogy things are conceived by expansion, for example, Tityos and the Cyclops, and by shrinking, for example, a Pygmy. And the centre of the earth is conceived through analogy with smaller spheres. On the basis of transposition, for example, eyes in the chest. On the basis of composition the Hippocentaur is conceived of; and death on the basis of opposition [to life]. Some things too are conceived of on the basis of transference, for example, the things said [*lekta*] and place. And there is a natural origin too for the conception of something just and good. Also on the basis of privation, for example, a man without a hand. These are their doctrines on presentation, sense-perception and conception.

54. They say that the graspable presentation, i.e. the one from what exists, is a criterion of truth, as Chrysippus says in book 2 of the *Physics* and Antipater and Apollodorus too. For Boethus says that there are a number of criteria: mind, sense-perception, desire, and knowledge. But Chrysippus, disagreeing with him in book one of *On Rational Discourse*, says that sense-perception and the basic grasp are criteria. (A basic grasp is a natural conception of things which are universal.) And other older Stoics say that right reason is a criterion, as Posidonius says in his *On the Criterion*.

55. Most of them are agreed that the study of dialectic should begin from the topic of utterance. An utterance is air which has been struck, or the proper sensible of hearing, as Diogenes of Babylon says in his *Treatise on Utterance*. An animal's utterance is air struck by an impulse, while a human [utterance] is articulate and emitted from the intellect, as Diogenes says; and this [the intellect] is completed from the age of fourteen on. And utterance is a body, according to the Stoics, as Archedemus says in his *On Utterance* and Diogenes and Antipater, and Chrysippus in book two of his *Physics*. 56. For everything which acts is a body, and voice does act when it comes to the listeners from the utterers. As Diogenes says, speech, according to the Stoics, is an utterance in letters, for example 'day'. Rational discourse [*logos*] is an utterance which signifies, emitted from the intellect; ⟨for example, 'It is day'.⟩ And dialect is speech marked both as Greek and as distinctive of a [specific] ethnic group; or speech from a particular region, i.e., which is peculiar in its dialect. For example, in Attic [one says] *thalatta* [for *thalassa*], and in Ionic *hemere* [for *hemera*].

The elements of speech are the twenty-four letters. Letter is used in three sense, ⟨the element⟩, the character and the name, for example alpha. 57. There are seven vowels among the elements, alpha, epsilon, eta, iota, omicron, upsilon, omega; and six mutes: beta, gamma, delta, kappa, pi, tau. Utterance and speech differ in that utterance also includes echoes, while only what is articulate [counts as] speech. And speech differs from rational discourse in that rational discourse is always significant, and speech [can] also [be] meaningless, like the 'word' *blituri*, while rational discourse cannot be. There is a difference between saying and verbalizing. For utterances are verbalized, while what is said are facts (which [is why they] are also 'things said' [*lekta*]).

There are five parts of rational discourse, as Diogenes says in *On Utterance* and also Chrysippus: name, noun, verb, conjunction, article. And Antipater also adds the participle in his *On Speech and Things Which are Said*.

58. According to Diogenes, a noun is a part of rational discourse which signifies a common quality, for example 'man', 'horse'; a name is a part of rational discourse which reveals an individual quality, for example 'Diogenes', 'Socrates'; a verb as Diogenes says, is a part of rational discourse which signifies an incomposite predicate, or as others [say], it is an undeclined element of rational discourse which signifies something put together with [lit. of] some thing or things, for example 'write', 'speak'; a conjunction is an undeclined part of rational discourse which joins together the parts of rational discourse; an article is a declined element of rational discourse which distinguishes the genders and numbers of names, for example *ho, he, to, hoi, hai, ta.*[7]

59. There are five virtues of rational discourse: good Greek, clarity, brevity, propriety, elaboration. Good Greek, then, is diction which is in conformity not with any common usage but one sanctioned by the art [of grammar]; clarity is speech which presents what is thought in a recognizable fashion; brevity is speech which includes exactly what is necessary for the revelation of its object; propriety is speech which is appropriate to its object; elaboration is speech which has transcended ordinariness. Of the vices, barbarism is a [form of] speech which violates the normal usage of reputable Greeks; solecism is rational discourse which is put together incongruently.

60. According to Posidonius in his *Introduction to Speech*, a poem is metrical speech, or rhythmical speech together with elaboration which escapes being prosaic. The rhythmical is:[8]

Greatest Earth and Zeus' sky.

---

7. The six nominative forms of the Greek article 'the', given in singular and plural numbers and masculine, feminine and neuter genders.

8. The metre of the Greek (fr. 839 of Euripides in Nauck) cannot be reproduced in translation.

But a 'poesis' is a poem which signifies in virtue of containing an imitation of divine and human affairs.

A definition is, as Antipater says in book one of his *On Definitions*, an analytical statement [*logos*] expressed precisely, or as Chrysippus says in his *On Definitions*, the rendering of what is proper [to the thing]. An outline is a statement which introduces [us] to the objects by a [general] impression, or a definition which introduces the force of the definition [proper] in simpler form. A genus is a conjunction of several inseparable concepts, for example, 'animal'; for this includes the particular animals.

61. A concept is a phantasm of the intellect, and is neither a something nor a qualified thing, but [rather] a quasi-something and a quasi-qualified thing; for example, there arises an impression of a horse even when no horse is present.

A species is that which is included by a genus, as man is included in animal. The most generic is that which, being a genus, does not have a genus, i.e., being; the most specific is that which, being a species, does not have a species, for example, Socrates.

Division is the cutting of a genus into its immediate species, for example: of animals, some are rational and some are irrational. Counterdivision is a division of the genus into a species in virtue of its opposite, as when things are divided by negation, for example: of beings, some are good and some are not good. Subdivision is a division following on a division, for example: of beings some are good and some are not good, and of things not good some are bad and some are indifferent.

62. A partitioning is an arrangement of a genus into its topics, according to Krinis; for example: of goods some belong to the soul and some belong to the body.

Ambiguity is a speech which signifies two or even more things, linguistically and strictly and in virtue of the same usage, so that by means of this speech several things are understood at the same time.[9] For example, *auletrispeptoke*; for by means of this [speech] are indicated something like this "a house fell three times" and something like this "a flute girl fell".

According to Posidonius, dialectic is a knowledge of what is true, what is false and what is neither. And, as Chrysippus says, it is concerned with signifiers and what is signified. This, then, is the sort of thing said by the Stoics in their study of utterance.

63. In the topic of objects and things signified are placed the account

---

9. 'Speech' is utterance articulable in letters (§ 56 above). Our translation has been improved by reflection on ch. 4 of Catherine Atherton's excellent book, *The Stoics on Ambiguity* (Cambridge 1993). The ambiguity in the example which follows is untranslatable, but stems from alternate divisions into words of the same syllables.

of *lekta* [things said], complete ones and propositions and syllogisms, and the account of incomplete [*lekta*] and predicates both active and passive. And they say that a *lekton* is what subsists in accordance with a rational presentation. And of *lekta* the Stoics say that some are complete and some are incomplete. Incomplete are those which are unfinished in their expression, such as 'writes'; for we go on to ask 'Who?' Complete are those which are finished in their expression, such as 'Socrates writes'. So predicates are placed among the incomplete *lekta*, and propositions and syllogisms and questions and enquiries are placed among the complete.

64. A predicate is what is said of something, or a thing put together with [lit. about] some thing or things, as Apollodorus says; or an incomplete *lekton* put together with a nominative case to generate a proposition. Of predicates, some are events, such as 'to sail through the rocks' . . . [There is a lacuna here.] And some predicates are active, some passive, some neither. Active are those put together with one of the oblique cases to generate a predicate, such as 'hears', 'sees', 'discusses'. Passive are those put together with the passive form, such as 'am heard', 'am seen'. Neither are those which fit in neither group, such as 'to be prudent', 'to walk'. Reflexive passives are those which, being passive, are [nevertheless] actions, such as 'gets his hair cut'. For the man getting his hair cut includes himself [in his action]. **65.** The oblique cases are the genitive, the dative and the accusative.

A proposition is that which is true or false; or a complete object which can be asserted on its own, as Chrysippus says in his *Dialectical Definitions*: "a proposition is what can be asserted or denied on its own, for example, 'It is day' or 'Dion is walking'." The proposition gets its name [*axioma*] from being accepted;[10] for he who says 'It is day' seems to accept [*axioun*] that it is day. So when it is day, the present proposition becomes true, and when it is not [day], it becomes false. **66.** There are differences among propositions, questions, enquiries, imperatives, oaths, curses, hypotheses, addresses, and objects similar to a proposition. For a proposition is what we say when we reveal something and it is this which is true or false. A question is a complete object, like the proposition, which asks for an answer; for example, 'Is it day?' This is neither true nor false, so that 'it is day' is a proposition and 'Is it day?' is a question. An enquiry is an object to which one cannot give an answer with a gesture, as one can to a question [by indicating] 'Yes', but [in response to which one must] say [for example,] 'He lives in this place'.

---

10. The words which follow "or rejected" seem wrong and we omit them at the suggestion of Michael Frede.

67. An imperative is an object which we say when we give an order, for example,[11]

'You, go to the streams of Inachus.'

An oath is an object . . . . . [There is a lacuna here.] ⟨and an address is an object⟩ which, if one were to say, one would be addressing [someone]; for example,[12]

'Noblest son of Atreus, lord of men Agamemnon!'

[An object] similar to a proposition is what has a propositional [form of] utterance, but because of the excessiveness or emotional quality of one part of it falls outside the class of propositions; for example,

'Fair is the Parthenon!'

'How similar to Priam's sons is the cowherd!'[13]

68. There is also a dubitative object which is different from a proposition, and if one were to say it one would be expressing puzzlement:[14]

'Are pain and life somehow akin?'

Questions, enquiries and things like these are neither true nor false, while propositions are either true or false.

Of propositions, some are simple, some not simple, as the followers of Chrysippus and Archedemus and Athenodorus and Antipater and Krinis say. So, the simple are those which are composed of a proposition which is not doubled,[15] such as 'It is day'. The not simple are those composed of a doubled proposition or of propositions. **69.** From a doubled proposition: for example, 'If it is day, it is day'; from propositions, for example, 'If it is day, it is light'.

Among simple propositions are the contradictory and the negative and the privative and the predicative and the predicational and the indefinite;

---

11. A fragment of an unknown Greek tragedy, 177 Nauck 2.

12. *Iliad* 2.434.

13. A fragment of an unknown Greek tragedy, 286 Nauck.

14. Kock iii, Men. 281 v. 8

15. The reading *diphoroumenoi* which yields this sense is found in Alexander of Aphrodisias (SVF 2.261, 263).

and among the non-simple propositions are the conditional and the para-conditional and the compound and the disjunctive and the causal and that which indicates the more and that which indicates the less . . . . [There is a lacuna here.] and a contradictory, for example, 'It is not the case that it is day.' A species of this is the double contradictory. A double contradictory is the contradictory of a contradictory, for example, 'It is not the case that it is ⟨not⟩ day'. It posits that it is day.

70. A negative [proposition] is that which is composed of a negative particle and a predicate, for example, 'no-one is walking'. A privative is that which is composed of a privative particle and a potential proposition, for example, 'This [man] is unphilanthropic'. A predicative is that which is composed of a nominative case and a predicate, for example, 'Dion is walking'. A predicational is that which is composed of a demonstrative nominative case and a predicate, for example, 'This [man] is walking'. An indefinite is that which is composed of an indefinite particle or indefinite particles ⟨and a predicate⟩, for example, 'someone is walking' and 'that [man] is in motion'.

71. Of the non-simple propositions, a conditional is, as Chrysippus says in his *Dialectics* and Diogenes in his *Art of Dialectic*, that which is compounded by means of the conditional conjunction 'if'. This conjunction indicates that the second [proposition] follows the first, for example, 'if it is day, it is light'. A paraconditional [inference] is, as Krinis says in his *Art of Dialectic*, a proposition which is bound together by the conjunction 'since', and which begins with a proposition and ends with a proposition, for example, 'since it is day, it is light.' The conjunction indicates that the second [proposition] follows the first and that the first is the case. 72. A compound is a proposition which is compounded by certain compounding conjunctions, for example, 'both it is day and it is night'. A disjunctive is that which is disjoined by the disjunctive conjunction, for example, 'either it is day or it is night'. This conjunction indicates that one of the two propositions is false. A causal proposition is one put together by means of 'because', for example, 'because it is day, it is light'. For the first is, as it were, the cause of the second. A proposition which indicates the more is one put together by means of the conjunction which indicates 'more', and the [conjunction] 'than' put between the propositions, for example, 'It is more day than it is night'. 73. The proposition indicating the less is the opposite of the preceding, for example, 'It is less night than it is day'.

Again, among propositions, those are opposed to each other with respect to truth and falsehood where one is the contradictory of the other; for example, 'it is day' and 'it is not day'. A conditional is true if the opposite of the conclusion conflicts with the antecedent, for example, 'if it is day, it is light'. This is true; for 'it is not light', being the opposite of the conclusion, conflicts with 'it is day'. A conditional is false if the opposite of the conclusion does not conflict with the antecedent, for example, 'if it is day, Dion is walking'; for 'it is not the case that Dion is walking' does not conflict with 'it is day'.

74. A paraconditional is true if it begins with a true [proposition] and concludes with one which follows [from it], for example, 'since it is day, the sun is over the earth.' A false [paraconditional] is one which either starts with a false [proposition] or concludes in one which does not follow from it, for example, 'since it is night, Dion is walking', if it is said when it is day. A true causal [proposition] is one which begins from a true [proposition] and concludes in one which follows from it, but whose first [proposition] does not follow from the conclusion; for example, 'because it is day, it is light'. For 'it is light' follows from 'it is day' and 'it is day' does not follow from 'it is light'. A false causal [proposition] is one which either [1] begins from a falsehood or [2] concludes in a [proposition] which does not follow from it or [3] one whose first [proposition] follows from the consequent.

75. A persuasive proposition is one which leads to assent, for example, 'if someone gave birth to something, she is its mother'. But this is false; for the bird is not the mother of the egg.

Again, some [propositions] are possible and some are impossible; and some are necessary and some are not necessary. That [proposition] is possible which admits of being true, if external factors do not prevent it from being true, for example, 'Diocles is alive'. That [proposition] is impossible which does not admit of being true, for example, 'the earth flies'. The necessary is that which, being true, is not receptive of being false, or is receptive of being false but external factors prevent it from being false, for example, 'virtue is beneficial'. The non-necessary is that which both is true and is able to be false, with external factors not opposing it at all, for example, 'Dion is walking'.

76. A reasonable proposition is one which has more chances at being true [than not], such as 'I will be alive tomorrow'.

And there are other differences among propositions and changes of them from true to false, and conversions; these we discuss in a general fashion.

As the followers of Krinis say, an argument is what is composed of a premiss, an additional statement, and a conclusion. For example, something like this:

> If it is day, it is light.
> It is day.
> Therefore, it is light.

For the premiss is "if it is day, it is light"; the additional statement is "it is day"; and the conclusion is "therefore, it is light". A mode is a sort of schema for an argument, such as this:

> If the first, the second.
> But the first.
> Therefore, the second.

77. An argument-mode is what is compounded of both [the argument and the schema], for example,

> If Plato is alive, Plato breathes.
> But the first.
> Therefore, the second.

The argument-mode was added in order to avoid having to repeat the long additional statement and the conclusion in a somewhat lengthy series of arguments, so that the conclusion can be given briefly: The first; therefore, the second.

Of arguments, some are non-conclusive, others are conclusive. Non-conclusive are those where the opposite of the conclusion is not in conflict with the conjunction of the premisses, for example, arguments like this:

> If it is day, it is light.
> It is day.
> Therefore, Dion is walking.

78. Of conclusive arguments, some are called conclusive homonymously with the genus. Others are syllogistic. Syllogistic arguments, then, are those which are either indemonstrable or reducible to the indemonstrables by one or more of the *themata*, for example, ones like this:[16]

> If Dion is walking, ⟨Dion is moving.
> But Dion is walking.⟩
> Dion is, therefore, moving.

Those conclusive in the specific sense are ones which reach a [valid] conclusion non-syllogistically, for example, ones like this:

---

16. The textual supplement is by Hicks.

It is false that it is day and it is night.
It is day.
Therefore, it is not night.

Unsyllogistic are those which are persuasively similar to syllogistic arguments, but do not conclude [validly], for example,

If Dion is a horse, Dion is an animal.
But Dion is not a horse.
Therefore, Dion is not an animal.

79. Again, of arguments some are true, some false. True arguments, then, are those which conclude [validly] by means of true premisses, for example,

If virtue is helpful, vice is harmful.
⟨But virtue is helpful.
Therefore, vice is harmful.⟩

False arguments are those having at least one false premiss or those which are non-conclusive, for example,

If it is day, it is light.
It is day.
Therefore, Dion is alive.

And there are possible arguments and impossible and necessary and non-necessary. And there are indemonstrable arguments, because they do not need demonstration, different ones being given by different authors. In Chrysippus there are five, through which every argument is formed. These are used in conclusive arguments, in syllogisms and in mode-arguments.
    80. The first indemonstrable is that in which every argument is made up of a conditional and the antecedent from which the conditional begins, and concludes to the consequent, for example,

If the first, the second.
But the first.
Therefore, the second.

The second indemonstrable is that which, through a conditional and the opposite of the consequent, draws as its conclusion the opposite of the antecedent, for example,

> If it is day, it is light.
> But it is not light.
> Therefore, it is not day.

For the additional statement is formed from the opposite of the consequent and the conclusion from the opposite of the antecedent. The third indemonstrable is that which, through a negated conjunction and one of the elements in the conjunction, concludes the opposite of the other element, for example,

> It is not the case that Plato is dead and Plato is alive.
> But Plato is dead.
> Therefore, Plato is not alive.

81. The fourth indemonstrable is that which, through a disjunction and one of the disjuncts, has as its conclusion the opposite of the other, for example,

> Either the first or the second.
> But the first.
> Therefore, not the second.

The fifth indemonstrable is that in which every argument is formed from a disjunction and the opposite of one of the disjuncts and concludes the other, for example,

> Either it is day or it is night.
> It is not night.
> Therefore, it is day.

According to the Stoics a truth follows from a truth, as 'it is light' follows from 'it is day'. And a falsehood follows from a falsehood, as 'it is dark' follows from the falsehood 'it is night'. And a truth follows from a falsehood, as 'the earth exists' follows from 'the earth flies'. A falsehood, however, does not follow from a truth. For 'the earth flies' does not follow from 'the earth exists'. 82. And there are certain puzzling arguments, the Hooded Man, the Hidden Man, the Sorites, the Horned Man, and the

Nobody. And the Hooded Man is like this . . . [There is a lacuna here, which includes the introduction of the sorites.] 'It is not the case that two are few and that three are not [few]; and it is not the case these are [few] but four (and so on up to ten) are not [few]; but two are few; therefore, so is ten.' . . . . [There is a lacuna here.] The Nobody is an argument which draws a conclusion and is composed of an indefinite and a definite, having an additional statement and a conclusion, for example, 'If someone is here, that [someone] is not in Rhodes; ⟨but someone is here; therefore, there is not someone in Rhodes⟩.' . . . [There is a lacuna here.]

83. And this is what the Stoics are like in logical matters, so that they can maintain that the wise man is always a dialectician. For *everything* is seen through consideration of it in arguments: both what belongs to the topic of physics and again what belongs to ethics. For if the logician is supposed to say something about the correct use of terms, how could he fail to say what are the proper names for things? There are two customary facets of the virtue [i.e. dialectic]; one considers what each existent thing is, the other what it is called. And this is what their logic is like.

Cicero *Academica* 1.40–42   [II-4]

40. But in that third part of philosophy [i.e., logic] he [Zeno] made quite a few changes. First, he made some new claims here about the senses themselves, which he held were joined to a sort of stimulus received from the outside world (he called this a *phantasia* but we may call it a presentation—and let us hold on to this term, for we will have to use it often in the rest of our discussion). But to these presentations which are, as it were, received by the senses he joined the assent given by our minds, which he claims is in our power and voluntary. 41. He said that not all presentations are reliable, but only those which have a distinctive kind of clear statement to make about the objects of presentation; when this presentation is discerned all on its own, then it is "graspable". . . But when it had been received and approved then he said it was a "grasping"— like those things gripped by one's hand. Indeed, that is how he derived the word, since no one had previously used this term in this connection; and Zeno used quite a few new terms (for he was advancing new theories). What had been grasped by sense-perception, he called this itself a "sense-perception" and if it was grasped in such a way that it could not be shaken by argument he called it knowledge; if not, he called it ignorance, which is also the source of opinion which is weak and a state shared with what is false and not known. 42. But between knowledge and ignorance

he placed that "grasp" which I just mentioned and said it was neither right nor wrong but that it alone deserved to be believed. Therefore, he said the senses too were reliable because, as I said above, he thought that a grasp made by the senses was true and reliable, not because it grasped everything about the object but because it left out nothing [about it] which could be grasped and because nature had provided this grasp as a standard for knowledge and a basis for understanding nature itself. From such [perceptual grasps] conceptions of things are subsequently impressed on the soul, and these provide not just the foundations but also certain broader paths leading to the discovery of reason. Error, however, and rashness and ignorance and opinion and conjecture—in a word, all that is hostile to a solid and stable assent—all these he banned from the sphere of wisdom and virtue. On these points rests all of Zeno's departure from and disagreement with his predecessors.

Cicero *Academica* 2.24–26 [II-5]

24. . . . And, moreover, this point is obvious, that there must be a principle which wisdom follows when it begins to do something and this principle must be according to nature. For otherwise impulse (for that is the translation we use for *horme*), by which we are driven to act and pursue what is presented, cannot be stimulated. 25. But that which stimulates must first be presented [to the agent] and it must be believed; and this cannot happen if what is presented cannot be distinguished from what is false. For how can the mind be moved to an impulse if there is no judgement as to whether what is presented is according to nature or contrary to it? Similarly, if the mind does not realize what is appropriate to it, it will never do anything at all, will never be driven to anything, will never be stimulated. But if it is ever to be moved, what occurs to the agent must be presented as being true.

26. And what of the fact that, if the sceptics are right, all reason is abolished, which is like the light and illumination of life? Will you persist in *that* kind of perversity? For reason provides a starting point for inquiry, which perfects virtue when reason itself has been strengthened by inquiring. And inquiry is an impulse to knowledge and discovery is the goal of inquiry. But no one discovers what is false, nor can matters which remain uncertain be discovered; but when things which were previously veiled are revealed, then they are said to be discovered, and thus both the starting point of inquiry and the conclusion of perception and understanding are obtained by the mind. A demonstration (the Greek is *apodeixis*) is defined thus: "an argument which leads from things perceived to that which previously was not perceived."

Cicero *Academica* 2.144–5   [II-6]

144. . . . First I shall expound those odious theories, in which you
[i.e., Stoics] say that all of those [ordinary people] who stand in the
assembly are exiles, slaves and madmen. Then I shall move on to the
theories which pertain not to the mass of people but to you yourselves
who are present now: Zeno and Antiochus deny that you know anything.
"How so?" you will ask, "for we hold that even an unwise man grasps
many things." **145.** But you deny that anyone except the wise man *knows*
anything. And Zeno used to make this point by using a gesture. When
he held out his hand with open fingers, he would say, "this is what a
presentation is like." Then when he had closed his fingers a bit, he said,
"assent is like this." And when he had compressed it completely and
made a fist, he said that this was grasping (and on the basis of this
comparison he even gave it the name *katalepsis* [grasp], which had not
previously existed). But when he put his left hand over it and compressed
it tightly and powerfully, he said that knowledge was this sort of thing
and that no one except the wise man possessed it. But they themselves
are not in the habit of saying who is or has been wise.

Porphyry *De Anima* (in Stobaeus *Anthology*   [II-7]
1.49.25, vol. 1 p. 349.23–27 W-H; SVF 2.74)

The Stoics did not make sense-perception consist in presentation alone,
but made its substance depend on assent; for perception is an assent to
a perceptual presentation, the assent being voluntary.

Sextus *M* 7.227–236 (SVF 2.56)   [II-8]

227. Since the Stoic doctrine remains, let us next speak of it. These
men, then, say that the graspable presentation is a criterion of truth. We
shall know this if we first learn what presentation is, according to them,
and what its specific differentiae are. **228.** So, according to them, a
presentation is an impression in the soul. And they differed immediately
about this. For Cleanthes took "impression" in terms of depression and
elevation—just like the impression on wax made by seal-rings. **229.** But
Chrysippus thought that such a view was absurd. For first, he says, this
will require that when our intellect has presentations at one time of a
triangle and a tetragon, the same body will have to have in itself at the
same time different shapes—triangular and tetragonal together, or even
round; which is absurd. Next, since many presentations exist in us at
the same time the soul will also have many configurations. This is worse

than the first problem. **230.** [Chrysippus] himself speculated, therefore, that "impression" was used by Zeno to mean "alteration"; so that the definition becomes like this: 'presentation is an alteration of the soul'; for it is no longer absurd that the same body at one and the same time (when many presentations exist in us) should receive many alterations. **231.** For just as air, when many people speak at once, receiving at one time an indefinite number of different blows, also has many alterations, so too the leading part of the soul will experience something similar when it receives varied presentations.

232. But others say that even Chrysippus' corrected definition is not right. For if a presentation exists, then it is an impression and an alteration in the soul. But if an impression in the soul exists, it is not necessarily a presentation. For if a blow to the finger or a scratch to the hand occurs, an impression and alteration are produced in the soul, but not a presentation, since the latter occurs not in any chance part of the soul, but only in the intellect, that is, in the leading part of the soul. **233.** In response, the Stoics say that 'impression in the soul' implies 'insofar as it is in the soul'. . . . **234.** Others, starting from the same basic position, have defended their position more subtly. For they say that 'soul' is meant in two senses, one referring to that which holds together the entire, continuous composite, and the other referring particularly to the leading part. For whenever we say that man is composed of soul and body, or that death is the separation of soul from body, we are speaking particularly of the leading part. . . . **236.** Therefore, when Zeno says that presentation is an impression in the soul, he should be understood to mean not the whole soul but only a part of it, so that what is said is "presentation is an alteration in the leading part of the soul".

Sextus *M* 7.372–373 (SVF 2.56; 1.64, 484)   [II-9]

372. . . . For if presentation is an impression in the soul, either the impression is in terms of depressions and elevation, as Cleanthes and his followers think, or it is in terms of simple alteration, as Chrysippus and his followers thought. **373.** And if on the one hand these exist in terms of depression and elevation, then the absurdities alleged by the Chrysippeans will follow. For if the soul in experiencing a presentation is stamped like wax, the most recent change will always obscure the previous presentation, just as the outline of the second seal wipes out the former one. But if this is the case, then memory, which is a storehouse of presentations, is destroyed, and so is every craft. For craft was defined as a complex and a collection of grasps, and it is impossible for several different presentations to exist in the leading part [of the soul] since different impressions are conceived in it at different times. Therefore, an impression, strictly conceived, is not a presentation.

Sextus *M* 8.56–58 (SVF 2.88)   [II-10]

56. . . . For every thought comes from sense-perception or not without sense-perception and either from direct experience or not without direct experience. 57. Hence, we shall find that not even the so-called false presentations (for example, those occurring in sleep or madness) are independent of things known to us through sense-perception by direct experience. . . . 58. And in general one can find nothing in our conceptions which is not known to oneself in direct experience. For it is grasped either by similarity to what is revealed in direct experience or by expansion or reduction or compounding.

Sextus *M* 8.275–6   [II-11]

275. But if the sign is neither sensible, as we have shown, nor intelligible, as we have established, and there is no third possibility beyond these, one must say that the sign is not a something. The dogmatists are silenced by each of these arguments and in their effort to prove the opposite they say that man differs from the irrational animals not in virtue of verbalized reason (since crows and parrots and jays verbalize articulate utterances) but in virtue of internal reason; 276. and not in virtue of just a simple presentation (since they too receive presentations) but in virtue of a presentation which is based on transference and composition. And that is why, having a conception of logical consequence, man immediately derives a conception of a sign as a result of the logical consequence. For the sign itself is something like this: "if this, this". Therefore, the existence of a sign follows on the nature and constitution of man.

Aetius 4.11.1–5 (= *Dox. Gr.* pp. 400–401;   [II-12] SVF 2.83) The origin of sense-perception, conceptions and internal reason.

1. The Stoics say: When man is born, the leading part of his soul is like a sheet of paper in good condition for being written on. On this he inscribes each and every one of his conceptions.

2. The first manner of writing on it is through the senses. For when one perceives something, white, for example, one retains a memory after it goes away. When there are many memories similar in kind then we

say one has experience. For experience is the plurality of presentations similar in kind.

3. Of conceptions, some come into being naturally in the stated ways and without technical elaboration, but others, already, come into being through our teaching and efforts. The latter are called just conceptions, while the former are also called basic grasps.

4. But reason, according to which we are termed rational, is said to be completely filled out with basic grasps at the age of seven years. And a concept is a phantasm of the intellect of a rational animal. For when a phantasm occurs in a rational soul, then it is called a concept, taking its name from "mind" [*ennoema*, from *nous*].

5. Therefore, all the phantasms which strike irrational animals are *only* phantasms and those which occur in us and in the gods are phantasms in general and specifically concepts. (Just as denarii and staters, on their own, are denarii and staters, but when they are given to pay for a ship-passage, then they are called "ship money" in addition to being denarii [and staters].)

Aetius 4.12.1–6 (=*Dox. Gr.* p. 401–402; SVF 2.54) What the difference is between the presentation, the presented object, the 'phantastic', and the phantasm. [II-13]

1. Chrysippus says that these four things differ from each other. Presentation, then, is an experience which occurs in the soul and which, in [the experience] itself, also indicates that which caused it. For example, when we observe something white by means of vision, there is an experience which has occurred in the soul by means of vision; and ⟨in virtue of⟩ this experience we are able to say that there exists something white which stimulates us. And similarly for touch and smell.

2. Presentation [*phantasia*] gets its name from light [*phos*]; for just as light reveals itself and the other things which are encompassed in it, so too presentation reveals itself and that which caused it.

3. The presented object is that which causes the presentation. For example, the presented object is the white and the cold, and everything which is able to stimulate the soul.

4. The 'phantastic' is a groundless attraction, an experience in the soul which occurs as the result of no presented object, as in the case of people who fight with shadows and punch at thin air. For a presented object underlies the presentation, but no presented object [underlies] the 'phantastic'.

5. A phantasm is that to which we are attracted in the 'phantastic'

groundless attraction. This occurs in the melancholic[17] and in mad men; at any rate when Orestes in the tragedy[18] says,

> Mother! I beg you, do not shake at me
> those bloody, snakelike maidens!
> They, they are leaping at me!

he says this like a madman, and sees nothing, but only thinks that he does. 6. That is why Electra says to him,

> Stay, poor wretch, peacefully in your bed;
> for you see none of those things which you think you clearly
> know.

Similarly, there is Theoclymenus in Homer.[19]

Pseudo-Galen *Medical Definitions* 126   [II-14]
(19.381 K. = SVF 2.89)

A conception is a stored-up thought, and a thought is a rational presentation.

Augustine *City of God* 8.7 (SVF 2.106)   [II-15]

. . . those who placed the criterion of truth in the bodily senses, and thought that every object of learning should be measured by their standards, like the Epicureans and all others of the sort, including even the Stoics. For although they passionately loved the skill of debating, which they call dialectic, they thought it should be derived from the bodily senses, asserting that it was from this source that the soul acquired conceptions, which they call *ennoiai*, i.e., those things which are clarified by definition; from this source (they said) the entire system of teaching and learning is generated and the links within it are forged.

Origen *Against Celsus* 7.37 (SVF 2.108)   [II-16]

. . . [Celsus] dogmatically asserts, like the Stoics who abolish intelligible substances, that everything which is grasped is grasped by the senses and every act of [mental] grasping is dependent on the senses. . . .

---

17. Those affected by an excess of black bile, not the melancholic in our sense.
18. Euripides *Orestes* 255–259.
19. *Odyssey* 20.350 ff.

Plutarch *Stoic Self-Contradictions* 1037b [II-17]
(SVF 2.129)

Having said in his book *On the Use of Argument* that one must not use the power of argument for inappropriate ends, just as is the case with weapons, he [Chrysippus] said this in addition: "One must use it for the discovery of truths and for coordinated training in them, but not for the opposite purposes, although many do this". By "many" he presumably means those who suspend judgement [i.e., sceptics].

Plutarch *Stoic Self-Contradictions* [II-18]
1035f–1036a (SVF 2.127)

(1035f) . . . He [Chrysippus] says that he does not absolutely reject arguments to opposite conclusions, but he does advise that this technique be used with caution, as in the law courts—(1036a) not with a sense of advocacy but to dissolve the plausibility of these arguments. "It is appropriate," he says, "for those who urge suspension of judgement on all things to do this, and it is helpful for their aim. But for those who work to produce knowledge according to which we may live consistently, the opposite is appropriate, to give instruction in basic principles to beginners, from beginning to end. In this context it is timely to mention the opposite arguments too, dissolving their plausibility just as in the law courts."

Sextus *M* 7.440–442 (SVF 2.118) [II-19]

440. But in reply the dogmatists are accustomed to ask how the sceptic can ever show that there is no criterion. For he says this either without a criterion or with one. If without a criterion he will be untrustworthy; and if with a criterion he will be turned upside down; while saying that there is no criterion he will concede that he accepts a criterion to establish this. 441. And we in turn ask, "if there is a criterion, has it been judged [by a criterion] or not?"; and we conclude one of two things: either that there is an infinite regress or that, absurdly, something is said to be its own criterion. Then they say in reply that it is not absurd to allow that something is its own criterion. 442. For the straight is the standard for itself and other things and a set of scales establishes the equality of other things and of itself and light seems to reveal not just other things but also itself. Therefore, the criterion can be the criterion both of other things and of itself.

Physics

Diogenes Laertius 7.132–160   [II-20]

132. They divide the account of physics into topics on bodies and on principles and elements and gods and limits and place and void. And this is the detailed division; the general division is into three topics, concerning the cosmos, concerning the elements and the third on causal explanation.

They say that the topic concerning the cosmos is divided into two parts; for the mathematicians share in one branch of its investigations, the one in which they investigate the fixed stars and the planets, for example, [to ascertain] whether the sun is as big as it appears to be, and similarly if the moon is; and concerning the revolution [of the cosmos] and similar enquiries.

133. The other branch of the investigation of the cosmos is the one which pertains *only* to natural scientists, the one in which the substance [of the cosmos] is investigated and whether it is generated or ungenerated and whether it is alive or lifeless and whether it is destructible or indestructible and whether it is administered by providence; and so forth.

The topic concerning causal explanations is itself also bipartite. For medical investigation shares in one branch of its investigations, the one in which they investigate the leading part of the soul, what happens in the soul, the [generative] seeds, and questions like these. The mathematicians also lay claim on the other, for example, [investigation into] how we see, into the cause of how things appear in a mirror, how clouds are formed, and thunder and rainbows and the halo and comets and similar topics.

134. They believe that there are two principles of the universe, the active and the passive. The passive, then, is unqualified substance, i.e., matter, while the active is the rational principle [*logos*] in it, i.e., god. For he, being eternal and [penetrating] all of matter, is the craftsman of all things. Zeno of Citium propounds this doctrine in his *On Substance*, Cleanthes in his *On Atoms*, Chrysippus towards the end of book one of his *Physics*, Archedemus in his *On Elements* and Posidonius in book two of his *Account of Physics*. They say that there is a difference between principles and elements. For the former are ungenerated and indestructible, while the elements are destroyed in the [universal] conflagration. And the principles are bodies[20] and without form, while the elements are endowed with form.

20. So the mss; some editors prefer the emendation "incorporeal".

135. According to Apollodorus in his *Physics*, body is that which is extended in three [dimensions], length, breadth and depth; this is also called solid body; surface is the limit of a body or that which has only length and breadth, but no depth; Posidonius, in book 5 of his *On Meteorological Phenomena*, says that it exists both in conception and in reality. A line is the limit of a surface or a length with no breadth, or that which has only length. A point is the limit of a line, and it is the smallest [possible] mark.

God and mind and fate and Zeus are one thing, but called by many different names. 136. In the beginning, then, he was by himself and turned all substance into water via air; and just as the seed is contained in the seminal fluid, so this, being the spermatic principle of the cosmos, remains like this in the fluid and makes the matter easy for itself to work with in the generation of subsequent things. Then, it produces first the four elements, fire, water, air, earth. And Zeno discusses this in his *On the Universe* and Chrysippus [does so] in book one of his *Physics* and Archedemus in some work entitled *On Elements*.

An element is that from which generated things are first generated and that into which they are dissolved in the end. 137. The four elements together are unqualified substance, i.e., matter; and fire is the hot, water the wet, air the cold, and earth the dry. Nevertheless, there is still in the air the same part. Anyway, fire is the highest, and this is called aither; in this is produced first the sphere of the fixed stars, and then the sphere of the planets. Next comes the air, then the water, and, as the foundation for everything, the earth, which is in the middle of absolutely everything.

They use the term 'cosmos' in three senses: [1] the god himself who is the individual quality consisting of the totality of substance, who is indestructible and ungenerated, being the craftsman of the organization, taking substance as a totality back into himself in certain [fixed] temporal cycles, and again generating it out of himself; 138. [2] they also call the organization itself of the stars cosmos; and [3] thirdly, that which is composed of both.

And the cosmos in the sense of the individual quality of the substance of the universe is either, as Posidonius says in his *Elements of the Study of Meteorological Phenomena*, a complex of heaven and earth and the natures in them, or a complex of gods and men and the things which come to be for their sake. Heaven is the outermost periphery in which everything divine is located.

The cosmos is administered by mind and providence (as Chrysippus says in book five of his *On Providence* and Posidonius in book thirteen of his *On Gods*), since mind penetrates every part of it just as soul does us. But it penetrates some things more than others. 139. For it penetrates some as a condition [*hexis*], for example, bones and sinews, and others as mind, for example, the leading part of the soul. In this way the entire cosmos too, being an animal and alive and rational, has aither as its leading part, as Antipater of Tyre [says] in book eight of his *On the Cosmos*. Chrysippus in book one of his *On Providence* and Posidonius in his *On Gods* say that the heaven is the leading part of the cosmos, while Cleanthes says it is the sun. Chrysippus, however, in the same work, again somewhat differently, says it is the purest part of the aither, which they also call the first god in a perceptible sense, [saying also] that it, as it were, penetrates the things in the air and all the animals and plants; and [it penetrates] even the earth in the form of a condition.

140. [They say] that the cosmos is one, and limited at that, having a spherical shape; for that sort of thing is most fit for movement, as Posidonius, in book five of his *Account of Physics*, and the followers of Antipater, in their treatises on the cosmos, say.

Spread around the outside of it is the unlimited void, which is incorporeal. And the void[21] is what can be occupied by bodies but is not occupied. Inside the cosmos there is no void, but it is [fully] unified. For this is necessitated by the sympathy and common tension of heavenly things in relation to earthly things. Chrysippus speaks about the void in his *On Void* and in the first of his *Arts of Physics* and [so do] Apollophanes in his *Physics* and Posidonius in book two of his *Account of Physics*.

Things said [*lekta*][22] are incorporeal in the same way. **141.** Again, so too is time an incorporeal, being the interval of the movement of the cosmos. Of time, the past and future are unlimited, while the present is limited. They believe too that the cosmos is destructible, on the grounds that it is generated; ⟨and⟩[23] on the basis of ⟨this⟩ argument: in the case of things conceived of by sense-perception, that whose parts are destructible is also destructible as a whole; but the parts of the cosmos are destructible, since they change into each other; therefore, the cosmos is destructible. And if something is capable of change for the worse, it is destructible; and the cosmos is [capable of such change], since it is dried out and flooded.

142. The cosmos comes into being when substance turns from fire through air to moisture, and then the thick part of it is formed into earth and the thin part is rarefied and this when made even more thin produces fire. Then by a mixing from these are made plants and animals and the rest of the [natural] kinds. Zeno, then, speaks about the generation and

---

21. An emendation for the repeated "incorporeal".

22. An emendation for "These things".

23. The supplements are by Michael Frede.

destruction in his *On the Universe*, Chrysippus in book one of the *Physics*, Posidonius in book one of his *On the Cosmos*, and [so does] Cleanthes and [also] Antipater in book ten of his *On the Cosmos*. Panaetius, though, claims that the cosmos is indestructible.

Chrysippus in book one of *On Providence*, Apollodorus in his *Physics* and Posidonius say that the cosmos is also an animal, rational and alive and intelligent; **143.** an animal in the sense that it is a substance which is alive and capable of sense-perception. For an animal is better than a non-animal; and nothing is better than the cosmos; therefore, the cosmos is an animal. And [it is] alive, as is clear from the fact that the soul of [each of] us is a fragment derived from it. Boethus says that the cosmos is not an animal. And Zeno says that it is one in his *On the Universe*, and so do Chrysippus and Apollodorus in his *Physics* and Posidonius in book one of his *Account of Physics*. According to Apollodorus, the totality is said to be the cosmos, and in another sense it is said to be the composite system of the cosmos and the void outside it. Anyway, the cosmos is limited and the void is unlimited.

144. The fixed stars are carried around with the entire heaven, and the planets move with their own unique motions. The sun makes its elliptical journey through the circle of the zodiac; similarly, the moon makes its journey in a spiral. And the sun is pure fire, as Posidonius says in book seven of *On Meteorological Phenomena*; and it is bigger than the earth, as the same [philosopher] says in book six of his *Account of Physics*; and it is also spherical, as the followers of this same man say, just like the cosmos. So [they say] it is fire, because it does everything that fire does; and that it is bigger than the earth, because the entire earth is illuminated by it—but so is the heaven. And the fact that the earth produces a conical shadow also shows that [the sun] is bigger; and because of its size it is seen from all over [the earth].

145. The moon is more like the earth, since it is closer to the earth. And these fiery [phenomena] and the other stars are nourished, the sun [being nourished] by the great sea, as it is an intelligent kindling [of its exhalations]; and the moon [is nourished] by bodies of potable water, since it is mixed with air and is closer to the earth, as Posidonius says in book six of his *Account of Physics*; the others [are nourished] by the earth. [The Stoics] believe that both the stars and the immovable earth are spherical. The moon does not have its own light, but receives its light from the sun by being shone upon.

The sun is eclipsed when the moon covers it on the side which is towards us, as Zeno writes in his *On the Universe*. **146.** For at the conjunctions it [the moon] is seen gradually to approach [the sun] and to occlude it and then to pass by. This is observed in a pan of water.

And the moon [is eclipsed] when it falls into the earth's shadow; and that is why there is only an eclipse at the full moon. Although [the moon] is diametrically opposite to the sun once a month, because it moves in [an orbit which is] oblique with relation to the sun's, it [usually] diverges in latitude [and so is not eclipsed every month], being either too far to the north or too far to the south. But it is eclipsed whenever its latitude lines up with that of the sun and the ecliptic and is then diametrically opposite to the sun. And its latitude lines up with that of the ecliptic in Cancer, Scorpio, Aries and Taurus, as the followers of Posidonius say.

147. God is an animal, immortal, rational, perfect[24] in happiness, immune to everything bad, providentially [looking after] the cosmos and the things in the cosmos; but he is not anthropomorphic. [God] is the craftsman of the universe and as it were a father of all things, both in general and also that part of him which extends through everything; he is called by many names in accordance with its powers.[25] They say that *Dia* [a grammatical form of the name Zeus] is the one 'because of whom' all things are; they call [god] *Zena* [a grammatical form of the name Zeus] in so far as he is cause of life or because he penetrates life; and Athena by reference to the fact that his leading part extends into the aither; Hera because he extends into the air; Hephaestus because he extends into craftsmanlike fire; Poseidon because he extends into the fluid; and Demeter because he extends into the earth. Similarly they also assign the other titles [to god] by fastening onto one [of his] peculiarities.

148. Zeno says that the entire cosmos and the heaven are the substance of god, and so does Chrysippus in book one of his *On Gods* and Posidonius in book one of *On Gods*. And Antipater, in book seven of *On the Cosmos*, says that his substance is airy. Boethus [says] in his *On Nature* that the sphere of the fixed stars is the substance of god.

Sometimes they explain 'nature' as that which holds the cosmos together, and other times as that which makes things on earth grow. And nature is a condition which moves from itself, producing and holding together the things it produces at definite times, according to spermatic principles, and making things which are of the same sort as that from which they were separated. 149. They say that this [i.e., nature] aims at both the advantageous and at pleasure, as is clear from the craftsmanlike [structure or activity] of man.

Chrysippus says, in his *On Fate*, that everything happens by fate, and so does Posidonius in book two of *On Fate*, and Zeno, and Boethus in book one of *On Fate*. Fate is a continuous string of causes of things

24. We excise the words "or intelligent" as a gloss.
25. The etymologies which follow involve untranslatable word plays.

which exist, or a rational principle according to which the cosmos is managed. Moreover, they say that all of prophecy is real, if providence too exists; and they even declare that it is a craft, on the grounds that sometimes it turns out [true], as Zeno says, and Chrysippus in book two of his *On Prophecy* and Athenodorus and Posidonius in book twelve of his *Account of Physics* and in book five of his *On Prophecy*. Panaetius, though, denies the reality of prophecy.

150. They say that primary matter is the substance of all things which exist, as Chrysippus says in book one of his *Physics* and [so too does] Zeno. Matter is that from which anything at all can come into being. And it has two names, 'substance' and 'matter', both as the matter of all things [as a whole], and as the matter of individual things. The matter of all things [as a whole] does not become greater or smaller, but the matter of the individual things does. Substance is, according to the Stoics, body, and it is limited, according to Antipater in book two of *On Substance* and Apollodorus in his *Physics*. And it is capable of being affected, as the same man says; for if it were immune to change, the things generated from it would not be generated. From this it follows that [matter] can be divided to infinity. Chrysippus says that this division is infinite, ⟨but not to infinity⟩; for there is no infinity for the division to reach; rather, the division is unceasing.

151. As Chrysippus says in book three of the *Physics*, mixtures are total and not a matter of being surrounded or being juxtaposed. For a bit of wine thrown into the sea is for a certain time extended through it reciprocally; but then it is destroyed into it.

And they say that there also exist daimons who have a sympathy with men and are overseers of human affairs; and the surviving souls of virtuous men are heroes.

Of things which occur in the [region of the] air, they say that winter is the air above the earth cooled by the withdrawal of the sun; and spring is the temperate blend of the air which is a result of the [sun's] journey towards us; **152.** summer is the air above the earth warmed by the journey of the sun towards the north; and fall is caused by the return journey of the sun away from us. ⟨The winds are flows of the air; they have different names⟩ in accordance with the regions from which they flow. The cause of the generation of [the winds] is the sun's evaporation of the clouds. The rainbow is a refraction of the rays [of light] from moist clouds, or as Posidonius says in his *Meteorological Phenomena*, a reflection (which appears rounded in a circle) of a portion of the sun or moon in a moist and hollow cloud, continuous in its presentation. Comets and 'bearded' stars and 'torch' stars are fires which come into existence when thick air is borne up to the region of aither. **153.** A meteor is a kindled mass of fire moving quickly in the air, creating the presentation [i.e., appearance] of length. Rain is a change from cloud to water, when moisture is borne up from earth or sea and is not consumed by the sun. When it is cooled, it is called frost. Hail is a frozen cloud broken up by the wind. Snow is moisture from a frozen cloud, as Posidonius says in book eight of his *Account of Physics*. Lightning is a kindling of clouds which are rubbed together or broken by the wind, as Zeno says in his *On the Universe*. Thunder is the noise produced by these [clouds] when they are rubbed together or broken. **154.** A thunderbolt is a vigorous kindling of clouds which falls on the earth with great violence when clouds are rubbed together or broken by the wind. Others say it is a compacted mass of fiery air which descends violently. A typhoon is a great thunderbolt, violent and windlike, or a wind like smoke from a broken cloud. A tornado is a cloud split by fire together with wind. ⟨Earthquakes occur when wind flows⟩ into the hollows of the earth, or when wind is closed up in the earth, as Posidonius says in book eight. Some of them are 'shaking' [earthquakes], some 'openings', some 'slippings', and others are 'bubblings'.

155. They believe that the organization is like this: in the middle is earth, playing the role of centre, after which is water spherically arranged with the same centre as the earth so that the earth is inside the water. After water is a sphere of air. There are five circles in the heaven; of these the first, the arctic, is always apparent; the second is the summer tropic; the third is the equinoctial circle; the fourth the winter tropic; the fifth is the antarctic, which is invisible. They are called parallels in that they do not converge; still, they are inscribed about a common centre. The zodiacal [circle] is oblique, since it crosses the parallel circles. There are five zones on the earth; **156.** the first is the northern zone, beyond the arctic circle, uninhabited because of the cold; the second is temperate; the third is uninhabited because of scorching heat and is called the torrid zone; the fourth is the counter-temperate; the fifth is the southern, uninhabited because of cold.

They believe that nature is a craftsmanlike fire, proceeding methodically to generation, i.e., a fiery and craftsmanly *pneuma*. And soul is a ⟨nature⟩ capable of sense perception. And this [soul] is the inborn *pneuma* in us. Therefore, it is a body and lasts after death. It is destructible, but the soul of the universe, of which the souls in animals are parts, is indestructible. **157.** Zeno of Citium and Antipater in their treatises *On the Soul* and Posidonius [say] that the soul is a warm *pneuma*. For by means of this we live and breathe and by this we are moved. So Cleanthes says that all [souls] last until ⟨the⟩ conflagration, but Chrysippus says that only those of the wise do so.

They say that there are eight parts of the soul, the five senses, the spermatic principles in us, the vocal part and the reasoning part. We see when the light which is the medium between the [power of] vision and the external object is tensed in a conical fashion, as Chrysippus, in book two of his *Physics*, and Apollodorus say. The conical part of the [tensed] air meets our visual organ, and its base meets the object seen. So the observed object is 'announced' [to us] by the tensed air, just as [the ground is revealed to a blind man] by his walking stick. **158.** We hear when the air which is the medium between the speaker and the hearer is struck in spherical fashion, and then forms waves and strikes our auditory organs, just as the water in a cistern forms circular waves when a stone is thrown into it. Sleep occurs when the perceptual tension is relaxed in the region of the leading part of the soul. They say that alterations of the *pneuma* are the causes of the passions. They say that a seed is that which is able to generate other things which are of the same sort as that from which it itself [the seed] was separated. Human seed, which a human emits together with a moist [carrier], is blended with the parts of the soul in a mixture of the [spermatic or rational] principles of his ancestors. **159.** In book two of his *Physics* Chrysippus says that it is *pneuma* in its substance, as is clear from seeds which are sown in the earth: when they get old they no longer germinate, obviously because their potency has evaporated. And the followers of Sphaerus say that the seed is derived from the whole body; at any rate, [the seed] is able to generate all the parts of the body. But they claim that the [seed] of the female is sterile; for it lacks tension, is limited in quantity, and is watery, as Sphaerus says. And the leading part is the most authoritative [or: dominant] part in the soul; in it occur the presentations and impulses, and from it rational discourse is emitted. It is in the heart.

160. These are their physical doctrines, as far as seems sufficient for us [to relate], keeping in view [the need for] due symmetry in [the plan of] my work. . . .

The Hymn to Zeus by Cleanthes (Stobaeus [II-21] Anthology 1.1.12 p. 25.3–27.4; SVF 1.537)

> Most glorious of the immortals, called by many names, ever all-mighty
> Zeus, leader of nature, guiding everything with law,
> Hail! For it is right that all mortals should address you,
> since all are descended from you and imitate your voice,
> alone of all the mortals which live and creep upon the earth.
> So I will sing your praises and hymn your might always.

This entire cosmos which revolves around the earth obeys
    you,
wherever you might lead it, and is willingly ruled by you;
such is [the might of] your thunderbolt, a two-edged helper
in your invincible hands, fiery and everliving;
for by its blows all deeds in nature are ⟨accomplished⟩.
By it you straighten the common rational principle which
    penetrates
all things, being mixed with lights both great and small.
By it you have become such a lofty power and king forever.
Nor does any deed occur on earth without you, god,
neither in the aithereal divine heaven nor on the sea,
except for the deeds of the wicked in their folly.
But you know how to set straight what is crooked,
and to put in order what is disorderly; for you, what is not
    dear is dear.
For thus you have fitted together all good things with the
    bad,
so that there is one eternal rational principle for them all—
and it is this which the wicked flee from and neglect,
ill-fated, since they always long for the possession of good
    things
and do not see the common law of god, nor do they hear it;
and if they obeyed it sensibly they would have a good life.
But fools they be, impelled each to his own evil,
some with a strife-torn zeal for glory,
others devoted to gain in undue measure,
others devoted to release and the pleasures of the body.
. . . they are swept off in pursuit of different things at
    different times
while rushing to acquire the exact opposites of these things
    above all.
But Zeus, giver of all, you of the dark clouds, of the blazing
    thunderbolt,
save men from their baneful inexperience
and disperse it, father, far from their souls; grant that they
    may achieve
the wisdom with which you confidently guide all with justice
so that we may requite you with honour for the honour you
    give us
praising your works continually, as is fitting
for mortals; for there is no greater prize, neither for mortals

nor for gods, than to praise with justice the common law for ever.

From another hymn by Cleanthes: Epictetus [II-22]
Enchiridion 53 (SVF 1.527)

Lead me, O Zeus, and you O Fate,
to whatever place you have assigned me;
I shall follow without reluctance, and if I am not willing to,
because I have become a bad man, nevertheless I *will* follow.

Cicero *On the Nature of the Gods* 2 [II-23]
(selections)

3. Then Balbus [the Stoic] said, "I shall indulge you, and deal with things as briefly as I can; indeed, once one has exposed the errors of Epicurus my speech is stripped of all [excuse for] length. Our school exhaustively divides this whole question about the immortal gods into four parts: first they teach that there are gods, then what they are like, then that the cosmos is governed by them, and finally that they take thought for the affairs of human beings. . . .

4. Then Lucilius [Balbus] said, "The first part hardly even seems to require discussion. For what is so obvious or clear, when we have gazed up at the heaven and contemplated the heavenly bodies, as that there exists some divine power of most exceptional intelligence by which these phenomena are governed? . . . If someone were to doubt this, I do not at all understand why the same fellow could not also doubt whether there is a sun or not; 5. for how is this any more evident than that? And unless [such a conception] were known and grasped in our minds, our opinion would not persist in such a stable fashion, nor would it be confirmed by the passage of time, nor could it have become fixed as the centuries and generations of mankind passed. We notice that other opinions, which are ungrounded and empty, have faded away with the passage of time. . . .

. . . 12. Augurs have great authority; is the craft of the soothsayers not divine? Is not someone who witnesses these things [cases of successful prediction] and countless others of the same sort not compelled to admit that there are gods? For it is certainly necessary, if there are spokesmen for certain beings, that those beings themselves exist; but there are spokesmen for the gods; let us, therefore, admit that there are gods. But perhaps not all predictions are fulfilled. Well, just because not all sick men recover it does not follow that there is no craft of medicine. Signs of future events are shown by the gods; if some people make mistakes in [interpreting] them, it is not the nature of the gods which erred, but human inference.

And so the general issue is agreed upon by all people of all nations; for in the minds of all there is an inborn and, as it were, engraved [conviction] that there are gods. 13. There is disagreement about what they are like, but no one denies that they exist. Cleanthes, [a leader of] our [school] said that four causes accounted for the formation of conceptions of the gods in the minds of men. First, he cited the cause I was just mentioning, which is derived from the premonition of future events; second, one we have derived from the magnitude of the benefits we receive from our temperate climate, the fertility of the land and the bounty of many other benefits; 14. third, one which strikes fear into our minds because of thunderbolts, storms, cloudbursts, snowstorms, hail, natural devastation, plagues, earthquakes and underground rumblings, showers of stones and blood-coloured raindrops, and monstrosities which violate nature, whether human or animal, and flashes of light seen in the sky, and the stars which the Greeks call 'comets' and we [Romans] call 'curly-haired' [stars] . . . when frightened by these men came to believe that there is a certain divine power in the heavens; 15. the fourth cause, and also the most effective, is the regularity of the motions and revolutions of the heaven, and the distinctive and varied, yet orderly beauty of the sun, moon and all the stars; just looking at them indicates clearly enough that these things are not the result of chance. When someone goes into a house or gymnasium or public forum and sees the orderliness of everything, and its regularity and systematic character, he cannot judge that these things happen with no cause, but he understands that there is someone who is in charge and runs things; in the same way, but much more so, in the midst of so many motions and changes, and the orderly patterns of so many things of such great size which since the beginning of time have never belied themselves, one must decide that natural motions on such a scale are governed by some intelligence.

16. For all his intellectual acuity, Chrysippus nevertheless puts these points in such a way that they seem to be the teachings of nature and not his own discoveries. "If," he says, "there is something in nature which the human mind, reason, strength and power cannot accomplish, then certainly that which does accomplish it is better than man; but the heavenly bodies and everything which is part of the eternal natural order cannot be created by man; therefore, that by which they are created is better than man; but what would you call this thing if not god? Indeed, if there are no gods, what can there be in nature which is better than man? For reason exists in man alone, and there is nothing more splendid than that; but it is arrogant lunacy for there to be a man who supposes

that there is nothing in the whole cosmos better than he; therefore, there is something better; therefore, obviously, there is a god."

17. If you see a large and beautiful house, you could not be induced to think that it was built by mice and polecats, even if you do not see the master of the house. If, then, you were to think that the great ornament of the cosmos, the great variety and beauty of the heavenly bodies, the great power and vastness of the sea and land, were your own house and not that of the immortal gods, would you not seem to be downright crazy? Or do we not understand even this, that everything above is better and that the earth is in the lowest position and is surrounded by the densest form of air? As a result, for the same reason that applies when we observe that some regions and cities have duller-witted inhabitants because of the more congested nature of their climatic conditions, the human race too is afflicted by this because men are located on the earth, i.e., in the densest part of the universe. 18. And yet, we ought to infer from the very cleverness of man that there is some intelligence [in the universe as a whole], indeed one which is more acute and divine. For where did man 'snatch' his own intelligence from (as Socrates puts it in Xenophon)?[26] Indeed, if someone were to inquire about the source of the moisture and heat which is distributed throughout our bodies, and of the earthy solidity of our organs, and finally about [the source of] the air-like spirit [i.e., *pneuma*] which we have, it appears that we derived one from the earth, another from the moisture, another from fire, and another from the air which we inhale as we breathe. But the most important of these, I mean reason and (if it is all right to use a number of words) intelligence, planning, thought and prudence, where did we find this? where did we derive it from? Or does earth have all the rest and not have this one thing which is of the highest value? And yet, it is certain that nothing at all is superior to or more beautiful than the cosmos; and not only *is* there nothing better, but nothing can even be conceived of which is better. And if nothing is better than reason and wisdom, it is necessary that these be present in that which we have granted to be the best.

19. What? Who is not compelled to accept what I say by [consideration of] the tremendous sympathy, agreement and interconnected relationships [of the cosmos]? Could the earth bloom at one time, and be barren at another in turn? Could the approach and retreat of the sun at the summer and winter solstices be known by the manifold changes of things? Could the sea tides in channels and straits be moved by the risings and settings of the moon? Or could the variable orbits of the heavenly bodies

26. *Memorabilia* 1.4.8.

be maintained despite the uniform revolution of the entire heavens? These things, and the mutual harmony of the parts of the cosmos, certainly could not happen as they do unless they were bound together by one divine and continuously connected *pneuma*.[27]

20. When these doctrines are expounded in a fuller and more flowing fashion, as I intend to do, they more easily escape the captious criticisms of the Academy; but when they are demonstrated in the manner of Zeno, in shorter and more cramped syllogisms, then they are more open to attack; for just as a flowing river is virtually free of the risk of pollution while a confined body of water is polluted quite readily, in the same way the reproaches of a critic are diluted by a flowing oration while a cramped syllogistic demonstration cannot easily protect itself.

Zeno used to compress the arguments which we expand upon, in the following manner. 21. "That which is rational is better than that which is not rational; but nothing is better than the cosmos; therefore, the cosmos is rational." It can be proven in a similar manner that the cosmos is wise, happy and eternal, since all of these are better than things which lack them, and nothing is better than the world. From all of this it will be proven that the cosmos is a god. Zeno also used this argument: 22. "If something lacks the ability to perceive, no part of it can have the ability to perceive; but some parts of the cosmos have the ability to perceive; therefore, the cosmos does not lack the ability to perceive." He goes on and presses his point even more compactly. He says, "nothing which lacks life and reason can produce from itself something which is alive and rational; but the cosmos produces from itself things which are alive and rational; therefore, the cosmos is alive and rational." He also argues by means of a comparison, as he often does, as follows: "If flutes playing tunefully grew on olive trees, surely you would not doubt that the olive tree possessed some knowledge of flute playing? What if plane trees bore lyres playing melodiously? surely you would also decide that there was musical ability in plane trees. Why, then, is the cosmos not judged to be alive and wise, when it produces from itself creatures which are alive and wise?"

23. But since I have already begun to digress from the mode of discussion which I announced at the beginning—for I said that this first part of [our theme] did not require discussion, since it was obvious to everyone that there are gods—well, despite this I want to support the same point by proofs drawn from physics, i.e., from the study of nature. For the

---

27. Cicero uses the term *spiritus*, but the Greek term he has in mind is obviously *pneuma*, which has been transliterated where it occurs in Greek sources. Similarly, Cicero's *mundus* has been rendered by 'cosmos' for the sake of uniformity with the Greek sources.

fact is that everything which is nourished and grows contains within itself a large measure of heat, without which these things could neither be nourished nor grow. For everything which is warm and fiery is set going and kept in motion by its own characteristic motion; but that which is nourished and grows makes use of a certain definite and regular motion; as long as this remains in us our power of sense-perception and life remains, but when this heat is cooled and extinguished, then we ourselves die and are extinguished. **24.** On this point, Cleanthes also uses these arguments to show how great is the power of heat in every body. He says that there is no food which is so heavy that it cannot be digested[28] within a night and a day, and even the residues of the food, which are naturally eliminated, contain heat. Moreover, the veins and arteries do not cease to pulsate with a certain flame-like motion; and it has often been observed that when some animal's heart is removed it continues to beat as rapidly as a flickering flame. Therefore, everything which lives, whether an animal or a vegetable, lives because of the heat contained within it. From this one should understand that the nature of heat has within itself the power of life which penetrates the entire cosmos.

25. This will be easier to see if we give a more detailed account of this all-pervasive fiery stuff as a whole. All parts of the cosmos (though I will only deal with the most important parts) are supported and sustained by heat. This can be seen first in the nature of earth. For we see that fire is produced when stones are struck or rubbed together, and when a hole has just been dug we see 'the warm earth steaming'; and warm water is drawn even from spring-fed wells, especially in winter, because the hollow parts of the earth contain a great deal of heat and in winter [the earth] is denser and so confines the heat which is native to it more tightly. **26.** It could be shown, by a long discourse and many arguments, that all the seeds which the earth receives and all the plants which are generated from her and which she holds rooted in her are born and grow because of her temperate heat.

And that heat is also blended with water is shown first of all by the fluidity of water, which would neither be frozen by the cold nor solidified into snow and frost if it did not also dissolve and liquify itself when heat is added. Thus moisture hardens when it is affected by the blasts of the north wind and other sources of cold, and in turn is softened when warmed and is [even] dried up by heat. Even the seas, when tossed by the winds, warm up to such an extent that one can easily see that heat is enclosed in these vast bodies of water; and one must not suppose that the warmth in question comes from some external and extraneous source,

---

28. The word literally means 'cooked'; hence the point about heat.

but rather that it is stirred up by the [wind-induced] motion from the deepest parts of the sea. This also happens to our own bodies, when they warm up with motion and exercise.

Air itself, which is by nature the coldest [element], is hardly devoid of heat. 27. Indeed, it is mixed with a very great deal of heat, since it arises from the evaporation of bodies of water and air should be held to be a kind of vapour arising from them; anyway, air comes to be as a result of the motion of the heat contained in bodies of water. We can see something like this when water is brought to a boil by putting a fire beneath it.

What now remains is the fourth part of the cosmos; it itself is in its entirety a hot nature and it communicates its salutary and life-giving heat to all other natures. 28. From this it is argued that, since all the parts of the cosmos are sustained by heat, that the cosmos itself is preserved for an immense time by an exactly similarly nature, all the more so since one ought to understand that this hot and fiery nature is blended throughout all of nature in such a way that it contains in itself the procreative power and cause of generation; all animals and everything which is rooted in the earth must be born from and nourished by this [principle of heat].

29. There is, therefore, a nature which holds the entire cosmos together and preserves it, and which is endowed with sense-perception and reason. For every nature which is not isolated and simple, but rather is joined and connected with something else, must have in itself some 'leading part', like the mind in man and in a brute beast something analogous to mind which is the source of its desires for things; in trees and plants which grow in the earth the leading part is thought to reside in their roots. By 'leading part' I mean that which the Greeks call *hegemonikon*; in each type of thing there cannot and should not be anything more excellent than this. Necessarily, then, that in which the leading part of nature as a whole resides must be the best of all, and the most worthy of power and authority over all things. 30. We see, moreover, that the parts of the cosmos (and there is nothing in the whole cosmos which is not a part of the whole) contain the powers of sense-perception and reason. These powers must, then, be present in that part of the cosmos which contains its leading part—and in a more acute and powerful form. That is why the cosmos must be wise and why the nature which contains in its grasp all things must surpass them in the perfection of its reason; so the cosmos is a god and all the powers of the cosmos are held together by the divine nature. . . .

32. . . . One can also see that the cosmos contains intelligence from the fact that it is without doubt better than any other nature. Just as

there is no part of our body which is not of less value than we ourselves are, so the cosmos as a whole must be of more value than any part of it; but if this is so, the cosmos must necessarily be wise, for if it were not, then man, who is a part of the cosmos, would have to be of more value than the entire cosmos in virtue of his participation in reason.

33. And if we want to proceed from primary and rudimentary natures to those which are highest and perfect, it is necessary that we arrive at the nature of the gods. We notice first that nature sustains things produced from the earth, to whom she gave nothing more than the ability to nourish themselves and to grow. 34. But she gave to beasts the powers of sense-perception and motion and the ability to use a kind of impulse to acquire beneficial things and avoid dangerous things. Her gifts to man were greater in that she added reason, by which the soul's impulses could be governed by being alternately set loose and restrained. The fourth and highest level belongs to those who are by nature born good and wise, those in whom right and consistent reason is inborn from the very beginning. This kind of reason must be thought of as beyond human capacity and should be assigned to a god, i.e., the cosmos, which must necessarily contain that perfected and completed form of reason.

35. Nor can one say that in any complex system ultimate perfection does not occur. In the case of vines or cattle we see that, unless some [external] force interferes, nature follows its own path to its final goal; in painting, building and the other crafts we can point to the completion of a perfect piece of workmanship; similarly, (but much more so) it is necessary that something be completed and perfected in nature as a whole. Indeed, other natures can be prevented by many external factors from achieving perfection, but nature as a whole cannot be hindered by anything, for the very reason that it itself embraces and contains all [other] natures. That is why it is necessary that there be this fourth and highest level which is immune to all outside force. 36. It is on this level that we find the nature of the universe; and since this nature is superior to all things and is immune to hindrance by anything, it is necessary that the cosmos be intelligent and even wise.

And what is more foolish than to deny that the nature which contains all things is best, or to say that, although it is best, it is not, in the first place, alive, secondly, equipped with reason and deliberative ability, and finally, wise? How else could it be best? For if it resembles plants or even the lower animals, it must be thought of not as the best but as the worst. And if it is rational but not wise from the very beginning, the condition of the cosmos is worse than that of human beings; for a man can become wise, but if the cosmos has been foolish throughout the eternity of preceding time, surely it will never achieve wisdom—and so it will be worse than man. And since this is absurd, one must hold that the cosmos is both wise from the very beginning and a god.

37. Nor does anything else exist which lacks nothing and is completely equipped, perfect and fulfilled in all aspects and parts of itself, except the cosmos. Chrysippus put the point well when he said that just as the cover was made for the sake of the shield and the sheath for the sword, in the same way everything else except the cosmos was made for the sake of other things. For example, the crops and fruits which the earth bears exist for the sake of animals, but animals for the sake of men; the horse exists for riding, the ox for plowing and the dog for hunting and guarding, but man himself was born for the sake of contemplating and imitating the cosmos; he is not at all perfect, but he is a certain small portion of what is perfect. 38. But since the cosmos embraces everything and since there is nothing which is not in it, it is perfect in all respects. How, then, can it lack what is best? But nothing is better than mind and reason. Therefore, the cosmos cannot lack these things. Chrysippus also uses comparisons to show effectively that everything is better in perfected and full-grown [specimens], for example, better in a horse than in a colt, in a dog than in a puppy, in a man than in a boy; similarly, what is best in the cosmos as a whole ought to exist in something which is perfected and completed; 39. but nothing is more perfect than the cosmos, nothing better than virtue; therefore, virtue is a property of the cosmos. Indeed, man's nature is not perfect, and for all that virtue is produced in man; how much more easily, then, could it be produced in the cosmos; therefore, it contains virtue. Therefore, it is wise and consequently a god.

Now that we have seen that the cosmos is divine, we should assign the same sort of divinity to the stars, which are formed from the most mobile and pure part of the aither and have no additional elements mixed into their nature; they are totally hot and bright, so that they too are also said quite correctly to be animals and to perceive and to have intelligence. 40. And Cleanthes thinks that the evidence of two senses, touch and sight, shows that they are totally fiery. For the sun's light is brighter than that of any fire, seeing that it shines so far and wide across the boundless cosmos, and the effect of its contact is such that it not only warms but also often burns things; it could not do either of these things unless it were fiery. "Therefore," he says, "since the sun is fiery and is nourished by the moisture from the ocean (since no fire can persist without fuel), it is necessary either that it be similar to the fire which we use for our daily purposes or to the fire which is contained in the bodies of animals. 41. But the fire which we are familiar with and which we need for the purposes of daily life consumes and destroys everything and wherever it penetrates it upsets and scatters everything. By contrast, the fire found in bodies is life-giving and beneficial, and in everything it preserves, nourishes, promotes growth, sustains, and provides the power of sense-perception."

Consequently, he says that there is no doubt about which sort of fire the sun is like, since it too causes everything to flourish and mature according to its kind. Therefore, since the sun's fire is like those fires which are in the bodies of animals, the sun too should be alive, and indeed so too should the rest of the heavenly bodies which take their origin from the celestial heat, which is called aither or heaven [sky].

42. So, since some animals are born on earth, some in the water, some in the air, it seems absurd to Aristotle[29] to suppose that no animals are born in that part [of the cosmos] which is most suited for the production of animal life. But the stars reside in the aither, and since this is the rarest element and is always alive and moving, it is necessary that an animal born there should also have the most acute senses and the most rapid motion. And since the heavenly bodies are born in the aither, it is reasonable that they should possess the powers of sense-perception and intelligence. From which it follows that the heavenly bodies should be counted among the gods.

Indeed, one may observe that people who live in lands blessed with pure and thin air have keener intellects and greater powers of understanding than people who live in dense and oppressive climatic conditions. **43.** Indeed, they also think that the food one eats makes a difference to one's mental acuity. So, it is plausible that the stars should have exceptional intelligence, since they inhabit the aitherial part of the cosmos and are nourished by moisture from the land and sea which is rarified by the great distance it has travelled. The orderliness and regularity of the heavenly bodies is the clearest indication of their powers of sense-perception and intelligence. For nothing can move rationally and with measure except by the use of intelligence, which contains nothing haphazard or random or accidental. But the orderliness and perpetual consistency of the heavenly bodies does not indicate a merely natural process (for it is full of rationality) nor one produced by chance, which tends to produce haphazard change and is hostile to consistency. It follows, therefore, that they move on their own, by their own wills, perceptions and divinity. **44.** And Aristotle is to be praised for his opinion that everything which moves does so either by nature or force or will; now the sun and moon and all the heavenly bodies move; things which move by nature either move straight down because of weight or straight up because of lightness; but neither of these applies to the heavenly bodies, since their motion is

29. In the lost work *On Philosophy*.

circular revolution; nor can it be said that the heavenly bodies are compelled by some greater force to move contrary to their nature—for what
force could be greater? The only remaining possibility is that the motion
of the heavenly bodies is voluntary.

Anyone who [so much as] sees them would be not only ignorant but
even impious to deny that there are gods. Nor does it really make much
difference whether he denies that or merely deprives them of all providential concern and activity; for in my view [a god] who does nothing might
as well not exist. Therefore, it is so obvious that there are gods that I
can hardly consider anyone who denies it to be in his right mind. . . .

57. So I hardly think that I will go wrong to take my lead in discussing
this subject from a leading investigator of truth. Zeno, then, defines nature
thus: he says that it is a craftsmanlike fire which proceeds methodically to
the task of creation. For he thinks that creating and producing are most
characteristic of a craft and that nature (i.e., the craftsmanlike fire, as I
said, which is the instructor of all the other crafts) accomplishes the same
sort of thing as our hands do when they are used in human crafts, but
much more skillfully. And on this theory nature as a whole is craftsmanlike, because it has a kind of method and path to follow; 58. but the
nature of the cosmos itself, which constrains and contains all things in
its embrace, is said by the same Zeno not only to be craftsmanlike but,
to put it directly, a craftsman, since it looks out for and is provident
about all kinds of usefulness and convenience. And just as all other
natural entities are produced, grow and are held together each by its own
seeds, so too the nature of the cosmos has all the voluntary motions,
endeavours and impulses (which the Greeks call *hormai*) and carries out
the actions consequent on them, just as we ourselves do who are set in
motion by our minds and senses. For since the mind of the cosmos is
like this and can for this reason properly be called prudence or providence
(in Greek the term is *pronoia*), the principal concern of this providence
and its greatest preoccupation is, first, that the cosmos be as well suited
as possible for remaining in existence, second, that it be in need of
nothing, but most of all that it should possess surpassing beauty and
every adornment.

59. The cosmos as a whole has been discussed; so have the heavenly
bodies. We now have a pretty clear picture of a large number of gods
who are not idle, but who do not have to carry out the tasks they perform
with laborious and unpleasant effort. For they are not held together by
veins and nerves and bones; nor do they consume the sort of food and
drink which would make their humours either too sharp or too dense;
nor do they have the sorts of bodies which would lead them to dread

falls or blows or fear diseases produced by physical exhaustion. It was for fear of this sort of thing that Epicurus invented his insubstantial and idle gods. **60.** Endowed with that most beautiful of shapes, located in the purest region of the heaven, they move and steer their courses in such a way that they seem to have come to an agreement to preserve and protect everything. . . .

73. The next thing is for me to explain that the world is governed by the providence of the gods. This is a large topic indeed, and one on which we are challenged by your school [i.e., the Academics], Cotta; to be sure the whole debate is with you . . . . **75.** So I say that the cosmos and all its parts were in the beginning constituted by the providence of the gods and are governed by it for all time; our school usually divides the discussion of this topic into three parts. The first is derived from the argument used to show that the gods exist; when that is granted one must admit that the cosmos is governed by their rational planning. The next shows that all things are subordinate to a perceptive nature and are managed by it most beautifully; when that point is settled it follows that they were produced by first principles endowed with life. The third topic is derived from our feelings of admiration for celestial and terrestrial phenomena.

76. First of all, then, either one must deny that there are gods, as Democritus does in a way, by bringing in his effluences and Epicurus his images, or those who admit that there are gods must concede that they do something impressive. But nothing is more impressive than the governance of the cosmos; therefore, it is governed by the rational planning of the gods. But if this is not so, certainly there must be something which is better and endowed with greater power than a god—whatever it is, a lifeless nature or necessity set in motion with great force—which produces all these most beautiful works which we see; **77.** it follows then that the nature of the gods is not preeminently powerful or excellent, since it is subordinated to that other power, whether it be necessity or nature, by which the heaven, seas and earth are ruled. But nothing is superior to god; therefore, it is necessary that the world be ruled by god. Therefore, god is not obedient to nature and is not subjected to it; and so god himself rules all of nature.

Indeed, if we grant that the gods are intelligent, we grant also that they are provident, especially about the most important things. Are the gods, then, ignorant about which things are the most important and about how they are to be handled and preserved? Or do they lack the power to sustain and carry out such great tasks? But ignorance of things is foreign to the nature of the gods, and it is inconsistent with the gods' majesty to have difficulty carrying out their duties because of some weakness. From these premisses our desired conclusion follows, that the cosmos is governed by the providence of the gods.

78. And yet, since there are gods (if they really exist, as they certainly do) it is necessary that they be alive, and not only alive but also rational and bound to each other by a kind of political bond [i.e., congeniality][30] and society, governing this single cosmos like some shared republic or city. 79. It follows that they possess the same kind of reason as is present in mankind, that the same truth is found in both [gods and men] and the same law, which consists in injunctions to do what is right and avoid what is wrong. From this one can see that the gods are the source of man's prudence and intelligence; and that is why our ancestors consecrated and publicly dedicated temples to [gods such as] Intelligence, Faith, Virtue and Concord. How can we deny that [such things] exist among the gods when we worship their revered and sacred images? But if mankind possesses intelligence, faith, virtue and concord, from where could they have come down [to us] here on earth if not from the [gods] above? And since we have deliberative ability and reason it is necessary that the gods have them in even greater abundance, and not just have them but also use them in matters of the greatest value and import. 80. But nothing is of greater value or import than the cosmos; therefore, it is necessary that it be administered by the deliberation and providence of the gods. Finally, since we have shown clearly enough that those whom we see to possess remarkable power and extraordinary beauty are gods (I mean the sun and moon and the planets and the fixed stars and the heaven and the cosmos itself, and the multitude of things which are present throughout the cosmos and are of great utility and convenience for mankind), it follows that everything is ruled by the intelligence and providence of the gods. But enough has been said about the first topic.

81. Next I must show that everything is subordinate to nature and is ruled by it in the finest possible manner. But first, I must give a brief explanation of what nature is, to facilitate the understanding of what I want to show. For some think that nature is a type of non-rational force which induces necessary motions in bodies; others that it is a force endowed with reason and orderliness, proceeding methodically, as it were, and showing what the cause of each thing brings about and what follows upon it, [a force] whose cleverness could not be emulated by any craft, skill or craftsman. [They say] that the power of a seed is such that, despite its minute size, if it meets with a receptive and favourable nature, and gets hold of the sort of matter which can nourish it and foster its

---

30. The Latin is *conciliatio*, usually Cicero's translation for the Greek *oikeiosis*.

growth, the seed can produce each sort of thing, according to its kind—some things which are nourished only via their roots, others which can set themselves in motion and perceive and desire and produce others like themselves. 82. And there are also those who use the term 'nature' to refer to everything, like Epicurus, who makes the following division: the nature of all things which exist is bodies and void and their attributes. But since we say that the cosmos is constituted and governed by nature, we do not mean that it is like some lump of mud, piece of stone or anything else with only a natural power of cohesion, but rather that it is like a tree or animal. For nothing is random in them; rather, it is evident that they possess a certain orderliness and craftsmanlike quality.

83. But if nature's craft is responsible for the life and vigour of plants which are held together by being rooted in the earth, certainly the earth itself is held together by the same force, since when the earth is impregnated by seeds she gives birth to and brings forth all things, embraces their roots, nourishes them, fosters their growth and is herself nourished in turn by external and superior natural elements. And the air and the aither and all superior entities are nourished by vapours produced from the earth. So, if the earth is held together by nature and owes its vigour to nature, then the same rational force is present in the rest of the cosmos. For the roots [of plants] are bound to the earth, while animals are sustained by inhalation of air and the air itself helps us to do our seeing, helps us to do our hearing and speaking; for none of these functions can be carried out without air. Indeed, it even helps us to move, since wherever we go or we move to, it seems to give way and yield to us.

84. And the motion of things to the central, i.e., lowest, region of the cosmos, and the motion of other things from the middle to the upper regions, and the circular orbit of others around this mid point all combine to make the nature of the cosmos a single and continuous whole. And since there are four kinds of bodies, nature is rendered continuous by their mutual interchange. For water comes from earth, air from water and aither from air; then in reverse air comes from aither, then water and from water comes earth, the lowest element. Thus the union of the parts of the cosmos is held together because the elements from which everything is composed move up and down and back and forth. 85. And this union must either be everlasting, exhibiting the very order which we now see, or at the very least very stable, enduring for a long, nearly boundless expanse of time. And either way it follows that the cosmos is governed by nature.

Consider the sailing of a fleet of ships, the formation of an army, or (to return to examples drawn from the works of nature) the reproduction of vines or trees, or furthermore the shape and organization of the limbs of an animal: which of these points to as great a degree of cleverness as the cosmos itself does? Either, therefore, there is nothing ruled by a nature capable of perception or one must admit that the cosmos is so ruled. 86. Moreover, how can that which contains all natures and the seeds which produce them fail to be itself governed by nature? So, if someone were to say that the teeth and body hair exist by nature but that the man to whom they belong was not constituted by nature, he would simply be failing to understand that those things which produce something from themselves have natures more perfect than the things produced from themselves. But the cosmos is the sower and planter and (if I may so put it) the parent and nurse and nourisher of all things governed by nature; the cosmos nourishes and holds together everything as though those things were its limbs and parts of itself. But if the parts of the cosmos are governed by nature, it is necessary that the cosmos itself be governed by nature. And the governance of the cosmos contains nothing which is subject to criticism; the best possible result which could be produced from those natures which existed was indeed produced. 87. Let someone, then, show that something better could have been produced! But no one will ever show this. And if someone wants to improve on something [in the cosmos], either he will make it worse or he will be longing for something which simply could not have happened.

But if all parts of the cosmos are so constituted that they could neither have been more useful nor more beautiful, let us see whether they are the products of chance or of such a character that they could never even have held together if not for the control exerted by a perceptive and divine providence. If, therefore, the products of nature are better than those of the crafts and if the crafts do nothing without the use of reason, then nature too cannot be held to be devoid of reason. When you look at a statue or a painting, you know that craftsmanship was applied; and when you see from afar the course steered by a ship, you do not doubt that it is moved by rational craftsmanship; when you gaze on a sundial or waterclock, you understand that the time is told as a result of craft and not as a result of chance. So what sense does it make to think that the cosmos, which contains these very crafts and their craftsmen and all else besides, is devoid of deliberative ability and reason? . . .

94. . . . So Aristotle puts it splendidly:[31] 95. "If," he says, "there were people who lived under the earth in fine and splendid houses adorned with statues and paintings and outfitted with all those things which those who are considered happy have in great abundance, but who had never come out onto the surface of the earth, though they had heard by rumour

31. In the lost work *On Philosophy*.

and hearsay that some divine force and godly power existed; and then one day the earth opened its maw and they could emerge from those hidden places and come out into the regions which we inhabit, and they then became aware of the huge clouds and the force of the winds and saw the sun in all its great size and beauty, and also became aware of its creative power (for it created the day by spreading its light throughout the entire heaven); and then when night darkened the earth they could see the whole heaven adorned and ornamented with stars, and the changes in the illumination of the moon as it waxed and waned, and the risings and settings of all those heavenly bodies moving in courses immutably fixed for all of eternity—when they saw all of this, certainly they would think that both that there are gods and that these things are their handiwork."

115. . . . And not only are these things amazing, but there is nothing more so than the fact that the cosmos is so stable and so internally coherent that nothing can even be conceived of which is more suited to permanent existence. For all of its parts from every direction exert an equal effort to reach the centre. Moreover, compound bodies maintain their existence most effectively when they are surrounded by a kind of bond which ties them together; and this is done by that nature which penetrates the entire cosmos and causes everything with its intelligence and rationality, rapidly drawing the outermost parts [of the cosmos] back towards the centre. 116. So if the cosmos is spherical, and as a result all its parts from every direction are held together in an equal balance by each other and with each other, then it is necessary that the same thing must apply to the earth too; consequently, since all the parts of the earth tend towards the centre (and the centre is the lowest point in a sphere), there is no break in its continuity which might cause such a large and coordinated system of weight and gravity to crumble. And similarly the sea, which lies above the earth and yet strives to reach the centre of the earth, is evenly balanced on all sides and so forms a sphere; it never overflows or exceeds its bounds. 117. Air is continuous with the sea and is borne aloft by its lightness; but still it distributes itself in all directions; and so it is both continuous with the sea and joined to it, and by nature it moves upwards to the heavens, whose rareness and heat blend with it and so enable the air to provide to animals life-giving and beneficial *pneuma*. The highest part of the heaven, which is termed aitherial, embraces the air and also retains its own rarefied heat, being compounded with nothing else, and [yet] it is conjoined with the boundaries of the air. And the heavenly bodies revolve in the aither; by their own effort they hold themselves together in their spherical shape, and in virtue of their shape and form they sustain their movements—for they are round

and, as I think I said before, things which have this shape are least susceptible to harm. **118.** The stars, moreover, are by nature fiery and so are nourished by vapours which rise from the earth, sea and bodies of water, having been produced by the sun's warming of the fields and waters. The stars, and the entire aitherial region, are nourished and renewed by these vapours; and then they pour them forth again, and in turn draw them back from the same source, with virtually no loss [to the vapours] except for a very little bit which is consumed by the fire of the heavenly bodies and the flames of the aither. And for this reason our school [the Stoics] thinks that there will someday occur the event which they say Panaetius had his doubts about, i.e., the final conflagration of the entire cosmos. This will happen when all the moisture is used up and the earth cannot be nourished [any longer] and the air cannot return— for air cannot arise if all the water is consumed; so there will be nothing left except fire. This, though, is an animal and a god and so in turn it produces the renewal of the cosmos and the emergence of the same beautiful order. . . .

127. . . . A great deal of care was taken by divine providence to assure the eternity of the adornment of the cosmos, by working to assure the constant existence of the races of beasts, of trees and of all the plants whose roots are bound in the earth. All of these possess a seminal power which enables one [living thing] to produce many offspring, and this seed is is closed up in the inmost core of the fruits produced by each kind of plant; these same seeds give a good supply of food to men, as well as filling the earth with new stock of the same type. **128.** Why should I even mention the high degree of reason displayed in the efforts of beasts to assure the perpetual preservation of their species? First, some are male and others female—a plan devised by nature to promote their perpetuity; and their organs are very well suited for the tasks of procreation and conception; and then there is the astounding desire that both feel for copulation. When the seed [i.e., the semen] has settled in place, it draws virtually all the [mother's] nutrition to itself and protected within it it produces a [new] animal. And when the offspring is born, then in mammalian species virtually all of the mother's food begins to turn to milk and the offspring which are newly born seek [their mother's] breasts under the sole guidance of nature, being taught by no one, and are satisfied by their rich abundance. And to prove that none of this is a matter of chance but rather that all of these arrangements are the work of provident and intelligent nature, [note that] those animals who bear many offspring at once (such as pigs and dogs) have been given a large number of teats; those animals who bear fewer offspring have fewer teats. **129.** What should I say about the love there is in beasts for rearing and caring for the young they have produced, until such time as the young can defend themselves? Although fish are said to abandon their eggs once they have laid them, it is easy for them to be supported by the water and to hatch in it. Turtles, though, and crocodiles are said to bear their young on land, then bury the eggs and go away, leaving them to be born and raised all by themselves. But hens and other birds seek a peaceful place for bearing their young and there build dwellings and nests, making them as soft as possible a support for the eggs in order to promote their survival. And when the chicks hatch, [the adults] protect them and cuddle them with their wings so that the cold will not hurt the young; or if it is hot, they shade them from the sun. But when the chicks can first make use of their wings, then their mothers accompany them on their flights but otherwise need care for them no further. **130.** Human care and intelligence is also a factor contributing to the preservation and well-being of several species of animals and of plants born from the earth; for there are many kinds of domesticated animals and plants which could not survive without the care of human beings.

The agricultural activities of men and their success are made easier by a variety of different factors in different regions. The Nile irrigates Egypt, keeping the land flooded all summer until it recedes and leaves the fields softened and muddy for the planting season. The Euphrates makes Mesopotamia fertile by bringing new soil to the fields every year. And the Indus River, the largest of all, not only fertilizes the fields and softens them but even sows them; for it is said to bring with its waters a great quantity of seeds which resemble those of grain. **131.** I could mention many other noteworthy things from a variety of areas, and many regions all of which are fertile for different kinds of crops.

But how great is nature's generosity! She produces so many different kinds of appetizing food, at all different times of the year, that we are always delighted by both its abundance and its novelty. She has given us the Etesian winds; how fitting to their season and how salutary not just for mankind but also for the animal species and even for plants which grow from the earth. Excessive heat is moderated by their [gentle] breath and they also help our ships to steer a swift and certain course at sea. I must pass over many points. **132.** For the blessings provided by rivers are beyond counting, as are those of the tides which ebb and flow, of the mountains clad in forests, of salt pools found far from the sea shore, regions where the very soil teems with medicinal substances, and finally, [so are the blessings] of numberless crafts which are essential for our life and well-being. Even the alternation of day and night helps to preserve animal life by setting aside different times for action and for rest. Thus from every angle and by every line of reasoning, our minds prove that everything in this cosmos is wonderfully governed by the intelligence and deliberative ability of the gods for the purpose of the well-being and preservation of all.

133. Here someone will ask, for whose benefit was such a complex system created? For the sake of trees and plants, which despite their lack of sense-perception are nevertheless sustained by nature? But surely that is absurd. For the beasts then? It is no more likely that the gods should have worked so hard for mute animals which understand nothing. So for whose sake will we say that the cosmos was made? Surely for the sake of those of those animals which use reason, and those are gods and men; surely nothing is better than they are, since reason is superior to all other things. So it turns out to be plausible that the cosmos and everything in it were created for the sake of gods and men.

It will be easier to see that man has been well provided for by the immortal gods if the entire structure of a human being is considered along with the entire form and perfection of human nature. . . .

140. This catalogue of nature's painstaking and intelligent providence could be greatly enriched by a consideration of how many rich and splendid gifts have been bestowed on men by the gods. First of all, she lifted men up from the earth and gave them a lofty and erect posture, in order that they might gaze upon the heavens and so acquire knowledge of the gods. For men come from the earth, not to be its inhabitants and tenants, but to be, as it were, spectators of higher, indeed celestial, things, the contemplation of which belongs to no other race of animals. . . .

145. . . . All of man's senses are far better than those of the lower animals. First, in those crafts in which the eyes make the crucial distinctions, painting, sculpture and engraving, and also in distinguishing bodily motion and gestures, [in all of these] the [human] eye makes many distinctions more subtly; for the eyes judge the beauty and order and, I may say, the propriety of colours and figures; and there are other, even more important distinctions which it makes, since it recognizes the virtues and the vices, and an angry or friendly person, a happy or sad one, a brave or cowardly one, a bold or timid one. **146.** The ears too possess a remarkably craftsmanlike sense of judgement, by which we can distinguish, in vocal music and in wind or string instruments, timbre, pitch and key, and a great many vocal qualities as well: a melodious or 'dark' voice, a smooth or rough one, a flexible or inflexible one. These distinctions are made only by the human ear. Smell, taste and touch also possess ⟨to some extent⟩ great powers of judgement. . . .

147. Moreover, he who does not see the divine effort which was put into the perfection of man's mind, intelligence, reason, deliberative ability and prudence, seems to me to lack these same qualities. And in discussing this topic, I wish, Cotta, that I had your eloquence. How [wonderfully] you could describe, first of all, human understanding; and then our ability to link conclusions with premisses and grasp the result, i.e., the ability by which we judge what follows from what and prove it in the form of a syllogism, and define in a compact description each kind of thing. And from this we can grasp the power and characteristics of knowledge, a thing whose excellence even the gods cannot surpass. How extraordinary, indeed, are those powers which you Academics try to undermine and even to destroy: the ability to perceive and grasp external objects with our senses and mind. **148.** It is by comparing and contrasting these with each other that we can produce the crafts, some of which are necessary for the practicalities of life and some for the sake of pleasure.

Indeed, the mistress of all, as you call it, is the power of eloquence— how wonderful and divine it is! First, it enables us to learn what we do not know and to teach others what we do know; next, we use it to exhort and persuade, to comfort the unfortunate and to distract the timid from their fears, to calm those who are passionate and dampen their desires and anger; it is the bond which unites us in law, legislation and civil society; it is eloquence which has raised us from a state of uncouth savagery. . . .

153. What then? Does human reason not penetrate even to the heavens? For we are the only animals who know the risings, settings and courses of the heavenly bodies; it is the human race which has defined the day, the month and the year, has learned about solar and lunar eclipses and predicted their dates of occurrence and degree for all time to come. By contemplating these things our mind attains to knowledge of the gods, and that is the origin of piety, which is closely linked with justice and the other virtues, which are in turn the source of a life which is happy and similar, even equivalent, to that of the gods—yielding to the heavenly beings only in respect to immortality, which is quite irrelevant to the good life. After explaining this, I think that I have shown clearly enough by how much human nature is superior to the [other] animals. And from that one ought to see that chance could never have created the form and arrangement of our limbs or the power of our mind and intelligence.

154. It remains for me to come to my conclusion at last by showing that everything in this cosmos which is of use to men was in fact made and provided for their sake. First of all, the cosmos itself was made for the sake of gods and men, and the things in it were provided and discovered for the use of men. For the cosmos is like a common home for gods and men, or a city which both [gods and men] inhabit. For only creatures who use reason live by law and justice. So just as one must hold that Athens and Sparta were founded for the sake of the Athenians and Spartans and everything in these cities is properly said to belong to those peoples, in the same way one must hold that everything in the entire cosmos belongs to gods and men. 155. Moreover, although the orbits of the sun and moon and the other stars help the cosmos hold together, they also serve as a [wonderful] spectacle for men. For no sight is less likely to become boring, none is more beautiful and none more outstanding with respect to rationality and cleverness; for by measuring out their courses we learn when the various seasons change and reach their peaks. And if men alone know these things, one must judge that they were created for the sake of men.

156. The earth is rich with grain and other kinds of vegetables and pours them forth with the greatest generosity; do you think that it was made for the sake of beasts or of men? What should I say about vines and olive trees? Their most rich and fertile fruits are of no use at all to beasts. Beasts have no knowledge of sowing, cultivating, of reaping and bringing in the harvest at the proper time, nor of putting it up and storing it; only men can use and care for these things. 157. Just as we should say that lyres and flutes are made for the sake of those who can use them, so one must admit that the things I have been talking about are provided only for the sake of those who use them; and if some animals steal or snatch some of it from them, we shall still not say that those things were made for their sake. For men do not store grain for the sake of mice or ants, for rather for the sake of their wives, children and households. So animals use such things by stealth, as I said, but their masters do so openly and freely. 158. So one must concede that this generous supply of goods was provided for the sake of men, unless the great richness and variety of fruits, and their pleasant taste, odour and appearance, leaves any doubt about whether nature presented them to men alone.

So far is it from being true that these things were provided for the sake of the beasts, that we can see that even the beasts themselves were created for man's sake. What are sheep for except to provide wool which can be worked and woven into clothes for men? And without man's cultivation and care they could not have been nourished or maintained, nor produced anything of use to others. What can be the meaning of the faithful guard service of dogs, their loving admiration of their masters, their hatred of outsiders, and their remarkable skill in tracking and speed in the hunt? Only that they were created to serve man's needs. . . . .

159. . . . It would take too long to recount the useful services provided by mules and asses, which were certainly provided for man's use. 160. What is there in pigs, except food? Chrysippus says that the pig was given a soul in place of salt, to keep the meat from spoiling. Because it

is well-suited for feeding humans, no other type of animal is more prolific of offspring. ... **161.** ... You can scan the land and all the seas with your mind, as though with your eyes, and you will immediately see huge expanses of land which bear fruit [for man], and densely forested mountains, pasture land for cattle, and also sea-lanes for ships to sail in with remarkable speed. **162.** It is not just on the earth's surface either; but even in the deepest, darkest bowels of the earth there lies hidden a great store of useful materials which were made for man and are only discovered by man.

There is another point too, which both of you[32] will perhaps seize on for criticism, you Cotta because Carneades loved to attack the Stoics, Velleius because Epicurus ridiculed nothing so much as the prediction of future events; but I think that it proves better than anything else that divine providence takes thought for human affairs. For divination certainly does exist, since it shows up in many different places and at many different times, in both private and public affairs. **163.** ... This power, or art, or natural ability of knowing future events was certainly given to man and to no other animal by the immortal gods. ... **164.** And the immortal gods do not limit themselves to taking thought for mankind as a whole, but they even concern themselves with individual men. For one may gradually reduce the scope of universality, from mankind to smaller and smaller numbers of men, and finally get down to single individuals [applying the same arguments at each stage]. ...

Aetius 1.6.1–16 (= *Dox. Gr.* pp. 292–297;   [II-24]
SVF 2.1009)

The Source of Man's Conception of the Gods

1. The Stoics define the substance of god thus: it is an intelligent and fiery *pneuma*, which does not have a shape but changes into whatever it wishes and assimilates itself to all things. **2.** They [sc. men] acquired the conception of god first by getting it from the beauty of the things which appear to them. For nothing beautiful becomes so at random and haphazardly but rather by a craft which acts as an artisan. And the cosmos is beautiful; this is clear from its shape and its colour and its size and the varied adornment of the heavenly bodies around the cosmos. **3.** For the cosmos is spherical and this is the best shape of all. For this shape alone is similar to its own parts. And since it is rounded, it contains parts which are round. For it is for this reason that Plato held that the most sacred [part of man], his mind, is in the head. **4.** And its colour is beautiful

---

32. The two other speakers in the dialogue are an Epicurean and an Academic sceptic.

too. For it has a bluish colour, which is darker than purple but has a shining quality. And for this reason it can be observed from such great distances, because it cuts through so great an expanse of air in virtue of the intensity of its colour. 5. And it is also beautiful because of its size. For among things which are of the same type, the one which includes [or: surrounds] [the others] is beautiful, as in the case of animal or a tree.

6. And these phenomena too complete the beauty of the cosmos; for the ecliptic in the heavens is adorned with a variety of different constellations:[33]

> Cancer is there, and so is Leo, and after him Virgo and
> Libra, and Scorpio himself and Sagittarius and Capricorn too,
> and after Capricorn comes Aquarius; and Pisces with its
> shining stars is next, after which come Aries and Taurus and
> Gemini.

7. And [god] has produced thousands of other [constellations] by similar revolutions of the cosmos. Hence Euripides too says,[34]

> The starry gleam of heaven
> the fair adornment of Time, the wise craftsman.

8. From this we have acquired the conception of god. For the sun and the moon and the rest of the heavenly bodies moving around the earth always rise [displaying] the same colours, the same sizes, and in the same places at the same times. 9. Therefore, the initiators of religious observance expounded it for us in three forms. First, that based on physics, second, that based on myths, and third, that based on the testimony of customs. The philosophers teach the one which is based on physics and the poets the one based on myths, while the customary forms of religious observance are always established by individual cities.

10. Their entire teaching is divided into seven 'species'. The first is that based on the phenomena of the heavens; for we acquired our conception of god from the phenomena of the heavenly bodies, by seeing that they are the cause of great harmony, and [by seeing] the regularity of day and night, winter and summer, risings and settings, and of the birth of animals and plants in the earth. 11. Therefore, they thought that the heaven was a father, while earth was a mother. Of these, the one is father because the effusions of water play the role of seeds, while the other is mother

---

33. Aratus *Phainomena* 545–549.
34. Actually the poet Critias, fr. 1.33–34 p. 771 Nauck.

because she receives these [seeds] and bears [offspring]. And seeing that the heavenly bodies are always moving and are the cause of our ability to observe [things], they called the sun and moon gods.

12. For the second and third types they divided the gods into the harmful and the beneficial; the beneficial ones are Zeus, Hera, Hermes and Demeter, while the harmful ones are the Penalties, the Furies, Ares; these they abhor since they are difficult to deal with and violent.

13. They assigned a fourth and a fifth [type of gods] to activities and passions, Eros, Aphrodite and Longing being passions and Hope, Justice and Good Order being activities.

14. As a sixth type they added the fictions of the poets. For when Hesiod wanted to make gods fathers of gods who were born, he introduced sires for them like these:[35]

Coeus, Krios, Hyperion and Iapetos

15. And it is for this reason that it is called mythical.

As a seventh, in addition to all these, there are [gods who were] born human but were honoured because of their good deeds which benefitted the life of all men; for example, Heracles, the Dioscuri and Dionysus.

16. They said that they were anthropomorphic on the grounds that the divine is the most authoritative of all things and that man is the most beautiful of animals, being adorned in a distinctive way by virtue, in accordance with the constitution of his mind. So they thought that what is best [in the cosmos] would be similar to those who are superior [among animals].

Origen *On Principles* 3.1.2–3 (=SVF 2.988) [II-25]

2. Of things that move, some have the cause of motion in themselves, while others are moved only from the outside. Thus things which are moved by being carried, such as sticks and stones and every form of matter held together by *hexis* [condition] alone, are moved from the outside . . . Plants and animals, and in a word everything held together by nature and soul have within themselves the cause of motion. They say that this category includes veins of metal and, in addition, that fire and perhaps springs of water are also self-moved. Of things which contain the cause of motion in themselves, they say that some move from themselves and others by themselves. 'From themselves' applies to soulless objects, 'by themselves' to things with soul. For ensouled things move

---

35. *Theogony* 134.

by themselves when a presentation occurs which stimulates the impulse.
. . . 3. But the rational animal has reason too in addition to the power
of presentation. Reason judges the presentations and rejects some and
admits others.

Origen *On Prayer* 6.1 (= SVF 2.989)   [II-26]

Of things that move, some have the mover external to them as do
soulless things and those held together by *hexis* [condition] alone. And
those things that move by nature or by soul sometimes also move not as
beings of this sort, but in a manner similar to those held together by
hexis alone. For stones and sticks, [i.e.,] things which are cut off from a
vein of metal or have lost the power to grow, are held together only by
hexis and have their motive power external to them. And the bodies of
animals and the moveable parts of plants which are shifted by someone
are not shifted *qua* animal or plant, but in a manner similar to sticks and
stones which have lost the power to grow . . . . After those, second are
those objects moved by the nature or the soul within them, which are
also said to move 'from themselves' by those who use words in their
stricter senses [i.e., the Stoics]. Third is the motion in animals which is
termed motion 'by itself'. I think that the motion of rational animals is
motion 'through themselves'. And if we deprive an animal of motion 'by
itself' it is impossible to go on thinking of it as an animal. Rather, it will
be similar either to a plant moved only by nature or a stone carried along
by an external agent. And if the animal is aware of its own motion, this
animal must be rational, since we have called this motion 'through itself'.

Simplicius *Commentary on Aristotle's*   [II-27]
Categories 1b1 p. 306.19-27 (=SVF 2.499)

They [the Stoics] say that the differences between kinds [of motion]
are: [1] moving 'from themselves', as a knife has the ability to cut because
of its special structure (for the doing is carried out in accordance with
its shape and form); [2] and the activation of motion 'through oneself',
as natural organisms and curative powers carry out their action: for the
seed is sown and unfolds its proper [rational] principle and attracts the
matter nearby and fashions the principles in it; [3] and also doing 'by
oneself', which in general terms is doing by a thing's own impulse. But
another sense [4] is doing by a rational impulse, which is called action.
And [5] even more specific than this is activity according to virtue.

Sextus *M* 8.263 (SVF 2.363) [II-28]

According to them, the incorporeal can neither do anything nor have anything done to it.

Cicero *Academica* 1.39 (SVF 1.90) [II-29]

[Zeno] disagreed with the same men [Peripatetics and Academics] in that he thought it totally impossible for anything to be effected by what lacked body; . . . and indeed he held that whatever effected something or was affected by something must be body.

Aetius 1.10.5 (= *Dox. Gr.* p. 309; SVF 2.360) [II-30]

Zeno's followers, the Stoics, said that the Ideas [i.e., Platonic Forms] were our own thoughts.

Syrianus *Comm. On Aristotle's Metaphysics* [II-31]
1078b12, *CIAG* 6.1, p. 105.22–23 (SVF 2.364)

. . . that the Forms were not introduced, as Chrysippus and Archedemus and the majority of the Stoics thought, by these godlike men [Socrates, Plato, the Parmenideans, the Pythagoreans] to account for our customary use of the names of things [i.e., common nouns] . . .

Seneca *Letters on Ethics* 58.11–15 (SVF 2.332) [II-32]

11. Moreover, there is something higher than body; for we say that some things are corporeal, some incorporeal. What, therefore, is that from which these are derived? That to which we just now assigned the technical term 'that which is'. It will be divided into species so that we say 'that which is' is either corporeal or incorporeal. 12. . . . That genus, 'that which is', has no genus above it; it is the first principle of things; everything is subordinate to it. 13. But the Stoics want to set yet another genus above this one, which is a higher principle; I will speak of it now . . . 15. Some Stoics held that the first genus is the "something"; I shall add an explanation of why they held this. They say that in the nature of things, some things are and some are not; and nature also includes those things which are not but which occur to our mind, such as Centaurs, Giants and whatever, being formed by a false concept, begins to take on a certain image [in our minds], although it does not have substance.

Alexander of Aphrodisias *Comm. on*   [II-33]
Arisotle's Topics 121a10, 127a26 (*CIAG* 2.2,
p. 301.19–25, 359.12–16 = SVF 2.329)

301.19 In this way you might show that the Stoics do not properly
posit the something as a genus of 'that which is'; for obviously, if it is
a something, it is something which is. And if it is something which is, then
the definition of being would apply to it. But they made an idiosyncratic
stipulation to the effect that 'that which is' applies only to bodies and
so tried to evade the paradox. For thus they say that the 'something' is
its highest genus and is predicated not just of bodies but also of incorporeals. . . . 359.12 In this way it will be shown that the something is not
the genus of everything. For it will also be the genus of the one, which
is either co-extensive with it or of even wider extent, if indeed the one
also applies to the concept; but the something applies only to bodies and
incorporeals, while the concept, according to the proponents of this
theory, is neither of these.

Sextus *M* 10.218 (SVF 2.331)   [II-34]

The Stoics, though, thought that time is incorporeal. For they say
that of "somethings" some are bodies and some are incorporeals and they
listed four kinds of incorporeals: *lekton* [thing said] and void and place
and time. From which it is clear that in addition to supposing that time
is incorporeal they also believe that it is a thing conceived of as existing
on its own.

Plutarch *Common Conceptions* 1081c–1082a   [II-35]
(SVF 2.518, 2.519)

(1081c) It is paradoxical for the future and past time to exist and for
present time not to exist, but for the recent and more remote past to
subsist and for the "now" not to exist at all. But this result does obtain
for the Stoics, who do not allow a minimal time to exist and do not want
to have a partless "now"; but they say that whatever one thinks one has
grasped and conceived as present is in part future and in part past.
Consequently there neither remains nor is left in the "now" any part of
present time (1081d), if the time which is called present is divided up,
some of it being future and some past. . . .
(1081f) . . . Chrysippus wishing to be subtle about the division [of
time] says in his *On Void* and in some other writings, that the past part
of time and the future part do not exist but subsist and only the present
exists. But in the third, fourth and fifth books of *On Parts* he posits that

part of the present time is future and part is past. (1082a) Consequently it turns out that he divides the existing part of time into the non-existing parts and the existing part; or rather, he leaves absolutely no part of time in existence if the present has no part which is not future or past.

Arius Didymus fr. 26 (= *Dox. Gr.* pp. 461–2; [II-36] SVF 2.509)

Chrysippus says that time is the interval of motion according to which the measure of speed and slowness is spoken of; or, time is the interval which accompanies the motion of the cosmos. And each and every thing is said to move and to exist in accordance with time, unless of course time is spoken of in two senses, as are earth and sea and void and the universe and its parts. And just as void as a whole is infinite in every direction, so too time as a whole is infinite in both directions; for both the past and the future are infinite. He says most clearly that no time is wholly present; for since the divisibility of continuous things is infinite, time as a whole is also subject to infinite divisibility, by this method of division. Consequently no time is present in the strictest sense, but only loosely speaking. He says that only the present exists, whereas the past and future subsist but do not at all exist—unless it is in the way that predicates are said to exist, though only those which actually apply; for example, walking 'exists for me' when I am walking, but when I am reclining or sitting it does not 'exist for me'. . . .

Aetius 1.18.5, 1.20.1 (= *Dox. Gr.* p. 316, 317; [II-37] SVF 1.95)

1.18.5 Zeno and his followers say that there is no void within the cosmos but an indefinite void outside it. . . . 1.20.1 The Stoics and Epicurus say that void, place and space are different. Void is the privation of body, place is what is occupied by body and space is what is partly occupied, as in the case of wine in a jar.

Arius Didymus fr. 25 (*Dox.Gr.* p. 460–461 = [II-38] SVF 2.503)

Chrysippus proclaimed that place was that which is occupied through-out by what exists or what is such as to be occupied by what exists and is occupied throughout by some thing or things. And if what is such as to be occupied is partly occupied by what exists and partly not, the whole will be neither void nor place, but another unnamed thing. For the void is spoken of similarly to empty containers, and place similarly to full ones.

Is space what is such as to be occupied by what is, only bigger, and, as it were, a larger container for a body, or is it what has space for a larger body? Anyway, the void is said to be unlimited. For what is outside the cosmos is like this and place is limited because no body is unlimited. Just as the bodily is limited, so the incorporeal is unlimited, for time is unlimited and so is void. For just as the nothing *is* no limit, so [there is no limit] of the nothing, which is what the void is like. For it is unlimited in its own substance. And again, this is limited by being filled. If what fills it is removed, it is not possible to conceive of a limit for it.

Sextus *M* 7.38–45 (SVF 2.132)   [II-39]

38. Some, and especially the Stoics, think that truth differs from the true [or what is true] in three ways: in substance, composition and power. In substance, in that truth is corporeal and the true is incorporeal. And reasonably so, they say; for the true is a proposition and a proposition is a thing said [*lekton*]; a thing said is incorporeal. And again truth is a body in that it seems to be knowledge which declares all which is true; 39. and all knowledge is the leading part of the soul in a certain state (as the hand in a certain state is thought of as a fist). And the leading part of the soul, according to them, is a body. Therefore, truth too is corporeal in kind. 40. In composition, in that the true is conceived of as something single and simple in nature, such as "it is day" and "I am speaking"; and truth is conceived thought of in the opposite way as systematic and a collection of several things, in that it is knowledge. . . . 42. In power, these things differ from one another since the true is not always connected to truth (for a fool and an idiot and a madman sometimes say something true but do not have knowledge of the true) and truth is contemplated in knowledge. Hence, he who has this is a wise man (for he has knowledge of true things) and never lies even if he says something false since he utters it not from a bad disposition but from a good one. . . . 44. . . . In this way the wise man, i.e., the man who has knowledge of the true, will sometimes say what is false but will never lie since his mind will not assent to a falsehood. . . . 45. . . . Saying a falsehood is very different from lying in that the former comes from good intention, whereas lying comes from bad intention.

Sextus *M* 8.11–12 (SVF 2.166)   [II-40]

11. . . . And there was yet another quarrel among the dogmatists; for some located the true and false in the thing signified, some located it in the utterance and some in the motion of the intellect. And the Stoics championed the first view, saying that three things are linked with one

another: the thing signified, the signifier, and the object. **12.** Of these, the signifier is the utterance, for example, "Dion"; the thing signified is the thing indicated by the utterance and which we grasp when it subsists in our intellect and which foreigners do not understand although they hear the utterance; the object is the external existent, for example, Dion himself. Two of these are bodies, the utterance and the object, and one incorporeal, the signified thing, i.e., the thing said [*lekton*] which is true or false. This last point is not of unrestricted application, but some *lekta* are incomplete and some complete. One kind of complete *lekton* is the so-called proposition, which they describe thus: a proposition is that which is true or false.

Sextus *M* 8.70 (SVF 2.187) [II-41]

They say that what subsists in accordance with a rational presentation is a thing said [*lekton*] and that a rational presentation is one according to which the content of a presentation can be made available to reason.

Ammonius *Comm. on Aristotle's De* [II-42] *Interpretatione* 16a3 *CIAG* 4.5 pp. 17.24–28 (SVF 2.168)

Here [*De Interpretatione*] Aristotle teaches what is primarily and immediately signified by utterances, saying that it is thoughts, and that through these as intermediaries, objects are signified. And we need think of nothing beyond these which is between the thought and the object. But the Stoics hypothesized that such a thing exists and thought it should be called a "thing said".

Stobaeus *Anthology* 1.13.1c, vol. 1 [II-43] p. 138.14–22 W-H (SVF 1.89)

Zeno says that a cause is "that because of which". That of which it is the cause is an event [or accident]. And the cause is a body and that of which it is the cause is a predicate. It is impossible for the cause to be present and that of which it is the cause not to be the case. What is said amounts to this: a cause is that because of which something comes about, for example, prudent thinking occurs because of prudence, living because of soul, and temperate behaviour because of temperance. For if someone has temperance or soul or prudence it is impossible for there not to be temperate behaviour, life, or prudent thinking.

Sextus *M* 9.211 (SVF 2.341)   [II-44]

. . . The Stoics say that every cause is a body which causes something incorporeal in a body. For example, a scalpel, which is a body, causes in flesh, which is a body, the incorporeal predicate "being cut". Again, fire, which is a body, causes in wood, which is a body, the incorporeal predicate "being burned".

Simplicius *Comm. on Aristotle's Categories*   [II-45]
1b25 (= *CIAG* 8.66.32–67.2; SVF 2.369)

The Stoics think it right to reduce the number of primary categories. And among this reduced number they include some which have been changed. For they divide them into four: substrates [underlying things], and qualities [qualified things], dispositions [things in a certain state] and relative dispositions [things in a certain state with respect to something]. . .

Galen *On Incorporeal Qualities* 1, 19.463–464   [II-46]
K. (SVF 2.377)

There was a discussion of qualities and of all accidents, which the Stoics say are bodies.

Aetius 1.15.6 (=*Dox. Gr.* p. 313, SVF 1.91)   [II-47]

Zeno the Stoic says that colours are primary arrangements of matter.

Galen *Comm. On Hippocrates On Humours* 1,   [II-48]
16.32 K. (SVF 1.92)

Zeno of Citium believed that, like qualities, substances were totally mixed.

Aetius 4.20.2 (=*Dox. Gr.* p. 410, SVF 2.387)   [II-49]

The Stoics say that voice is a body. For everything which acts or has effects is a body. And voice acts and has effects. For we hear it and perceive it striking our ears and making an impression like a seal-ring on wax. Again, everything which stimulates or disturbs is a body; and good music stimulates us and bad music disturbs us. Again, everything which is in motion is a body; and voice is in motion and strikes smooth surfaces and is reflected as in the case of a ball thrown against a wall. At any rate, inside the Egyptian pyramids, one utterance produces four or even five echoes.

Plutarch *Stoic Self-Contradictions* [II-50]
1053f–1054b (SVF 2.449)

(1053f) . . . again in *On Conditions* [Chrysippus] says that conditions [*hexeis*] are nothing but [parcels] of air. For bodies are held together by these, and it is air which holds together and is responsible for the quality of each of the things held together by a condition. They call this air "hardness" in iron, "denseness" in stone, "whiteness" in silver. (1054a) . . . And yet they claim all the time that matter, which is in itself inactive and unmoving, underlies the qualities and that the qualities, which are *pneumata* and airy tensions, produce forms and shapes (1054b) in whatever parts of matter they are in.

Pseudo-Galen *Introduction* 9, 13 14.697 and [II-51]
726 K. (SVF 2.716)

9. According to the ancients, there are two [forms of] *pneuma*: that of the soul and that of nature. And the Stoics add a third, that of *hexis*, which they call a condition. . . .

13. There are two forms of the inborn *pneuma*, that of nature and that of soul; and some add a third, that of *hexis*. The *pneuma* which holds things is what makes stones cohere [hold together], while that of nature is what nourishes animals and plants, and that of the soul is that which, in animate objects, makes animals capable of sense-perception and of every kind of movement.

Aetius 1.3.25 (= *Dox. Gr.* p. 289; SVF 1.85) [II-52]

Zeno of Citium, son of Mnaseas, says the principles are god and matter, the former being responsible for acting, the latter for being acted upon. And there are four elements.

Achilles *Introduction to Aratus* p. 3, 1–3 [II-53]
(SVF 1.85)

—Zeno of Citium says that the principle of the universe is god and matter, god being the active and matter what is acted upon. From these the four elements came into being.

Calcidius *Comm. on Plato's Timaeus* c. 290 [II-54]
(SVF 1.86)

But several philosophers distinguish matter and substance, such as Zeno and Chrysippus. They say that matter is that which underlies all those things which have qualities; however, the primary matter of all things or their most primeval foundation is substance—being in itself without qualities and unformed. For example, bronze, gold, iron, etc. are matter of those things which are manufactured from them, but are not substance. But that which is cause of the existence of both the former and the latter is itself substance.

Arius Didymus fr. 20 (= *Dox. Gr.* pp.   [II-55]
457–458; SVF 1.87)

Zeno: The primary matter of all things which exist is substance and all of this is everlasting and becomes neither greater nor smaller. Its parts do not always stay the same, but are divided and fused together. Through this runs the rational principle of the universe, which some call fate, being just like the seed in seminal fluid.

Chalcidius *Comm. on Plato's Timaeus* c. 294   [II-56]
(SVF 1.87)

[The Stoics say] that god is that which matter is or that god is the inseparable quality of matter and that he moves through matter just as semen moves through the genital organs.

Chalcidius *Comm. on Plato's Timaeus* c. 292   [II-57]
(SVF 1.88)

Then Zeno said that this substance itself is finite and that only this substance is common to all things which exist, but that it is divisible and changeable in every place. Its parts change but do not perish in such a way that they turn into nothing from being existents. But he thinks that there is no form or shape or quality which is proper to the foundation of the matter of all things (just as there is no proper shape for the innumerable shapes which wax too takes on), but that nevertheless this matter is always joined with and inseparably bonded to some quality. And since it is as birthless as it is deathless because it neither comes into being from the non-existent nor turns into nothing, it does not lack an eternal spirit [*pneuma*] and liveliness which will move it in a rational manner, sometimes all of it, sometimes a proportional part of it, and which is the cause of such frequent and powerful changes in the universe. Moreover, this spirit which moves will not be nature but soul—and indeed rational soul, which gives life to this sentient cosmos and gave it the beauty which is now visible. And they call this [i.e., the cosmos] a happy animal and a god.

Alexander of Aphrodisias *On Mixture* [II-58]
224.32–225.9 (SVF 2.310)

At this point in the argument one might charge that, while saying that there are two principles for all things, matter and god, the latter being active and the former passive, they [the Stoics] also say that god is mixed with matter, extending through all of it and shaping it, forming it and making it into a cosmos in this manner. If, according to them, god is a body, being intelligent and everlasting *pneuma*, and matter too is a body, then in the first place a body once more will extend through a body; and second, this *pneuma* will either be one of the four simple bodies which they also call elements, or a compound mixture of them, as they themselves also seem to say, I suppose (for they postulate that *pneuma*'s substance is composed of air and fire); or, if it is something else, then the divine body will be some fifth substance.

Alexander of Aphrodisias *On Mixture* [II-59]
p. 223.25–224.14 (SVF 2.441)

. . . This being so, how could it be true that the totality is unified and held together because some *pneuma* extends through all of it? Next, it would be reasonable that the coherence produced by the *pneuma* should be found in all bodies; but this is not so. For some bodies are coherent and some discrete. Therefore, it is more reasonable to say that each of them is held together and unified with itself by the individual form in virtue of which each of them has its being, and that their sympathy with each other is preserved by means of their communion with the matter and the nature of the divine body which surrounds it, rather than by the bond of the *pneuma*. For what is this 'pneumatic tension' by which things are bound and so both possess coherence with their own parts and are linked to adjacent objects? For [according to the Stoics] it is when *pneuma* is forced by something that it takes on a kind of strength as a result of the concentrated movement, because it is naturally suited to this (since owing to its flexibility it can offer no resistance to what moves it). And being flexible in its own nature it is fluid and easily divisible, and so too is the nature of all other things with which *pneuma* is mixed; it is in virtue of *pneuma* above all that they are divided so very easily. For this reason, at any rate, some thought it was something void and an intangible nature, while others thought it had a lot of void in it.

Moreover, if the *pneuma* which holds bodies together is the cause of their persistence and not disintegrating, it is clear that bodies which do disintegrate would not possess *pneuma* binding them together.

And how, in the first place, could the divisibility of bodies be preserved, if division is the separation of what is united, and according to them all things stay united with each other, all the same even when they are divided? And how could one avoid the inconsistency of saying that objects which are adjacent to each other and can easily be separated from each other are all the same united with each other, being coherent and never being able to be separated from each other without division?

Plotinus 2.4.1 (SVF 2.320) [II-60]

And those who postulate that the only things that exist are bodies and that substance consists in them say that matter is one and that it underlies the elements and that matter itself is substance. All other things are, as it were, modifications of matter and even the elements are matter in a certain state. Moreover, they dare to bring matter into the realm of the gods. And finally, they say that their god himself is this matter in a certain state and they give it [matter] a body, saying that body itself is qualityless, and magnitude too.

Aristocles, in Eusebius *Prep. Ev.* 15.14, [II-61] 816d–817a (SVF 1.98)

They say that fire is an element of the things that exist, as does Heraclitus, and that the principles of this are matter and god (as Plato said). But he [Zeno] said that both (the active and the passive) were bodies, while Plato's first active cause was said to be incorporeal. And then, at certain fated times, the entire cosmos goes up in flames and then is organized again. And the primary fire is like a kind of seed, containing the rational principles and cause of all things and events, past, present, and future. And the interconnection and sequence of these things is fate and knowledge and truth and an inescapable and inevitable law of what exists. Thus, all things in the cosmos are organized extremely well, as in a very well-managed government.

Stobaeus *Anthology* 1.10.16c, vol. 1 [II-62] p. 129.1–130.20 W-H (SVF 2.413)

Chrysippus. Concerning the elements which come from substance, he holds views of this sort, following Zeno the leader of the school. He says there are four elements, ⟨fire, air, water, and earth, from which all animals are formed⟩ and plants and the whole cosmos and the things contained in it, and into which these same things are resolved. And ⟨fire⟩ is said to be an element par excellence because the others are first formed from it by qualitative change and finally are dissolved and resolved into it, while fire itself is not subject to dissolution or breakdown into anything else. So on this theory fire is said independently to be an element, since it is not formed together with another one, while according to the earlier theory fire is formed with other elements. For first there occurs the change in form from fire to air, second occurs the analogous change from water to earth. Again, from earth as it is resolved and dissolved the first dissolution is into water, second from water to air, third and last to fire. Everything fiery is called fire, and everything airy air and so forth. "Element" is used in three senses by Chrysippus: in one sense fire is the element since the others are formed from it by change of quality and the breakdown is back into fire; in another sense there are said to be four elements (fire, air, water, and earth)—since from one or more of these or all of them everything else is formed: through the four, for example, animals and all terrestrial compounds; through two, for example, the moon is formed of fire and air; or through one, as the sun which is formed of only fire—the sun being pure fire. And a third sense [here there is a lacuna] to be what was first formed in this way, so that it methodically produced generation from itself until the end [was reached] and [then returning] from that point it received the breakdown into itself by the same method. And he said that there have also been the following descriptions of the element, that it is most mobile on its own, and the principle ‹and the spermatic› principle and the eternal power which has a nature such as to move itself both downwards towards conversion and upwards away from the conversion again in a complete circle, both absorbing all things into itself and again restoring them from itself in a regular and methodical way.

Seneca *Letters on Ethics* 92.30 (SVF 2.637) [II-63]

Why shouldn't you think that there is something divine in him who is a part of god? All of that which contains us is one and is god. And we are his allies and parts.

Nemesius *On the Nature of Man* 2 [II-64] (SVF 2.773)

Practically all the ancients disagree on the theory of the soul. For Democritus and Epicurus and the entire Stoic school claim that the soul is a body. And these same people who claim that the soul is a body disagree about its substance. For the Stoics say it is a warm and fiery *pneuma*.

Arius Didymus fr. 39 (= *Dox. Gr.* 471.18–24,   [II-65]
SVF 2.809)

. . . They say the soul is generated and destroyed; it is not destroyed
as soon as it leaves the body but lasts for a while on its own. The soul
of the virtuous man lasts until the breakdown of everything into fire, but
that of fools [only] for a certain length of time. They say that the enduring
of souls works like this, i.e., that we last by becoming souls separated
from the body, changing into a more limited substance, that of the soul.
But the souls of imprudent and irrational animals are destroyed together
with their bodies. . . .

Nemesius *On the Nature of Man* 2   [II-66]
(SVF 2.790)

And Chrysippus says, "Death is a separation of soul from body. But
nothing incorporeal can be separated from a body. For neither does
anything incorporeal touch a body, and the soul both touches and is
separated from the body. Therefore the soul *is* a body."

Tertullian *On the Soul* 5.3 (SVF 1.137)   [II-67]

Then Zeno, defining the soul as the inborn *pneuma* [*spiritus*], teaches
as follows: that, he says, because of the departure of which the animal
dies, is a body. But when the inborn *pneuma* departs the animal dies.
But the inborn *pneuma* is the soul. Therefore, the soul is a body.

Chalcidius *Comm. on Plato's Timaeus* c. 220   [II-68]
(SVF 1.138)

The Stoics grant that the heart is the seat of the leading part of the
soul, but nevertheless that it is not the blood which is created together
with the body. To be sure, Zeno argues that the soul is [inborn] *pneuma*
thus: that whose withdrawal from the body causes the animal to die is
certainly the soul; furthermore, the animal dies when the inborn *pneuma*
withdraws; therefore, the inborn *pneuma* is the soul.

Alexander *De Anima Mantissa* CIAG Supp.   [II-69]
2.1 p. 117–118 (SVF 2.792)

[Alexander cites and rejects Stoic arguments.]—117.1–2. For it [the
soul] is not a body just because the same thing is predicated of it [as of
the body].—117.9–11. But the argument which says that something
incorporeal does not share an experience with a body, and purports to
show that the soul is not incorporeal, is also false.—117.21–23. Nor is
the argument sound which says that nothing incorporeal is separated

from a body, but the soul is separated from the body, so that it is not incorporeal.—117.28–29. Nor is it true to say that only those things which touch each other can be separated from each other.—117.30–118.2. Nor is this true: 'we are animate because of that by which we breathe; but we are animate because of the soul.' Not even if [it is true] that animals cannot exist without inborn *pneuma* does it follow that this is the soul.

Alexander *De Anima CIAG* Supp. 2.1   [II-70] p. 18.27–19.1 (SVF 2.793)

Nor does the argument which says, "that of which a part is a body is itself also a body; but perception is a part of soul and is a body; so [the soul] itself is a body,' prove anything.

Galen *On the Habits of the Soul* 4, 4.783–784   [II-71] K. (SVF 2.787)

For they [the Stoics] claim that the soul is a kind of *pneuma*, as is nature too; the *pneuma* of nature is more fluid and cool, while that of the soul is drier and hotter. Consequently, [they also think this]: that *pneuma* is a kind of matter proper to the soul, and in form the matter is either a symmetrical blend of airy and fiery substance; for it is not possible to say that it is either air alone or fire alone, since the body of an animal does not appear to be either extremely cold or extremely hot, but rather it is not even dominated by a great excess of either of these; for if there is even a minor deviation from symmetry [in the blend] the animal becomes feverish because of the unmeasured excess of fire, and it becomes chilled and livid, or completely incapable of sense-perception as a result of blending [excessively] with the air. For [air] itself in its own right is cold, and becomes temperate as a result of mixture with the fiery element. So it is immediately clear that the substance of the soul is a certain kind of blend of air and fire, according to the Stoics, and that Chrysippus was rendered intelligent because of a temperate mixture of these [elements].

Nemesius *On the Nature of Man* 2.   [II-72] (SVF 1.518)

76. Cleanthes weaves a syllogism of this sort: not only, he says, are we like our parents in respect to the body, but also in respect to the soul, in our passions, characters and dispositions; but similarity and dissimilarity are [properties] of body, and not of the incorporeal; therefore, the soul is a body. . . . 78. Again, [Cleanthes] says: nothing incorporeal shares an experience with a body, nor does a body with an incorporeal,

but [only] a body with a body; but the soul suffers with the body when [for example,] it is ill and when it is cut. And the body [suffers] with the soul—at any rate when [the soul] is ashamed it [the body] turns red, and pale when [the soul] is frightened; therefore, the soul is a body.

Aetius 4.21.1–4 (= *Dox. Gr.* pp. 410–411;   [II-73] SVF 2.836)

1. The Stoics say that the leading part [of the soul], i.e., that which produces presentations and assents and sense-perceptions and impulses, is the highest part of the soul. And they call this "reason". 2. Seven parts grow out of the leading part and extend to the body, just like the tentacles from the octopus. Of the seven parts of the soul, five are the senses— sight, smell, hearing, taste and touch. 3. Of these, sight is a *pneuma* extending from the leading part to the eyes, hearing a *pneuma* extending from the leading part to the ears, smell a *pneuma* extending from the leading part to the nostrils, taste a *pneuma* extending from the leading part to the tongue and touch a *pneuma* extending from the leading part to the surface [of the skin] for the sensible contact with objects. 4. Of the remaining parts, one is called "seed", which is itself a *pneuma* extending from the leading part to the testicles and the other, which was called "vocal" by Zeno (which they also call "voice"), is a *pneuma* extending from the leading part to the throat and tongue and the related organs. The leading part itself, like ⟨the sun⟩ in the cosmos, dwells in our head which is round.

Plotinus 4.7.7 (SVF 2.858)   [II-74]

When a man is said to be in pain with respect to his finger, the pain is surely in the finger, while surely they [the Stoics] will admit that the perception of pain is in the leading part of the soul. Though the distressed part is different from the *pneuma*, it is the leading part which perceives and the whole soul suffers the same experience. How then does this happen? They will say, by a transmission of the *pneuma* of the soul in the finger which suffered first and passed it on to the next *pneuma* and this one to another, until it arrives at the leading part.

Philo *On the Posterity of Cain* 126   [II-75] (SVF 2.862)

No one, at least no one in his senses, would say that the eyes see, but rather that the mind [sees] through the eyes, nor that the ears hear, but that the mind [hears] through the ears, nor that the nostrils smell but that the leading part of the soul [smells] through the nostrils.

On Fate

Epictetus *Discourses* 2.19.1–5   [II-76]

1. The Master Argument [of Diodorus Cronos] seems to be be based on premisses of this sort. There is a general conflict among these three statements: [1] everything past and true is necessary; [2] the impossible does not follow from the possible; [3] there is something possible which neither is nor will be true. Seeing this conflict, Diodorus used the plausibility of the first two statements to establish that only that which is or will be true is possible. 2. But from among the [consistent] pairs [of statements] one man will retain these: [3] that there is something possible which neither is nor will be true and [2] that the impossible does not follow from the possible; but [he would not concede] that [1] everything past and true is necessary. This seems to be the position of Cleanthes and his followers, and Antipater generally agreed with it. 3. Others [will accept] the other two, [3] that there is something possible which neither is nor will be true and [1] that everything past and true is necessary; [and they will concede] that the impossible follows from the possible. 4. But it is impossible to retain all three of those statements because of their general conflict with each other. 5. So if someone asks me, "which pair do you retain?". I will answer him by saying that I do not know. I have learned from research that Diodorus retained one pair, the followers of Panthoides and Cleanthes another, and the followers of Chrysippus another.

Pseudo-Plutarch *On Fate* 574ef (SVF 2.912)   [II-77]

(547e) According to the opposing argument, the first and most important point would seem to be that nothing happens uncaused, but according to prior causes. Second, that this cosmos, which is itself coordinated and sympathetic with itself, is administered by nature. Third, which would seem rather to be additional evidence, is the fact that divination is in good repute with all men because it really does exist, with divine cooperation, and second that wise men are contented in the face of events, (547f) since all of them occur according to [divine] allotment; and third, the much-discussed point, that every proposition is true or false.

Theodoretus *Graecarum Affectionum Cura* 6.14 (SVF 2.916)   [II-78]

And Chrysippus the Stoic said that what is necessitated is no different from what is fated, and that fate is an eternal, continuous and ordered motion [or change]. Zeno of Citium called fate a power capable of moving matter, and gave to the same [force] the names providence and nature. His successors said that fate was a rational principle for the things administered by providence within the cosmos, and again in other treatises they called fate a string of causes.

Aetius 1.28.4 (= *Dox. Gr.* p. 324; SVF 2.917)   [II-79]

The Stoics say it is a string of causes, i.e., an ordering and connection which is inescapable.

Alexander *De Anima Mantissa CIAG* Supp.   [II-80]
2.1 p. 185.1–5 (SVF 2.920)

But it is conceded that all things which happen by fate occur in a certain order and sequence and have an element of logical consequence in them... Anyway, they say that fate is a string of causes.

Plutarch *Stoic Self-Contradictions.* 34,   [II-81]
1049f–1050d (SVF 2.937)

(1049f) But nevertheless one will have not just one or two occasions but thousands, to address to Chrysippus this remark, which is now praised: "You have said the easiest thing, in blaming the gods." For first, in book one of his *Physics* he compares the eternity of motion to a posset[36] which spins and agitates the various things which come to pass in various ways; then he says: (1050a) "Since the organization of the universe proceeds thus, it is necessary for us to be such as we are, in accordance with it, whether we are ill or lame, contrary to our individual nature, or whether we have turned out to be grammarians or musicians." And again, a bit further on: "and on this principle we will say similar things about our virtue and our vice and, in general, about our skills or lack of them, as I have said". And a bit further on, removing all ambiguity: "for it is impossible for any of the parts, even the smallest one, to turn out differently than according to the common nature and its reason". That the common nature and the (1050b) common reason of nature are fate and providence and Zeus, even the Antipodeans know this; for the Stoics prattle on about this everywhere and he says that Homer correctly said[37] "and Zeus' plan was being fulfilled", referring it to fate and the nature of the universe according to which everything is ordered.

---

36. A drink composed of a suspension of solid particles in a fluid base.
37. *Iliad* 1.5.

How, then, can it be the case at one and the same time that god is not partly responsible for anything shameful and that not even the smallest thing can occur otherwise than according to the common nature and its reason? For in everything which occurs surely there are some shameful things too. And yet, Epicurus twists this way and that and exercises his ingenuity (1050c) in his attempt to free and liberate voluntary action from the eternal motion, so as not to leave vice free of blame, while Chrysippus gives vice blatant freedom to say not only that it is necessary and according to fate but even that it occurs according to god's reason and the best nature. And this too is plain to see, when we provide the following literal quotation: "for since the common nature extends into everything, it will be necessary that everything which occurs in any way in the universe and in any of its parts should occur according to it [the common nature] and its reason, in proper and unhindered fashion, because there is nothing outside it which could hinder its organization nor (1050d) could any of its parts be moved or be in a state otherwise than according to the common nature."

Simplicius *Comm. On Aristotle's Categories* [II-82] 13a37 *CIAG* 8, pp. 406.34–407.5 (SVF 2.198)

Concerning [pairs of] contradictories which bear on the future the Stoics accept the same principle as they do for other statements. For what is true of [pairs of] contradictories concerning things present and past is also true, they say, for future contradictories themselves and their parts. For either "it will be" or "it will not be" is true if they must be either true or false. For they are fixed by the future events themselves. And if there will be a sea-battle tomorrow, it is true to say that there will be. But if there will not be a sea-battle, it is false to say that there will be. Either there will or there will not be a battle; therefore, each statement is either true or false.

Plutarch *Stoic Self-Contradictions* 1055de [II-83] (SVF 2.202)

(1055d) . . . Surely his [Chrysippus'] account of possibility is in conflict with his account of fate. (1055e) For if Diodorus' view of the possible as "what either is or will be true" is not right but [Chrysippus' view is], that "everything which permits of occurring even if it is not going to occur is possible", then many things are possible which are not according to fate. ⟨Therefore, either⟩ fate loses its character as unconquerable, unforceable, and victorious over all things, or, if fate is as Chrysippus claims, then "what permits of occurring" will often turn out to be impossible. And everything true will be necessary, being gripped by the most sovereign of necessities; while everything false will be impossible, since the greatest cause opposes its being true.

Cicero *On Fate* 28–33 (SVF 2.955–956)   [II-84]

28. . . . Nor will the so-called "Lazy Argument" stop us. For a certain argument is called the *argos logos* by the philosophers, and if we listened to it we would never do anything at all in life. For they argue in the following fashion: "if it is fated for you to recover from this illness whether you call the doctor or not, you will recover; 29. similarly, if it is fated for you not to recover from this illness whether you call the doctor or not, you will not recover. And one of the two is fated. Therefore, there is no point in calling the doctor". It is right to call this kind of argument "lazy" and "slothful", because on the same reasoning all action will be abolished from life. One can also change the form of it, so that the word "fate" is not included and still keep the same sense, in this way: "if from eternity this has been true, 'you will recover from that disease whether you call a doctor or not', you will recover; similarly, if from eternity this has been false, 'you will recover from that disease whether you call the doctor or not' you will not recover. Et cetera."

30. Chrysippus criticizes this argument. "For," he says, "some things are simple, some conjoined. 'Socrates will die on that day' is simple. Whether he does anything or not, the day of death is fixed for him. But if it is fated, 'Oedipus will be born to Laius', it cannot be said 'whether Laius lies with a woman or not'. For the events are conjoined and co-fated." For that is how he refers to it, since it is fated thus, *both* that Laius will lie with his wife *and* that Oedipus will be produced by her. Just as, if it had been said, "Milo will wrestle at the Olympics" and someone reported "therefore, he will wrestle whether or not he has an opponent", he would be wrong. For "he will wrestle" is conjoined, because there is no wrestling match without an opponent. "Therefore, all the sophistries of that type are refuted in the same way. 'Whether you call a doctor or not, you will recover' is fallacious; for calling the doctor is fated just as much as recovering". Such situations, as I said, he calls co-fated.

31. Carneades [the Academic] did not accept this entire class [co-fated events] and thought that the above argument had been constructed with insufficient care. And so he approached the argument in another way, not using any fallacious reasoning. This was the result: if there are antecedent causes for everything that happens, then everything happens within a closely knit web of natural connections. If this is so, then necessity

causes everything. And if this is true there is nothing in our power. There is, however, something in our power. But if everything happens by fate, everything happens as a result of antecedent causes. Therefore, it is not the case that whatever happens happens by fate. 32. This argument cannot be made tighter. For if someone wished to turn the argument around and say: if every future event is true from eternity so that whatever should happen would certainly happen, then everything happens within a closely knit web of natural connections, he would be speaking nonsense. For there is a great difference between a natural cause making future events true from eternity and future events which might be understood to be true, without natural [cause] from eternity. Thus Carneades said that not even Apollo is able to pronounce on any future events unless it were those the causes of which are already contained in nature, so that they would happen necessarily. 33. On what basis could even a god say that Marcellus, who was three times a consul, would die at sea? This was indeed true from eternity, but it did not have efficient causes. Thus [Carneades] was of the opinion that if not even past events of which no trace existed would be known to Apollo, how much less would he know future events, for only if the efficient causes of any thing were known would it then be possible to know what would happen in the future. Therefore, Apollo could not predict anything regarding Oedipus, there not being the requisite causes in nature owing to which it was necessary that he would kill his father, or anything of this sort.

Aetius 1.29.7 (= *Dox. Gr.* p. 326; SVF 2.966) [II-85]

Anaxagoras and the Stoics say that chance is a cause non-evident to human calculation. For some things happen by necessity, some by fate, some by intention, some by chance and some automatically.

Plutarch *On Stoic Self-Contradictions* [II-86]
1045b–c (SVF 2.973)

(1045b) . . . Some philosophers think that they can free our impulses from being necessitated by external causes if they posit in the leading part of the soul an adventitious motion which becomes particularly evident in cases where things are indistinguishable. For when two things are equivalent and equal in importance and it is necessary to take one of the two, there being no cause which leads us to one or the other since they do not differ from each other, this adventitious cause generates a swerve in the soul all by itself (1045c) and so cuts through the stalemate. Chrysippus argues against them, on the grounds that they are doing violence to nature by [positing] something which is uncaused, and frequently cites dice and scales and many other things which cannot fall or settle in different ways at different times without some cause or difference, either something which is entirely in the things themselves or something which occurs in the external circumstances. For he claims that the uncaused and the automatic are totally non-existent, and that in these adventitious [causes] which some philosophers make up and talk about there are hidden certain non-evident causes and they draw our impulse in one direction or another without our perceiving it.

Alexander *De Anima Mantissa* CIAG Supp.   [II-87]
2.1 p. 179.6–18 (SVF 2.967)

To say that chance is a cause non-evident to human calculation is not the position of men who posit some nature called chance, but of men who say that chance consists in the relational disposition of men to the causes. . . . For if they were to say not that chance is the cause which is non-evident to some men, but the cause which is universally non-evident to all men, they would not be admitting that chance exists at all, although they grant that divination exists and suppose that it is able to make known to other men the things which seemed to be non-evident.

Alexander of Aphrodisias *On Fate* 26,   [II-88]
196.21–197.3 Bruns (SVF 2.984)

Perhaps it would not be a bad idea for us to take in hand and examine how matters stand with the puzzles they put most confidence in; for perhaps they will appear not too difficult to solve. One of these [difficulties] is as follows: If, they say, things are in our power when we can also do the opposite of those things, and it is upon such things that praise and blame and encouragement and discouragement and punishment and honours are bestowed, then it follows that being prudent and virtuous will not be in the power of those who are prudent and virtuous; for [such men] are no longer capable of receiving the vices opposite to their virtues. And the same point applies to the vices of bad men; for it is no longer in the power of such men to cease being bad. But it is absurd to say that the virtues and vices are not in our power, and that they are not the objects of praise and blame. Therefore, 'what is in our power' is not like that.

Aulus Gellius 7.2 (SVF 2.1000)   [II-89]

1. Chrysippus, the chief Stoic philosopher, defines fate (*heimarmene* in Greek) roughly as follows: "Fate," he says, "is a sempiternal and

unchangeable series and chain of things, rolling and unravelling itself through eternal sequences of cause and effect, of which it is composed and compounded". . . .

4. But authors from other schools make this objection to this definition. **5.** "If," they say, "Chrysippus thinks that everything is moved and governed by fate and the sequences and revolutions of fate cannot be turned aside or evaded, then men's sins and misdeeds should not rouse our anger, nor should they be attributed to men and their wills but to a kind of necessity and inevitability which comes from fate, mistress and arbiter of all things, by whose agency all that will be is necessary. And therefore the penalties applied by the law to the guilty are unfair, if men do not turn to misdeeds voluntarily but are dragged by fate."

6. Against this position Chrysippus made many sharp and subtle arguments. But this is the gist of all he said on the topic: **7.** although, he said, it is true that by fate all things are forced and linked by a necessary and dominant reason, nevertheless the character of our minds is subject to fate in a manner corresponding to their nature and quality. **8.** For if our minds were originally formed by nature in a sound and useful manner then they pass on all the force of fate which imposes on us from outside in a relatively unobjectionable and more acceptable way. But if, on the other hand, they are rough and untrained and uncouth, supported by no good training, then even if the blows of fated misfortune which strike them are trivial or non-existent these men will plunge headlong into constant misdeeds and errors because of their own ineptitude and their voluntary impulse. **9.** But this state of affairs is itself brought about by that natural and necessary sequence of cause and effect which is called fate. **10.** For it is by the very nature of the case fated and determined that bad characters should not be free of misdeeds and errors.

11. He then uses a quite appropriate and clever illustration of this state of affairs. "Just as," he says, "if you throw a cylindrical stone down a steep slope, you are indeed the cause and origin of its descent, nevertheless the stone afterwards rolls down not because you are still doing this, but because such is its nature and the 'rollability' of its form: similarly, the order and reason and necessity of fate sets in motion the general types and starting points of the causes, but each man's own will [or decisions] and the character of his mind govern the impulses of our thoughts and minds and our very actions."

12. He then adds these words, which are consistent with what I have said: "So the Pythagoreans too said, 'You shall know that men have woes which they chose for themselves', since the harm suffered by each man is in his own power and since they err and are harmed voluntarily and by their own plan and decision."

13. Therefore he says that we ought not to tolerate or listen to men who are wicked or lazy and guilty and shameless, who when convicted of misdeeds take refuge in the necessity of fate as in the asylum of a religious sanctuary and say that their worst misdeeds should be laid at the door, not of their own recklessness, but of fate.

14. And that most wise and ancient poet [Homer] was the first to make this point, in the verses which follow:

> It makes me furious! how mortals blame the gods! For they
> say that their troubles come from us; but they incur pains on
> their own beyond their allotment, because of their
> wickedness.[38]

15. And so Cicero, in his book entitled *On Fate*, when he said that the question was very obscure and complex, says also in these words that even the philosopher Chrysippus did not get clear on the problem: "Chrysippus, sweating and toiling to discover how he might explain that everything happens by fate and yet that there is something in our own power, gets tangled up in this manner."

Cicero *On Fate* 39–44 (SVF 2.974)   [II-90]

39. Since there were two opinions of the older philosophers, one belonging to those men who believed that everything occurred by fate in such a way that the fate in question brought to bear the force of necessity (this was the view of Democritus, Heraclitus, Empedocles and Aristotle), the other of those who held that there were voluntary motions of the mind without fate, Chrysippus, it seems to me, wanted to strike a middle path, like an informal arbitrator, but attached himself more to the group which wanted the motions of the mind to be free of necessity. But while employing his own terms he slipped into such difficulties that he wound up unwillingly confirming the necessity of fate.

40. And, if you please, let us see how this occurs in the case of assent, which we discussed at the start of our discourse. For the older philosophers who held that everything occurred by fate said that it occurred by force and necessity. Those who disagreed with them freed assent from fate and denied that if fate applied to assent it could be free of necessity and so they argued thus: "if everything happens by fate, everything occurs by an antecedent cause and if impulse [is caused], then also what follows from impulse [is caused]; therefore, assent too. But if

38. *Odyssey* 1.32–34.

the cause of impulse is not in us then impulse itself is not in our own power; and if this is so, not even what is produced by impulse is in our power; therefore, neither assent nor action is in our power. From which it follows that neither praise nor blame nor honours nor punishments are fair". Since this is wrong, they think that it is a plausible conclusion that it is not the case that whatever happens happens by fate.

41. Chrysippus, however, since he both rejected necessity and wanted that nothing should occur without prior causes, distinguished among the kinds of causes in order both to escape from necessity and to retain fate. "For," he said, "some causes are perfect and principal, while others are auxiliary and proximate. Therefore, when we say that all things occur by fate by antecedent causes, we do not want the following to be understood, viz. that they occur by perfect and principal causes; but we mean this, that they occur by auxiliary and proximate causes". And so his response to the argument which I just made is this: if everything occurs by fate it does indeed follow that everything occurs by antecedent causes, but not by principal and perfect causes. And if these are not themselves in our power it does not follow that not even impulse is in our power. But this would follow if we were saying that everything occurred by perfect and principal causes with the result that, since these causes are not in our power, ⟨not even [impulse] would be in our power⟩. **42.** Therefore, those who introduce fate in such a way that they connect necessity to it are subject to the force of that argument; but those who will not say that antecedent causes are perfect and principal will not be subject to the argument at all.

As to the claim that assents occur by antecedent causes, he says that he can easily explain the meaning of this. For although assent cannot occur unless it is stimulated by a presentation, nevertheless since it has that presentation as its proximate cause and not as its principal cause, it can be explained in the way which we have been discussing for some time now, just as Chrysippus wishes. It is not the case that the assent could occur if it were not stimulated by a force from outside (for it is necessary that an assent should be stimulated by a presentation); but Chrysippus falls back on his cylinder and cone. These cannot begin to move unless they are struck; but when that happens, he thinks that it is by their own natures that the cylinder rolls and the cone turns.

43. "Therefore," he says, "just as he who pushed the cylinder gave it the start of its motion, he did not, however, give it its "rollability", so a presentation which strikes will certainly impress its object and as it were stamp its form on the mind, but our assent will be in our own power and the assent, just as was said in the case of the cylinder, when struck from without, will henceforth be moved by its own force and nature. But if something were produced without an antecedent cause, then it would be false that everything occurs by fate. But if it is probable that a cause precedes all things which occur, what could block the conclusion that all things occur by fate? Let it only be understood what difference and distinction there is among causes."

44. Since Chrysippus has clarified this, if his opponents who say that assents do not occur by fate were nevertheless to concede that they do not occur without a presentation as antecedent [cause]—then that is a different argument; but if they grant that presentations precede and nevertheless that assents do not occur by fate, on the grounds that it is not that proximate and immediate [kind of] cause which moves the assent, note that they are really saying the same thing [as Chrysippus]. For Chrysippus, while granting that there is in the presentation a proximate and immediate cause of assent, will not grant that this cause necessitates assent in such a way that, if all things occur by fate, all things would occur by antecedent and *necessary* causes. And similarly the opponents, who disagree with him while conceding that assents do not occur without prior presentations, will say that, if everything occurs by fate in the sense that nothing occurs without a prior cause, it must be granted that all things occur by fate.

From this it is easy to understand, since both sides get the same result once their opinions are laid out and clarified, that they disagree verbally but not in substance.

Plutarch *Stoic Self-Contradictions* 47, 1055f–1056d (SVF 2.935, 937, 994, 997)   [II-91]

(**1055f**) . . . Moreover, what is said about presentations is also in powerful opposition to [Chrysippus' view of] fate. For wanting to prove that presentation is not a sufficient cause of assent, he has said that wise men will be doing harm by producing false presentations in others *if* presentations are sufficient to produce acts of assent; for wise men often use a falsehood when (**1056a**) dealing with base men and produce a persuasive presentation which is, however, not the cause of assent (since in that case [a presentation] would also be the cause of false belief and deception). So, if someone transfers this statement from the wise man to fate and should say that the assents do not arise because of fate, since in that case false assents and beliefs and deceptions would arise because of fate, and people would be harmed because of fate, then the argument which exempts the wise man from doing harm demonstrates at the same time that fate is not the cause of everything. For if people do not hold opinions and are not harmed because of fate, (**1056b**) it is clear that they also do not act correctly or have correct opinions or hold stable beliefs or get benefit because of fate, but instead the claim that fate is the cause of everything goes up in smoke. And someone who says that Chrysippus did not make fate the sufficient cause of these things but only the initiating cause will also prove that he is in contradiction with himself where he extravagantly praises Homer[39] who speaks about Zeus, "So accept whatever he sends to each of you, of evil" or of good; and Euripides[40] [who says], "O Zeus, why then should I say that miserable men have any intelligence? For we depend on you and do whatever you happen to think."

(1056c) And Chrysippus himself writes many things in agreement with these views and finally says that nothing, not even the smallest thing, is in any state or motion otherwise than according to the reason of Zeus, who is the same as fate.

Again, then, the initiating cause is weaker than the sufficient and is feeble when it is dominated by other causes which impede it, but by claiming that fate is an unconquerable, unhinderable, and unswerving cause, he calls it Unturning, Inevitable, Necessity, and Firmly Fixed (since it sets a limit on everything).

Should we, then, say that assents are not in our power, and neither are virtues, vices, (1056d) [morally] perfect actions, and [moral] errors; or should we say that fate is deficient and that the Firmly Fixed is indeterminate and that Zeus' motions and dispositions are unfulfilled? For some of these result from fate being a sufficient cause, some from it merely being an initiating cause. For if it is a sufficient cause of all things it destroys what is in our power and the voluntary, and if it is initiating, it ruins the unhinderable and fully effective character of fate. For not once or twice but everywhere, and especially in all his treatises on physics he has written that there are many hindrances to particular natures and motions, but that there are no obstacles to the nature and motion of the universe as a whole.

Hippolytus *Philosophoumena* 21 (= *Dox. Gr.* [II-92] 571.11–16, SVF 2.975)

They [Zeno and Chrysippus] support the claim that everything happens by fate by using this example. It is as though a dog is tied behind a cart. If he wants to follow, he is both dragged and follows, exercising his autonomy in conjunction with necessity. But if he does not wish to

---

39. *Iliad* 15.109.
40. *Suppliants* 734–6, slightly altered.

follow, he will nevertheless be forced to. The same thing happens in the
case of men. Even if they do not want to follow, they will nevertheless
be forced to go along with what has been destined.

Diogenianus in Eusebius *Prep. Ev.* 6.8,   [II-93]
265d–266d (SVF 2.998)

So in book one of his [Chrysippus'] *On Fate* he used proofs of this
nature, and in book two he tries to resolve the absurdities which seem
to follow on the thesis that all things are necessitated, which we listed
at the beginning: for example, the destruction of our own initiative
concerning criticism and praise and encouragement and everything which
seems to happen by our own agency.

So, in book two he says that it is obvious that many things occur by
our own initiative, but nonetheless these are co-fated with the administration of the universe. And he uses illustrations like these.

The non-destruction of one's coat, he says, is not fated simply, but
co-fated with its being taken care of, and someone's being saved from
his enemies is co-fated with his fleeing those enemies; and having children
is co-fated with being willing to lie with a woman. For just as if, he says,
someone says that Hegesarchus the boxer will leave the ring completely
untouched, it would be strange for him to think that Hegesarchus should
fight with his fists down because it was fated that he should get off
untouched (the man who made the assertion saying this because of the
fellow's extraordinary protection from being punched), so too the same
thing holds in other cases. For many things cannot occur without our
being willing and indeed contributing a most strenuous eagerness and
zeal for these things, since, he says, it was fated for these things to occur
in conjunction with this personal effort. . . . But it will be in our power,
he says, with what is in our power being included in fate.

Ethics

Diogenes Laertius 7.84–131   [II-94]

84. They divide the ethical part of philosophy into these topics: on
impulse, on good and bad things, on passions, on virtue, on the goal, on
primary value, on actions, on appropriate actions, on encouragements
and discouragements to actions. This is the subdivision given by the
followers of Chrysippus, Archedemus, Zeno of Tarsus, Apollodorus,

Diogenes, Antipater and Posidonius. For Zeno of Citium and Cleanthes, as might be expected from earlier thinkers, made less elaborate distinctions in their subject matter. But they did divide both logic and physics.

85. They say that an animal's first [or primary] impulse is to preserve itself, because nature made it congenial to itself from the beginning, as Chrysippus says in book one of *On Goals*, stating that for every animal its first [sense of] congeniality is to its own constitution and the reflective awareness of this. For it is not likely that nature would make an animal alienated from itself, nor having made the animal, to make it neither congenial to nor alienated from itself. Therefore, the remaining possibility is to say that having constituted the animal she made it congenial to itself. For in this way it repels injurious influences and pursues that which is congenial to it.

The Stoics claim that what some people say is false, viz. that the primary [or first] impulse of animals is to pleasure. 86. For they say that pleasure is, if anything, a byproduct which supervenes when nature itself, on its own, seeks out and acquires what is suitable to [the animal's] constitution. It is like the condition of thriving animals and plants in top condition. And nature, they say, did not operate differently in the cases of plants and of animals; for it directs the life of plants too, though without impulse and sense-perception, and even in us some processes are plant-like. When, in the case of animals, impulse is added (which they use in the pursuit of things to which they have an affinity), then for them what is natural is governed by what is according to impulse. When reason has been given to rational animals as a more perfect governor [of life], then for them the life according to reason properly becomes what is natural for them. For reason supervenes on impulse as a craftsman. 87. Thus Zeno first, in his book *On the Nature of Man*, said that the goal was to live in agreement with nature, which is to live according to virtue. For nature leads us to virtue. And similarly Cleanthes in *On Pleasure* and Posidonius and Hecaton in their books *On the Goal*.

Again, "to live according to virtue" is equivalent to living according to the experience of events which occur by nature, as Chrysippus says in book one of his *On Goals*. 88. For our natures are parts of the nature of the universe. Therefore, the goal becomes "to live consistently with nature", i.e., according to one's own nature and that of the universe, doing nothing which is forbidden by the common law, which is right reason, penetrating all things, being the same as Zeus who is the leader of the administration of things. And this itself is the virtue of the happy man and a smooth flow of life, whenever all things are done according to the harmony of the daimon in each of us with the will of the administrator of the universe. So Diogenes says explicitly that the goal is reasonable behaviour in the selection of things according to nature, and Archedemus [says it is] to live carrying out all the appropriate acts.

89. By nature, in consistency with which we must live, Chrysippus understands both the common and, specifically, the human nature. Cleanthes includes only the common nature, with which one must be consistent, and not the individual. And virtue is a disposition in agreement. And it is worth choosing for its own sake, not because of some fear or hope or some extrinsic consideration. And happiness lies in virtue, insofar as virtue is the soul [so] made [as to produce] the agreement of one's whole life.

And the rational animal is corrupted, sometimes because of the persuasiveness of external activities and sometimes because of the influence of companions. For the starting points provided by nature are uncorrupted.

90. Virtue in one sense is generally a sort of completion [or: perfection] for each thing, for example, of a statue. And there is also non-intellectual virtue, for example, health; and intellectual virtue, for example, prudence. For in book one of his *On Virtues* Hecaton says that those virtues which are constituted out of theorems are knowledge-based and intellectual, for example prudence and justice; but those which are understood by extension from those which are constituted out of theorems are non-intellectual, for example health and strength. For it turns out that health follows on and is extended from temperance, which is intellectual, just as strength supervenes on the building of an arch. 91. They are called non-intellectual because they do not involve assent, but they supervene even in base people, as health and courage do.

Posidonius (in book one of his *Ethical Discourse*) says that a sign that virtue exists is the fact that the followers of Socrates, Diogenes, and Antisthenes were making [moral] progress; and vice exists because it is the opposite of virtue. And that it is teachable (virtue, I mean) Chrysippus says in book one of his *On the Goal*, and so do Cleanthes and Posidonius in their *Protreptics* and Hecaton too. It is clear that it is teachable because base men become good.

92. Panaetius, anyway, says that there are two [kinds of] virtues, theoretical and practical; others [divide virtue into] logical, physical and ethical. Posidonius' followers [say there are] four, and those of Cleanthes and Chrysippus and Antipater [say there are even] more. But Apollophanes says there is one virtue, viz. prudence.

Of virtues, some are primary and some are subordinate to these. The primary are these: prudence, courage, justice and temperance. Forms of these are magnanimity, self-control, endurance, quick-wittedness, and deliberative excellence. And prudence is the knowledge of which things are good and bad and neither; courage is knowledge of which things are to be chosen and avoided and neither; and . . . . [There is a lacuna here.] **93.** magnanimity is knowledge or a condition which makes one superior to those things which happen alike to base and virtuous men; self-control is an unsurpassable disposition [concerned with] what accords with right reason, or a condition which cannot be defeated by pleasures; endurance is knowledge of or a condition [concerned with] what one is to stand firmly by and what is not and neither; quick-wittedness is a condition which instantly finds out what the appropriate action is; and deliberative excellence is a knowledge of how to consider the type and manner of actions which we must perform in order to act advantageously.

Correspondingly, of vices too some are primary and some are subordinate. For example, imprudence, cowardice, injustice and wantonness are primary, and lack of self-control, slow-wittedness and poor deliberation are subordinate. Those vices whose [counterpart] virtues are forms of knowledge are forms of ignorance.

94. Good is in general that from which there is something beneficial; in particular it is either the same as or not different from benefit. Hence, virtue itself and the good, which participates in it, are spoken of in these three ways: [1] the good is that *from which* being benefitted is a characteristic result; [2] it is that *according to which* [being benefitted] is a characteristic result, for example, action according to virtue; [3] it is he *by whom* [being benefitted is a characteristic result]; and "by whom" means, for example, the virtuous man who participates in virtue.

They give another particular definition of the good, as follows: "that which is perfectly in accord with nature for a rational being, qua rational". And virtue is such a thing, so that virtuous actions and virtuous men participate [in it]; and its supervenient byproducts are joy and good spirits and the like. **95.** Similarly, of bad things some are imprudence, cowardice, injustice and the like; and vicious actions and base men participate in vice; and its supervenient byproducts are low spirits and depression and the like.

Again, some goods are in the soul, some are external, and some are neither in the soul nor external. The ones in the soul are virtues and virtuous actions; the external are: having a virtuous fatherland and a virtuous friend and their happiness; those which are neither external nor in the soul are: for someone, in and for himself, to be virtuous and to be happy. **96.** Conversely, some bad things are in the soul, i.e., vices and vicious actions; the external ones are having an imprudent fatherland and an imprudent friend and their unhappiness; those which are neither external nor in the soul are for someone, in and for himself, to be base and to be unhappy.

Again, of goods some are final and some are instrumental and some are both final and instrumental. So a friend and the benefits derived from him are instrumental; but confidence and prudence and freedom and enjoyment and good spirits and freedom from pain and every virtuous action are final. 97. ⟨The virtues⟩ are both instrumental and final goods. For in that they produce happiness they are instrumental goods, and in that they fulfil it, such that they are parts of it, they are final goods. Similarly, of bad things some are final and some are instrumental and some are both. For an enemy and the harm derived from him are instrumental; but feelings of shock and lowliness and servitude and lack of enjoyment and low spirits and pain and every vicious action are final. ⟨The vices⟩ are both, since in that they produce unhappiness they are instrumental, and in that they fulfil it, such that they are parts of it, they are final.

98. Again of goods in the soul some are conditions and some are dispositions and some are neither conditions nor dispositions. The virtues are dispositions, practices are conditions, and activities are neither conditions nor dispositions. Generally, having good children and a good old age are mixed goods, while knowledge is a simple good. And the virtues are constant [goods], but there are ones which are not constant, such as joy and walking.

Every good is advantageous and binding and profitable and useful and well-used and honourable and beneficial and worth choosing and just. 99. [A good is] advantageous because it brings such things as we are benefitted by when they occur; binding because it holds together in cases where this is needed; profitable because it pays back what is expended on it, so that it exceeds in benefit a mere repayment of the effort; useful because it makes available the use of a benefit; well-used because it renders the use [of it] praiseworthy; honourable because it is symmetrical with its own use; beneficial because it is such as to benefit; worth choosing because it is such that it is reasonable to choose it; just because it is consonant with law and instrumental to a [sense of] community.

100. They say that the perfect good is honourable because it has all the features sought by nature or because it is perfectly symmetrical. There are four forms of the honourable: just, courageous, orderly, knowledgeable. For honourable actions are completed in these [forms]. Analogously, there are also four forms of the shameful: the unjust, the cowardly, the disorderly and the senseless. The honourable uniquely means that which makes those who possess it praiseworthy; or a good which is worthy of praise; otherwise: what is naturally well suited for its own function; otherwise: that which adorns [its possessor], [as] when we say that only the wise man is good and honourable.

101. They say that only the honourable is good, according to Hecaton in book three of his *On Goods* and Chrysippus in his book *On the Honourable*; and this is virtue and that which participates in virtue; this is the same as [saying] that everything good is honourable and that the good is equivalent to the honourable—which is equal to it. For "since it is good, it is honourable; but it is honourable; therefore, it is good." They think that all goods are equal and that every good is worth choosing in the highest degree and does not admit of being more or less intense. They say that of existing things, some are good, some bad, and some neither.

102. The virtues—prudence, justice, courage, temperance and the others—are good; and their opposites—imprudence, injustice and the others—are bad; neither good nor bad are those things which neither benefit nor harm, such as life, health, pleasure, beauty, strength, wealth, good reputation, noble birth, and their opposites death, disease, pain, ugliness, weakness, poverty, bad reputation, low birth and such things, as Hecaton says in book seven of his *On the Goal*, and Apollodorus in his *Ethics* and Chrysippus. For these things are not good, but things indifferent in the category of preferred things. **103.** For just as heating, not cooling, is a property of the hot, so benefitting, not harming, is a property of the good; but wealth and health do not benefit any more than they harm; therefore, neither wealth nor health is good. Again, they say that what can be used [both] well and badly is not good; but it is possible to use wealth and health [both] well and badly; therefore, wealth and health are not good. Posidonius, however, says that these things too are in the class of goods. But Hecaton in book nine of *On Goods* and Chrysippus in his *On Pleasure* deny even of pleasure that it is a good; for there are also shameful pleasures, and nothing shameful is good. **104.** To benefit is to change or maintain something in accordance with virtue, while to harm is to change or maintain something in accordance with vice.

Things indifferent are spoken of in two senses; in the simple sense, those things which do not contribute to happiness or unhappiness [are indifferent], as is the case with wealth, reputation, health, strength and similar things. For it is possible to be happy even without these things, since it is a certain kind of use of them which brings happiness or unhappiness. But in another sense things indifferent are what do not stimulate an impulse either towards or away from something, as is the case with having an odd or even number of hairs on one's head, or with extending or retracting one's finger; the first sort [of indifferents] are no longer called indifferent in this sense; for they do stimulate impulses towards or away from [themselves]. **105.** That is why some of them are selected ⟨and some⟩ are rejected, while those others leave one equally balanced between choice and avoidance.

Of things indifferent, they say that some are preferred and some rejected; preferred are those which have value, rejected are those which have disvalue. They say that one sort of value is a contribution to the life in agreement, which applies to every good; but another sort is a certain intermediate potential or usefulness which contributes to the life according to nature, as much as to say, just that [value] which wealth and health bring forward for [promoting] the life according to nature. And another sense of value is the appraiser's value, which a man experienced in the facts would set, as when one says that wheat is exchanged for barley with a mule thrown in.

106. Preferred things are those which also have value; for example, among things of the soul, natural ability, skill, [moral] progress and similar things; among bodily things life, health, strength, good condition, soundness, beauty and the like; among external things wealth, reputation, noble birth, and similar things. Rejected are, among things of the soul, natural inability, lack of skill and similar things; among bodily things death, disease, weakness, bad condition, being maimed, ugliness and similar things; among external things poverty, lack of reputation, low birth and the like. Those things which are in neither category are neither preferred nor rejected.

107. Again, of preferred things, some are preferred for themselves, some because of other things, and some both for themselves and because of other things. For themselves, natural ability, [moral] progress and similar things; because of other things, wealth, noble birth, and similar things; for themselves and because of other things, strength, good perceptual abilities, soundness. [Those which are preferred] for themselves [are preferred] because they are according to nature; [those which are preferred] because of other things, [are preferred] because they produce a significant amount of utility; the same applies to the rejected conversely.

Again, an appropriate [action], they say, is that which, when done, admits of a reasonable defence, such as what is consistent in life, and this extends also to plants and animals. For appropriate [actions] are observable in these too.

108. The appropriate was first so named by Zeno and the term is derived from [the expression] "extending [or applying] to certain people". It is an action congenial to arrangements which are according to nature. For of actions performed according to impulse [i.e., voluntarily], some are appropriate and some inappropriate ⟨and some are neither appropriate nor inappropriate⟩.

Appropriate [actions], then, are those which reason constrains [us] to do, such as honouring our parents, brothers, fatherland, and spending time with friends. Inappropriate are those which reason constrains [us] not [to do], such as things like this: neglecting our parents, ignoring our brothers, being out of sympathy with our friends, overlooking [the interests of] our fatherland and such things. **109.** Neither appropriate nor inappropriate are those which reason neither constrains us to perform nor forbids, such as picking up a small stick, holding a writing instrument or scraper and things similar to these.

And some are appropriate without regard to [special] circumstances, while some are conditioned by circumstances. Those which [are appropriate] without regard to [special] circumstances are these: looking out for one's health and sense organs, and similar things. Those which are conditioned by circumstances are maiming oneself and throwing away one's possessions. The analogous [distinctions apply] too for the things which are contrary to what is appropriate. Again, of appropriate [actions], some are always appropriate and some not always. And living according to virtue is always appropriate, but asking questions and answering and walking and similar things are not always [appropriate]. The same reasoning applies to inappropriate [actions]. **110.** And there is also a kind of appropriate [action] among intermediates, such as the obedience of boys to their attendants.

They say that the soul has eight parts; for its parts are the five sense organs and the vocal part and the thinking part (which is the intellect itself) and the generative part. And corruption afflicts the intellect because of falsehoods, and from [such a mind] there arise many passions and causes of instability. Passion itself is, according to Zeno, the irrational and unnatural movement of a soul; or, an excessive impulse.

According to Hecaton in book two of his *On Passions* and Zeno in his *On Passions*, the most general [classification] of the passions is into four types: **111.** pain, fear, desire, pleasure. They believe that the passions are judgements, as Chrysippus says in his *On Passions*; for greed is a supposition that money is honourable, and similarly for drunkenness and wantonness and the others.

And pain is an irrational contraction; its forms are: pity, grudging, envy, resentment, heavy-heartedness, congestion, sorrow, anguish, confusion. Pity is a pain [felt] for someone who is suffering undeservedly; grudging is a pain at the goods of other people; envy is a pain at someone else having things which one desires oneself; resentment is a pain at someone else too having what one also has oneself; **112.** heavy-heartedness is a pain which weighs one down; congestion is a pain which crowds one and makes one short of room; sorrow is a persistent or intensifying pain caused by brooding on something; anguish is a laborious pain; confusion is an irrational pain which gnaws at one and prevents one from getting a comprehensive view of one's current circumstances.

Fear is the expectation of something bad. These [forms] are brought under fear: dread, hesitation, shame, shock, panic, agony. Dread is a fear which produces fright; shame is a fear of bad reputation; hesitation is a fear of future action; shock is a fear arising from the appearance of an unfamiliar thing; 113. panic is fear in conjunction with a hastening of the voice; agony is a fear . . . [There is a lacuna here.]

Desire is an irrational striving, and these [forms] are ranged under it: want, hatred, quarrelsomeness, anger, sexual love, wrath, spiritedness. Want is an unsuccessful desire and is as though it were separated from its object yet vainly straining for and drawn to it; hatred is a progressive and increasing desire for things to go badly for someone; quarrelsomeness is a desire concerned with one's [philosophical] school; anger is a desire for revenge on one who seems to have done an injustice inappropriately; sexual love is a desire which does not afflict virtuous men, for it is an effort to gain love resulting from the appearance of [physical] beauty. 114. Wrath is long-standing and spiteful anger which just waits for its chance, as is apparent in these lines [*Iliad* 1.81–2]:

> For even if he swallows his resentment for today,
> still he will retain his spite in the future, until it is satisfied.

And spiritedness is anger just beginning.

Pleasure is an irrational elation over what seems to be worth choosing; under it are ranged enchantment, mean-spirited satisfaction, enjoyment, rapture. Enchantment is a pleasure which charms one through the sense of hearing; mean-spirited satisfaction is pleasure at someone else's misfortunes; enjoyment is, as it were, a turning,[41] a kind of incitement of the soul to slackness; rapture is a breakdown of virtue.

115. As there are said to be ailments in the body, such as gout and arthritis, so too in the soul there are love of reputation and love of pleasure and the like. For an ailment is a disease coupled with weakness and a disease is a strong opinion about something which seems to be worth choosing. And as in the body there are certain predispositions [to disease], for example catarrh and diarrhoea, so too in the soul there are tendencies, such as proneness to grudging, proneness to pity, quarrelsomeness and the like.

116. There are also three good states [of the soul], joy, caution, and wish. And joy is opposite to pleasure, being a reasonable elation; and caution to fear, being a reasonable avoidance. For the wise man will not be afraid in any way, but will be cautious. They say that wish is opposite

---

41. The pun is untranslatable.

to desire, being a reasonable striving. So just as there are certain passions which are forms of the primary ones, so too there are good states subordinate to the primary; forms of wish are good will, kindliness, acceptance, contentment; forms of caution are respect, sanctity; forms of joy are enjoyment, good spirits, tranquillity.

117. They say the wise man is also free of passions, because he is not disposed to them. And the base man is 'free of passions' in a different sense, which means the same as hard-hearted and cold. And the wise man is free of vanity, since he is indifferent to good and ill repute. And there is another type of freedom from vanity, i.e., heedlessness; such is the base man. And they say that all virtuous men are austere because they do not consort with pleasure nor do they tolerate hedonistic [actions and attitudes] from others; and there is another kind of austerity, in the same sense that wine is said to be 'austere' [harsh] (which is used medicinally, but not much for drinking).

118. The virtuous are sincere and protective of their own improvement, by means of a preparation which conceals what is base and makes evident the good things which are there. And they are not phony; for they have eliminated phoniness in their voice and appearance. And they are uninvolved; for they avoid doing anything which is not appropriate. And they will drink wine, but not get drunk. Again, [the wise man] will not go mad, although he will get strange presentations because of an excess of black bile or delirium—not in accordance with the account of what is worth choosing, but rather contrary to nature. Nor indeed will the wise man feel pain (since pain is an irrational contraction of the soul), as Apollodorus says in his *Ethics*.

119. And they are godly; for they have in themselves a kind of god. And the base man is godless. And the godless are of two kinds, the one opposite to him who is godly, and the one who denies that the godly exists [i.e., the atheist]—and this is not a feature of every base man. The virtuous are also pious, for they have experience of what is lawful with respect to the gods and piety is a knowledge of how to serve the gods. And indeed they will also sacrifice to the gods and be sanctified, since they will avoid [moral] mistakes concerning the gods. And the gods admire them, since they are holy and just towards the divine. And only wise men are priests, for they have conducted an investigation into sacrifices, foundations, purifications and the other matters which are proper for the gods.

120. The [Stoics] think that he [the wise man] will honour his parents and brothers in the second place, after the gods. They also say that love for one's children is natural to them and does not exist among the base. They also see fit to believe that [moral] mistakes are equal, according to

Chrysippus, in book four of his *Ethical Investigations*, and Persaeus and Zeno. For if one truth is not more [true] than another, then neither is one falsehood [falser] than another. So, neither is one deception [more of a deception] than another nor is one [moral] mistake more [of a moral mistake] than another. For he who is a hundred stades from Canopus and he who is one stade away are [both] equally not in Canopus. So too he who makes a larger [moral] mistake and he who makes a smaller one are [both] equally not acting correctly. **121.** But Heracleides of Tarsus, the student of Antipater of Tarsus, and Athenodorus say that [moral] mistakes are not equal.

They say that the wise man will participate in politics unless something prevents him, according to Chrysippus in book one of *On Ways of Life*; for he will restrain vice and promote virtue. And he will marry, as Zeno says in his *Republic*, and have children. Again, the wise man will not hold opinions, that is, he will not assent to anything which is false. And he will live like a Cynic. For the Cynic life is a short road to virtue, as Apollodorus says in his *Ethics*. And he will even taste human flesh in special circumstances. He alone is free, and the base men are slaves; for freedom is the authority to act on one's own, while slavery is the privation of [the ability] to act on one's own. **122.** There is also another kind of slavery, in the sense of subordination [to another]; and a third, in the sense of subordination [to] and possession [by another]; its opposite is mastery [or: despotism], and this too is base. Not only are the wise free, but they are also kings, since kingship is a form of rule not subject to review, which only the wise could have, as Chrysippus says in his book *On the Fact That Zeno Used Terms in Their Proper Senses*. For he says that the ruler must know about good and bad things and that none of the base understands these things. Similarly they alone are fit for office or for jury duty, and [they alone are] public speakers, but none of the base are. Again, they are also free of [moral] mistakes, since they are not subject to making [moral] mistakes. **123.** And they do no harm; for they harm neither others nor themselves. But they are not prone to pity and forgive no one. For they do not relax the penalties which the law fixes as relevant, since giving in and pity and equity itself are the vapidity of a soul which aims to substitute niceness for punishment; nor does he think that [such punishments] are too severe. Again, the wise man is astonished at none of the things which appear to be wonders, such as the caves of Charon or tidal ebbs or hot springs or fiery exhalations [from the earth]. Moreover, the virtuous man will not, they say, live in solitude; for he is naturally made for [living in a] community and for action. He will, moreover, submit to training for the sake of [building] bodily endurance. **124.** They say that the wise man will pray, asking for good things from the gods, according to Posidonius in book one of his *On Appropriate Actions* and Hecaton in book three of *On Paradoxes*. And they say that friendship exists only among virtuous men, because of their similarity. They say that it is a sharing [or: community] of things needed for one's life, since we treat our friends as ourselves. They declare that one's friend is worth choosing for his own sake and that having many friends is a good thing. And there is no friendship among base men and that no base man has a friend. And all the imprudent are mad; for they are not prudent, but do everything in accordance with madness, which is equivalent to imprudence.

125. The wise man does everything well, as we also say that Ismenias plays all the flute tunes well. And everything belongs to wise men; for the law has given them complete authority. Some things are *said* to belong to the base, just as things are also *said* to belong to men who are unjust; in one sense we say they belong to the state, in another sense to those who are using them.

They say that the virtues follow on each other and that he who has one has them all. For their theoretical principles are common, as Chrysippus says in book one of his *On Virtues*, and Apollodorus in his *Physics in the Old Stoa*, and Hecaton in book three of *On Virtues*. **126.** For he who has virtue has a theoretical knowledge of what is to be done and also practises it. And what one is to do and choose is also what one is to endure for and stand firmly by and distribute, so that if he does some things by way of choosing and others by way of enduring and others by way of distributing and others by standing firmly by [something], one will be prudent and courageous and just and temperate. Each of the virtues is demarcated by a particular sphere of relevance, such as courage which is concerned with what is to be endured for, prudence with what is to be done and what not and what is neither; similarly, the other virtues revolve around their proper objects. Deliberative excellence and understanding follow on prudence, organization and orderliness on temperance, even-handedness and fairness on justice, constancy and vigour on courage.

127. They believe that there is nothing in between virtue and vice, while the Peripatetics say that [moral] progress is between virtue and vice. For, they say, just as a stick must be either straight or crooked, so must a man be either just or unjust and neither 'more just' nor 'more unjust'; and the same for the other virtues. And Chrysippus says that virtue can be lost, while Cleanthes says that it cannot be lost; [Chrysippus says] that it can be lost owing to drunkenness and an excess of black bile, while [Cleanthes says it] cannot, because [it consists in] secure [intellectual] grasps; and it is worth choosing for its ⟨own⟩ sake. At any rate, we are ashamed at things we do badly, as though we knew that only the honourable is good. And it is sufficient for happiness, as Zeno says, and Chrysippus in book one of *On Virtues* and Hecaton in book two of *On Goods*. 128. "For if," he says, "magnanimity is sufficient for making one superior to everything and if it is a part of virtue, virtue too is sufficient for happiness, holding in contempt even those things which seem to be bothersome." Panaetius, however, and Posidonius say that virtue is not sufficient [for happiness], but that there is a need for health and material resources and strength.

They think that one employs virtue constantly, as the followers of Cleanthes say. For it cannot be lost and the virtuous man always employs a soul which is in perfect condition. And justice is natural and not conventional, as are the law and right reason, as Chrysippus says in *On the Honourable*. 129. They think that one [should] not give up philosophy because of disagreement [among philosophers], since by this argument one would give up one's whole life, as Posidonius too says in his *Protreptics*. And Chrysippus says that general education is very useful.

Again, they think that there is no justice between us and the other animals, because of the dissimilarity [between us and them], as Chrysippus says in book one of *On Justice* and Posidonius in book one of *On Appropriate Action*. And that the wise man will fall in love with young men who reveal through their appearance a natural aptitude for virtue, as Zeno says in the *Republic* and Chrysippus in book one of *On Ways of Life* and Apollodorus in his *Ethics*.

130. And sexual love is an effort to gain friendship resulting from the appearance of beauty; and it is not directed at intercourse, but at friendship. At any rate Thrasonides, although he had his beloved in his power, kept his hands off her because she hated him. So sexual love is directed at friendship, as Chrysippus says in his *On Sexual Love*; and it is not to be blamed; and youthful beauty is the flower of virtue.

There being three ways of life, the theoretical, the practical, and the rational, they say that the third is to be chosen; for the rational animal was deliberately made by nature for theory and action. And they say that the wise man will commit suicide reasonably [i.e., for a good reason], both on behalf of his fatherland and on behalf of his friends, and if he should be in very severe pain or is mutilated or has an incurable disease.

131. They think the wise men should have their wives in common, so that anyone might make love to any woman, as Zeno says in the *Republic* and Chrysippus says in his *On the Republic*; and again, so do Diogenes the Cynic and Plato. And we shall cherish all the children equally, like fathers, and the jealousy occasioned by adultery will be removed. The

best form of government is that which is a blend of democracy and monarchy and aristocracy.

And this is the sort of thing they say in their ethical opinions, and even more than this, together with the accompanying proofs. But let this be our summary and elementary account.

John Stobaeus *Anthology* 2, 5–12 [II-95] (pp. 57–116 W-H.)

5. The views of Zeno and the rest of the Stoics about the ethical part of philosophy.

5a. Zeno says that whatever participates in substance exists, and that of things which exist some are good, some bad and some indifferent. Good are things like this: prudence, temperance, justice, courage, and everything which either is virtue or participates in virtue. Bad are things like this: imprudence, wantonness, injustice, cowardice and everything which either is vice or participates in vice. Indifferent are things like this: life and death, good and bad reputation, pleasure and pain, wealth and poverty, health and disease, and things similar to these.

5b. Of goods, some are virtues, some are not. Prudence, then, and temperance ⟨and justice⟩ and courage ⟨and great-heartedness and strength of body and soul⟩ are virtues; joy and good spirits and confidence and wish and such things are not virtues. Of virtues, some are kinds of knowledge of certain things and crafts, and some are not. Prudence, then, and temperance and justice and courage are kinds of knowledge of certain things and crafts; great-heartedness and strength of body and soul are neither kinds of knowledge of certain things nor crafts. Analogously, of bad things some are vices and some are not. Imprudence, then, and injustice and cowardice and pusillanimity and powerlessness are vices; pain and fear and such things are not vices. Of vices, some are kinds of ignorance of certain things and the absence of skill, some are not. Imprudence, then, and wantonness and injustice and cowardice are kinds of ignorance of certain things and the absence of skill. Pusillanimity and powerlessness ⟨and weakness⟩ are neither kinds of ignorance nor lacks of skill.

5b1. Prudence is knowledge of what one is to do and not to do and what is neither; or the knowledge in a naturally social ⟨and rational⟩ animal of good things, bad things and what is neither (and they say that this [definition] is to be understood [to apply] in the case of the rest of the virtues too). Temperance is knowledge of what is to be chosen and avoided and what is neither. Justice is knowledge of the distribution of proper value to each person. Courage is knowledge of what is terrible and what is not terrible and what is neither. Folly is ignorance of good things, bad things and what is neither, or ignorance of what one is to do and not to do and what is neither. Wantonness is ignorance of what is worth choosing and worth avoiding and what is neither. ⟨Injustice is ignorance of the distribution of proper value to each person⟩. Cowardice is ignorance of what is terrible and what is not terrible and what is neither. They define the other virtues and vices similarly, following what has been said.

5b2. Of virtues some are primary, some subordinate to the primary. There are four primary virtues: prudence, temperance, courage, justice. And prudence concerns appropriate acts; temperance concerns man's impulses; courage concerns instances of standing firm; justice concerns distributions. Of those subordinate to these, some are subordinate to prudence, some to temperance, some to courage, some to justice. To prudence are subordinate: deliberative excellence, good calculation, quick-wittedness, good sense, ⟨a good sense of purpose⟩, resourcefulness. To temperance: organization, orderliness, modesty, self-control. To courage: endurance, confidence, great-heartedness, stout-heartedness, love of work. To justice: piety, good-heartedness, public-spiritedness, fair-dealing. They say, then, that deliberative excellence is a knowledge of the type and manner of actions which we must perform in order to act advantageously; good calculation is knowledge which draws up a balance and summarizes [the value of] what happens and is produced; quick-wittedness is knowledge which instantly finds out what the appropriate action is; good sense is knowledge ⟨of what is better and worse; a good sense of purpose is knowledge⟩ which achieves its goal in each action; resourcefulness is knowledge which discovers a way out of difficulties; organization is knowledge of when one is to act and what [to do] after what, and in general of the ordering of actions; orderliness is ⟨knowledge⟩ of appropriate and inappropriate motions; modesty is knowledge which is cautious about proper criticism; self-control is an unsurpassable knowledge of what is revealed by right reason; endurance is knowledge which stands by correct decisions; confidence is knowledge in virtue of which we know that we shall meet with nothing which is terrible; great-heartedness is knowledge which makes one superior to those things which naturally occur among both virtuous and base men; stout-heartedness is knowledge in a soul which makes it [the soul] invincible; love of work is a knowledge which achieves its goal by labour, not being deterred by hard work; piety is knowledge of service to the gods; good-heartedness is knowledge which does good [to others]; public-spiritedness is knowledge of fairness in a community; fair-dealing is knowledge of how to deal with one's neighbours blamelessly.

5b3. The goal of all these virtues is to live consistently with nature. Each one enables man to achieve this [goal] in its own way; for [man] has from nature inclinations to discover what is appropriate and to stabilize his impulses and to stand firm and to distribute [fairly]. And each of the virtues does what is consonant [with these inclinations] and does its own job, thus enabling man to live consistently with nature.

5b4. They say, then, that these virtues just listed are perfect in our lives and consist of theorems; but others supervene on them, which are no longer crafts but rather certain capabilities which come as a result of practice; for example, health of the soul and its soundness and strength and beauty. For just as the health of the body is a good blend of the hot and cold and wet and dry elements in the body, so too the health of the soul is a good blend of the beliefs in the soul. And similarly, just as strength of the body is a sufficient tension in the sinews, so too the strength of the soul is a sufficient tension in judging and acting and in not doing so. And just as beauty of the body is a symmetry of its limbs constituted with respect to each other and to the whole, so too the beauty of the soul is a symmetry of reason and its parts with respect to the whole of it and to each other.

5b5. All the virtues which are forms of knowledge and crafts have common theorems and the same goal, as was said; and consequently they are inseparable; for he who has one has them all, and he who acts with one virtue acts with all. They differ from each other in their topics. For the topics of prudence are, in the first instance, considering and doing what is to be done, and in the second instance considering what one should distribute ⟨and what one should choose and what one should endure⟩, for the sake of doing what is to be done without error. The topic of temperance is, in the first instance, to make the impulses stable and to consider them, and in the second instance [to consider] the topics of the other virtues, for the sake of behaving without error in one's impulses; and similarly courage in the first instance [considers] everything which one should endure and in the second instance the topics of the other virtues; and justice in the first instance looks to what is due to each person, and in the second instance the other topics too. For all the virtues consider the topics of all [the virtues] and those which are subordinate to each other. For Panaetius used to say that what happened in the case of the virtues was like what would happen if there were one target set up for many archers and this target had on it lines which differed in colour; and then each man were to aim at hitting the target—one by striking the white line, it might be, another by striking the black and another by striking another coloured line. For just as these [archers] make their highest goal the hitting of the target, but each sets before himself a different manner of hitting it, in the same way too all the virtues make being happy their goal (and this lies in living in agreement with nature) but each [virtue] achieves this in a different manner.

5b6. Diogenes [of Babylon] says that there are two senses of 'things worth choosing for their own sake and worth choosing in the final sense':[42] those set out in the previous division and those which have in themselves the cause of being worth choosing (and this is a property of every good thing).

5b7. They say that there are several virtues and that they are inseparable from each other. And that in substance they are identical with the leading part of the soul; accordingly, [they say] that every virtue is and is called a body; for the intellect and the soul are bodies. For they believe that the inborn *pneuma* in us, which is warm, is soul. And they also want [to claim] that the soul in us is an animal, since it lives and has sense-perception; and especially so the leading part of it, which is called intellect. That is why every virtue too is an animal, since in substance it is the same as the intellect; accordingly, they say also that prudence acts prudently. For it is consistent for them to speak thus.

5b8. There is nothing between virtue and vice. For all men have from nature inclinations towards virtue and, according to Cleanthes, are like half-lines of iambic verse; hence, if they remain incomplete they are base, but if they are completed [or: perfected] they are virtuous. They also say that the wise man does everything in accordance with all the virtues; for his every action is perfect, and so is bereft of none of the virtues.

5b9. Consistently with this they hold also that he [the wise man] acts with good sense and dialectically and sympotically and erotically; but the erotic man is so called in two senses, the one who is virtuous and gets his quality from virtue, and the one who is blamed, who gets his quality from vice—a sort of sex-fiend. And sexual love is . . . . [There is a lacuna here.] And being worthy of sexual love means the same as being worthy of friendship and not the same as being worthy of being enjoyed;[43] for

---

42. *telika*, which probably means 'having the character of an ultimate goal'. The two senses seem to be a narrow sense, which applies only to the virtues (below at 5g the virtues are again said to be *telika* as well as instrumental) and a broader sense which includes all good things, even the prudent man and the friend excluded from this category at 5g. We dissent from Wachsmuth-Hense's correction of the the evidently corrupt text and follow Heeren's emendation.

43. See II-94 (D.L. 7.130).

he who is worthy of virtuous sexual love is [properly] worthy of sexual love. They understand virtue exercised at a symposium as similar to virtue in sexual matters, the one being knowledge which is concerned with what is appropriate at a symposium, viz. of how one should run symposia and how one should drink at them; and the other is knowledge of how to hunt for talented young boys, which encourages them to virtuous knowledge; and in general, knowledge of proper sexual activity. That is why they say that the sensible man will engage in sexual activity. And sexual activity just by itself is an indifferent, since at times it also occurs among base men. But sexual love is not desire nor is it directed at any base object, but is an effort to gain friendship resulting from the appearance of beauty.

5b10. And they also say that the wise man does everything which he does well; obviously. For in the sense that we say that the flute player or kithara player does everything well, it being understood that we refer to what the one does in his flute playing and the other in his kithara playing, in the same sense we say that the prudent man does everything well, both what he does and, by Zeus, what he does not do too.[44] For they thought that the opinion that the wise man does everything well follows from his accomplishing everything in accordance with right reason and, as it were, in accordance with virtue, which is a craft concerned with one's entire life. Analogously, the base man too does everything which he does badly and in accordance with all the vices.

5b11. They call 'practices' the love of music, of letters, of horses, of hunting, and, broadly speaking, the so-called general crafts; they are not knowledge, but they leave them in the class of virtuous conditions, and consistently they say that only the wise man is a music lover and a lover of letters, and analogously in the other cases. They give an outline [definition] of a 'practice' as follows: a method using a craft or some part [of a craft] which leads [us] to what is in accord with virtue.

5b12. They say that only the wise man is a good prophet and poet and public speaker and dialectician and critic, but not every [wise man], since some of these [crafts] also require a mastery of certain theorems. And prophecy is a theoretical knowledge of signs significant for human life given by the gods or daimons. The forms of prophecy are similarly [described].

They say that only the wise man is a priest, but that no base man is.

---

44. The text is corrupt here and we translate the emendation of Hense; with their own emendation Long and Sedley (*The Hellenistic Philosophers* [Cambridge 1987] vol. 1, 61G1 p. 380) translate: "does everything well, so far as concerns what he does, and not of course also what he does not do."

For the priest must be experienced in the laws concerning sacrifices and prayers and purifications and foundations and all such things, and in addition he also needs ritual sanctity and piety and experience of service to the gods and [needs] to be intimate with the nature of divinity. And the base man has not one of these features, and that is why all imprudent men are impious. For impiety, being a vice, is ignorance of the service to the gods, while piety is, as we said, a knowledge of service to the gods.

Similarly they say that the base are not holy either; for holiness is defined in outline as justice towards the gods, while the base deviate in many respects from just action towards the gods, which is why they are unholy and impure and unsanctified and defiled and to be barred from festivals.

For they say that participating at a festival is a [prerogative] of the virtuous man, a festival being a time in which one should be concerned with the divine for the sake of honouring [the gods] and for the sake of the appropriate observations; and that is why the participant in a festival should accommodate [himself] to this sort of role with piety.

5b13. Again, they say that every base man is mad, being ignorant of himself and his own concerns; and that is madness. And ignorance is the vice opposite to prudence; and a certain relative disposition of this, which makes one's impulses unstable and fluttery, is madness. That is why they give an outline [definition] of madness as follows: a fluttery ignorance.

5c. Again, of good things, some are attributes of all prudent men all the time, and some are not. Every virtue and prudent sense-perception and prudent impulse and the like are attributes of all prudent men on every occasion; but joy and good spirits and prudent walking are not attributes of all prudent men and not all the time. Analogously, of bad things too, some are attributes of all imprudent men all the time, and some are not. Every vice and imprudent sense-perception and imprudent impulse and the like are attributes of all imprudent men all the time; but pain and fear and imprudent answering are not attributes of all imprudent men and not on every occasion.

5d. All good things are beneficial and well-used and advantageous and profitable and virtuous and fitting and honourable and congenial; conversely, all bad things are harmful and ill-used and disadvantageous and unprofitable and base and unfitting and shameful and uncongenial.

They say that 'good' is used in many senses; the primary sense, which plays a role like that of a source [for the other senses], is that which is stated as follows: that from which it characteristically results that one is benefitted or he by whom [it results that one is benefitted] (and what is good in the primary sense is the cause). The second sense is that in accordance with which it characteristically results that one is benefitted.

A more general sense and one extending also to the previous cases is: that which is such as to benefit. Similarly, the bad too is defined in outline by analogy with the good: that from which or by whom it characteristically results that one is harmed; and that in accordance with which it characteristically results that one is harmed; more general than these is that which is such as to harm.

5e. Of good things, some are in the soul, some external, and some neither in the soul nor external. In the soul are the virtues and ⟨the⟩ virtuous conditions and in general praiseworthy activities. External are friends and acquaintances and things like that. Neither in the soul nor external are virtuous men and in general those who have the virtues. Similarly, of bad things, some are in the soul, some external, and some neither in the soul nor external. In the soul are the vices together with wicked conditions and in general blameworthy activities. External are enemies together with their various forms. Neither in the soul nor external are base men and all those who have the vices.

5f. Of the goods in the soul, some are dispositions, some are conditions but not dispositions, and some are neither conditions nor dispositions. All the virtues are dispositions, while practices are only conditions but not dispositions, for example, prophecy and the like. Virtuous activities, for example, prudent action and the possession of temperance and the like, are neither conditions nor dispositions. Similarly, of the bad things in the soul, some are dispositions, some are conditions but not dispositions, and some are neither conditions nor dispositions. All the vices are dispositions, while tendencies, such as enviousness, resentfulness and such things, are only conditions and not dispositions; so too for diseases and ailments, such as greed, love of drink, and the like. Vicious activities such as imprudent action, unjust action and things like that are neither conditions nor dispositions.

5g. Of good things, some are final, some are instrumental, and some are both. For the prudent man and one's friend are only instrumental goods, but joy and good spirits and confidence and prudent walking are only final goods; all the virtues are both instrumental and final goods, since they both produce happiness and fulfil it, becoming parts of it. Analogously, of bad things some are instrumental to unhappiness, some are final, and some are both. For the imprudent man and one's enemy are only instrumental bad things, but pain and fear and theft and imprudent questioning and similar things ⟨are only⟩ final ⟨bad things⟩; the vices are both instrumental and final bad things, since they produce unhappiness and fulfil it, becoming parts of it.

5h. Again, of good things some are worth choosing for their own sakes, while some are instrumental; all those which are subject to reasonable

choice for the sake of nothing else are worth choosing for their own
sakes, while those [which are subject to reasonable choice] because they
produce other things are said [to be worth choosing] in the instrumental sense.

5i. And every good is worth choosing; for it is pleasing, and approved
of and praiseworthy. And every bad thing is worth avoiding. For the
good, in so far as it stimulates reasonable choice, is worth choosing; and
in so far as it is subject to choice without suspicion, it is pleasing . . .
[There is a lacuna here.] . . . and, moreover, in so far as one would
reasonably suppose that it is one of the products of virtue, ⟨it is praise-
worthy⟩.

5k. Again, of good things some consist in motion and some consist in
a state. For such things as joy, good spirits and temperate conversation
consist in motion, while such things as a well-ordered quietude, undisturbed rest and a manly attention consist in a state. Of things which
consist in a state, some also consist in a condition, such as the virtues;
others are only in a state, such as the above-mentioned. Not only the
virtues consist in a condition, but also the crafts which are transformed
in the virtuous man by his virtue and so become unchangeable; for they
become quasi-virtues. And they say that the so-called practices are also
among the goods which consist in a condition, such as love of music,
love of letters, love of geometry, and the like. For there is a method
which selects those elements in such crafts which are congenial to virtue
by referring them to the goal of life.

5l. Again, of good things, some are [things which exist] in themselves
and some are relative dispositions. Knowledge, just action, and similar
things are [things which exist] in themselves. Honour, good will, friendship and ⟨agreement⟩ are relative. And knowledge is a grasp which is
secure and unchangeable by argument; another definition: knowledge is a
complex system of grasps of this sort, such as knowledge of the particulars,
which is, in the virtuous man, rational; another definition: a complex
system of craftsmanlike knowledge, which provides its own stability,
which is what the virtues are like; another definition: a condition receptive
of presentations which is unchangeable by argument, which they say
consists in a tension and power [of the soul]. Friendship is a community
of life. Agreement is a sharing of opinions about things relevant to life.
Within friendship, familiarity is friendship with people who are well
known to you; habituation is friendship with people you have become
accustomed to; companionship is friendship by choice, such as that with
one's contemporaries; guest-friendship is friendship with foreigners; there
is also a kind of family friendship between relatives; and an erotic friendship based on sexual love. And painlessness and organization are the

same as temperance, just as insight and wits are [the same] as prudence and sharing and generosity are [the same] as good-heartedness; for they have been given names by reference to their relative dispositions. And one must note this too in each of the other virtues.

5m. Again, of good things, some are unmixed, such as knowledge, while others are mixed, such as having good children, a good old age, a good life. Having good children is the natural and virtuous possession of children; good old age is the natural and virtuous use of old age; and similarly for a good life.

5n. It is always clear in these cases that there will be similar divisions of [the corresponding] bad things.

5o. They say that what is worth choosing and what is worth taking are different. For what stimulates an unconditional impulse is worth choosing, ⟨while what is worth taking is what we reasonably select⟩. In so far as what is worth choosing differs from what is worth taking, to the same degree what is in itself worth choosing differs from what is in itself worth taking, and in general for what is good by comparison with what has value.

6. Since man is a rational, mortal animal, social by nature, they say also that all human virtue and happiness constitute a life which is consistent and in agreement with nature.

6a. Zeno defined the goal thus: 'living in agreement'. This means living according to a single and consonant rational principle, since those who live in conflict are unhappy. Those who came after him made further distinctions and expressed it thus: 'living in agreement with nature', supposing that Zeno's formulation was an incomplete predicate. For Cleanthes, who first inherited [the leadership of] his school, added 'with nature' and defined it thus: 'the goal is living in agreement with nature'. Chrysippus wanted to make this clearer and expressed it in this way: 'to live according to experience of the things which happen by nature.' And Diogenes: 'to be reasonable in the selection and rejection of natural things'. And Archedemus: 'to live completing all the appropriate acts'. And Antipater: 'to live invariably selecting natural things and rejecting unnatural things'. He often defined it thus as well: 'invariably and unswervingly to do everything in one's power for the attainment of the principal natural things'.

6b. 'Goal' is used in three senses by the members of this school: for the final good is said to be the goal in standard scholarly language, as when they say that agreement is the goal; and they say that the target is the goal, for example, they speak of the life in agreement by reference to the associated predicate; in the third sense they say that the ultimate object of striving is a goal, to which all others are referred.

6c. They think that the goal and the target are different. For the target is the physical state [lit. body] set up [for people] to try to achieve . . . [lacuna] . . . those who aim at happiness, since every virtuous man is happy and every base man is, by contrast, unhappy.

6d. And of good things, some are necessary for happiness and some are not. And all the virtues and the activities which employ them are necessary; joy and good spirits and the practices are not necessary. Similarly, of bad things some are necessary, as being bad, for the existence of unhappiness, and some are not necessary. All the vices and the activities based on them are necessary; all the passions and ailments and things like this are not necessary.

6e. They say that being happy is the goal for the sake of which everything is done and that it is itself done for the sake of nothing else; and this consists in living according to virtue, in living in agreement, and again (which is the same thing) in living according to nature. Zeno defined happiness in this manner: 'happiness is a smooth flow of life'. Cleanthes too used this definition in his treatises, and so did Chrysippus and all their followers, saying that happiness was no different from the happy life, although they do say that while happiness is set up as a target, the goal is to *achieve* happiness, which is the same as being happy.

So it is clear from this that [these expressions] are equivalent: 'living according to nature' and 'living honourably' and 'living well' and again 'the honourable and good' and 'virtue and what participates in virtue'; and that every good thing is honourable and similarly that every shameful thing is bad. That is also why the Stoic goal is equivalent to the life according to virtue.

6f. They say that what is worth choosing differs from what is to be chosen. For every good is worth choosing, but every advantage is to be chosen, and [advantage] is understood with reference to having the good. That is why we choose what is to be chosen, for example being prudent, which is understood with reference to having prudence; but we do not choose what is worth choosing, but if anything, we choose to have it.

Similarly too all goods are worth enduring [for] and worth standing firmly by, and analogously in the case of the other virtues, even if there is no name for them. And all advantages are to be endured [for] and to be stood firmly by. And in the same manner for the others which are in accordance with the vices.

7. After giving a sufficient account of good things and bad things and what is worth choosing and what is worth avoiding and the goal and happiness, we think it necessary to go through in their proper order what is said about things indifferent. They say that things indifferent are

between good things and bad things, saying that the indifferent is conceived of in two ways: in one way it is what is neither good nor bad nor worth choosing nor worth avoiding; in the other it is what is stimulative of impulse neither towards nor away from [itself]. In this sense some are said to be absolutely indifferent, such as ⟨having an odd or even number of hairs on one's head, or⟩ extending one's finger this way or that way, or to picking off some annoying object, such as a twig or a leaf. In the first sense one must say that, according to the members of this school, what is between virtue and vice is indifferent, but not [indifferent] with respect to selection and rejection; and that is why some have selective value, and some have rejective disvalue, but make no contribution at all to the happy life.

7a. And some are natural, some unnatural and some neither unnatural nor natural. Natural, then, are such things: health, strength, soundness of one's sense organs, and things like this. Unnatural are such things: disease, weakness, impairment and such things. Neither unnatural nor natural are: a stable condition of soul and body according to which the one is receptive of false presentations and the other receptive of wounds and impairments; and things like these. They say that the account of these matters is based on the primary natural and unnatural things. For what makes a difference and the indifferent are relative. That is why, they say, even if we say that bodily matters and external things are indifferent, we [also] say that they are indifferent with respect to living a beautifully ordered life (and in this consists a happy life), but not, by Zeus, [indifferent] with respect to being in a natural state nor with respect to impulse towards or away from [something].

7b. Again, of indifferent things, some have more value and others have less; and some are [valuable] in themselves and some instrumentally; and some are preferred and some are rejected, and some neither. Preferred are all things indifferent which have a lot of value as indifferents; rejected are all things indifferent which have a lot of disvalue, in the same sense; neither preferred nor indifferent are all which have neither a lot of value nor a lot of disvalue.

Of preferred things, some are in the soul, some in the body, and some external. In the soul are things like this: natural ability, [moral] progress, good memory, mental sharpness, a condition which enables one to stand firm in appropriate actions, and the crafts which can contribute substantially to the natural life. Preferred things in the body are health, good sense-perception, and things like these. Among externals are parents, children, possessions in due measure, acceptance among men.

The opposites of those mentioned are rejected things in the soul; [rejected things] in the body and externally are those which are similarly opposed to the above-mentioned preferred things in the body and externally.

Neither preferred nor rejected in the soul are presentation, assent and things like that; in the body: fair or dark complexion, having blue eyes and all pleasure and pain and anything else of this sort; in external things what is neither preferred ⟨nor rejected⟩ are things like this: whatever, being cheap and bringing nothing useful, provides by itself an utterly tiny amount of usefulness.

Since the soul is more important than the body, they also say that the things of the soul which are natural and preferred have more value for the natural life than bodily and external things; for example, natural ability in the soul is more helpful for virtue than natural ability in the body, and similarly for the others.

7c. Again, of things indifferent, they say that some are stimulative of impulse towards [themselves], some stimulative of impulse away from [themselves], and some stimulative of impulse neither towards nor away from [themselves]. Those things which we said are natural are stimulative of impulse towards [themselves]; those which are unnatural are stimulative of impulse away from [themselves]; those which are neither are stimulative of impulse neither towards nor away from [themselves]; for example, having an odd or even number of hairs.

7d. Of things which are indifferent and natural, some are primary natural things, some natural by participation. Primary natural things are a motion or state which occurs in accordance with the spermatic principles, such as ⟨soundness and⟩ health and sense-perception (I mean an act of grasping) and strength. By participation: everything which participates in a motion or state which is in accordance with the spermatic principles, for example, a sound hand and a healthy body and senses which are not impaired. Similarly, for the unnatural things [the situation is] analogous.

7e. Everything which is natural is worth taking and everything which is ⟨un⟩natural is worth not taking. Of natural things, some are worth taking in themselves, some because of other things. In themselves: everything which is stimulative of impulse in such a manner as to encourage [someone] to pursue it or to hang on to it, such as health, good sense perception, freedom from pain, bodily beauty. Instrumentally: everything which is stimulative of impulse by reference to other things and not in such a manner as to encourage [someone to pursue] it, such as wealth, reputation, and things like these. Similarly, of unnatural things some are in themselves not worth taking and some because they are instrumental to things which are in themselves not worth taking.

7f. Everything which is natural has value and everything which is unnatural has disvalue. Value has three senses: [1] the estimation and honour [for something] in itself, and [2] the exchange-value of its appraised worth; and [3] third what Antipater calls selective value, according to which when circumstances permit we choose these things rather than those, for example, health rather than disease and life rather than death and wealth rather than poverty. Analogously, they also say that disvalue has three senses, if one inverts the senses [of the definitions] given for the three kinds of value.

Diogenes says that the 'estimation' is a judgement of the extent to which something is natural or provides something useful to nature. 'Appraised worth' is not interpreted in the sense in which the things [themselves] are said to have 'appraised worth', but as we say that he who puts an appraisal on things is the 'appraiser'. For he says that such a man is the 'appraiser' of exchange-value. And these are the two [senses of] value according to which we say that something is preferred in value, and he says that the third is that according to which we say that something has valuable merit and value, which does not apply to things indifferent but only to virtuous things. He says that we sometimes use the word 'value' in place of 'what is fitting', as it was used in the definition of justice when it is said to be a condition which distributes to each person what is accordance with his value; for this is like saying 'what is fitting' for each person.

7g. Of things which have value, some have a lot of value, some have little. Similarly, of things which have disvalue, some have a lot of disvalue, some have little. Those which have a lot of value are called preferred things, while those which have a lot of disvalue are called rejected, Zeno being the first one to apply these terms to the things. They say that the preferred is that which, being indifferent, we select in accordance with the principal reason. The same kind of account applies to what is rejected, and the examples are the same by analogy. None of the good things is preferred, since they have the greatest value. The preferred, which holds the second rank and has value, is in a way close to the nature of good things. For at a court the king is not among those who are preferred, but those below him in rank are. They are called preferred, not because they contribute to happiness and help to produce it, but because it is necessary to select them in preference to the rejected things.

8. The topic of appropriate action follows [naturally] on the discussion of the preferred things. Appropriate action is defined [thus]: 'what is consistent in life, which when done admits of a reasonable defence'. What is contrary to the appropriate is the opposite. This extends even to irrational animals, for they too do thing[s] consistently with their nature. In rational animals it is expressed thus: 'what is consistent in a life'. And

of appropriate actions, some are complete [or perfect], and they are
called [morally] perfect actions. [Morally] perfect actions are activities
in accordance with virtue, such as being prudent and acting justly. Things
which are not of this character are not [morally] perfect actions, and they
do not call them complete appropriate actions either, but intermediate
ones, such as getting married, going on an embassy, engaging in dialectic,
and similar things.

8a. Of [morally] perfect actions some are requirements and some not.
Requirements are advantages, expressed in predicate form, such as being
prudent and being temperate. Things which are not of this character are
not requirements. The same technical distinctions apply similarly to
inappropriate actions.

Every inappropriate action which occurs in a rational ⟨animal⟩ is a
[moral] mistake; and an appropriate action when perfected [or completed]
is a [morally] perfect action. The intermediate appropriate action is
measured by [reference to] certain indifferent things, which are selected
according to or contrary to nature, and which bring prosperity of such
a sort that if we were not to take them or were to reject them, except
under abnormal circumstances, we would not be happy.

9. They say that what stimulates impulse is nothing but a hormetic
presentation of what is obviously [or: immediately] appropriate. And
impulse is, in general, a movement of the soul towards something. The
impulse occurring in rational animals and that in irrational animals are
understood to be its forms. But they have not been named. For striving
is not rational impulse but a form of rational impulse. And one would
properly define rational impulse by saying that it is a movement of
intellect towards something which is involved in action. Opposed to this
is an impulse away from [something], a movement ⟨of intellect away from
something involved in action.⟩ They say in a special sense too that
planning is impulse, being a form of practical impulse. And planning is
a movement of intellect to something in the future.

So, thus far impulse is used in four senses, and impulse away from
in two. When you add the hormetic condition too, which indeed they
also call impulse in a special sense, and which is the source of the active
impulse, then 'impulse' is [seen to be] used in five senses.

9a. There are several forms of practical impulse, among which are
these: purpose, effort, preparation, endeavour, ⟨choice,⟩ forechoice, wish,
wanting. So they say that purpose is an indication of accomplishment;
effort is an impulse before an impulse; preparation is an action before
an action; endeavour is an impulse in the case of something already in
hand; choice is wish based on analogy; forechoice is a choice before a
choice; wish is a rational striving; wanting is a voluntary wish.

9b. All impulses are [acts of] assent; ⟨there are other kinds of assent⟩,[45] but the practical ones also include the power to set [the agent] in motion. Now, [acts of] assent are directed at one thing and impulses at another; and [acts of] assent are directed at certain propositions, while impulses are directed at predicates which are, in a way, included in the propositions to which assent is given.

Since passion is a form of impulse, let us speak next about the passions.

10. They say that a passion is an impulse which is excessive and disobedient to the reason which constrains, or an ⟨irrational⟩, unnatural motion of the soul (and all passions belong to the leading part of the soul). And that is why every 'flutter' is a passion ⟨and⟩ again ⟨every⟩ passion is a 'flutter'. Since this is what a passion is like, one must suppose that some are primary and principal, and the others are referred to these. The primary are these four kinds: desire, fear, pain, and pleasure. Desire and fear, then, are principal, one [being concerned with] the apparent good, the other with the apparent bad. Pleasure and pain supervene on these, pleasure when we achieve what we desired or escape what we were afraid of; pain when we miss achieving what we desired or meet with what we were afraid of. With all the passions of the soul, since they say that they are opinions, the [word] opinion is used instead of 'weak supposition', and 'fresh' is used instead of 'what stimulates irrational contraction ⟨or⟩ elation'.

10a. The terms 'irrational' and 'unnatural' are not used in their common senses, but 'irrational' means the same as 'disobedient to reason'. For every passion is violent, since those who are in a state of passion often see that it is advantageous not to do this, but are swept away by the vehemence [of the passion], as though by some disobedient horse, and are drawn to doing it; in this connection people often concede [that this is going on] when they cite that familiar tag:[46] "Nature compels me, though I am aware [of what I am doing]". For he here calls the realization and consciousness of what is right "awareness". And the term 'unnatural' was used in the outline [definition] of passion, since it is something which happens contrary to the right and natural reason. Everyone in a state of passion turns his back on reason, not like those who are deceived on some point or other, but in a special sense. For those who are deceived, about atoms being principles for instance, when they are taught that they do not exist, then abandon their belief. But those who are in a state of passion, even if they do learn and are taught that one should not suffer

---

45. For the suggested supplement see B. Inwood, *Ethics and Action in Early Stoicism* (Oxford 1985) pp. 287–288 n. 271.

46. Euripides fr. 837 Nauck.

pain or fear or generally experience any of the passions of the soul, still
do not abandon them but are drawn by the passions into being dominated
by their tyrannical rule.

10b. They say, then, that desire is a striving which is disobedient to
reason; its cause is believing that a good is approaching, and that when
it is here we shall do well by it; this opinion itself ⟨that it really is worth
striving for⟩ has a ⟨fresh⟩ [power] to stimulate irregular motion. Fear is
an avoidance disobedient to reason, and its cause is believing that a bad
thing is approaching; this opinion that it really is worth avoiding has a
'fresh' [power] to stimulate motion. Pain is a contraction of the soul
disobedient to reason, and its cause is believing that a 'fresh' bad thing
is present, for which it is appropriate to ⟨suffer contraction [in the soul].
Pleasure is an elation of the soul disobedient to reason, and its cause is
believing that a fresh good thing is present, for which it is appropriate
to⟩ suffer elation [in the soul].

Under desire are subsumed such [passions] as these: anger and its
forms (spiritedness and irascibility and wrath and rancour and bitterness
and such things), vehement sexual desire and longing and yearning and
love of pleasure and love of wealth and love of reputation and similar
things. Under pleasure are mean-spirited satisfaction, contentment,
charms, and similar things. Under fear are hesitation, agony, shock,
shame, panic, superstition, fright, and dread. Under pain are envy, grudging, resentment, pity, grief, heavy-heartedness, distress, sorrow, anguish,
and vexation.

10c. Anger, then, is a desire to take revenge on someone who appears
to have wronged [you] contrary to what is appropriate; spiritedness is
anger just beginning; irascibility is swollen anger; wrath is anger laid by
or saved up for a long time; rancour is anger which watches for an
opportunity for vengeance; bitterness is anger which breaks out immediately; sexual desire is an effort to gain love resulting from the appearance
of [physical] beauty; longing is a sexual love for someone who is absent;
yearning is a desire for contact with a friend who is absent; love of
pleasure is a desire for pleasures; love of wealth [is a desire] for wealth;
love of reputation for reputation.

Mean-spirited satisfaction is pleasure at someone else's misfortunes;
contentment is pleasure at what is unexpected; charm is deceptive pleasure
which comes via vision.

Hesitation is a fear of future action; agony is a fear of failure or,
otherwise, a fear of defeat; shock is a fear arising from a presentation of
something unfamiliar; shame is a fear of bad reputation; panic is fear
which hastens with the voice; superstition is a fear of gods and daimons;

fright is a fear of something dreadful; dread is a fear which produces fright.[47]

Grudging is a pain at the goods of other people; envy is a pain at the other fellow getting what one desires oneself, and not getting it oneself; there is another sense of 'envy' [zeal], i.e., the congratulation of someone who is [there is a corrupt word here] or the imitation of someone thought of as better [than oneself]; resentment is a pain at the other fellow also getting what one desired oneself; pity is a pain at someone's seeming to suffer undeservedly; grief is a pain at an untimely death; heavy-heartedness is a pain which weighs one down; distress is a pain which makes one unable to speak; sorrow is a pain which comes by brooding [on something]; anguish is a pain which penetrates and settles in; vexation is a pain accompanied by tossing about.

10d. Of these passions, some indicate the object they are concerned with, such as pity, grudging, mean-spirited satisfaction, shame; some indicate the peculiar qualities of the motion, such as anguish and dread.

10e. A predisposition is a tendency towards [having a] passion, such as one of the activities contrary to nature; for example, proneness to pain, proneness to grudging, proneness to irascibility, and similar things. There are also predispositions to other activities which are contrary to nature, such as to theft and adultery and arrogant behaviour; it is in virtue of these that people are said to become thieves, adulterers and arrogant men. A disease is an opinion connected to a desire which has settled and hardened into a condition, in virtue of which people think that things not worth choosing are extremely worth choosing; for example, love of women, love of wine, love of money; there are also certain states opposite to ⟨these⟩ diseases which turn up as antipathies, such as hatred of women, hatred of wine, hatred of mankind. Those diseases which occur in conjunction with weakness are called ailments.

11a. They say that a [morally] perfect action is an appropriate action which covers all the features,[48] or as we said before, a complete [perfect] appropriate action. What is done contrary to right reason is a [moral] mistake; or, an [action] in which something appropriate has been omitted by a rational animal [is a moral mistake].

11b. They say that all good things belong ⟨in common⟩ to the virtuous, in that he who benefits one of his neighbours also benefits himself. Concord is a knowledge of common goods, and that is why all virtuous men are in concord with each other, because they are in agreement about

47. Restored from D.L. 7.112.
48. Literally "numbers".

matters concerned with life. The base are enemies and do harm to each other and are hostile, because they are in discord with each other. They say that justice exists by nature and not by convention. Consequent on this is [the belief] that the wise man participates in political life, especially in the sort of governments which show some [moral] progress towards becoming perfect governments. Again, it is congenial to the virtuous to legislate and to educate men and again to compose [books] which can help those who encounter their writings; and so are condescending to marry and have children, both for his own sake and for that of his fatherland; and he will endure both pain and death for the sake of [his fatherland], if it is moderate. Juxtaposed to these traits are base ones, courting the people and practicing sophistry and composing books which are harmful to those who read them. These are traits which would not occur in virtuous men.

11c. There are three senses of friendship. In one sense it is for the sake of common benefit that people are said to be friends; this kind of friendship is not that of good men, because for them there is no good which is composed out of separate components. They say that friendship in the second sense, a friendly attitude from one's neighbours, is one of the external goods. They claim that a personal friendship, according to which one *is* a friend of one's neighbours, is one of the goods in the soul.

11d. There is another sense in which all good things are common. For they believe that anyone who benefits anyone, by that very fact, receives equal benefit, but that no base man either benefits or is benefitted. For benefitting is ⟨to change⟩ or maintain something in accordance with virtue and being benefitted is to be changed in accordance with virtue.

They say that only the virtuous man is a household economist and a good household economist, and again a money-maker. For household economy is a condition which contemplates and practices what is advantageous to a household; and economy is an arranging of expenditures and tasks and a care for possessions and for the work that is done on the farm. And money-making is experience of acquiring money by means of the actions by which one should do so, and a condition which causes one to behave 'in agreement' in the collection and preservation and expenditure of money with the aim of [achieving] prosperity. And some think that money-making is an intermediate [activity], others that it is virtuous. And no base man is a good guardian of a household, nor can he arrange it that a house is well run. And only the virtuous man is a money-maker, since he knows the sources from which one is to get money and when and how and up to what point [one should continue doing so].

They say that ⟨the sensible man⟩ forgives ⟨no one; for it is characteristic of the same man to forgive⟩ and to think that the man who has made a [moral] mistake did not do so because of himself, although [in fact] everyone who makes a [moral] mistake does so because of his own vice. And that is why it is quite proper for them to say that he does not even forgive those who make [moral] mistakes. Nor, they say, is the good man equitable, since the equitable man is prone to ask for a reduction of the punishment which is due; and it is characteristic of the same man to be equitable and to suppose that the punishments established by the law for wrong-doers are too harsh, and to believe that the lawgiver established punishments which are unduly [severe].

They say that the law is virtuous, being right reason which commands what is to be done and forbids what is not to be done. And since the law is virtuous, the lawful man would be virtuous; for he is a man who is lawful and follows the law and does what is commanded by it. He who interprets the law is a man of the law; and none of the base is either lawful or a man of the law.

11e. Again, they say that some activities are [morally] perfect actions, some are [moral] mistakes, and some are neither. [Morally] perfect actions are such things: being prudent, being temperate, acting justly, feeling joy, doing good works, being in good spirits, walking prudently, and everything which is done in accordance with right reason. [Moral] mistakes are: being imprudent, being wanton, unjust action, feeling pain and fear, stealing, and in general whatever is done contrary to right reason. Such things as these are neither [morally] perfect actions nor [moral] mistakes: speaking, asking, answering, walking, going out of town, and similar things. All [morally] perfect actions are just actions and lawful actions and orderly actions and good practices and acts of good fortune and acts of a happy life and opportune actions and beautifully-ordered actions. They are, however, not yet acts of prudence, but only those which are performed on the basis of prudence and similarly for all the other virtues—even if they do not have proper names, such as acts of temperance which are performed on the basis of temperance and acts of justice which are performed on the basis of justice. By contrast, [moral] mistakes are unjust actions and unlawful actions and disorderly actions.

11f. They say that just as there is a difference between what is worth choosing and what is to be chosen, so there is a difference between what is worth striving for and what is to be striven for and what is worth wishing for and what is to be wished for and what is worth accepting and what is to be accepted. For ⟨good things⟩ are worth choosing and wishing for and striving for ⟨and accepting; but advantages are to be chosen and wished for and striven for⟩ and accepted, since they are predicates corresponding to the good things. For we choose what is to be chosen and want what is to be wanted and strive for what is to be striven for. For acts of choice and striving and wishing are directed at predicates, just as impulses are. But we choose and wish, and similarly strive, to *have* good things, which is why good things are worth choosing and wishing for and striving for. For we choose to have prudence and temperance, but not, by Zeus!, being prudent and being temperate, since these are incorporeals and predicates.

Similarly, they say that all goods are worth abiding in and cleaving to and analogously for the other virtues, even if they do not have proper names. But all the advantages and similar things are to be abided in and cleaved to. In the same way they suppose there is a difference between things worth being cautious over and things which one is to be cautious over and things which are not worth abiding in and things which are not to be abided in; the same account applies to the other terms which go with the vices.

11g. They say that every honourable and good man is complete [perfect] because he lacks none of the virtues. The base man, by contrast, is incomplete, since he participates in none of the virtues. That is why good men are always and under all conditions happy, and the base unhappy. And ⟨their⟩ happiness does not differ from divine happiness; and Chrysippus says that momentary [happiness] does not differ from the happiness of Zeus, ⟨and⟩ that the happiness of Zeus is in no respect more worth choosing or more honourable or more majestic that that of wise men.

Zeno and the Stoic philosophers who follow him believe that there are two classes of men, the virtuous and the base. And men of the virtuous class employ all the virtues throughout their entire life, while the base [employ] the vices. Hence, the one group is always [morally] perfect in everything they apply themselves to, but the other group [always] makes [moral] mistakes. And the virtuous man always uses his experience of life in what he does, and so does everything well, insofar [as he acts] prudently and temperately and in accordance with the other virtues. And the base man by contrast [does everything] badly. And the virtuous man is big and powerful and lofty and strong. Big, because he is able to achieve his purposes and aims; powerful, because he is well developed in all respects; lofty, because he participates in the height fitting for a man who is noble and wise; and strong, because he has acquired the fitting strength, being invincible and unbeatable in contests. Accordingly, he is not compelled by anyone nor does he compel anyone; he neither hinders nor is hindered; he is forced by no one and forces no one; he neither dominates nor is dominated; neither harms nor is himself harmed; neither meets with misfortune ⟨nor makes others do so⟩; is neither deluded nor deceives another; is neither deceived nor ignorant nor unaware of himself nor, in general, believes anything which is false. He is happy most of all, and fortunate and blessed and prosperous and pious and god-loving and worthy, like a king and a general, a politician and a household economist and a money-maker. And the base are the opposite of all of these.

In general, the virtuous have all good things and the base have all bad things. One must not suppose that they mean it in this sense: that if there exist good things, they belong to the virtuous, and similarly for the base; but rather [they mean that] they have so many good things that they are in no way lacking with respect to having a perfect [complete] ⟨and happy⟩ life, and the others have so many bad things that their life is incomplete [imperfect] and unhappy.

11h. They call virtue by many names.[49] For they say that it is something good, because it draws us to the correct life. And pleasing, because it is approved of without suspicion; and worth a lot, ⟨because⟩ its value is unsurpassable; and virtuous, for it is worth much virtuous effort; and worthy of praise, for one would be reasonable in praising it; and honourable, because by nature it summons to itself those who strive for it; and advantageous, for it brings the sort of things which contribute to living well; and useful because it is advantageous when used; and worth choosing, for its characteristic results are those things which one would reasonably choose; and necessary, because when it is present it benefits and when it is absent it is not possible to be benefitted; and profitable, for the advantages which come from it are greater than the effort which produces them; and self-sufficient, for it suffices for the man who possesses it; and not lacking, because it removes one from all lack; and it suffices, because when used it is sufficient and applies to every kind of use relevant to one's life.

11i. The base participate in none of the good things, since the good is virtue or what participates in virtue; and the requirements which correspond to the good things, being benefits, occur only in the virtuous; just as the non-requirements corresponding to the bad things [occur] only in the base; for they are forms of harm, and for this reason all good men are free of harm in both senses, unable to either do harm or to suffer it; and conversely for the base.

They say that true wealth is a good thing and that true poverty is a bad thing; and that true freedom is a good thing and true slavery a bad

---

49. Most of these appellations and their explanations exploit fanciful and inimitable etymological connections.

thing. That is why the virtuous man is also the only wealthy and free man, and the base man, conversely, is a pauper (since he is deficient in the requirements for wealth) and a slave (because of his suspect disposition).

All good things are common to the virtuous, and bad things to the base. That is why he who benefits someone else is also benefitted himself, and he who harms someone also harms himself. All virtuous men benefit each other, even though they are not in all cases friends of each other or well disposed [to each other] or in good repute [with each other] or receptive [of each other], because they do not have a [cognitive] grasp of each other and do not live in the same place. They, however, are disposed to be well disposed and to be friendly to each other and to hold [each other] in good repute and to be receptive [of each other]. The imprudent are in a condition opposite to this.

Since the law, as we said, is virtuous (because it is right reason which commands what is to be done and forbids what is not be done), they say that only the wise man is lawful, since he does what is commanded by the law and is the only interpreter of it, and that is why he is a man of the law. And silly men are in the opposite condition.

Again, they also assign to the virtuous the supervisory function of a ruler and its forms: kingship, generalship, naval command, and forms of rule like these. Accordingly, only the virtuous man rules, and even if he does not in all circumstances do so in actuality, still in all circumstances he does so by disposition. And only the virtuous man is obedient, since he is prone to follow a ruler. But none of the imprudent is like this; for the imprudent man is not able either to rule or to be ruled, since he is stubborn and intractable.

The sensible man does everything well, since he continuously makes use of his experience of life in a prudent and self-controlled and orderly and organized fashion. But the base man, since he has no experience of the right use [of things] does everything badly, acting in accordance with the disposition he has, being prone to change [his mind] and seized by regret about each thing [he does]. And regret is [a feeling of] pain [one has] about actions which have been performed, because [of the belief that] they were [moral] mistakes made by oneself; and this is a passion of the soul which produces unhappiness and internal strife. For in so far as the regretful man loathes what has happened, to that extent he is angry at himself for having been responsible for these events. And this is why the base man is dishonoured, since he is neither worthy of honour nor honoured. For honour is worthiness of reward and reward is the prize for virtue which does good for others. Thus what does not participate in virtue would justly be called dishonoured.

They say that every base man is an exile, in so far as he is deprived of law and a naturally fitting government. For the law is, as we said, virtuous and so too is the [corresponding] state. And it was enough that Cleanthes posed this sort of argument about the [claim that] the state [*polis*] is virtuous: If the state is a contrivance for dwelling in which one takes refuge in order to give and receive justice, is not the state a virtuous thing? But the state is such a dwelling place. Therefore, the state is a virtuous thing. And 'state' is used in three senses: as a dwelling place, as a complex system of men, and third as the combination of these two senses. In two of these senses the state is said to be virtuous: as a complex system of men and in the combination [of the two senses], because ⟨of the⟩ [implicit] reference to its inhabitants.

11k. They say that every base man is a boor; for boorishness is inexperience of the habits and laws of the state, and every base man is subject to this. And he is also wild, since he is a man hostile to the lawful way of life, beastlike, and harmful. This same fellow is untamed and tyrannical, having a disposition to perform despotic actions, as well as ferocious and violent and illegal actions, when he gets the chance. He is also ungrateful, not finding it congenial either to return or to offer gratitude since he does nothing for the common good or for friendship or without calculation.

Nor is the base man a lover of learning [*philologos*] or of listening, because in the first place he is not prepared for the reception of right accounts [or arguments: *logoi*] because of the imprudence which derives from his corruption, and because no base man has been encouraged [to turn] to virtue nor does he encourage [others to turn] to virtue; for he who has been encouraged [to turn] to virtue or who is encouraging others [to turn] to virtue must be prepared for philosophizing, and he who is prepared for it faces no impediments; but none of the base is like that. For it is not the man who listens eagerly and memorizes what philosophers say who is prepared for philosophizing, but the man who is prepared to carry into action what is pronounced in philosophy and to live by it. But none of the base is like that, since they are already in the grip of the opinions of vice. For if any of the base had been encouraged to [turn to virtue], he would also have turned away from vice. And no one who possesses vice has turned to virtue; just as no one who is sick has turned to health. Only the wise man has been encouraged to [turn to virtue], and only he is able to encourage [others to turn to virtue], and none of the imprudent—for none of the imprudent lives by the precepts ⟨of virtue⟩. Nor is he a lover of learning [*philologos*], but rather a lover of talk [*logophilos*], since he only proceeds as far as a superficial [sort of] chatter and does not yet confirm the talk [*logos*] about virtue by means of deeds.

Nor is any of the base a lover of toil; for love of toil is a disposition which produces what is fitting by means of toil in a manner which is unapprehensive; but none of the base is unapprehensive with regard to toil.

Nor does any of the base make the estimation of virtue which is in accordance with its value; for the estimation is a virtuous thing, since it is knowledge in accordance with which we think we are acquiring something worth considering. But none of the virtuous things belongs to the base, so that none of the base makes the proper estimation of virtue. For if any of the imprudent made the estimation which is in accordance with the value of virtue, then in so far as they honoured this, they would regulate vice out [of their lives]. But every imprudent man is pleasantly inured to his own vice. For one should not consider their external [i.e., verbalized] discourse, which is base,[50] but rather the discourse of their actions. For by their actions it is proven that they are not committed to honourable and virtuous actions, but rather to slavish and unmeasured pleasures.

They hold that every [moral] mistake is an act of impiety; for to do anything contrary to the wish of god is a sign of impiety. For since the gods find virtue and its works congenial and find vice and its products uncongenial, and since a [moral] mistake is an action in accordance with vice, obviously every [moral] mistake turned out to be displeasing to the gods—and that [sort of thing] is an act of impiety; for in every [moral] mistake the base man does something displeasing to the gods.

Again, since every base man does all that he does in accordance with vice, just as the virtuous man [does all that he does] in accordance with virtue, [it is] also [true that] he who has one vice has all. And among these [vices] one sees impiety, not the impiety which is classified as an activity, but the condition opposite to piety. And what is done in accordance with impiety is an act of impiety; ‹therefore›, every [moral] mistake is an act of impiety.

Again, they also hold that every imprudent man is an enemy to the gods. For hostility is a lack of consonance and lack of concord ‹concerning› the [practical] concerns of life, just as friendship is consonance and concord. But the base disagree with the gods about the [practical] concerns of life; and that is why every imprudent man is an enemy to the gods. Again, if every one believes that those who are opposed to them are enemies, and if the base man is opposed to the virtuous, and if god is virtuous, then the base man is an enemy to the gods.

50. This word is probably corrupt; perhaps the text should say 'deceptive' or something similar.

111. They say that all [moral] mistakes are equal, but not, however,[51] similar. For by nature they all derive from vice as from a single source, since in all [moral] mistakes the decision is the same; but [moral] mistakes do differ in quality with regard to the external cause, since there are differences among the intermediate things which are the subject of the decisions.

You could get a clear image of the point being demonstrated by attending to the following: every falsehood is equally a falsehood; for one is no more in error than another; for the statement "it is ⟨always⟩ night" is a falsehood, just as is the statement "a centaur lives"; and it is no more possible to say that the one is a falsehood than to say that the other is; but the falseness in each is not equally false, and those who are in error are not equally in error. And it is not possible to be making a [moral] mistake to a greater or lesser degree, since every [moral] mistake is performed in virtue of being in error. Moreover, it is not the case that a [morally] correct action does not admit of being greater or lesser while a [moral] mistake does admit of being greater or lesser; for they [i.e., moral mistakes and morally correct actions] are all complete and that is why they could not be deficient or excessive with respect to each other. Therefore, all [moral] mistakes are equal.

11m. As to natural ability and noble birth, some members of this school were led to say that every wise man is endowed with these attributes; but others were not. For some think that men are not only endowed with a natural ability for virtue by nature, but also that some are such by training, and they accepted this proverbial saying:[52] "practice, when aged by time, turns into nature." And they made the same supposition about noble birth, so that natural ability is a condition congenial to virtue which comes from nature or training, or a condition by which certain men are prone to acquire virtue readily. And noble birth is a condition congenial to virtue which comes from birth or training.

Since the virtuous man is affable in conversation and charming and encouraging and prone to pursue good will and friendship through his conversation, he fits in as well as possible with the majority of men; and that is why he is lovable and graceful and persuasive, and again flattering and shrewd and opportune and quick-witted and easy-going and unfussy and straightforward and unfeigned. And the base man is subject to all the opposite traits. And they say that being ironic is a trait of base men and that no free and virtuous man is ironic. Similarly for sarcasm, which

---

51. Literally, "not yet" or "no longer".
52. From an unknown tragedy, 227 Nauck.

is irony combined with a kind of mockery. They say that friendship only exists among the wise, since it is only among them that there is concord about the [practical] matters of life; and concord is a knowledge of common goods. For it is impossible for there to be genuine friendship (as opposed to falsely named friendship) without trust and reliability; but since the base are untrustworthy and unreliable and have hostile opinions there is no friendship among them, although there are certain other kinds of association and bonding which are held together from the outside by necessity and opinions. And they say that cherishing and welcoming and love belong to the virtuous alone.

And only the wise man is a king and regal, but none of the base is. For regal rule is not subject to review and is supreme and is superior to all [other forms of rule].

And they say that the virtuous man is the best doctor of himself; for he is a careful observer of his own nature and is knowledgeable about the factors which contribute to health.

The sensible man cannot get drunk; for drunkenness includes an element of [moral] error, for there is babbling over drink; but the virtuous man makes a [moral] mistake in no situation, which is why he does everything in accordance with virtue and right reason which depends on it.

There are three principal ways of life [for a wise man], the regal, the political and third, the life devoted to knowledge. Similarly, there are three principal ways to make money: by kingship, in which one is either a king oneself or commands the resources of a monarch; second, by political life, for, in accordance with the principal reason, he will participate in political life; for indeed he will also marry and have children, ⟨since⟩ these things follow on the ⟨nature⟩ of the rational and social and philanthropic animal. So he will make money both from politics and from his friends, [at least] those who are in elevated positions. On the topic of being a sophist[53] and doing well financially from sophistry, the members of this school disagreed over the meaning. For they agreed that [the wise man] would make money from his students and sometimes receive fees from those who wanted to learn; but there arose among them a debate about the meaning; some said that this very practice was sophistry, [i.e.,] sharing the doctrines of philosophy in return for a fee; others surmised that there was something base about the term 'sophistry', as though it meant setting up a retail market in arguments, and so they said that one not ought to make money from the education of whoever came along [to study], that this manner of making money was beneath the dignity of philosophy.

53. A professional intellectual.

They say that sometimes suicide is appropriate for virtuous men, in many ways; but that for base men, [it is appropriate] to remain alive even for those who would never be wise; for in [their mode of] living they neither possess virtue nor expel vice.[54] And [the value of] life and death is measured by [a reckoning of] appropriate and inappropriate actions.

They say that the wise man is free of arrogance; for he neither suffers arrogant behaviour nor inflicts it, since arrogance is a shameful act of injustice and harm. And the virtuous man does not suffer injustice or harm (although [it is true that] some people behave unjustly and arrogantly towards him), and in this he acts justly. In addition, arrogance is no ordinary form of injustice, but one which is shameful and arrogant. And the sensible man is immune from these things and is never shamed. For he has the good and divine virtue within himself, which is why he escapes all vice and harm.

And the sensible man will sometimes be a king and live with a king if he shows natural ability and a love of learning. We said[55] that it is possible for him to participate in political life in accordance with the principal reason, but that he will not do so if there is a ⟨hindrance⟩ and especially if it is going to provide no benefit to his fatherland and he supposes that great and difficult risks will follow from political activity.

They say that the wise man does not lie, but is truthful in all [circumstances]; for lying does not consist in saying something false, but in saying something false in order to make someone be in error and with intent to mislead one's neighbours. They believe, however, that he will sometimes employ falsehood in several ways without assenting [to it]; for [he will do so] when a general, against his adversaries, and in the provision of what is advantageous and in many other aspects of managing life. They say that wise man will never believe a falsehood, nor indeed will he assent at all to anything which is not graspable, because he neither holds [mere] opinions nor is ignorant in any respect. For ignorance is a changeable and weak assent. Nor does he hold any belief weakly, but rather securely and stably, and that is why the wise man holds no [mere] opinion. For there are two [kinds of] opinion: one is assent to something which is not graspable; the other is weak belief. And these are alien to the disposition of the wise man, and that is why hastiness and assenting

---

54. The base should refrain from suicide since it is in general appropriate for all animals to maintain their own lives, and the base (who are not wise) could not *know* when suicide would be appropriate for them. The wise, however, could recognize the exceptional circumstances which justify suicide.

55. 11b. above.

before he has a grasp are traits of the hasty and base man, and are not attributes of the man of natural ability who is perfect [complete] and virtuous. Nor does anything escape his notice, for to fail to notice is to have a belief which asserts a false thing.[56]

Following on these traits, he is not distrustful, for distrust is a belief in a falsehood; and trust is a virtuous thing, for it is a strong grasp which secures what is believed. Similarly, knowledge is unchangeable by argument; and that is why they say that the base man neither knows nor trusts in anything. Consequently, the wise man is not greedy nor does he cheat or deliberately miscount (nor does anyone cheat him by miscounting either); for all of these involve deception and commitment to falsehoods about the topic in question. And none of the virtuous men makes a mistake about about the road or his house or his target. But they believe that the wise man neither mis-sees nor mis-hears nor, generally, makes a mistake when using any of his sense-organs; for they believe that each of these depends on false assent. Nor does the wise man make conjectural interpretations, for a conjectural interpretation is in the class of assent to something which is not grasped. Nor do they suppose that the sensible man changes his mind, for changing one's mind depends on false assent, ⟨as though⟩ one had previously made a mistake. Nor does he change in *any* respect or shift his position or err. For all of these are characteristic of those who change their doctrines, and that is alien to the sensible man. Nor, they say, does he have any opinions similar to those discussed.

11n. They believe that a wise man does not at first notice that he is becoming one, nor does he strive for anything or believe that he wishes any of the special objects of wishing; [this is] because he does not judge that he has the requirements. Such distinctions also apply in the case of the other crafts, and not just to prudence.

11o. Since all [moral] mistakes and [morally] perfect actions are equal, all imprudent men are also equally imprudent, since they possess a disposition which is equal and identical. Although all [moral] mistakes are equal, there are some differences among them, in so far as some come from a hardened disposition which is difficult to cure and some do not.

11p. And some virtuous men are better than others at encouraging [people to virtue] and persuading them; again, some are more quick-witted than others, the increases being a result of the inclusion of interme-diate steps.

11q. Only the virtuous man has good children, though not all have virtuous children since it is necessary for him who has good children to

---

56. A difficult sentence. Alternatively, one might emend *apophantike* to *apophatike* and translate: for failure to notice is a belief in a falsehood which [implicitly] denies a fact.

use them as such. Only the virtuous man has a good old age and a good death; for a good old age is conducting oneself virtuously at a certain age, and a good death is to make one's end virtuously with a certain kind of death.

11r. And things are called healthy and unhealthy relative to man, [as are] what serves as nutriment and what is laxative or astringent, and things like these. For things which are naturally inclined to produce or preserve health are healthy; unhealthy are those which are in the opposite condition. A similar account applies to the others.

11s. And only the virtuous man is a prophet since he has a knowledge which distinguishes the signs relevant to human life which come from the gods and daimons. And that is why he also has the forms of the prophetic art, i.e., dream-reading and bird-interpretation and sacrificial prophecy and any other types like these.

And the virtuous man is said to be austere in so far as he neither uses on another nor admits for himself discourse directed at winning gratitude. And they say that the wise man will live a Cynic life, this ⟨being⟩ equal to remaining in one's Cynicism [after becoming wise]; however, once one becomes wise one will not *begin* to practice Cynicism.

They say that sexual love is an effort to produce friendship resulting from the appearance of [physical] beauty of young men in their prime; and that is why the wise man makes sexual advances and will have sexual intercourse with those who are worthy of [true] sexual love, [i.e.,] those who are well-born and endowed with natural ability.

They say that nothing happens to the wise man which is contrary to his striving and impulse and effort, since he does all such things with reservation and none of the events which oppose his [plans] befalls him unexpectedly.

And he is also gentle, gentleness being a condition according to which they are gentle about doing what is fitting in all circumstances and do not get swept away to anger in any circumstances. And he is calm and orderly, orderliness being knowledge of fitting motions and calmness being a proper organization of states of motion and rest of the soul and body in accordance with nature; the opposites of these are traits of all base men.

Every honourable and good man is free of slander, since he is immune to slander and so is free of slander in this sense and also in the sense that he does not slander someone else. And slander is a falling out among apparent friends because of a false utterance; this does not happen to good men, but only base men slander and are slandered, and that is why true friends neither slander nor are slandered, but [only] seeming and apparent friends.

Nor does the virtuous man ever stall on anything, since stalling is a deferral of action because of hesitation; but he defers some things only when the deferral is free of blame; for Hesiod said this of stalling: "do not stall until tomorrow and the next day;" and "a man who puts off his work always wrestles with disaster"[57] since stalling produces an abandonment of one's proper jobs.

12. So much for this. For Chrysippus discussed all the paradoxes in many other works: in his *On Doctrines* and in the *Outline [Definition] of Rational Discourse* and in many other treatises on special topics. But I have already gone through in an adequate fashion as much as I intended to deal with in the summary account of the ethical doctrines of ⟨those⟩ who belong to the Stoic school of philosophy; [so] I shall put an end to this notebook forthwith.

Sextus Empiricus *M* 11.200–201, 207   [II-96] (SVF 3.516)

200. In reply to this they say that all men have the same functions, though it makes a difference whether they are carried out from a craftsmanlike disposition or an uncraftsmanlike one. For taking care of one's parents and otherwise honouring them is not the special function of a virtuous man, but doing so from prudence is. **201.** And just as healing is common to the doctor and the layman, but doing so medically is the special function of the craftsman, in the same way too honouring one's parents is common to the virtuous man and the non-virtuous man; but honouring one's parents from prudence is the special function of the wise man; consequently he has a craft of life whose special function it is to do each of the things which are done from a virtuous disposition. . . . **207.** Just as in the intermediate crafts it is the special function of a craftsman to do things regularly and to produce the same results consistently (for even a layman could carry out the function of a craftsman, but rarely and not all the time, and certainly not consistently in the same manner), so too it is the function of a prudent man, they say, to be consistent in his [morally] perfect actions, and just the opposite for the imprudent man.

Stobaeus *Anthology* 4.39.22 vol. 5   [II-97] p. 906.18–907.5 W-H (SVF 3.510)

Chrysippus says: "he who makes [moral] progress to the highest degree performs all the appropriate actions in all circumstances and omits none."

---

57. *Works and Days* 410, 413.

And he says that his life is not yet happy, but that happiness supervenes on him when these intermediate actions become secure and conditioned and acquire a special sort of fixity.

Epictetus *Discourses* 2.6.6–10   [II-98]

6. "Go and salute Mr. So-and-so." "All right, I salute him." "How?" "Not in an abject fashion." "But you were shut out." "That's because I haven't learned how to enter through the window. And when I find the door shut [against me], I must either go away or enter through the window." 7. "But speak with the man too!" "I do so." "How?" "Not in an abject fashion." 8. "But you did not succeed."—Now surely that was not your business, but his. So why do you encroach on what concerns someone else? If you always remember what is yours and what concerns someone else, you will never be disturbed. 9. That's why Chrysippus was right to say, "As long as what comes next is non-evident to me, I always cling to what is better suited to getting what is in accordance with nature. For god himself made me such as to select those things. 10. But *if* I knew for sure that it was fated for me now to be ill, I would even seek [illness]. For my foot, if it had brains, would seek to be muddied."

Epictetus *Discourses* 2.10.1–6   [II-99]

1. Consider who you are. First of all a man, i.e., you have nothing more authoritative than your power of moral choice and all else is subordinate to it, but it itself is free and independent. 2. Consider, then, what you are separate from in virtue of your rationality. You are separate from wild beasts and from sheep. 3. And in addition you are a citizen of the cosmos and a part of it—not one of the servile parts but one of its principal parts. For you are able to follow the divine administration and figure out what comes next. 4. So, what is the role of a citizen? To have no private advantage, not to deliberate about anything as though one were a separate part, but just as if the hand or foot had reasoning power and were able to follow the arrangements of nature, they would never have sought or desired anything except after referring to the whole. 5. That is why the philosophers are right to say that if the honourable and good man knew what was going to happen, he would even collaborate with disease and death and lameness, being aware that these things are dispensed by the arrangement of the whole and that the whole is more authoritative than the part and the state more authoritative than the citizen. 6. But now, because we do not have this foreknowledge, it is appropriate for us to cling to what is better suited for selection, since we are also born for this.

Cicero *On Goals* 5.16–21

16. Since there is so much disagreement about this [the goal of life] we should employ the division of Carneades, which our friend Antiochus is so fond of using. Carneades discerned not only all the views which philosophers had yet held about the highest good, but also all the views which are possible. So he claimed that no craft took its starting point from itself, since there is always something external which is the object of the craft. We need not prolong this point with examples; for it is obvious that no craft is concerned with itself, but the craft is distinct from its object. So just as medicine is the craft of health and helmsmanship is the craft of navigation, in the same way prudence is the craft of living; therefore it too must be constituted by and take its principle from something else. 17. It is a matter of general agreement that the concern of prudence and its goal must be what is adapted and accommodated to nature and such as to stimulate and stir up, all by itself, an impulse in the mind (which the Greeks call *horme*). But there is no agreement about what it is which thus moves us and which nature seeks from the moment of birth—and that is the source of all the disagreement among philosophers when they are considering what the highest good is. For the source of the entire debate about the limits of good and bad, when they investigate the extreme limits of each, is to be found in the primary natural affiliations; and when that is found, the whole debate about the highest good and [worst] bad [thing] is derived from it as from a source.

18. Some philosophers think that our first impulse is to pleasure and that our first avoidance is of pain. Others think that freedom from pain is what we first welcome and that pain is the first object of avoidance. Others again take their start from the things which they call primary according to nature—a class in which they include the integrity and preservation of all of our parts, health, sound sense organs, freedom from pain, strength, good looks, and other things of this kind; similar to these are the primary natural things in the soul, which are as it were the sparks and seeds of the virtues. Since it is some one of these three which first stirs nature into action, either to pursue something or to avoid it, and since there can be no additional possibility beyond these three, it follows necessarily that the tasks of pursuit and avoidance are to be referred to one of these. Consequently, that prudence which we called the craft of living is concerned with some one of those three things and takes from it the basic principle for all of life.

19. One's theory of what is right and honourable is derived from whichever of these three which one has decided is the thing which stimulates nature into action, and this theory can correspond with any

one of the three. As a result, honourableness is either a matter of doing everything for the sake of pleasure, even if you do not achieve it; or for the sake of avoiding pain, even if you cannot manage this; or for the sake of acquiring primary natural things even if you succeed in getting none of them. So it is that disagreements about the starting points of nature exactly correspond to disagreements about the limits of good and bad things. Others again will start from the same principles and refer every [question about] appropriate action either to [the actual attainment of] pleasure or freedom from pain, or to the acquisition of the primary natural things.

20. So six views about the highest good have now been set forth, and the chief spokesman for the last three are: for pleasure, Aristippus, for freedom from pain, Hieronymus; and for the enjoyment of those things which we have termed primary natural things it is Carneades himself— not indeed that he believes in the view, but he does defend it for the sake of argument. The other three were views which *could* be held, though only one of them has ever been defended, but it has been defended with great vigour. For no one has said that the plan of acting in such a way that one does everything for the sake of pleasure, even if we do not achieve anything, is nevertheless worth choosing for its sake and honourable and the only good thing. Nor has anyone held that the very act of trying to avoid pain was something worth choosing, unless one could actually escape it. But that doing everything in order to acquire the primary natural things, even if we do not succeed, is honourable and the only thing worth choosing and the only good thing—that is what the Stoics say.

21. These are the six simple views about the greatest good and bad things; two without spokesmen, four which have actually been defended. There has been a total of three composite or double accounts of the highest good, and if you consider the nature of things carefully you will see that there could not have been any more. For either pleasure can be coupled with the honourable, as Callipho and Dinomachus held; or freedom from pain, as Diodorus held; and so can the primary natural things, which is the view of the ancients, as we call the Academics and Peripatetics.

Galen *On the Doctrines of Hippocrates and* [II-101] *Plato* 5.6.9–12 (5.470–471 K; SVF 3.12)

Not satisfied with this, Posidonius made a clearer and stronger criticism of Chrysippus for not having given a proper explanation of the goal. This is what he said: "Some ignore this and limit living in agreement to 'doing whatever one can for the sake of the primary natural things' by doing which they are doing much the same thing as they would be doing if they claimed that the goal was pleasure or freedom from pain or something else of the sort. There is something which reveals an internal conflict in the very utterance [of this formulation of the goal], but there is nothing which is honourable or could promote happiness. For this is a consequence of the goal but is not the goal. But if one gets [the formulation of] the goal right, one can use it to defeat the puzzles which the sophists advance, but one cannot so use the [formula] 'living according to experience of what happens in the whole of nature,' which is equivalent to saying living in agreement, since this makes no small contribution to achieving things indifferent."

Cicero *On Goals* 3.16–34   [II-102]

16. The school whose views I follow [a Stoic speaks] holds that every animal, as soon as it is born (for this should be our starting point), is congenial to itself and inclined to preserve itself and its constitution, and to like those things which preserve that constitution; but it finds uncongenial its own death and those things which seem to threaten it. They confirm this by [noting] that before pleasure or pain can affect them, babies seek what is salutary and spurn what is not, and this would not happen unless they loved their constitution and feared death. They could not, however, desire anything unless they had a perception of themselves and consequently loved themselves. From this one ought to see that the principle [of human action] is derived from self-love. 17. Most Stoics do not think that pleasure should be classed among the primary natural things; and I strongly agree with them, for fear that, if nature seemed to have classed pleasure among the primary objects of impulse, then many shameful consequences would follow. It seems, however, to be a sufficient argument as to why we love those things which were first accepted because of nature [to say] that there is no one (when he has a choice) who would not prefer to have all the parts of his body in a sound condition to having them dwarfed or twisted, though equally useful.

They think, moreover, that acts of cognition (which we may call grasps or perceptions or, if these terms are either displeasing or harder to understand, *katalepseis*) are, then, to be accepted for their own sake, since they have in themselves something which as it were includes and contains the truth. And this can be seen in babies, who, we see, are delighted if they figure something out for themselves, even if it does not do them any good. 18. We also think that the crafts are to be taken for their own sake, both because there is in them something worth taking and also because they consist of acts of cognition and contain something which is rational and methodical. They think, though, that we find false assent more uncongenial than anything else which is contrary to nature. . . .

20. Let us move on, then, since we began from these natural principles and what follows should be consistent with them. There follows this primary division: they say that what has value (we are to call it that, I think) is that which is either itself in accordance with nature or productive of it, so that it is worthy of selection because it has a certain 'weight' which is worth valuing (and this [value] they call *axia*); by contrast, what is opposite to the above is disvalued. The starting point being, then, so constituted that what is natural is to be taken for its own sake and what is unnatural is to be rejected, the first appropriate action (for that is what I call *kathekon*) is that it should preserve itself in its natural constitution; and then that it should retain what is according to nature and reject what is contrary to nature. After this [pattern of] selection and rejection is discovered, there then follows appropriate selection, and then constant [appropriate] selection, and finally [selection] which is stable and in agreement with nature; and here for the first time we begin to have and to understand something which can truly be called good. 21. For man's first sense of congeniality is to what is according to nature; but as soon as he gets an understanding, or rather a conception (which they call an *ennoia*) and sees the ordering and, I might say, concord of things which are to be done, he then values that more highly than all those things which he loved in the beginning, and he comes to a conclusion by intelligence and reasoning, with the result that he decides that this is what the highest good for man consists in, which is is to be praised and chosen for its own sake. And since it is placed in what the Stoics call *homologia*, let us call it agreement, if you please. Since, therefore, this constitutes the good, to which all things are to be referred, honourable actions and the honourable itself—which is considered to be the only good—although it arises later [in our lives], nevertheless it is the only thing which is to be chosen in virtue of its own character and value; but none of the primary natural things is to be chosen for its own sake. 22. Since, however, those things which I called appropriate actions proceed from the starting points [established] by nature, it is necessary that they be referred to them; so it is right to say all appropriate actions are referred to acquisition of the natural principles, not however in the sense that this is the highest good, since honourable action is not among the primarily and naturally congenial things. That, as I said, is posterior and arises later. But [such action] is natural and encourages us to choose it much more than all the earlier mentioned things.

But here one must first remove a misunderstanding, so that no one might think that there are two highest goods. For just as, if it is someone's purpose to direct a spear or arrow at something, we say that his highest goal is to do everything he can in order to direct it at [the target], in the same sense that we say that our highest goal is a good. The archer in this comparison is to do all that he can to direct [his arrow at the target]; and yet doing all that he can to attain his purpose would be like the highest goal of the sort which we say is the highest good in life; actually striking [the target], though, is as it were to be selected and not to be chosen.

23. Since all appropriate actions proceed from the natural principles, it is necessary that wisdom itself proceed from them as well. But just as it often happens that he who is introduced to someone puts a higher value on the man to whom he is introduced than on the man by whom he was introduced, just so it is in no way surprising that we are first introduced to wisdom by the starting points [established] by nature, but that later on wisdom itself becomes dearer to us than the things which brought us to wisdom. And just as our limbs were given us in such a way that they seem to have been given for the sake of a certain way of life, similarly the impulse in our soul, which is called *horme* in Greek, seems not to have been given for the sake of any old type of life but for a certain kind of living; and similarly for reason and perfected reason. 24. Just as an actor or dancer has not been assigned just any old [type of] delivery or movement but rather a certain definite [type]; so too life is to be lived in a certain definite manner, not in any old [manner]. And we call that manner 'in agreement' and consonant. And we do not think that wisdom is like navigation or medicine, but rather like the craft of acting or dancing which I just mentioned; thus its goal, i.e., the [proper] execution of the craft, depends on it itself and is not sought outside itself. There is also another point of dissimilarity between wisdom and these crafts, viz. that in them proper actions do not contain all the components [lit. parts] which constitute the art; but things called 'right' or 'rightly done', if I may call them that, though the Greeks call them *katorthomata* [morally perfect actions], contain all the features of virtue. Only wisdom is totally self-contained, and this is not the case with the other crafts. 25. But it is misguided to compare the highest goal of medicine or navigation with that of wisdom; for wisdom embraces magnanimity and justice and an ability to judge that everything which happens to a [mere] human being is beneath it—and this does not apply to the rest of the crafts. But no one can possess the very virtues which I just mentioned unless he has firmly decided that there is nothing except what is honourable or shameful which makes a difference or distinguishes one [thing or situation] from another.

26. Let us now see how splendidly these further points follow from what I have already expounded. . . . So, since the goal is to live consistently and in agreement with nature, it follows necessarily that all wise men always live happy, perfect and fortunate lives, that they are impeded by nothing, hindered by nothing and in need of nothing. The key not only to the doctrines of which I am speaking, but also to our life and fortune is that we should judge that only what is honourable is good. This point can be elaborated and developed fully and copiously, with all the choicest words and profoundest sentiments which rhetorical art can produce; but I prefer the short and pointed syllogisms of the Stoics.

27. Their arguments go like this: everything which is good is praiseworthy; but everything which is praiseworthy is honourable; therefore, that which is good is honourable. Does this argument seem valid enough? Surely it does; for as you see the argument concludes with a point which is proven by the two premises. Generally speaking, people attack the former of the two premises and claim that it is not the case that everything which is good is praiseworthy; for they concede that what is praiseworthy is honourable. But it is totally absurd [to claim] that something is good but not worth choosing, or worth choosing but not pleasing, or pleasing but not also to be loved; and so it is also to be approved of; so it is also praiseworthy; but that is [the same as] honourable. So it turns out that what is good is also honourable.

28. Next, I ask who can boast of a life if it is wretched or even just not happy. So we boast only of a happy life. From this it results that the happy life is, if I may put it so, worth boasting about; and this cannot properly [be said to] happen to any life but one which is honourable. So it turns out that an honourable life is a happy life. Moreover, since someone who is justly praised must have about him something remarkable, either in point of honour or glory, so that he can justly be called happy on account of these very valuable attributes, the same thing can be said most properly about the life of such a man. So if the honourable is a criterion for a happy life, one must hold that what is honourable is also good.

29. What? Could anyone deny that we could never have a man who is of steadfast and reliable spirit, a man you could call brave, unless it is firmly established that pain is not a bad thing? For just as someone who regards death as a bad thing cannot help but fear it, in the same way no one can be indifferent to and despise something which he regards as bad. Once this point is established and assented to, our next premiss is that magnanimous and strong-hearted men are able to despise and ignore everything which fortune can bring to bear against man. Consequently, it is proven that there is nothing bad which is not also shameful.

But the man we refer to is lofty and superior, magnanimous, truly brave, looks down on all merely human concerns; the man, I say, whom we wish to produce, whom we are looking for, should certainly have faith in himself and his life, both past and future, and should think well of himself, believing that nothing bad can happen to a wise man. And from this one can again prove the same old point, that only the honourable is good, i.e., that to live happily is to live honourably, i.e., virtuously.

30. I am not unaware that there is a variety of views held by philosophers, by which I mean those who place the highest good, which I call the goal, in the mind. Even though some of them have gone wrong, still I prefer them, whatever their views, who locate the highest good in the mind and virtue, to those three who have separated the highest good from virtue by placing either pleasure or freedom from pain or the primary natural things among the highest goods; I even prefer them to the other three who thought that virtue would be deficient without some addition and so added to it one or other of the three things mentioned above. 31. But those who think that the highest good is to live with knowledge and who claim that things are absolutely indifferent and that this was why the wise man would be happy, because he did not prefer one thing to any other in even the slightest degree—they are particularly absurd; so too are those who, as certain Academics are said to have held, believe that the highest good and greatest duty of the wise man is to resist his presentations and steadfastly to withhold his assent. Normally one gives a full answer to each of these views separately. But there is no need to prolong what is perfectly clear; and what is more obvious than that the very prudence which we are seeking and praising would be utterly destroyed if there were no grounds for choosing between those which are contrary to nature and those which are according to nature? When we eliminate, therefore, those views I have mentioned and those which are similar to them, all that is left is [the view] that the highest good is to live by making use of a knowledge of what happens naturally, selecting what is according to nature and rejecting what is contrary to nature, i.e., to live consistently and in agreement with nature.

32. When in the other crafts something is said to be craftsmanlike, one must suppose that what is meant is something which is, in a way, posterior and consequent, which they [the Greeks] call *epigennematikon* [supervenient]; but when we say that something is done wisely we mean that it is from the outset thoroughly right. For whatever is undertaken by a wise man must immediately be complete in all its parts; for it is in this that we find what we call that which is worth choosing. For just as it is a [moral] mistake to betray one's country, to attack one's parents, to rob temples (and these are [moral] mistakes because of the outcome

[of the action]), so too it is a [moral] mistake to fear, to grieve, and to suffer desire, even quite independently of their outcome. Rather, just as the latter are not dependent on their posterior consequences, but are [moral] mistakes right from the outset, similarly the actions which proceed from virtue are to be judged to be right from the outset and not by their ultimate completion.

33. 'Good', which has been used so frequently in this discussion, is also explained with a definition. The definitions offered by [the Stoics] do differ from each other, but only very slightly; for all that, they are getting at the same point. I agree with Diogenes who defined good as that which is perfect in its nature. He followed this up by defining the beneficial (let us use this term for *ophelema*) as a motion or condition which is in accord with what is perfect in its nature. And since we acquire conceptions of things if we learn something either by direct experience or by combination or by similarity or by rational inference, the conception of good is created by the last method mentioned. For the mind attains a conception of the good when it ascends by rational inference from those things which are according to nature. 34. But the good itself is not perceived to be good or called good because of some addition or increase or comparison with other things, but in virtue of its own special character. For honey, although it is the sweetest thing, is nevertheless perceived to be sweet not because of a comparison with other things, but because of its own distinctive flavour; in the same way the good, which is the subject of our discussion, is indeed most valuable, but that value derives meaning from its distinctive type and not from its magnitude. For value (which is called *axia*) is not counted as either good or bad; consequently, however much you might increase it, it will still remain in the same general category. Therefore, there is one kind of value which applies to virtue, and it derives its meaning from its distinctive type and not from its magnitude.

Cicero *On Goals* 3.62–70 (selections) [II-103]

62. Again, they think it important to understand that nature has brought it about that children are loved by their parents. For from this starting point we can follow the development of the shared society which unites the human race. One ought to see this first of all from the form and organs of the body which show that nature has a rational scheme for reproduction; but it would be inconsistent for nature to want offspring to be born and yet not to see to it that they are loved once they are born. The power of nature can be seen even in the beasts; when we see the effort they go to in bearing and rearing their offspring, we seem to be listening to the voice of nature herself. So, just as it is obvious that we

naturally shrink from pain, so too it is apparent that we are driven by
nature herself to love those whom we bear. 63. From this it develops
naturally that there is among men a common and natural congeniality
of men with each other, with the result that it is right for them to feel
that other men, just because they are men, are not alien to them. . . . So
we are naturally suited to [living in] gatherings, groups and states.

64. They also hold that the cosmos is ruled by the will of the gods,
that it is like a city or state shared by gods and men, and that each and
every one of us is a part of this cosmos. From which it naturally follows
that we put the common advantage ahead of our own. For just as the
laws put the well-being of all ahead of the well-being of individuals, so
too the good and wise man, who is obedient to the laws and not unaware
of his civic duty, looks out for the advantage of all more than for that
of any one person or his own. . . .

67. But just as they think that the bonds of justice unite men with
each other, so too they deny that there is any bond of justice between
man and beast. Chrysippus expressed it well, saying that everything else
was born for the sake of men and gods, but they were born for the sake
of their own community and society, with the result that men can use
beasts for their own advantage without injustice. . . .

70. They also think that friendship should be cultivated because it
falls into the class of beneficial things. Although some [Stoics] say that
in a friendship a friend's reason is just as dear to the wise man as is his
own, while others say that each man's reason is dearer to himself, even
this latter group admits that to deprive someone of something in order
to appropriate it for oneself is inconsistent with justice, which is a virtue
we are naturally committed to. So the school I am speaking of does not
at all approve of the view that justice or friendship should be welcomed
or approved of because of its advantages. For the very same advantages
could just as well undermine and overthrow them. Indeed, neither justice
nor friendship can exist at all unless they are chosen for their own sakes.

Epictetus *Discourses* 1.22.1–4   [II-104]

1. Basic grasps are common to all men, and one basic grasp does not
conflict with another; for which of us does not suppose that the good is
advantageous and worth choosing and that one ought to go for it and
pursue it in all circumstances? Which of us does not suppose that the
good is honourable and fitting? So where does the conflict come from?
2. In the application of basic grasps to individual substances; 3. as when
one man says "He did well and is brave!" [and someone else says,] "No,
he is crazy." This is the source of the conflict between men. 4. The

conflict between the Jews and the Syrians and Egyptians and Romans is not about whether the sacred must be honoured above all else and pursued in all instances, but about whether this particular thing, eating pork, is sacred or not.

Epictetus *Discourses* 2.11.13, 16 [II-105]

13. Consider the starting point of philosophy: a perception of the mutual conflict among men and a search for the cause of the conflict; [plus] the rejection and distrust of mere opinion, an investigation of opinion to see if it is right, and the discovery of some canon, like scales which we discover for [measuring] heavy things and the ruler which [we discover for distinguishing] what is straight and crooked. . . .

16. So is there no canon here higher than mere opinion? But how is it possible for what is most vital to men to be undeterminable and undiscoverable?

Seneca, *On Peace of Mind* 13.2–14.2 [II-106]

13.2. For a man who does many things frequently puts himself in fortune's power. But the safest course is to tempt fortune rarely, and always to be mindful of her and never to put any trust in her promises. Say "I shall set sail unless something intervenes" and "I shall become praetor unless something hinders me" and "my enterprise will be successful unless something interferes". 13.3. This is why we say that nothing happens to a wise man contrary to his expectations; we free him not from the misfortunes but from the blunders of mankind, nor do all these things turn out as he has wished but as he has thought. But his first thought has been that something might obstruct his plans. Then, too, the suffering that comes to the mind from the frustration of desire must necessarily be much lighter if you have not certainly promised it success.

14.1. We ought also to make ourselves adaptable, so that we do not become too fond of the plans we have formed and we should pass readily to the condition to which chance has led us and not dread shifting either purpose or positions, provided we avoid fickleness, a vice which poses a most grave threat to mental equilibrium. For obstinacy, from which fortune often wrests some concession, must needs be anxious and unhappy, and fickleness is much worse if it does not restrain itself. Both are hostile to peace of mind: being unable to make any change and being unable to endure anything. 14.2. At all events the mind must be withdrawn from all externals into itself. Let it trust in itself, rejoice in itself, esteem its own possessions, retreat as much as it can from things not its own, devote itself to itself, feel no damage and even take setbacks in a generous spirit. When he received news of a shipwreck and heard that all his possessions had been lost with the ship, Zeno, the head of our school, said "fortune bids me to follow philosophy bearing a lighter load".

Seneca, *Letters on Ethics* 121.1–24   [II-107]

1. I can see that you will quarrel when I have expounded for you today's theme, which we have already spent quite some time with; yet again you will cry out, "what does this have to do with ethics?" Exclaim away, until I can, first, give you the names of others to quarrel with, Posidonius and Archidemus . . .

5. Meanwhile let me examine some questions which seem to be a bit too far removed [from your practical concerns]. We were asking whether all animals had an awareness of their own constitution. The best evidence that this is so was that they move their limbs in a fitting and efficient manner, as though they had been trained to do so; each animal has a nimble mastery of his various parts. A craftsman handles his tools with ease; a helmsman controls the rudder with skill; and a painter can very quickly apply the many and varied colours which he sets out on his palette for the purpose of capturing a likeness, and moves back and forth between the hot wax and the canvas with a ready hand and eye. In the same way an animal is expeditious in the use of himself. 6. We often admire skilled dancers because their hands are capable of expressing all kinds of objects and emotions and their gestures are responsive to the rapidly uttered words. What art gives to these men, nature provides to the animals. They do this as soon as they are born; they come into this world with this knowledge; they are born with a sound training.

7. "And so," he says, "animals move their parts in a fitting manner because if they moved them any differently they would feel pain. Thus, on your theory, they are forced [to act as they do] and it is fear which leads them to correct action, not choice." This is false; for things which are driven by necessity are slow; nimbleness belongs to those who move of their own free will. Far from it being fear of pain which drives them to this [behaviour], they even strive for their natural motions when pain discourages them. 8. Consider a baby who is practicing standing up and learning how to walk; as soon as he begins to try his strength he falls and, in tears, gets up again and again until despite the pain he trains himself to the [function] demanded by his nature. Some animals, who have hard shells, can be turned over on their backs and they will strain and push with their feet and twist themselves for a long time, until they get back in their [proper] posture. Yet the turtle feels no pain when on his back; he is uneasy, nevertheless, because he desires his natural

constitution and does not stop straining and flailing until he gets to his feet. 9. Therefore, all [animals] have an awareness of their own constitution and that is the source of their very expeditious handling of their limbs. We have no better evidence that they come into life equipped with this knowledge than the fact that no animal is clumsy in handling himself. 10. "The constitution is," he says, "according to you, the leading part of the soul in a certain disposition relative to the body. How can a baby understand this, which is so complex and subtle and hard even for you to explain? All animals ought to be born as dialecticians so that they can understand that definition, which is opaque to most Roman citizens." 11. Your objection would be valid if I were saying that animals understood the *definition* of constitution and not the constitution itself. Nature is more easily understood than explained. And so that baby does not know what a constitution is, but does know his constitution; he does not know what an animal is, but he knows that he is an animal. 12. Furthermore, he understands that constitution of his vaguely and in outline and dimly. We too know that we have a soul; what the soul is, where it is, what it is like or where it came from—that we do not know. Our awareness of our own soul (despite our ignorance of its nature and location) is to us in the same relation as the awareness of their constitution is to all animals. It is necessary that they be aware of that through which they are also aware of other things; it is necessary that they have an awareness of that thing which they obey, by which they are governed. 13. Every one of us understands that there is something which sets our impulses in motion; but we do not know what that thing is. Thus babies and animals also have an awareness, neither very clear nor distinct, of the leading part in them.

14. "You say," he says, "that every animal first finds his own constitution congenial [to himself]; but a man's constitution is rational and so man finds not his animality but his rationality congenial [to himself]; for man is dear to himself in virtue of that part which makes him a man. So how can a baby find congenial a rational constitution when he is not yet rational?" 15. There is a different constitution for every age; one for the baby, one for the child, ⟨one for the teen-ager⟩, one for the old man. All find the constitution which they are in congenial. A baby lacks teeth; he finds that constitution congenial. His teeth appear; he finds that constitution congenial. For the plant which will turn into mature crop has a different constitution when it is tender and barely poking its nose out of the furrow, another when it gains strength and stands, admittedly with an unripe stalk but one able to support its own weight, and another when it ripens and gets ready for the threshing floor and the ear firms up; it looks to and adapts itself to whatever constitution it achieves. 16.

There are different stages of life for a baby, a boy, a teen-ager, and an old man; yet I am, for all that, the same [person] as the baby and the boy and the teen-ager I used to be. Thus, although each man's constitution changes [from one stage to another], the congeniality he feels towards his constitution is the same. For nature does not commend to me a boy or a youth or an old man, but myself. Therefore, a baby finds his own constitution congenial, the one he then has and not the one which he will have as a youth; the fact that he will have something greater to change into some day does not mean that the state in which he is born is not according to nature. 17. First of all, the animal finds itself congenial; for there must be something to which all else can be referred. I seek pleasure. For whose sake? Mine. Therefore, I am looking out for myself. I flee pain. For whose sake? My own. Therefore, I am looking out for myself. If I do everything in order to look out for myself, then looking out for myself is prior to everything else. This concern for oneself is in all animals; it is not acquired, it is innate. 18. Nature brings forth her young, she does not abandon them. And since the most certain guardianship is the closest, everyone is entrusted to himself. Thus, as I said in my earlier letter, young animals, even those who have just recently emerged from their mother's womb or egg, know immediately what is dangerous and they avoid what is life-threatening. Animals which are at risk from birds of prey even avoid the shadows cast by predators as they fly over. No animal comes into life without a fear of death.

19. "How," he says, "can a newborn animal understand what is salutary or life-threatening?" First of all, the point at issue is whether it understands, not how it understands. It is clear that they do understand from the fact that they behave no differently than [they would] if they did understand. Why is it that a hen does not flee a peacock or a goose, but does flee a hawk, which is so much smaller and is not even known to it yet? Why do chicks fear a cat, but not a dog? Obviously, they have a knowledge of what is liable to harm them which is not acquired by experience; for before they can acquire any experience they are already cautious. 20. Next, in order that you should not think that this is an accident, they neither fear things which they need not fear nor do they ever forget this care and diligence; the avoidance of danger is their lifelong companion. Moreover, they do not become more timid as they live; from this it is obvious that they do not get this characteristic by practice but from a natural love of their own preservation. What practice teaches is late and various; whatever nature passes on is the same for all [members of a species] and instantaneous. 21. If, however, you insist, I shall tell how every animal is compelled to understand what is dangerous. It is aware that it is made of flesh; and so it is aware of what can cut and

burn and bruise flesh, of the animals which are equipped for hurting it; it regards their appearance as hostile and threatening. These things are closely connected; for as soon as each animal takes its safety to be congenial, it seeks what will help it and fears what will harm it. There are natural impulses to what is useful and natural rejections of the opposite. Whatever nature teaches comes without any thought to enunciate it, without planning. **22.** Do you not see how sophisticated bees are in building their hives, how much cooperation there is all round in the division of the necessary tasks? Do you not see that the weaving of a spider cannot be imitated by any mortal, [do you not see] how much work it takes to arrange the threads—some set in a straight line as a kind of framework, others spun in a circle to fill in the pattern, so that smaller animals (for whose destruction such webs are woven) might be caught and held as though in a net? **23.** That craft is born, not learned. Therefore, no one animal is any more skilled than any other; you will see that the webs of spiders are all the same, the cells in all the corners of honeycombs are all the same. What craft passes on is indefinite and uneven. What nature distributes comes equally. She passes on nothing more than care of oneself and skill in that, and that is also why they begin to live and learn at the same time. **24.** And it is not surprising that animals are born with those things without which it would be pointless for them to be born. Nature gave them this as their first tool for survival: congeniality with and love for themselves. They could not have been safe if they did not want to be; this would not have been beneficial all on its own, but without it nothing else would have been either. But in no animal will you find contempt for itself, nor even neglect; even silent and brutish animals have the cunning required to live, although they are stupid in all else. You will see that even animals which are useless to others do not let themselves down.

Farewell.

Seneca *Letters on Ethics* 117.2–3 [II-108]

2. Our school believes that the good is a body, because that which is good acts and whatever acts is a body. What is good benefits [someone]; but for something to benefit [someone] it ought to act; and if it acts, it is a body. They say that wisdom is good; it follows that it is also necessary to say that it is corporeal. **3.** But being wise is not in the same category. It is an incorporeal attribute of something else, viz. wisdom; consequently it neither acts nor benefits [anyone]. 'What then?' he says, 'do we not say that being wise is good?' We do say so, but only by reference to that on which it depends, i.e., to wisdom itself.

Seneca *Letters on Ethics* 120.3–14

So now I return to the topic you wish to have discussed, which is how we get our conception of what is good and honourable. **4.** Nature could not have taught us this: she has given us the seeds of knowledge, but not the knowledge itself. Some people say that we stumble onto the notion, but it is unbelievable that anyone should learn the form of virtue by chance. Our view is that it is the result of the observation and comparison to each other of frequently performed actions; our school thinks the honourable and the good are understood by analogy . . . Let me explain what this analogy is. **5.** We know what bodily health is; from this we suppose that there is also a kind of health of the soul. We know what bodily strength is; from this we infer that there is also a kind of strength of the soul. Certain generous and humane deeds, certain brave deeds struck us so forcefully that we began to admire them as though they were perfect. They contained many faults, but these were hidden by the shining beauty of a remarkable deed; these we ignored. Nature commands us to magnify what is praiseworthy, and everyone exaggerates what is glorious. It is from such actions that we derive the form of a great good. . . .

8. . . . I shall add a point which will perhaps seem amazing: sometimes bad things contribute to the form of the honourable and what is best shines forth from its opposite. As you know, the virtues are quite close to their opposites, and there is a similarity between what is right and things which are corrupt and shameful. Thus the spendthrift mimics the generous man, though there is a very great difference between someone who knows how to give and someone who does not know how to save. . . . Carelessness imitates easy-goingness; rashness imitates bravery. **9.** This similarity forced us to pay attention and to distinguish things which are formally quite close to each other but in fact radically different. While we were watching those who have been made famous by some outstanding deed, we began to note who has done something with a noble spirit and great effort, but only once. We saw a man brave in war, but a coward in politics, a man who endured poverty with spirit, but disgrace with shame. [In these cases] we praised the deed and held the man in contempt.

10. But we have [also] seen a different man, who is kind to his friends, moderate to his enemies, governing public and private affairs in a pious and religious manner; we saw that he did not lack patience in enduring what had to be endured or prudence in doing what had to be done. We have seen his generosity in distributing, his effort and determination (which relieve bodily weariness) in working. Moreover, he was always consistent in every action, not good by some plan, but by character the sort of person who was not only able to act properly, but could not act otherwise. 11. In this man we came to understand perfect virtue, and we distinguished it into parts: the desires were to be held in check, fears repressed, plans made for action, what was owed was to be distributed; so we grasped temperance, courage, prudence, and justice and we assigned to each its own appropriate role. So where did we get our understanding of virtue? It was shown to us by his orderliness, fittingness and consistency, by the mutual harmony of all his actions, and by his greatness which elevated itself above all else. This is the source for our understanding of the happy life which flows smoothly in its own course and is completely in control of itself.

12. So how did this make itself apparent to us? I shall tell you. This perfect and virtuous man never cursed fortune, was never sad about what happened, regarded himself as a citizen and soldier of the cosmos and so endured all his labours as though he were under orders. Whatever happened, he did not scorn it as inflicted upon him by chance, but took it as a job assigned to him. He says, "This, whatever it may be, is mine; it is harsh and difficult, but it is to this that I must devote my efforts." 13. A man who never whined over misfortune and never complained about his fate of necessity appears to be great. He provided many people with an understanding of himself, like a light shining in the darkness; he attracted attention from everyone, though he was quiet and mild, equally able to handle human and divine affairs. 14. He had a mind which was perfect and had achieved its full potential; there is nothing greater, except the mind of god, from whom some portion was diverted into his mortal breast. This part is never more divine than when contemplating its mortality and realizing that man was born for dying, that his body is not a home but a guest-house—and a brief one at that, since it must be vacated when you see that you are a burden to your host.

Seneca *Letters on Ethics* 124.1–20   [II-110]

1. . . . The question is whether the good is grasped with the senses or the mind; connected with this is the fact that the good is not found in dumb animals and infants. 2. Those who make pleasure supreme hold that the good is perceptible, but we on the other hand attribute it to the mind and hold that it is intelligible. If the senses made judgements about the good, we would not reject any pleasure; for no pleasure fails to attract us and every pleasure pleases us; conversely, we would not willingly suffer any pain; for every pain hurts our senses. 3. Moreover, those who are excessively pleased by pleasure and who fear pain more than anything else would not deserve criticism. But in point of fact we do disapprove of those who are devoted to their bellies and to pleasure and we hold in

contempt those whose fear of pain prevents them from ever daring to act in a manly fashion. What are they doing wrong if they obey their senses, i.e., the judges of what is good and bad? For you have handed over the decision about what is good and bad to the senses. **4.** But surely it is reason which is in charge of that matter; that is what makes the decisions about good and bad, just as it does about the happy life, about virtue and about the honourable. But [the hedonists] let the lowest part [of man] make the decisions about what is better, so that judgement is pronounced on the good by sense perception, which is blunt and lazy, and slower in men than it is in beasts. **5.** What [would we think] if someone wanted to discriminate tiny things not by the eyes but by touch? . . .

6. He says, "Just as every branch of knowledge and every craft takes something which is obvious and is grasped by sense perception as the starting point from which it will develop, similarly, the happy life must take something obvious as its foundation and starting point. Surely you say that the happy life has something obvious as its starting point." **7.** We say that those things which are in accordance with nature are happy. And what is in accordance with nature is out in the open and immediately apparent, just as is the case with what is healthy. I do not call the natural, [i.e.,] what immediately affects a newborn [animal], good, but rather the starting point of the good. You give over the highest good, i.e., pleasure, to infancy, so that a newborn starts out from the point which a fully accomplished man [might hope to] reach. You put the top of the tree where the roots ought to be. **8.** It would be a blatant error if someone said that the fetus hidden in its mother's womb, still of uncertain sex, immature, unfinished and not yet formed, were already in some good condition. And yet, how small is the difference between one who is just in the act of receiving life and one who lies as a hidden burden inside its mother's body. As far as an understanding of good and bad is concerned, both are equally mature; an infant is no more capable of the good than a tree or some dumb animal! But why is the good not found in a tree or a dumb animal? Because reason is not there either. That is also the reason why it is missing in an infant; for infants too lack reason. It attains the good when it attains reason.

9. There is such a thing as a non-rational animal; and such a thing as an animal which is not yet rational; and one which is rational but not yet perfect. In none of them can you find the good, which is brought with reason. What is the difference, then, between the [kinds of animal] I have mentioned? In the non-rational the good will never exist; in that which is not yet rational the good cannot exist just then; ⟨in the rational⟩ but imperfect the good is already *able* to ⟨exist⟩, but does not. **10.** I maintain, Lucilius, that the good is not found in just any body, nor in just any age; it is as far from the state of infancy as the last is from the first and as the perfect is from its starting point; so it is not found in a young body, still immature and in the process of formation. Of course it is not found there, any more than it is found in the seed!

11. You could put it like this: we are familiar with the good in a tree or a plant: it does not lie in the first sprouts which are just breaking the soil as they sprout. There is something good in a stalk of wheat, but it is not yet present in the sappy sprout nor when the tender ear [first] emerges from the husk, but when it ripens with the heat of summer and its proper maturity. Just as every nature refuses to bring forth its good until it is finished, so too man's good is not present in man until his reason is perfected. 12. But what is this good? I shall say: a free and upright mind, superior to other things and inferior to nothing. So far is infancy from having this good that childhood does not hope for it, and adolescence is wrong to hope for it. We are lucky if it comes with old age as a result of long and serious effort. If this is what is good, it is also intelligible.

13. He says, "You said that there was a certain [kind of] good which belongs to a tree and to a plant; so there can also be a certain [kind of] good in an infant." The true good is not in trees or dumb animals; what is good in them is called good by courtesy. "What is this?" you say. [Merely] that which is in accord with the nature of each. But the good can in no way apply to a dumb animal; it belongs to a happier and better nature. Where there is no room for reason, there is no good. 14. There are these four kinds of natures: that of a tree, of an animal, of a man and of a god. The latter two are rational and have the same nature and differ [only] in that the one is immortal and the other mortal. Nature perfects the goodness of one of these, i.e., god, while effort perfects the goodness of the other, i.e., man. The others, which lack reason, are perfect in their own natures, but not really perfect. For in the final analysis the only thing which is perfect is that which is perfect in accordance with universal nature; and universal nature is rational. The other things can [only] be perfect in their own kind. 15. And in this there cannot exist a happy life, nor that which produces a happy life. But a happy life is produced by good things. In a dumb animal the happy life does not exist, ⟨nor does that by which a happy life⟩ is produced: the good does not exist in a dumb animal.

16. A dumb animal grasps what is present by its senses; it remembers past events when it meets with something which reminds its senses, as a horse is reminded of the road when it is placed at its starting point. But when in the stable he has no recollection of the road, no matter how

often he has trodden it. The third [part of] time, i.e., the future, does not apply to dumb animals. 17. So how can their nature seem to be perfect when they cannot make use of the past?[58] For time consists of three parts, past, present and future. For animals the present is the briefest and most transitory time; they rarely recall the past, and then only when it is occasioned by the occurence of something in the present. 18. Therefore, the good of a perfected nature cannot exist in an imperfect nature, or if such a nature has it, so do plants. I do not deny that dumb animals have great and powerful impulses towards achieving what is according to their natures; but they are disorderly and confused. But the good is never disorderly or confused. 19. "What, then?" you say, "are dumb animals moved in a thoroughly confused and disorganized fashion?" I would say that they are moved in a thoroughly confused and disorganized fashion, if their nature were capable of orderliness; but as it is, each is moved according to his own nature. Disorganized is [a term] reserved for those things which can sometimes move in a non-disorganized fashion; troubled [a term reserved] for that which can be free of care. Nothing has a vice if it cannot have virtue; and such is the motion of dumb animals by their very nature. 20. But to avoid detaining you any longer, there will be a kind of good in a dumb animal, a kind of virtue, and a kind of perfection; but there will not be good or virtue or perfection in an absolute sense, since these properties apply only to rational animals, to whom it has been given to know why, to what extent, and how. So nothing which does not have reason can possess the good. . . .

Plutarch *On Common Conceptions* 1076ab   [II-111]
(SVF 3.246)

(1076a) . . . So the third element in their conception of the gods is that the gods are superior to men in respect to nothing so much as their happiness and virtue. But according to Chrysippus they do not have even this superiority, for Zeus does not surpass Dion in virtue, and Zeus and Dion are benefitted equally by each other when one meets with a motion of the other, since they are [both] wise. For this is the only good which men get from the gods and the gods get from men when they become wise. (1076b) They say that if a man is not deficient in virtue he in no way falls short in happiness, but Zeus the saviour is no more blessed than the unfortunate man who commits suicide because of his bodily diseases and impairments—providing that he is wise.

---

58. "Past time" in Latin is *tempus perfectum*. The pun on 'perfect' is not readily translated.

Plutarch *On Common Conceptions* 1069e [II-112]
(SVF 3.491)

[Chrysippus] says, "So where shall I start from? And what am I to take as the principle of appropriate action and the raw material for virtue, if I give up nature and what is according to nature?"

Plutarch *On Stoic Self-Contradictions* [II-113]
1035a–d (SVF 2.42, 30; 3.326, 68)

(1035a) Chrysippus thinks that young men ought to study logic first, ethics second and then physics, and theology last of all as the culmination of the others. He says this in many places, but it will suffice to cite literally what is said in book four of *On Lives*: "First of all I think, following the correct account given by the ancients, that there are three kinds of theorems to be studied by a philosopher, those of logic, those of ethics and those of physics; and then that we must put the logical first, the ethical second, and the physical third. And theology is last in physics. (1035b) That is why the teaching of theology has been called a 'final revelation'." But in practice he usually puts this topic, which he says ought to put last, at the beginning of his every ethical enquiry. For manifestly he never utters a word on any topic—the goal of life, justice, good and bad things, marriage, child-rearing, law, citizenship—without prefacing his remarks (just as those who introduce decrees in public assemblies preface their remarks with invocations of Good Fortune) with references to Zeus, fate, providence, and stating that the cosmos is one and finite, being held together by a single power. And none of this can be believed, (1035c) except by someone who is thoroughly immersed in physics. So listen to what he says about these matters in book three of *On Gods*: "for one can find no other starting point or origin for justice except the one derived from Zeus and that derived from the common nature; for everything like this must take that as its starting point, if we are going to say anything at all about good and bad things." And again in his *Propositions in Physics*: "there is no other, and certainly no more appropriate, way to approach the discussion of good and bad things or the virtues or happiness, ⟨except⟩ on the basis of common nature and the administration of the cosmos." (1035d) A bit further on again, "for the discussion of good and bad things must be linked to them, since there is no better starting point or reference point and since the study of physics is not to be taken up for any other reason than to distinguish good from bad."

Plutarch *On Stoic Self-Contradictions*   [II-114]
1037c–1038c (SVF 3.520,175,674,179;
2.171,724)

(1037c) . . . They say that a [morally] perfect action is what the law
commands and that a [moral] mistake is what the law forbids, and that
is why the law forbids the foolish to do many things (1037d) but commands them to do nothing; for they are unable to perform a [morally]
perfect action. And who is not aware that it is impossible for someone
who cannot perform a [morally] perfect action to avoid making a [moral]
mistake? So [the Stoics] put the law in conflict with itself by commanding
what they are unable to do and forbidding what they are unable to refrain
from. For the man who cannot be temperate cannot avoid being wanton,
and he who cannot be prudent cannot avoid acting imprudently. Indeed,
they themselves say that those who forbid say one thing, forbid another
and command yet another. For he who says "do not steal" says just this,
"do not steal", (1037e) forbids ⟨stealing and commands⟩ not stealing. So
the law won't be forbidding base men to do anything if it is not giving
them a command. Moreover, they say that the doctor commands his
apprentice to cut and burn, with the omission [of the specification] that
he should do so at the right time and in the right manner, just as the
music master [commands his student] to play the lyre or sing with the
omission [of the specification] that they do so tunefully and harmoniously.
The reason why they punish the students who do these things inartistically
and badly is that they were ordered to act on the understanding that it
be done so properly, but they did not act properly. Therefore, when the
wise man commands his servant to do or say something and punishes
him for doing it at the wrong time or in the wrong manner, obviously
he too is commanding him to an intermediate act and not a [morally]
perfect act. But if wise men command base men to perform intermediate
acts, (1037f) why can the commands of the law not be like this? And
indeed, impulse, according to [Chrysippus] is the reason of man commanding him to act, as he wrote in his treatise *On Law*. Therefore, an
impulse away from something is reason forbidding, ⟨and so is avoidance,
for it is reasonable, since it is the opposite of desire; and according to
him caution⟩ is reasonable avoidance. (1038a) So caution, then, is reason
which forbids the wise man [to do something]. For being cautious is
special to the wise man and does not belong to base men. So if the wise
man's reason is distinct from the law, then the wise men will have their
caution, i.e., their reason, in conflict with law. But if law is nothing other
than the wise man's reason, then the law is found to be forbidding wise
men to do those things which they are cautious about.

Chrysippus says that nothing is useful to base men, and that the base man makes use of nothing and needs nothing. After saying this in book one of his *On [Morally] Perfect Actions* he goes on to say later that utility and gratitude extend to intermediate actions, none of which is useful according to the Stoics. (1038b) Moreover, he also says that nothing is congenial or fitting for the base, in following words: "similarly, nothing is alien to the virtuous man and nothing is congenial to the base man, since one of these properties is good and the other is bad." So why does he grind on in every single book on physics, and even, by Zeus! on ethics, writing that as soon as we are born we are congenial to ourselves and to our parts and to our offspring? And in book one of *On Justice* he says that even beasts find their offspring congenial in accordance with the needs of the offspring, except in the case of fish; for even the unhatched eggs are nourished by themselves. (1038c) But there is no sense-perception for those to whom nothing is perceptible and there is no congeniality for those to whom nothing is congenial. For congeniality seems to be a perception and grasp of what is congenial.

Sextus Empiricus *M* 11.22–30 (SVF 3.75)   [II-115]

22. The Stoics cling to the common conceptions and define the good as follows: "good is benefit or what is not other than benefit." By benefit they mean virtue and virtuous action, and by not other than benefit they mean the virtuous man and a friend. **23.** For since virtue is the leading part of the soul in a certain state, and virtuous action is an activity in accordance with virtue, they are immediately beneficial. And the virtuous man and the friend, who themselves belong to the class of good things, would not properly be termed benefit, but neither would they be other than benefit, for the following reason. **24.** For, the followers of the Stoics say, the parts are not the same as the whole nor are they different in kind from the whole; for example, the hand is not the same as the whole man (for the hand is not a whole man), nor is it other than the whole, since the entire man is conceived of as a man together with his hand. So, since virtue is a part of the virtuous man and of the friend, and the parts are neither the same as the whole nor other than the whole, it is said that the virtuous man and the friend are not other than benefit. Consequently, every good thing is encompassed by the definition, whether it is immediately a benefit or is not other than benefit. **25.** Hence and consequently they say that good is said in three senses; and they outline each of its meanings in its own formulation. For one sense of good, they say, is that by which or from which it is possible to be benefitted, which is indeed the most fundamental sense and is [the same as] virtue; for from this as from a spring every other utility naturally flows. **26.** In another sense it is that according to which being benefitted is a characteristic result. In this not only will the virtues be called good but also virtuous actions, since it is characteristic of them that benefit results. **27.** In the third and final sense good is said to be that which is such as to benefit, this description encompassing the virtues, virtuous actions, friends, virtuous men and gods and excellent daimons. . . . . **30.** . . . and there were some who said that the good is that which is worth choosing for its own sake; and some who used this definition: "good is that which contributes to happiness"; and others who said that it is "that which fulfils happiness". And happiness is, according to definition given by the followers of Zeno, Cleanthes and Chrysippus, a smooth flow of life.

Sextus Empiricus *M* 11.61–67 (SVF 3.122)   [II-116]

61. In the third and final sense the indifferent is that which contributes neither to happiness nor to misery, and it is in this sense that they say that health and disease and everything bodily and most external things are indifferent, since they tend to produce neither happiness nor misery. For that which can be used well and badly would be indifferent. Virtue is always used well; vice is always used badly; but health and bodily things can be used sometimes well and sometimes badly, and that is why they would be indifferent. **62.** And of indifferents, they say, some are preferred and some are rejected; the preferred are those which have considerable value, the rejected are those which have considerable dis-value, and neither preferred nor rejected are things like holding one's finger straight or crooked and everything like this. **63.** Health and strength and beauty, wealth and reputation and things like these, are counted among the preferred things; disease and poverty and pain and similar things are counted among the rejected. That is what the Stoics say.

64. Ariston of Chios said that health and everything similar to it are not preferred indifferents. For to say that it is a preferred indifferent is tantamount to claiming that it is good, since they practically differ only in name. **65.** In general, things which are indifferent as between virtue and vice are indistinguishable, nor are some naturally preferred and others naturally rejected; rather [they vary] in accordance with different circumstances and occasions. Thus things which are said to be preferred are not unconditionally preferred, nor are things called rejected uncondi-tionally rejected. **66.** Anyway, if it were necessary for healthy men to serve a tyrant and for this reason to be executed, while sick men were released from service and so also freed from destruction, the wise man would choose sickness over health on such an occasion. And in this way health is not unconditionally a preferred thing, nor is disease rejected. 67. So just as when we write words we sometimes put one letter first, sometimes another, fitting them to their different circumstances (we write the D first for Dion's name, the I first for Ion, the O first for Orion); it is not that some letters are naturally preferred to others, but just that circumstances force us to do this. In the same way in matters which are intermediate between virtue and vice there is no natural preference for one set over the other, but this, rather, is determined by circumstances.

Galen *On the Doctrines of Hippocrates and* [II-117]
Plato 4.2.9–18 (5.368–370 K; SVF 3.462)

We shall see this more clearly if we quote his own [Chrysippus'] utterances. The first passage goes like this: "We must first keep in mind that the rational animal is by nature such as to follow reason and to act according to reason as a guide. Nevertheless, he often moves toward some things and away from some things in another way, disobediently to reason, when he is pushed too far [or to excess]. Both definitions [of passion, the one mentioning] the natural motion which arises irrationally in this way and [the one mentioning] the excessiveness in the impulses, are in terms of this motion. For this irrationality must be taken to be disobedient to reason and turning its back on reason. And it is in terms of this motion that we also say in ordinary usage that some people are 'pushed' and 'moved irrationally without reason and judgement'. For we do not use these expressions as if someone is moved mistakenly and because he overlooks something that is according to reason, but most especially according to the motion he [Zeno?] outlines, since the rational animal does not naturally move in accordance with his soul in this way, but rather in accordance with reason. . . . The excess of the impulse was also spoken of in terms of this, because they overstep the symmetry of impulses which is proper to themselves and natural. What I say would be made easier to understand by means of these examples. In walking according to impulse the motion of the legs is not excessive but is in a sense coextensive with the impulse, so that it can come to a standstill when he [the walker] wishes, or change direction. But in the case of those who are running according to impulse, this sort of thing is no longer the case, but the motion of the legs exceeds the impulse so that it is carried away and does not change direction obediently in this way as soon as they start to do so. I think something similar to these motions [of the legs] occurs in the impulses because of the overstepping of the symmetry which is according to reason, so that whenever one has an impulse he is not obedient with respect to it, the excess being beyond the impulse in the case of running and beyond reason in the case of impulse. For the symmetry of natural impulse is that according to reason and is as far as reason thinks proper. Therefore, since the overstepping is according to this [sc. standard] and in this way, the impulse is said to be excessive and an unnatural and irrational motion of the soul."

Galen *On the Doctrines of Hippocrates and*   [II-118]
Plato 4.4.16–18, 24–25 (5.385–387 K; SVF 3.476)

Chrysippus himself shows this in the following quotation: "That is why it is not off the mark to say, as some people do, that a passion of the soul is an unnatural motion, as is the case with fear and desire and things like that. For all such motions and conditions are disobedient to reason and reject it. And so we say that such people are irrationally moved, not as though they make a bad calculation, which would be the sense opposite to 'reasonably', but rather in the sense of a rejection of reason." . . . 4.4.24 "That is what such conditions are like, uncontrolled, as though they were not masters of themselves but were carried away in the manner as those who run strenuously are swept away and cannot control their motion. But those who move according to reason, as though it were their leader, and steer their course by it wherever it might lead, these people are in control of this sort of motion and the impulses that go with it."

Plutarch *On Moral Virtue* 446f–447a   [II-119]
(SVF 3.459)

But some say that passion is not something distinct from reason, and that there is no disagreement and strife between two things, but that the reason which is a single thing turns in both directions, (447a) and this escapes our notice because of the sharpness and speed of the change, since we do not realize that it is the same thing in the soul which gives us the ability to desire and to regret, to get angry and to fear, to be drawn to shameful acts by pleasure and to fight back against this temptation. For they say that desire and anger and fear and all such things are bad opinions and judgements, and that they do not arise in some one part of the soul, but are cases of the inclination, yielding, assent and impulse of the leading part of the soul, and in general are activities which can change in a very short time, just as the charging around of children is violent, very unstable and uncertain because of their weakness.

Galen *On the Doctrines of Hippocrates and* [II-120]
Plato 5.1.4, 4.3.2 (5.429, 5.377 K; SVF 1.209)

In book one of his *On Passions* Chrysippus tries to show that the passions are certain judgements [formed] by the leading part of the soul, but Zeno did not believe that the passions were the judgements themselves but contractions, relaxations, elations and depressions which supervene on the judgements. .... **4.3.2** [Chrysippus] is in conflict with Zeno on this point, and with himself and many other Stoics who did not suppose that the passions of the soul were judgements of the soul but rather the irrational contractions, depressions, 'bites', elations and relaxations which follow those [judgements].

Galen *On the Doctrines of Hippocrates and* [II-121]
Plato 5.2.49–5.3.8 (5.444–447 K; SVF 2.841)

[Chrysippus said,] "There do exist parts of the soul out of which the reason in it and the disposition in [the reason] are composed. And the soul is honourable or shameful in accordance with the condition of its leading part with respect to its proper divisions." What are these proper divisions, Chrysippus, which will you write about next to get us out of our difficulties? But you did not explain this here or in any of your books; but just as though the whole central issue of the discussion of the passions did not turn on this point, you immediately give up on teaching it and drag out your discussion with irrelevant considerations. But you ought to stick to the point and indicate just what these parts of the reasoning part of the soul are. But since you have abandoned the argument— whether intentionally or inadvertently I cannot guess—I shall try to follow your doctrines and discover your intention and then to consider its truth, and I shall take my start from the passage just quoted, which is: "There do exist parts of the soul out of which the reason in it is composed." Perhaps you are reminding us of what you wrote in your *On Rational Discourse*, where you explained that reason is an aggregation of certain conceptions and basic grasps. But if you think that each of the conceptions and basic grasps is a part of the soul, then you are making two mistakes. First of all, you should not have said that they were parts of soul but parts of reason, just as you have written in your *On Rational Discourse*. For surely soul and reason are not the same thing; besides, you proved in the preceding discussion that reason too is one of the components in the soul—and the soul and a component in it are not the same. And second, even if we let this first point go by without refutation, still one should not call conceptions and basic grasps *parts* of the soul but rather activities. But nothing is *composed* of its proper activities, neither the eye nor the ear nor the hand nor the leg nor any other bodily organ. . . . 5.3.7 For conceptions and basic grasps are activities of the soul, but its parts, as you yourself explain elsewhere, are the auditory *pneuma* and the visual *pneuma*, and again the vocal in addition to these and the reproductive, but above all the leading part of the soul, of which you said that the reason is a component and which is the part [of the soul] in virtue of which (more than any other part) you say that the shameful and the honourable come to inhere in it.

III: Scepticism

Academic Scepticism: Arcesilaus and Carneades

Diogenes Laertius 4.28–44 (selections) [III-1]

28. Arcesilaus, the son of Seuthos (or of Scythos according to Apollodorus, in the third book of his *Chronology*) was born in Pitane, in Aeolis. He is the founder of the Middle Academy and the first to suspend [making] assertions because of the contradictions among arguments. He was also the first to argue both sides of a question and the first to change the doctrine handed down by Plato, that is, to make it more eristic by the use of question and answer. . . .

32. . . . Some say that Arcesilaus never wrote a book because he suspended judgement about everything. Others say that he was discovered finishing up some work which, according to some, he published, but according to others, he burned. He seems to have admired Plato and he possessed his books. According to some, he also emulated Pyrrho, and practised dialectic and took up Eretrian argumentative procedures,[1] as a result of which, Ariston said of him, "Plato in front, Pyrrho in back, and Diodorus in the middle." . . .

37. He was most inventive at finding exactly the right words with which to counter opponents, at steering the course of argument back to the topic, and at saying the right thing on every occasion. He was more persuasive than anybody at all, which drew many to his school, even though they were chastened by his sharpness. Still, they bore it gladly, for he was an extremely good man and inspired his pupils with hopes. He was most generous in his way of living and was always quick to do a good deed and to conceal the favor, being a very modest man. For example, one time he went to see Ctesibius who was sick and, seeing that he was hard pressed for money, secretly put a purse under his pillow. When Ctesibius found it he said, "This is Arcesilaus' little joke." Another time he sent him 1000 drachmas. . . .

---

1. The Eretrian school, founded by Menedemus, seems to have been a continuation of the school of Elis and to have concentrated on dialectic; see Cicero *Academica* 2.129.

42. . . . He was, though, modest enough to advise his pupils to attend the lectures of others too. When some Chian youth was not satisfied with his approach, preferring that of the above-mentioned Hieronymus, Arcesilaus himself led him to that philosopher and introduced him, advising him to behave himself.

43. There is also this pleasant story about him. When asked by someone why people were defecting to the Epicurean school from the others, but never the other way around, he said, "Because eunuchs are made from men, not men from eunuchs." . . .

44. . . . According to Hermippus, he died having indulged in too much unmixed wine, which made him mad. He was already 75 years old by this time and had been accepted by the Athenians as no one else had been.

Numenius in Eusebius *Prep. Ev.* bk. xiv, ch. vi, 730b–731c   [III-2]

(730b) No one knew about Arcesilaus' stand any more than they knew about which side the son of Tydaeus was on,[2]—about whom Homer said that no one knew whether he sided with the Trojans or the Achaeans. (730c) He did not have it in him ever to express one and the same position nor, for that matter, did he think such a thing at all worthy of a shrewd man. And that is why he was called a "clever sophist, cutthroat of novices." For just like the Empusae,[3] he was enchanting and bewitching with his verbal apparitions, as a result of careful preparation and practice, and he would not allow that he or anyone else was in a position to know anything. He terrified and confused [others], and indeed took first prize for sophistical arguments and argumentative fraud, delighting in the charge, and priding himself marvellously on not knowing whether something is shameful or honourable, good or bad; (730d) but he would say whatever came into his head and then immediately reversing himself he would knock down that view in more ways than he had used to set it up.

Like a hydra, he decapitated himself and was decapitated by himself, not distinguishing which was which and with no consideration for propriety. Still, he satisfied his hearers, who could observe his handsome face while he lectured. He was therefore most pleasing to hear and see, at least once they became accustomed to hearing the words come from his beautiful face and mouth (not to mention the kindness in his eyes).

Don't think that this is a trivial matter, since he was like this from the very beginning. (731a) For when he was a boy he fell in with Theo-

---

2. *Iliad* 5.801 ff.

3. Bogey-women of antiquity.

phrastus, a kindly man and no stranger to the affairs of love; and because he still had his youthful beauty he became the beloved of Crantor, the Academic, to whom he devoted himself—but since he was not without natural gifts he employed them effortlessly as he went, and, enflamed with ambition, he acquired from Diodorus those clever, all-purpose persuasive arguments, while associating with Pyrrho too. **(731b)** (Pyrrho was inspired by Democritus in one way or another.) Being equipped from one source and another, Arcesilaus persisted in refuting everything, just like a Pyrrhonian except for the name. At any rate, Mnaseas and Philomelus and Timon, the Sceptics, called him a sceptic, just like themselves, since he abolished truth, falsity, and plausibility.

Thus, because of his Pyrrhonian arguments, he was called a Pyrrhonian, but out of deference to his lover he let himself continue to be called an Academic. So, whereas he was a Pyrrhonist except in name, he was not an Academic, except for being called one. For I am not persuaded of what Diocles of Cnidus says in his work called *Diatribes*, namely, that Arcesilaus, for fear of the disciples **(731c)** of Theodorus and Bion the sophist, who attacked philosophers and would stop at nothing to refute them, took precautions so that he would not have difficulties, never appearing to endorse a dogma, but rather emitting the suspension of judgement for his own protection, like the ink emitted by a squid. But I am not persuaded of this.

Diogenes Laertius 4.62–66 (selections) [III-3]

62. Carneades of Cyrene was the son of Epicomus or, according to Alexander in his *Successions*, of Philocomus. He read carefully the books of the Stoics, particularly those of Chrysippus. He countered these so persuasively and acquired thereupon so much renown that he remarked, "If there were no Chrysippus, I would not be." He was an industrious man if anybody was, applying himself less to physical matters and more to ethical. As a result of his occupation with his studies he let his hair and nails grow. He was so powerful in philosophy that even rhetoricians would dismiss their classes and go and listen to him. . . .

64. . . . He seems to have faced death rather fearfully for at that time he continually said "nature which has composed [me] will decompose [me]." When he learned that Antipater died by drinking poison, he was moved by his courageous demise and said, "Give it then to me too." "What?" he was asked. "A sweet drink," he said. They say that when he died there was an eclipse of the moon, a hint, one might say, of the sympathy of the most beautiful of heavenly bodies after the sun.

65. Apollodorus in his *Chronicles* said that he died in the fourth year of the 162nd Olympiad [129–128 B.C.] at 85 years of age. His letters to Ariarathes, king of Cappadocia are extant. As to the rest, his pupils wrote up his views. He himself left nothing.

Numenius in Eusebius *Prep. Ev.* bk. xiv, ch.   [III-4] vii–viii, 736d–739d (selections)

(736d) "After these [Lacydes, Evander, Hegesinus of Pergamum][4] Carneades inherited leadership of the school and founded the third Academy. In arguments he used the same approach as Arcesilaus. For he himself practiced the method of arguing on both sides of a question and demolished all the claims made by others. He set himself apart from [Arcesilaus] only in his account of suspension of judgement, saying that it was impossible for a human being to suspend judgement about absolutely everything, that there was a difference between 'non-evident' and 'ungraspable,' and that everything was ungraspable, but that not everything was non-evident. (737a) Carneades was acquainted with Stoic theories and by his eristic opposition to them grew in fame, by aiming not at the truth, but at what appeared to be plausible to the many. As a result, he provided much discomfort to the Stoics." This, then, is what Numenius too writes about him.

(737b) "Carneades, having succeeded Hegesinus, did not take care to defend what he should have, namely, the [distinction between which of] his doctrines were settled and which had changed, but rather, referring everything back to Arcesilaus, no matter if what he had said was better or worse, renewed the conflict [between Sceptics and Stoics] after a long interval." And next he (737c) adds, "Indeed, Carneades used to advance and put forward contradictory claims and he brought to the conflict subtle twists of argument of various sorts; he would deny, affirm, and contradict both sides. Whenever he needed something impressive for his arguments, he would rise up, roaring like a rushing river over-flowing both its banks, and would come crashing down and sweep away his hearers with his tumultuous voice. Sweeping aside the others, he never led himself astray, which was not the case with Arcesilaus. For he, while defrauding his frenzied companions with his quackery, did not notice that he had first deceived himself: because he had refuted absolutely everything, he had not (737d) noticed that he had come to believe that what he was saying was true.

Carneades was, with regard to Arcesilaus, an evil on top of an evil,

---

4. The text of Eusebius mistakenly gives Aristippus of Cyrene as the successor of Evander. The correct version is given below at 737b and by Diogenes Laertius (4.60).

not giving the slightest opening to his opponents whereby they might avoid being 'inactive'. [He argued] in accordance with positive and negative presentations (which he said were based on plausibility) that something was an animal or was not an animal. And so conceding this point, like wild animals which recoil to throw themselves more violently against the spears, he himself, having given in [about plausibility], was better able to attack. And when he withstood an attack and emerged victorious, he would go right ahead and disregard what he had previously held, and even forget about it. (738a) He would allow that truth and falsity were present in things, as though he were cooperating in the investigation; like a clever wrestler, he gave [his opponent] a good hold and then used it to get the upper hand. For, by granting either [side of a disagreement] in accordance with the weight of plausibility, he would then say that neither side could be securely grasped.

He was both a bandit and a rather clever sorcerer. For taking hold of a falsehood similar to a truth, and one graspable presentation similar to another, he would put them on the same footing and not grant that either the true one or the false one was the case or that one was more the case than the other, (738b) or that one had more plausibility than the other. It was then dreams for dreams, because false presentations were similar to true ones, as in the case of the wax egg compared with a real one. And the evils multiplied. And still Carneades, when he spoke, charmed men's souls and enslaved them. He was both a sneak thief and a brazen bandit, conquering by trickery or force even those who were very well prepared for him. At any rate, every idea of Carneades was victorious and no one else's was, since those with whom he did battle were less powerful in speaking.

(738c) "Antipater [the Stoic], for example, who lived at the same time as he, even intended to strain himself to write something in opposition to Carneades. He never made it public, however, in the face of the stream of arguments coming daily from Carneades. He did not say anything nor even utter a sound either in the schools or in the streets; in fact, they say that no one heard even a single syllable from him. But he kept threatening replies and kept to a corner where he wrote books which he left for posterity which are now useless and were then even more useless against a man like Carneades who appeared to be exceedingly great and renowned among the men of his time. (738d) Nevertheless, Carneades sowed confusion in public because of his rivalry with the Stoics, but in private with his friends he would agree to things, say that things were true, and make claims just like anyone else." . . .

(739a) And again he adds, "Carneades, expressing contradictory philosophical positions, as it were, decked himself out with falsehoods and concealed the truth beneath them. So, he used falsehoods as curtains and, hiding behind these, kept the truth in the back room, hiding it like a [crooked] shopkeeper. His nature, therefore, was like that of beans, where the empty ones float on water and rise to the top and the good ones sink and disappear."

This is what is said about Carneades. Clitomachus was installed as the successor in his school, and after him Philo, about whom Numenius remarks, **(739b)** "Philo, as soon as he acquired headship of the school, was filled with joy, and rendering homage, he honored and extolled the doctrines of Clitomachus, and, against the Stoics, **(739c)** he 'armed himself with gleaming bronze'."[5]

As time went by and their doctrine of suspension of judgement lost the impact of its novelty, Philo could not maintain his previous way of thinking, but rather the clarity and consistency of his experiences began to turn him around. Having so much clarity in his insights, he was extremely eager, you may be sure, to find someone who would refute him so that he would not appear to have turned his back and to have fled of his own accord. Antiochus became a pupil of Philo and founded another Academy. At any rate, he attended the lectures of Mnesarchus the Stoic, and adopted views contrary to **(739d)** those of Philo his teacher, foisting on the Academy countless alien views."

Diogenes Laertius 4.66–67   [III-5]

66. ... [Carneades] had many other students, the most famous of whom was Clitomachus. We should also speak of him ... 67. Clitomachus was a Carthaginian. His real name was Hasdrubal. He used to philosophize in Carthage in his native language. At 40 years of age he came to Athens where he heard Carneades. The latter, perceiving his industriousness, arranged for him to learn to read and write [Greek] and himself took part in his training. He exerted himself so much that he wrote more than 400 books. He succeeded Carneades and in his writings elucidated his [master's] views in particular. The man was trained in three systems: Academic, Peripatetic, and Stoic. ...

---

5. Homer *Iliad* 7.206.

Cicero *Academica* 2.28 [III-6]

Hence arose the demand made just now by Hortensius, that you [sceptics] should at least concede that the wise man has grasped that nothing can be grasped. But Antipater [the Stoic] demanded the very same thing, and said that it was consistent for him who affirmed that nothing could be perceived to say that [at least] this one thing could be perceived, even if other things could not. Carneades argued against him with greater acuity: for, he said that, far from being consistent, it was in fact totally self-contradictory. For he who denies that there is anything that can be grasped makes no exceptions; therefore, it is necessary that not even [the claim that nothing can be grasped] can in any way be grasped and perceived, since it has not been excepted [from the general claim].

Cicero *Academica* 2.40–42 [III-7]

40. But now let us look at the opposing arguments usually advanced by the other side [i.e., the Academics]. But first you can become acquainted with what are, as it were, the foundations of their entire system. So first of all they put together a sort of craft dealing with what we call presentations, and they define their character and types, and in particular they [define] what sort of thing can be perceived and grasped, at as great a length as the Stoics do. Then they elaborate the two propositions which, as it were, constitute this entire investigation. [1] When there are things which are so presented that other things can be presented in the same way, and that there is no difference between [the two presentations], it is not possible that the one group should be perceived and the other not. [2] However, [they say that] there is no difference, not just if they are of the same quality in all respects, but even if they cannot [in fact] be distinguished [by the perceiver]. When these premises are laid down, the whole issue is contained in one argument; and the argument is put together as follows. Some presentations are true, some false; what is false cannot be perceived; but every true presentation is such that there can be a false presentation of the same quality; and with presentations which are such that there is no difference between them it cannot happen that some can be perceived while others cannot; therefore, there is no presentation which can be perceived.

41. They think that of the premisses they assume in order to generate the desired conclusion, two will be granted to them (and in fact no one does reject these two); these are, [first] that false presentations cannot be perceived, and the other is that with presentations between which there is no difference it is not possible that some should be such as to

be perceived while others are not. The other premises they defend with a complex and lengthy discussion; these other premises are also two in number, first that some presentations are true while others are false, and second that every presentation coming from something true is such that it could also have come from something false.

42. They do not just fly past these two propositions; rather, they develop them with extraordinary care and diligence. For they first subdivide [the argument] into major parts: [1] first the senses, [2] then the inferences which we draw from the senses and ordinary experience (which they want to claim is obscure), and [3] finally they come to the part in which they claim that even with reason and inference it is not possible for anything to be perceived. They divide these general arguments even more finely; the method you saw them using on the senses yesterday is also used for the other parts; for in each and every case—and they subdivide very finely indeed—they want to show that true presentations are coupled with false ones which differ in no respect from the true; and since they are of this nature, they cannot be grasped.

Cicero *Academica* 2.59–60   [III-8]

59. But the real absurdity comes with your statement that you follow what is plausible, providing that you are not hindered by anything. First of all, how can you fail to be hindered by the very fact that falsehoods are not distinct from truths? Next, what criterion can there be of truth if it is shared with falsehood? This, necessarily, was the origin of the doctrine of *epoche* i.e., withholding of assent. Arcesilaus was more consistent on this, if what some people say about Carneades is true. For if nothing can be perceived—and this is what both of them thought— assent must be eliminated. For what is more pointless than that anything which is not *known* should be approved of? We kept hearing yesterday that Carneades was in the habit of slipping into the concession that the wise man would sometimes hold an opinion, i.e., make a [moral] mistake. But I am not as certain that there is something which can be grasped (and I have been arguing this thesis for quite some time now), as I am that the wise man does not hold [mere] opinions, i.e., the wise man never gives his assent to anything which is false or not known.

60. There remains their claim that one ought to argue pro and contra everything, for the sake of discovering the truth. All right, then, I want to see what they have discovered. He [Carneades] says, "it is not our custom to set forth [our views]." Well, whatever are those mysteries? Why do you hide your opinion as though it were something to be ashamed of? He says, "it is in order that our audience should be guided by reason and not by authority." . . .

Cicero *Academica* 2.66–67 [III-9]

66. . . . When presentations strike my mind or senses forcefully, I accept them and sometimes I even assent to them—not that I perceive them, for I do not think that anything can be perceived. I am not wise, and so I yield to presentations and cannot resist them; but Arcesilaus agrees with Zeno [the Stoic] and holds that the wise man's chief strength is that he is careful not to be tricked and sees to it that he is not deceived; for nothing is more alien to the conception which we have of the seriousness of a wise man than error, frivolity or rashness. What shall I say then of the wise man's steadfastness? Even you, Lucullus, concede that he never holds a [mere] opinion. And since you approve of this thesis . . . consider first the force of this argument: 67. If a wise man ever assents to anything, then he will sometimes hold [mere] opinions; but he will never hold [mere] opinions; therefore he will assent to nothing. Arcesilaus approved of this argument, for he argued in support of the first and second premisses. Carneades sometimes conceded the second premiss, i.e., that the wise man sometimes assents; hence it followed that the wise man holds [mere] opinions. You want to avoid this, and rightly so in my view. But the first premiss, that the wise man will have [mere] opinions if he gives assent, is held to be false by the Stoics and their supporter Antiochus, on the grounds that he [the wise man] can distinguish falsehoods from truths and what is not perceptible from what is perceptible.

Cicero *Academica* 2.76–78 [III-10]

76. . . . From what follows one can understand that Arcesilaus did not fight with Zeno for the sake of quarrelling but really wanted to discover the truth. 77. None of his predecessors ever formally claimed or even merely mentioned that it was possible for a man to hold no opinions, while it was not only possible but even necessary for a wise man to do so. Arcesilaus thought that this view was true, and respectable and worthy of a wise man. Perhaps he asked Zeno what would happen if [a] the wise man could not perceive anything, and [b] it was not fitting for the wise man to hold a [mere] opinion. I think that Zeno would have said that the wise man would indeed avoid forming an opinion because there *was* something which could be perceived. So what would this be? A

presentation, I believe. So what kind of presentation? Then Zeno defined it as a presentation which came from an existing thing and which was formed, shaped and moulded exactly as that thing was. Next question: could a true presentation be of the same quality as a false one? Here Zeno was quite sharp and saw that no presentation could be perceived if, though it came from something which exists, it could be of the same quality as that which came something which does not exist. Arcesilaus agrees that the addition to the definition was correct, since what is false cannot be perceived and neither can what is true if it is just like what is false. The burden of his argument in those debates was to show that there in fact existed no presentation coming from something true which was not such that one of the same quality could have come from something false.

78. This is the one dispute which has persisted [unchanged] until our own day. For the claim that the wise man would assent to nothing was not in the least essential to this debate. For he could well perceive nothing and yet still hold an opinion—which is the view of which Carneades is said to have approved. However, I follow Clitomachus, rather than Philo or Metrodorus, and so think that this thesis was advanced as a debating point rather than as something of which he really approved. But never mind that now. If opinion and perception are eliminated, suspension of all assent certainly follows; consequently, if I show that nothing can be perceived you should concede that [the wise man] will never assent.

Cicero *Academica* 2.95–98   [III-11]

95. . . . But I [a sceptic speaks] leave this point and ask the following question: if those propositions [i.e., the Liar paradox, etc.] cannot be explicated and there is no criterion for them such that you could answer that they are true or false, what is left of your [i.e., the Stoic] definition, which claims that a proposition is that which is true or false? For if one takes a group of propositions, I make the further claim that of these some are to be approved of and some rejected—i.e., the ones which are contradictory to the former. 96. So what do you make of how this argument works? 'If you say that it is now light and you speak the truth, then it is light; but you say that it is now light and you speak the truth; therefore it is light." Surely you approve of the general form of argument and say that it is a completely valid argument; that is why you treat it as the first argument form in your teaching of logic. So, either you will approve of every argument which uses the same form, or the entire craft [of logic] is nullified. So see whether you are going to approve of this

argument: 'if you say you are lying and you speak the truth, then you are lying; but you do say that you are lying and you speak the truth; therefore, you are lying'. How can you avoid approving of this argument when you have approved of the previous one which has the same form? These problems were put by *Chrysippus*, but even he did not solve them. For what would he make of this argument: 'if it is light, it is light; but it is light; therefore, it is light.' Surely he would allow it; for the very nature of the conditional is such that when you have granted the antecedent you are compelled to grant the consequent. How then does this argument differ from the following? 'If you are lying, you are lying; but you are lying; therefore, you are lying'. You say that you can neither approve of this nor disapprove of it; so how can you do any better with the other? If craft, reason, method, if rational inference itself have any force, then they are all found equally in both arguments.

97. Their final position is this: they demand that these [arguments] be excepted as inexplicable. I think they had better appeal to a tribune for their exception; they will certainly never get it from me. Further, they cannot get Epicurus, who disdains and scoffs at dialectic as a whole, to grant that statements of this form are true, 'either Hermarchus will be alive tomorrow or he will not', despite the declaration of the dialecticians that every utterance with this form, '*p* or not-*p*' is not just true but necessary; but notice the cleverness of the man whom those dialecticians think is slow-witted: 'if I grant that one of the two is necessary, then it will be necessary tomorrow for Hermarchus either to live or not to live; but there is no such necessity in the nature of things.'

So let your dialecticians, i.e., Antiochus and the Stoics, quarrel with Epicurus; for he undermines all of dialectic, since if a disjunction of contradictories (by contradictories I mean two statements, one of which says *p* and the other not-*p*)—if such a disjunction can be false then none is true. 98. So what is their quarrel with me, who follow their own teaching on the matter? When this sort of problem arose, Carneades used to tease them as follows: 'if my argument is sound, then I will stick to it; but if it is unsound, then Diogenes should give me my mina back.' For he had studied dialectic with this Stoic, and that was the fee which dialecticians used to charge. So I follow the methods which I learned from Antiochus; and therein I do not find any reason to judge that 'if it is light, it is light' is true (for the reason that I learned that every doubled conditional is true) and not to judge that 'if you are lying, you are lying' is a conditional of the same form. Either, then, I will make both judgements, or if I should not make the one, then I should not make the other either.

Plutarch *Against Colotes* 1122a–f   [III-12]

(1122a) . . . Not even those who concerned themselves a great deal
with this matter and wrote exhaustive books and tracts were able to shake
the doctrine of suspension of judgement on all questions. But at last the
Stoics brought against it like a Gorgon's head (1122b) the "argument
from inaction" and then gave up. For despite all their poking and twisting,
impulse refused to become assent and did not accept sense-perception
as the basic principle which tipped the scales [i.e., determined what one
would do], but it [i.e., impulse] turned out to lead to action all on
its own, not needing the assent [of the agent]. For debates with those
philosophers [i.e., sceptics] are carried out by the rules of dialectic and
"Such a word as you spoke, that you will hear as an answer".[6]

But the discussion about impulse and assent, I think, gets no better
hearing from [the Epicurean] Colotes than lyre music gets from an ass.
The argument [of the sceptics] runs like this—for those who listen to it
and are capable of following it: there are three movements in the soul,
that of presentation, that of impulse, and that of assent. Presentation
cannot be removed even by those who want to, (1122c) but it is necessary
that those who meet with objects should be impressed and affected by
them; and impulse is awoken by presentation, and moves man to act
with respect to what is appropriate for him, as though a tipping of the
scales and an inclination occurred in the leading part [of the soul]. Now,
those who suspend judgement on all matters do not abolish this second
motion either, but they use impulse, which naturally leads a man towards
what is presented as being congenial to him.

What, then, is the only thing which the sceptics avoid? Only that
which is linked to falsehood and deception, i.e., holding opinions and
making a premature assent, which is a kind of yielding to what is presented, owing to weakness and is quite useless. For action requires two
things, a presentation of something appropriate for a man and an impulse
towards the thing presented as [being] appropriate. (1122d) Neither of
these is incompatible with suspension of judgement. For the sceptical
argument rejects opinion, not impulse or presentation. So, when what
is congenial to a man is presented one needs no opinion in order to move
and progress towards it, but the impulse, which is a motion and progress
of the soul, immediately comes along.

Indeed, it is their own claim [i.e., the Epicureans] that one need only
have sense-perception and be made of flesh for pleasure to appear to be
good. Therefore it will appear good even to someone who suspends

6. Homer *Iliad* 20.250.

judgement. For he has sense-perception and is made of flesh, and when he receives a presentation of something good he desires and has an impulse, and does all that he can to prevent it from escaping him; as far as possible he will be in the company of what is congenial to him, being drawn by necessity which is natural rather than geometrical.[7] **(1122e)** No teacher is needed: all on their own these fine, smooth and agreeable movements of the flesh exert an attraction (as they themselves say) even on those who firmly refuse and reject being swayed and softened by them.

'But how can it be that he who suspends judgement does not run off to the mountain rather than to the baths, and does not stand up and walk into the wall when he wants to go the market-place, but rather walks to the door?' Do you [the Epicurean] ask this, although you claim that the sense organs are accurate and that our presentations are true? Surely it is because it is not the mountain which appears to him to be the baths, but the baths **(1122f)**; and it is not the wall which appears to him to be a door, but the door, and so on in each case. For the argument for suspension of judgement does not interfere with sense-perception, nor does it introduce into our irrational experiences and movements some change which disrupts our faculty of presentation. All it does is to remove opinions; the rest it makes use of in accordance with their natures.

Cicero *Academica* 2.108 [III-13]

The second point is that you deny that any action concerning anything can occur in someone who approves nothing with his assent. For first there must be a presentation, in which assent is involved—for the Stoics say that acts of sense-perception are themselves acts of assent and that because impulse follows on these [acts of assent], action also follows, and that all of this is removed if presentations are removed.

On this topic there have been many arguments, written and oral, on either side, but the whole issue can be dealt with briefly. For my part, although I agree that the highest activity is to fight against presentations, to resist opinions, and to suspend assent, which is a slippery sort of thing; and although I agree with Clitomachus when he writes that a veritably Herculean labour was performed by Carneades when he drove assent—i.e., [mere] opinion and rashness—out of our souls, as though it were a wild and ravening beast; despite all of this (to set aside this line of defence), what will hinder a man who follows what is plausible providing nothing hinders it?

7. Plutarch alludes to Plato, *Republic* 458d.

Cicero *Academica* 2.139   [III-14]

... [perhaps] I should follow the opinion of Calliphon, whose view Carneades used to argue for so assiduously that he even seemed to approve of it, though Clitomachus used to claim that he never could understand what Carneades really believed ...

Cicero *Academica* 2.148   [III-15]

[Catulus speaks] ... "I return to the view held by my father, who said that it was also Carneades' view: although I hold that nothing can be perceived, still I think that the wise man will assent to something which is not perceived, i.e., that he will hold a [mere] opinion; but that he will also understand that he is indeed opining and knows that there is nothing which can be grasped and perceived. And that is why, although I disapprove of their *epoche* on all matters, I give strong assent to the other view, viz. that there is nothing which can be perceived."

Cicero *On Goals* 2.2   [III-16]

But we know that the man I have mentioned [Gorgias] and the other sophists were mocked by Socrates, as we gather from Plato. For he [Socrates] used to draw out the opinions of his interlocutors by examination and questioning, in order that he might say what he thought in response to their answers. This method was not preserved by his [immediate] successors, but Arcesilaus revived it and required that those who wished to hear him not ask for [his opinion], but should themselves say what they thought; and when they had done so, he maintained the contrary position. And *his* interlocutors defended their own views to the best of their abilities; with other philosophers, by contrast, someone who asks a question must remain silent. And that is what happens today, even in the Academy. ...

Cicero *On Goals* 5.10   [III-17]

The same school [the early Peripatetics] handed down rules not just for dialectic but also for rhetoric. Their founder, Aristotle, established the exercise of arguing on both sides of each issue, not, however, like Arcesilaus, arguing against every [thesis] all the time, but just in order to set forth in every case all that could be said on either side of the issue.

Sextus *M* 7.150–189   [III-18]

150. Arcesilaus and his followers in the Academy did not in the proper sense define a criterion, whereas those who seem to have defined one

offered it as a move in their argument against the Stoics. **151.** For they hold that there are three things linked to each other: knowledge, opinion, and, placed between these, grasping. Of these, knowledge is sure and stable grasping unalterable by reasoning; opinion is weak and false assent; and grasping is what is between these, assent to a graspable presentation. **152.** According to the Stoics, a graspable presentation is true and such that there could not be a false one just like it. They say that knowledge is present only in the wise, opinion is present only in base men, but that grasping is common to both groups, and that this is the criterion of truth. **153.** These being the Stoics' views, Arcesilaus countered them by showing that grasping is in no respect a criterion midway between knowledge and opinion. For that which they call grasping and assent to a graspable presentation occurs either in a wise man or in a base man. But if it occurs in a wise man, it is knowledge, and if in a base man, it is opinion, and there is nothing else left besides these two but a name. **154.** And if grasping is assent to a graspable presentation, it is non-existent, first, because assent occurs not with respect to a presentation but with respect to a statement, for assents are given to propositions; second, because there is no true presentation such that there could not be a false one just like it, as is shown by many and varied examples. **155.** Since there is no graspable presentation, grasping will not occur either, for the assent has to be to a graspable presentation. And if there is no grasping, everything will be ungraspable. Everything being ungraspable, it will follow, even according to the Stoics, that the wise man suspends judgement.

156. Let us consider the matter in this way. Since everything is ungraspable because of the non-existence of the Stoic criterion, if the wise man gives assent, the wise man will opine, for since nothing is graspable, if he gives assent to something, he will give assent to the ungraspable, but assent to the ungraspable is opinion. **157.** So, if the wise man is one of those who give assent, the wise man will be one of those who opines. But the wise man is surely not one of those who opines, for, according to them, opining is a mark of imprudence and the cause of [moral] mistakes. Therefore, the wise man is not one of those who gives assent. If this is the case, he will have to refuse to give assent to everything. And refusal to give assent is nothing else but suspension of judgement. Therefore, the wise man will suspend judgement about everything. **158.** But since it was necessary after this [argument] to inquire into the conduct of life which naturally cannot be directed without a criterion, upon which happiness too, that is, the goal of life, depends for its reliability, Arcesilaus says that he who suspends judgement about everything regulates choices and avoidances and, generally, actions by reasonableness, and, proceeding according to this criterion, will act correctly [perform morally perfect actions].[8] For happiness arises because of prudence, and prudence resides in correct [morally perfect] actions, and a correct [morally perfect] action is that which, having been done, has a reasonable defence. Therefore, he who adheres to reasonableness will act correctly and will be happy.

159. This is the [argument] of Arcesilaus. Carneades marshalled his arguments concerning the criterion not only against the Stoics but against all those who came before him as well. His first argument actually applies to them all, according to which he shows that there is unqualifiedly no criterion of truth, neither reasoning nor sense-perception nor presentation nor any other thing, for all of these together deceive us. **160.** His second argument is that according to which he shows that even if there is a criterion, this does not exist separately from the experience [or state] produced by the clarity [of that which is perceived]. For since an animal differs from inanimate things by its perceptual power, it is certainly through this that it will become capable of grasping itself and things external to it. But sense-perception, if it is unmoved, unaffected, and unchanged, is neither [actual] sense-perception, nor can it grasp anything; **161.** rather, when it is changed and somehow affected in the respect in which it experiences clear [perceptual objects], only then does it indicate things. Therefore, the criterion should be sought for in the experience [or state] of the soul arising from a clear [perception]. But this experience [or state] ought to be indicative of itself and of the phenomenon which produces it, and this experience [or state] is nothing other than the presentation. **162.** For this reason, one should say that a presentation is a certain experience [or state] in the animal which reveals itself and the other object. For example, Antiochus says, when we look at something we are put into a certain condition with respect to our power of vision and we do not have our power of vision in the same condition as we did before we looked. In this sort of alteration we are aware of two things, one being the alteration itself [i.e., the presentation], the second being the object which causes this alteration [i.e., the visible thing]. And similarly in the case of the other senses. **163.** So, just as light reveals both itself and everything in it, in this way the presentation too, being the starting point of the animal's knowledge, like light, ought to make apparent both itself and the clear thing which makes it be indicative. But since it does not always indicate the truth, but frequently deceives us and disagrees with the things which send it [to us] like bad messengers, it necessarily follows

8. It is important that Arcesilaus, as reported by Sextus, is here using a Stoic technical term, *katorthoma*, in a non-Stoic sense, although the Stoic meaning (given in square brackets) is, we think, supposed to be in the reader's mind.

that we are not able to allow all presentations as a criterion of the truth, but only, if any, the true presentation.

164. Again, since no one of these is true such that there could not be a false one just like it, but rather for every one which is held to be true, one exactly like it is found which is false, the criterion will turn out to lie in a presentation common to the true and the false. But the presentation common to both of these is not graspable and, not being graspable, it will not be a criterion. **165.** And if there is no presentation capable of judging, reasoning too would not be a criterion, for reasoning is based on a presentation. And this makes sense, for that which is to be judged must first be presented to someone, and nothing is able to be presented apart from non-rational sense-perception. So, neither non-rational sense-perception nor reasoning would be a criterion.

166. These were the counter-arguments which Carneades set forth against the other philosophers to the effect that the criterion does not exist. But he himself when asked for some criterion for the conduct of life and for the attainment of happiness, is virtually compelled to take a position for himself on the topic, introducing the plausible presentation, and [the presentation] which is at the same time plausible, uncontroverted, and thoroughly tested. **167.** The difference between these should be summarily explained. The presentation is a presentation of something, i.e., of that from which it arises and of that in which it arises—that from which it arises being an external sensible object, and that in which it arises, being, say, a man. Being such, it has two relations, one its relation to the object presented, the other being its relation to the subject having the presentation. **168.** With respect to its relation to the object presented, it turns out to be either true or false, true whenever it is in harmony with the object presented, false whenever it is in disagreement with it. **169.** With respect to its relation to the subject having the presentation, the one [kind] is apparently true, the other apparently false. The apparently true presentation is called a [representational] image by the Academics or plausibility or a plausible presentation; the one not apparently true is designated as a non-[representational] image or implausibility or an implausible presentation. For it is not what immediately appears false nor what, though true, does not appear to us as such, [and so] does not naturally persuade us. **170.** Of these presentations, the sort that is clearly false and not apparently true is to be ruled out and is not a criterion, ⟨whether it does not come from an existing object or⟩ whether it does so but disagrees with that object and is not in accord with it, such as was the case with the presentation derived from Electra and striking Orestes when he thought that it was one of the furies and cried out,

"Away! One of my furies!" **171.** Of apparently true [presentations], one kind is obscure, as for example, the kind where, owing to the smallness of the object, or its considerable distance, or the weakness of sight, it is received confusedly and not clear in outline; another kind is where besides being apparently true, the presentation appears intensely so. **172.** Of the two kinds, the unclear and loose one would not be a criterion; for since it indicates distinctly neither itself nor that which causes it, it does not naturally persuade us nor induce us to assent to it. **173.** On the other hand, the presentation that is apparently true and adequately representative is a criterion of the truth according to Carneades' school. As a criterion, it admits of a fair degree of variation, and since it can be intensified [in its clarity], one presentation will stand up against another as more plausible and striking than another. **174.** 'Plausible' is used in three senses in the present discussion. In the first sense, it is true and apparently true; in the second, it is [in fact] false, but it appears true; and in the third, it is common to the two [i.e., appears to be true but could be either true or false]. For this reason, the criterion will be the apparently true presentation which the Academics call plausible, **175.** although it sometimes happens to be the case that it is really false, so that sometimes we have to use the presentation which is common to the true and the false. But still because of the rarity of the occurrence of this kind, I mean those that mimic the truth [by appearing to be true but really being false], one should not distrust the one which is true for the most part. For as it happens one's judgements and actions are regulated by what is so for most part.

This, then, is the first and general criterion according to the school of Carneades. **176.** Since, however, presentations are never isolated, but rather one depends upon another like links in a chain, that which will be added as the second criterion to plausibility is the presentation that is at the same time uncontroverted. For example, one who acquires a presentation of a man necessarily receives a presentation of his attributes, and of his external circumstances; **177.** among the former are colour, size, shape, movement, speech, dress, footwear, among the latter are the air, light, day, the heavens, earth, friends, and all the rest. Whenever none of these presentations drags us to and fro by appearing false, but rather all appear true and consistent, we trust more [in the initial presentation]. **178.** For that this man is Socrates we trust from [the presentation of] all the customary characteristics belonging to him, colour, size, shape, opinions, garment and his being in a place where there is no one else exactly like him. **179.** And just as some doctors do not conclude from one symptom that someone is really feverish, for example, a quickened pulse or just a high temperature, but from a combination of symptoms, for example, high temperature, quickened pulse, soreness of touch, a rash, thirst, and the like, so the Academic makes the judgement about the truth on the basis of a combination of presentations, and when no one of these [strikes] him as controverted [and so] false, he states that the [impression] he receives is true. **180.** And that the uncontrovertability resides in a combination that produces trustworthiness is clear from the case of Menelaus; for leaving behind on board the ship the apparition of Helen which he brought from Troy, thinking it really was Helen, and landing on the island of Pharos, he saw the real Helen and though he received from her a true presentation, nevertheless he did not trust this presentation, because of its being controverted by another, according to which he understood that he had left Helen on board the ship. **181.** The uncontroverted presentation is then this sort of thing. It seems to admit of some degree of variation, because of the fact that one presentation is found to be more uncontrovertable than another.

The presentation which produces judgement is most perfect and more trustworthy than the uncontroverted presentation; this is [the presentation] which, along with being uncontroverted, is thoroughly tested. **182.** What the character of this is should be explained next. In the case of the uncontroverted presentation, the only thing sought for is that no one of the combination of presentations should [strike us as] controverted [and so] false, but only that they should all appear to be true and not implausible. But in the case of a combination which is thoroughly tested, we scrutinize diligently each of the presentations in the combination, which is just what occurs in assemblies, whenever the people examine each would-be official or judge to see if he is worthy of being entrusted with the office or with the task of judging. **183.** For example, at the place of judgement there is the one who judges, the thing judged, the medium in which judgement occurs, [i.e.,] distance, interval, place, time, manner, disposition, and activity, and we discern precisely the particular character of each of this sort of thing. [Thus, we discern] whether the one judging has defective vision, for this would make his judgement defective; whether the thing judged is not excessively small; whether the medium of judgement is an atmosphere that is not murky; whether the distance from the thing judged is not too great; whether the interval is not disorienting; whether the place is not vast; whether the time is not brief; whether the disposition [of the subject] is not observed to be lunatic; whether the activity is not unacceptable.

184. All these together constitute one criterion, the plausible presentation, the simultaneously plausible and uncontroverted presentation, and the plausible, uncontroverted, and thoroughly tested presentation. And it is for this reason that just as in daily living, whenever we are investigating a small matter we interrogate one witness, and whenever we are investigating a greater matter we interrogate several witnesses, and whenever we are investigating an even more urgent matter we examine thoroughly each of the witnesses on the basis of their consistency with the others; so, similarly, the Carneadeans say that in trivial matters we employ only the plausible presentation as criterion, in more important matters the uncontroverted presentation, and in matters pertaining to our happiness the thoroughly tested presentation. **185.** Of course, they say that just as in different matters they utilize a different [kind of] presentation [as criterion], so in different circumstances they do not follow the same [kind of] presentation. They claim that they attend to the plausible presentation alone where circumstances do not afford an opportunity for accurate consideration of the matter. **186.** For example, someone is being pursued by his enemies and, coming upon a ditch, he receives a presentation that his enemies are lying in wait for him there too. Being seized by this presentation as plausible, he turns and flees the ditch, following the plausibility of the presentation before he could know accurately whether there is an ambush of his enemies in that place or not. **187.** But they follow the plausible and thoroughly tested presentation in those cases in which time allows for the judgement of what is occurring with care and thorough testing.

For example, someone seeing a coiled rope in a dark room jumps over it, thinking at first that it is a snake, but afterwards he turns around and searches for the truth, and finding that it is motionless, his intellect is already inclined to thinking that it is not a snake, **188.** but still reckoning that sometimes snakes do not move owing to winter frost, he prods the coil with a stick, and having thus tested the presentation that occurs, he assents to its being false that the body presented to him is a snake. And again, as I said, seeing something clearly we assent to its being true when our senses are thoroughly tested for their soundness, when we are looking while awake and not asleep, and when there exist at once a clear atmosphere, moderate distance, **189.** and immobility of the object presented, so that because of these factors the presentation is trustworthy, there being sufficient time for a thorough testing of that which is observed where the presentation occurs. The same sort of account pertains to the uncontroverted presentation. They allow it whenever nothing has been able to dislodge it, as was said in the case of Menelaus.

Cicero *Academica* 1.44–46   [III-19]

44. . . . It was with Zeno [the Stoic], we gather, that Arcesilaus started his whole quarrel. This was not, so it seems to me, because of stubbornness or zeal for victory, but because of the obscurity of the very matters that led Socrates to a confession of ignorance, and before Socrates, Democritus, Anaxagoras, Empedocles, and almost all the old philosophers. These had said that nothing could be understood or perceived or known, that the senses are narrow, minds are feeble, lives are short, and, according to Democritus, that truth is immersed in the depths, that everything is accepted on the basis of opinions and customs, no room is left for truth, and consequently they said that all things are enveloped in darkness.

45. So, Arcesilaus denied that there was anything that could be known, not even that very thing that Socrates thought was left for him to know, [namely, that he knew nothing]. He judged everything to reside in darkness and that nothing could be discerned or understood. For these reasons, one should neither profess nor affirm nor give approval with assent to anything, and should always hold back and restrain oneself from slipping into an unfounded position. It would be a rash mistake to approve of something false or unknown, and there is nothing more disgraceful than for assent and approval to outrun knowledge and perception. He acted consistently with this position: by arguing against everyone's opinions he led many to share his position, so that when equally weighty arguments were found for contrary positions on the same subject, it was easier to withhold assent from either position.

46. They call this the New Academy, but it seems to me to be Old, at least if we count Plato as belonging to the Old, for in his books nothing is affirmed and there are many arguments on both sides of an issue, everything is open to question, and nothing is said with certainty. Nevertheless, let that Academy which you described be called the Old and this one the New. This Academy continued up to Carneades, who was fourth in line from Arcesilaus, and maintained the same position as the latter. Carneades was not unacquainted with any area of philosophy, as I have learned from those who heard him, especially Zeno the Epicurean, who, although he disagreed with him greatly, admired him above others, for he had an incredible facility . . . [The text breaks off here.]

Cicero *Academica* 2.98–105 [III-20]

98. . . . But putting aside those cutting remarks and the entire tortuous class of argumentation, let us display our true position, for once all the views of Carneades are explicated, those of Antiochus will all collapse together. I will, however, say nothing such that anyone might suspect me of making it up. I shall take it from Clitomachus who was with Carneades until his old age—[Clitomachus was] a sharp man, a Carthaginian, and exceedingly studious and hard working. There are four books

of his on *Suspension of Assent* and the things I am about to say are taken
from book one.

99. According to Carneades, there are two kinds of presentations: one
kind is subdivided into those which can be perceived and those which
cannot: the other kind is subdivided into those that are plausible and
those that are not. So, the objections raised against the senses and clarity
belong to the first division, whereas no objection should be made to
the second. Therefore, he held that there is no presentation such that
perception follows, but many, however, such that plausibility does. For
it is contrary to nature that nothing should be plausible; the overthrow
of all life that you were referring to, Lucullus, follows [on that view].
Thus, many things are plausible to the senses, provided it is held that
there is nothing about the presentations such that there could not possibly
be a false one that did not differ from it. Thus, the wise man will employ
whatever apparently plausible presentations he meets with, provided
there is nothing which opposes its plausibility, and thus will every plan
of life be governed. In fact, even he who is introduced by you as a wise
man will follow many things as being plausible, but neither grasped nor
perceived nor assented to, but as being like truth. And unless he approves
of them, all life would be eliminated. **100.** What else? Surely when a
wise man goes on board a ship, he has not grasped with his mind or
perceived that he will sail away as intended. Who could? But if he were
to set out from here to Puteoli, a distance of 30 stades, with a sound
ship, a good captain, waters calm as they are now, it would seem plausible
to him that he would arrive safely at his destination. In this manner, he
takes presentations as guides for acting and not acting, and he will be
readier to approve of the claim that snow is white than was Anaxagoras
(who not only denied that snow was white but, because he knew that
the water from which it was composed was black, even denied that it
appeared white to himself), **101.** and will be moved by whatever thing
strikes him as a presentation that is plausible and not impeded by any
other thing. For he is not carved out of stone or hewn from wood; he
has a body, a soul, he is moved with his mind and senses, so that many
things *seem* true to him, although they do not have that distinctive and
peculiar mark of perceptibility, and for that reason the wise man does
not assent, for there can exist a false presentation indistinguishable from
a true one. Nor do we speak against the senses differently from the Stoics,
who say that many things are false and are very different from how they
appear to the senses.

If, however, it is the case that the senses receive even one false presentation, he is right here to deny that anything can be perceived with the
senses. In this way, without a word from us, but with one principle from

Epicurus and one from you [Lucullus], perception with the senses and grasping are eliminated. What is Epicurus' principle? If any presentation to the senses is false, nothing can be perceived. And yours? There are false presentations to the senses. What follows? Even if I should keep silent the argument itself declares that nothing can be perceived. "I do not admit Epicurus' principle," he [Lucullus] says. Well, then, quarrel with him, who differs from you totally, not with me, who assent to your claim that there is something false in the senses. 102. Still, nothing seems to me so strange as that those words should be spoken, especially by Antiochus, who was intimately acquainted with what I said a while ago. For anyone is allowed on the basis of his own judgement to take issue with our denial that anything can be perceived—that is certainly a less serious criticism; whereas our saying that some things are plausible seems inadequate to you. Perhaps so. In any case, we certainly ought to try to avoid the difficulties forcefully brought forward by you: "Do you discern nothing? Do you hear nothing? Is nothing clear to you?" I have explained a little while ago, on the authority of Clitomachus, how Carneades would respond to these questions. Listen to what Clitomachus says along the same lines in the book he dedicated to the poet Gaius Lucilius, although he had written the same things to Lucius Censorinus when he was consul with Manius Manilius. He wrote in just about these words—I know them because the first introduction and, as it were, the programme for the very matters we are discussing are contained in that book—anyway, he wrote as follows:

103. According to the Academics, things are dissimilar in a way such that some seem to be plausible and some otherwise. But that is not sufficient to allow you to say that some can be perceived and others not, for there are many false [presentations] that are plausible, whereas nothing which is false could be perceived or known. Therefore he says that those who say that the senses are taken away from us by the Academy are very much mistaken. For that school never said that color, taste, or sound were nothing, but they did argue that there was no peculiar feature in them which was a mark of certainty and truth which could not belong to something else. 104. When he had set out these claims, he added that there are two senses in which the wise man is said to suspend judgement. In one sense he gives assent to nothing at all; in the other sense, he suspends judgement by not responding to a query as to whether he approves of something or disapproves of it, so that he is not forced to deny or affirm anything. Since this is so, the one sense is accepted, so that he never assents to anything, and he holds to the other sense, so that, following plausibility wherever this should be present or absent, he is able to respond [to a question about acceptance] "yes" or "no" accord-

ingly. Indeed, since we believe that he who withholds assent from everything is nevertheless moved and does something, there remain presentations of the sort that excite us to action, and also those about which,
when questioned, we would be able to respond either way, following
only the claim that the presentation was like that, but still without assent.
However, we do not give assent to every presentation of this sort, but
only to those which nothing impedes.

105. If we do not persuade you with these arguments, since they may
well be false, still they are certainly not despicable; for we do not destroy
the light, but rather we merely say that those things which you say are
perceived and grasped, 'appear', so long as they are plausible.

Cicero *Academica* 2.7–9   [III-21]

7.... There remains one group of critics, by whom the Academic
argument is rejected. We would take this more seriously if anyone ever
approved of any philosophical school except the one which he himself
followed. But since it is our custom to advance our own views against
everyone else, we cannot object to others disagreeing with us.

Still, our case at least is straightforward; all we want to do is to discover
the truth without strife and this we pursue with the greatest care and
enthusiasm. For although all knowledge is beset by many hardships and
although there is so much unclarity in the things themselves and so much
weakness in our faculty of judgement that the most ancient and wise
thinkers were justified in doubting that they could discover what they
wished to, still, they did not give up and neither shall we weary and
abandon our enthusiasm for uncovering [what we seek]. The sole aim of
our discussions is to tease out—or, as it were, squeeze out—something
which is either true or comes as close to it as possible, by speaking on
both sides of the issue and listening [to our opponents]. **8.** The only
difference between us and those who think that they know something is
that they do not doubt that the positions which they defend are true,
while we say that many things are plausible, those which we can easily
follow [in practice] but can hardly affirm.

But we are freer and more flexible just in so far as our ability to decide
lies wholly in our own hands; we are not compelled by any necessity to
defend a whole set of positions which are laid down like orders. For the
others are tied down and committed before they can decide what is best;
furthermore, it is when they are at the most vulnerable time of life that
they either follow some friend or become captivated by one speech given
by the first person they happen to hear and so make decisions about
things which are unknown to them. Having been carried off to whatever

school it might be as though by a storm, they then cling to it as though to a rock. **9.** For I would approve of their saying that they believe in all respects him whom they judge to be a wise man, if they had been able to make such a judgement while so inexperienced and uneducated. To settle who is wise seems to be more than any other thing a job for the wise man. But grant that they were capable of making that assessment; either they made that judgement after hearing all the arguments and understanding the positions of the rest of the philosophical schools, or they delivered themselves into the authority of one man after one quick hearing. But for some reason or other most people prefer going astray and defending most aggressively that position which they have fallen in love with to the job of searching without stubbornness for what can most consistently be claimed.

Pyrrhonian Scepticism

Pyrrho

Life of Pyrrho: **Diogenes Laertius 9.61–108** [III-22]
(selections)

61. Pyrrho of Elis was the son of Pleistarchus, as Diocles too narrates. According to Apollodorus in his *Chronicles* he was formerly a painter; and, according to Alexander in his *Successions*, he attended the lectures of Bryson, son of Stilpo, then Anaxarchus', accompanying the latter everywhere in his travels, even spending time with the Gymnosophists in India and the Magi. From this experience, he seems to have theorized in a most noble way, introducing the idea of ungraspability and suspension of judgement, according to Ascanius of Abdera. For he said that nothing was either honourable or shameful, just or unjust; similarly for all cases he said that nothing exists in truth but that men do everything on the basis of convention and custom; for each thing is no more this than that.

62. He was consistent with this view in his manner of living, neither avoiding anything nor watching out for anything, taking everything as it came, whether it be wagons or precipices or dogs, and all such things, relying on his senses for nothing. He was kept alive by his acquaintances who followed him around, according to the school of Antigonus of Carystus. Aenesidemus, however, says that he only theorized about the suspension of judgement, whereas he did not actually act improvidently. He lived to be almost ninety years old.

Antigonus of Carystus in his book on Pyrrho says the following about him. In the beginning he was a poor and unknown painter. In fact, in

the gymnasium of Elis there are preserved some fair paintings of his of
torch-bearers. **63.** He isolated himself and lived like a hermit, rarely
showing himself to those in his household. He did this after he heard
some Indian reproach Anaxarchus that he would never be able to teach
someone else what is good so long as he served the royal courts. He
always maintained the same mental condition, so that even if someone
walked out on him in the middle of whatever he was saying, he just
finished speaking to himself, even though in his youth he had been
excitable and . . . [there is a lacuna in the text]. They say that many
times he would leave town without telling anyone beforehand, and ramble
around with whomever he might meet. And once, when Anaxarchus fell
into a ditch, he passed by him and did not give him any help. Some
blamed him for this, but Anaxarchus himself praised his indifference
and lack of sentimentality.

64. Once he was caught talking to himself and, when asked why, he
replied that he was practising to be a nice fellow. In investigative matters
he was scorned by no one, because he could both discourse at length
and respond to questions, so that even Nausiphanes when he was a youth
was immediately captivated by him; at least Nausiphanes used to say
that while one should acquire the disposition of Pyrrho, one should follow
his own theories. He often said that Epicurus marvelled at Pyrrho's
behavior and continually asked him about Pyrrho. He was so honoured
by his state that they made him the chief priest and for his sake decreed
that all philosophers should pay no taxes. . . .

66. Diocles says that the Athenians honoured him with citizenship for
having killed the Thracian Cotys. According to Eratosthenes, in his work
Wealth and Poverty, he lived piously with his sister, a midwife. Sometimes,
he himself actually used to bring poultry or maybe pigs to market to be
sold, and he did the household cleaning without complaint. He is said
to have washed a piglet himself because he was indifferent to what he
did. Once he became angry with someone in a matter regarding his sister,
whose name was Philista, and in reply to someone who blamed him for
this said that the manifestation of indifference was not suitable on behalf
of a mere woman. Once when a dog attacked him [Pyrrho] and he
panicked, he replied to someone who blamed him for this that it was
hard to shed completely one's humanity, but that one should struggle
against circumstances, as much as possible in one's actions, but if not
then at least in one's words.

67. They say that when septic medicines and surgical and caustic
procedures were applied to some wound of his, he did not even frown.
Timon further clarifies his disposition in his reply to Pytho. Philo of
Athens, who was an intimate of his, said that he most often mentioned

Democritus and after him, Homer, marvelling at the latter and saying continually, "As is the generation of leaves, so is that of man."[9] And he also marvelled at Homer because he compared men to wasps, fleas, and birds, quoting these words: "Ah, my friend, you die too; why do you weep so? Patroclus has fallen, a better man than you."[10] and all such passages pertaining to human insecurity, vanity, and puerility.

68. Posidonius also relates a similar story about him. One time his [Pyrrho's] fellow passengers on a ship were frightened by a storm. He, however, was calm and serene and, pointing to a little pig on the ship who was eating away, said that the wise man ought to repose in just such a state of freedom from disturbance. Only Numenius says that he has dogmas. He had notable pupils, one of whom, Eurylochus, is said to have failed him in that once he got so angry at his cook that he seized the cooking-spit with the meat still on it and chased him into the market. **69.** And in Elis he [Eurylochus] was once so pressured by his pupils' arguments, that he stripped off his cloak and swam across the Alpheus. . . .

71. Some say that Homer was the founder of this [i.e., the Pyrrhonian] system, since regarding the same matters he more than anyone pronounces differently at different times, and never definitively dogmatizes about the pronouncement. The sayings of the Seven Wise Men are also said to be sceptical such as "nothing in excess" and "a pledge is a curse" meaning that for someone who makes a pledge definitely and confidently, a curse follows. Even Archilochus and Euripides were held to be sceptics, for the former says,[11] "The soul of man, Glaucus, son of Leptines, is like a day sent by Zeus." And Euripides [addressing Zeus],[12]

> Why do they say that wretched mortals think?
> For we depend on you and do just
> What you happen to wish.

72. Furthermore, according to them, Xenophanes, Zeno of Elea, and Democritus are found to be sceptics. For of that group Xenophanes says,[13] "clear truth no man knows nor will ever know;" as for Zeno, he eliminates motion, saying,[14] "that which is moved is neither moved in the place it is nor in the place it is not;" as for Democritus, he throws

9. *Iliad* 6.146.
10. *Iliad* 21.106–7.
11. Fr. 131 West.
12. *Suppliants* 735–737.
13. Diels-Kranz B 34.1–2.
14. B 4.

out qualities, so that he says,[15] "cold by custom, hot by custom; atoms and void in truth," and again, "in truth we know nothing; for truth is in the depths."[16] Also, Plato who, although he grants truth to the gods and their sons, seeks [for himself] only a likely explanation.[17]

73. Euripides says,[18] "Who knows if life is death? Mortals think that dying is living?" So too Empedocles:[19] "Thus these things are neither beheld nor heard nor grasped with the mind by men;" and before that, "each one is persuaded only by that which he confronts." And even Heraclitus:[20] "Let us not agree carelessly about the most important matters." And even Hippocrates showed himself a mere doubting mortal. And before them all was Homer: "Pliant is the tongue of man, full of many tales" and "There is a great range of words, here and there" and "Whatever word you utter returns to you in kind,"[21] referring to the equal force of contradictory words.

74. The sceptics, then, spent their time overturning all the dogmas of the schools, whereas they themselves make no dogmatic pronouncements, and while they presented and set out in detail the views of others, they themselves expressed no determinate opinions, not even this itself [that they had no determinate opinions]. Thus, they even abolished the position of holding no determinate opinion, saying, for example, "we determine nothing" since otherwise they would be determining something; but, they say, they produce the pronouncements [of others] to display their absence of rashness, so that they could show this even if they inclined [to the view]. Thus, by means of the utterance "we determine nothing," they indicate the state of equilibrium [in their souls] and similarly, by means of the utterance "no more this than that" and the utterance "for every argument there is an opposing argument" and similar utterances.

75. Now "no more this than that" can also be understood positively, indicating that certain things are similar. For example, "the pirate is no more wicked than is a liar." But the sceptics say this negatively, not positively, as in refuting someone by saying "Scylla no more exists than does the Chimera." The words "more than" are sometimes used comparatively, as when we say "honey has more sweetness than grapes." Some-

---

15. See B 125.
16. B 117.
17. *Timaeus* 29c–d.
18. Fr. 638 Nauck.
19. B 2.7–8, 5.
20. B 47.
21. *Iliad* 20.248–250.

times they are used positively and negatively, as when we say "virtue benefits more than it harms," we signify that virtue benefits and does not harm.

76. The sceptics, however, even abolish the very utterance "no more this than that" for as providence is no more than it is not, so "no more this than that" is no more than it is not. So Timon says in the *Pytho*, the utterance ["no more this than that"] signifies determining nothing and refusing to assent. The very utterance "for every argument there is an opposing argument" also concludes to suspension of judgement, for when the facts are disputed, but there is equal force in the [opposing] arguments, ignorance of the truth follows. Even this argument [i.e., that every argument has an opposing argument] has an opposing argument, [namely, there is an argument which has no opposing argument] so that when it has destroyed every other argument it turns on itself and is destroyed by itself, just like purges which first purge the foreign matter and then themselves are purged and destroyed. . . .

78. The Pyrrhonian strategy, according to Aenesidemus in his *Outline for Pyrrhonian Topics*, is a kind of display of appearances or thoughts according to which they are all juxtaposed and when compared are found to have much inconsistency and confusion. As for the contradictions found in their investigations, first they show the modes by which things persuade us and then how confidence is eliminated by the same modes. For they say that we are persuaded when things are consistently perceived, when they never or at least rarely change, when they become familiar to us and when they are determined by customs and when they are delightful and marvellous. 79. They thus showed that on the basis of indications contrary to those that persuaded in the first place, [conclusions] opposite to those we accepted were equally plausible.

The problems which they raised for the [supposed] agreement of appearances or thoughts were set down according to ten modes [or dialectical moves, *tropoi*], corresponding to the ways in which the facts appeared to differ. These are the ten modes they laid down:

[1] The first mode is based on the differences among animals with respect to pleasure and pain and harm and benefit. By this mode it is inferred that animals do not receive the same presentations from the same things, and that for this reason suspension of judgement follows upon this conflict. For among animals some are conceived without intercourse, such as the animals that live in fire, the Arabian phoenix, and worms; whereas some are conceived through intercourse, such as men and other animals. 80. Further, some are structured in one way, some in another. Therefore, they differ in sense-experience; for example, hawks have the keenest sight, whereas dogs have the most acute sense of smell.

It is reasonable, then, that animals whose eyes are different should receive different appearances. So, for example, the shoot of a tree is edible for a goat, but bitter for a man; hemlock is nourishing for a quail, but fatal for a man; excrement is edible for a pig, but not for a horse.

[2] The second mode is based on the natures of men and their idiosyncracies. For example, Demophon, the table-servant of Alexander, used to get warm in the shade, but shivered in the sun. 81. Andron the Argive, according to Aristotle, went across the Libyan desert without drinking anything. Again, one man desires to be a doctor, another a farmer, and still another a businessman; and the same things that harm some benefit others. From these facts, suspension of judgement ought to follow.

[3] The third mode is based on the differences in the sensory passages. For example, the apple strikes sight as pale yellow, taste as sweet, and smell as fragrant. And something with the same shape appears different corresponding to the differences in mirrors that reflect it. Therefore, it follows that that which appears is no more one way than another.

[4] 82. The fourth mode is based on dispositions and, in general, changes; for example, health, sickness, sleep, waking, joy, sorrow, youthfulness, old age, courage, fear, emptiness, fullness, hatred, love, heat, cold; besides these, breathing [freely] and constriction of the passages. Things that strike the observer appear different corresponding to the quality of the dispositions. Even madmen do not have dispositions contrary to nature, for why should theirs be more so than ours? After all, we see the sun as standing still. Theon, the Tithorean Stoic, after going to bed, walked in his sleep and the slave of Pericles [sleepwalked] on the roof.

[5] 83. The fifth mode is based on ways of life, customs, mythical beliefs, agreements among various peoples, and dogmatic assumptions. In this mode are included views about things honourable and shameful, true and false, good and bad, the gods, and the generation and destruction of all phenomena. For the same thing is held to be just by some but unjust by others; good to some and bad to others. The Persians, for example, do not regard it as out of place for a father to have intercourse with his daughter; whereas for the Greeks, this is monstrous. The Massagetae, according to Eudoxus in the first book of his *Travels*, hold wives in common; the Greeks do not. The Cilicians delighted in being pirates, but not the Greeks. 84. Different people believe in different gods; some believe in providence, some do not. The Egyptians mummify their dead; the Romans cremate them; the Paeonians throw them into lakes. From these facts, suspension of judgement about the truth [ought to follow].

[6] The sixth mode is based on mixtures and combinations according to which nothing appears purely by itself, but only together with air,

light, moisture, solidity, heat, cold, motion, vapours and other powers. For example, purple appears different in its shade of colour in sunlight, moonlight and lamplight. Our own complexion appears different in the middle of the day and ⟨at dusk⟩. 85. Further, a rock which requires two men to lift it in the air, is easily shifted in the water, whether [the rock] is in its nature heavy but buoyed by the water, or light and weighed down by the air. So we are ignorant of properties, as we are of the oil [which is the base for] perfumes.

[7] The seventh mode is based on distances, kinds of positions, places and things in places. According to this mode, things that are held to be large now appear small, square things round, level things bumpy, straight things crooked, pale things differently coloured. The sun, at any rate, appears small from a distance, mountains appear misty and smooth from far away but jagged up close. 86. Further, the sun appears one way when rising but a different way when it is in the middle of the heavens and the same body appears one way in a grove and another in a clearing. Further, the image varies according to the sort of position [of the object], for example, the neck of a dove, depending on the way it is turned. Since these things are never observed outside of some place and position, their nature is not known to us.

[8] The eighth mode is based on quantities and [qualities of things, whether these be] hotness or coldness, swiftness or slowness, paleness or variety of colour. For example, wine drunk in moderate amount fortifies us but in excessive amount weakens; similarly, with food and the like.

[9] 87. The ninth mode is based on that which is unceasing, odd, or rare. At any rate, in those places where earthquakes happen continuously, they occasion no wonder, nor, for that matter, does [the presence of] the sun, because it is seen daily. (The ninth mode is eighth in the list of Favorinus and tenth in the lists of Sextus and Aenesidemus. And the tenth is eighth in Sextus and ninth in Favorinus.)

[10] The tenth mode is based on the comparison of things with each other, for example, the light in comparison with the heavy, the strong in comparison with the weak, the larger in comparison with the smaller, up in comparison with down. At any rate, right is not by nature right, but is so understood in relation to something else; at any rate if it moves, it won't be to the right any more. 88. Similarly, "father" and "brother" are relational terms and day is so designated in relation to the sun and, in general, everything in relation to the intellect. Therefore, things relative are, in themselves, unknowable.

These are the ten modes.

The school of Agrippa introduces, in addition to these, five other modes, one based on disagreement, one forcing an infinite regress, one based on relativity, one based on hypothesis and one based on circular reasoning.

[1] The one based on disagreement demonstrates that whatever question is advanced by philosophers or by everyday life is a matter of the greatest contention and full of confusion.

[2] The one based on infinite regress forbids that that which has been sought has been firmly established because confidence in it is based on establishing something else which is in turn based on establishing something else, and so on to infinity.

[3] **89.** The one based on relativity says that nothing is understood just by itself, but always with something else; for which reason, things are unknowable.

[4] The mode constructed on hypothesis is used when people think that the principles of things should be assumed as immediately plausible and not questioned. But this is in vain, for someone will hypothesize the opposite.

[5] The mode based on circularity occurs whenever that which ought to provide support for some claim needs to have its own establishment based on the plausibility of the claim, as, for example, if someone based the existence of pores on the occurrence of emanations and took the existence of pores as establishing the occurrence of emanations.

90. They also used to abolish all demonstration, criterion, sign, cause, motion, learning, generation and something being good or bad by nature. For every demonstration, they say, is constructed out of things [claimed to be] previously demonstrated or things not demonstrated. If the former, then they will need to produce the demonstration [for the things used as support], and this will go on indefinitely. If the latter, then if either all [of the undemonstrated supports], or some, or even a single one, is in doubt, then the whole argument is undemonstrated. If it is held that they say there are things in need of no demonstration, then those who hold this are mental marvels if they don't grasp that there must be a demonstration of the fact that these things are self-confirming.

91. Nor should the fact that there are four elements be established on the grounds that there are four elements. In addition, if particular demonstrations are untrustworthy, so is demonstration in general. And in order that we might know that there is [such a thing as] demonstration, a criterion is needed; and in order that we might know that there is a criterion, a demonstration is needed. So, the demonstration and the criterion, each dependent on the other, are ungraspable. How then could someone grasp non-evident things, being ignorant of the demonstration? For one seeks not to discover if things appear thus and so, but whether they are really so.

They pronounced the dogmatists to be simple-minded. For that which is concluded on the basis of an hypothesis has the status of an assumption, not an investigation. By means of this sort of argument, one may even argue about impossibilities.

92. As for those who think that one ought not to try to judge the truth on the basis of the circumstances or to legislate on the basis of what is natural, they say that such men make themselves the measure of all things and did not notice that every appearance appears in accordance with reciprocal circumstances and [our] disposition. Therefore, everything ought to be said to be true or everything false. For if [only] some things are true, by what means should they be distinguished? One will not distinguish sensibles by sense-perception, since they are all equally apparent to it; nor with one's intellect, for the same reason. But besides these, there is no power available for deciding. Therefore, they say that whoever is to make a firm assertion about a sensible or intelligible object, ought to first establish what opinions there are on the matter. For some have abolished one view and some another. 93. But [the truth] must be judged either by means of a sensible or an intelligible and each of these is disputed. So one cannot decide on the opinions concerning sensibles or intelligibles; and if, because of the conflict among thoughts, one ought to put no trust in any of them, the measure by means of which all things are to be [known] with precision will be destroyed. Therefore, all [claims] will be held to be equal. Further, they say, whoever investigates along with us that which appears, is either trustworthy or not. If he is trustworthy, he will have nothing to say to the man to whom the matter appears opposite. For just as he himself is to be trusted who says the appearance [is one way], so is the other man who says the opposite. If he is untrustworthy, he will not be trusted when he reports on the appearance.

94. One ought not to suppose that that which persuades us is true. For the same thing does not persuade everyone nor does it persuade the same people constantly. Persuasiveness sometimes arises on the basis of externals, the reputation of the speaker or his intellectual eminence or wiliness, or on the basis of his familiarity or charm. Further they abolish the criterion with this sort of argument. Either the criterion has been judged or it has not. If it has not been judged, then it is untrustworthy and it errs with respect to the true and the false. If it has been judged, it [the criterion] will become one of the particulars being judged, so that the same thing would [have to] judge and be judged, and that which has served as a criterion will have to be judged by something else, which itself will have to be judged by yet another and so on to infinity.

95. In addition to this, the criterion is subject to disagreement, some saying that man is the criterion, some saying that the senses are, others

saying reason, and a few the graspable presentation. But man [sometimes] disagrees with himself or with others, as is clear from the existence of different laws and customs. And the senses are deceived and reason is in disagreement. The graspable presentation is judged by the mind, and the mind is altered in a variety of ways. Therefore the criterion is unknowable, and because of this, so is the truth.

96. Further, there is no sign. For if a sign exists, they say, either it is sensible or intelligible. It is not sensible, since the sensible is public, but a sign is private. And the sensible is one of the differentiated things whereas the sign is relative. It is not intelligible, since the intelligible is the apparent [idea] of an appearance, or a non-apparent [idea] of that which is non-apparent, or a non-apparent [idea] of an appearance, or an apparent [idea] of that which is non-apparent. But the sign is none of these and so there is no sign. A sign is not the apparent [idea] of an appearance, since the apparent does not require a sign; it is not the non-apparent [idea] of the non-apparent, since that which is revealed by something must be apparent; **97.** it cannot be the non-apparent [idea] of an appearance because that which provides the starting-point for grasping something else must be apparent; nor is it the apparent [idea] of the non-apparent, because the sign, being relative, must be grasped along with that of which it is a sign, whereas it is not in this case. Thus, nothing non-evident could be grasped, because it is by means of signs that non-evident things are said to be grasped.

They abolish the cause in this way. A cause is a relative thing, for it is relative to something causable. But relatives are only conceptual objects, and do not exist. **98.** Therefore, a cause is only a conceptual object, since if it is a cause, it ought to accompany that of which it is a cause, otherwise it will not be a cause. Just as a father would not be a father should someone of whom he is the father not exist, so too for a cause: that in relation to which the cause is conceived does not exist; for generation or destruction or anything else [does not exist]. Therefore, a cause does not exist. Moreover, if a cause does exist, either a body is a cause of a body, or an incorporeal is a cause of an incorporeal, ⟨or an incorporeal is a cause of a body, or a body is a cause of an incorporeal⟩. But it is none of these; so there is no cause. A body could not be a cause of a body, since both have the same nature, and if either is said to be a cause, just insofar as it is a body, the other thing, being a body, will become a cause. **99.** But if both are causes, there will be nothing passive. The incorporeal is not a cause of the incorporeal for the same reason. An incorporeal is not a cause of a body since nothing incorporeal produces a body. A body is not a cause of something incorporeal, because whatever is generated must be in the category of passive matter. But if there is nothing passive because it is incorporeal, it would not come to be because of anything. So, there is no cause. With this the conclusion is also drawn that the first principles of the universe are non-existent, for that which acts and effects must be a something.

Moreover, there is no motion. For that which is moved is moved in the place in which it is or in the place in which it is not. But it cannot be moved in the place in which it is nor can it be moved in the place in which it is not. Therefore, there is no motion.

100. They also eliminated learning. For if, they say, something is taught, either what exists is taught by means of what is or what is not is taught by means of what is not. But what is is not taught by means of what is—for the nature of things appears to everyone and is known to all; nor is what is not taught by what is not; for what is not has no accidents, and consequently not even 'being taught'. Nor does it come to be, they say. For what is does not come to be, since it is; nor does what is not, since it does not exist; and that which neither exists nor is also comes off badly with respect to coming to be.

101. And there is nothing good or bad by nature. For if good and bad exist by nature, then it must be either good or bad for everyone, just as snow is something cold for everyone. But there is nothing which is good or bad for everyone in common; therefore, there is nothing good or bad by nature. For either one should say that everything which is thought [to be good] by anyone is good, or not everything. And one cannot say that everything is, since the same thing is thought to be good by one person (for example, pleasure [is thought to be good] by Epicurus) and thought to be bad by someone else, viz. Antisthenes. It will turn out, then, that the same thing is both good and bad. But if we say that not everything which is thought [to be good] by anyone is good, it will be necessary for us to make a distinction among opinions. But that is not possible because of the equal force of the arguments. So what is good by nature is unknowable.

102. The entirety of their approach can be comprehended from the extant treatises. For Pyrrho himself left no writings, but his associates, Timon, Aenesidemus, Numenius, Nausiphanes and others like them did.

The dogmatists, responding to them, say that they themselves [the sceptics] grasp things and dogmatize. For, insofar as they believe they have refuted someone, they are grasping [something], since by the same act they are confirming [their belief] and dogmatizing. Moreover, when they say that they determine nothing and that for every argument there is an opposing argument, they determine something and dogmatize about these very things. **103.** The sceptics reply: "We concede the point about what we experience qua human; for we acknowledge that it is daytime, that we are alive, and many other appearances in life. But concerning the things the dogmatists assert definitely with argument, saying that they have grasped them, we suspend judgement because of their being non-evident, acknowledging only the states which we find ourselves in. We concede that we see and acknowledge that we think, but as for how we see or think, we are ignorant. That this appears white we say colloquially without asserting definitely that it is really so. **104.** Regarding the utterance 'I determine nothing' and the like, we say that these are uttered but not as dogmas. For they are unlike the utterance 'the cosmos is round.' The latter is non-evident, whereas the former are mere admissions. So, when we say 'we determine nothing' we are not determining this very thing."

Again, the dogmatists say that they [the sceptics] abolish life, in the sense that they throw out everything that goes to make up a life. But the sceptics say that these charges are false. For they do not abolish, say, sight, but only hold that we are ignorant of its explanation. "For we do posit the phenomenon, but not as being what it appears to be. We do sense that fire burns, but we suspend judgement as to whether it is fire's nature to burn. **105.** Further, we do see that someone is moving, that someone perishes; but as for how these things occur, we do not know. We only object," they say, "to the non-evident things added on to the phenomena. For when we say that a picture has raised surfaces we are elucidating what is apparent; when we say that it does not [really] have them, we are no longer speaking about what appears, but something else. For this reason, Timon in his *Pytho* says that he has not diverged from what is customary. And in his *Likenesses* he says, 'But the apparent utterly dominates wherever it goes.' And in his work *On the Senses* he says, 'That honey is sweet I do not posit; that it appears so I concede.' "

106. Aenesidemus too in the first book of his *Pyrrhonian Arguments* says that Pyrrho determines nothing dogmatically because of the existence of contradictory arguments, but rather follows appearances. He says the same thing in *Against Wisdom* and in *On Investigation*. And Zeuxis, an associate of Aenesidemus, in *On Twofold Arguments* and Antiochus of Laodicea and Apellas in his *Agrippa* posit the phenomena alone. Therefore, according to the sceptics, the appearance is a criterion, as Aenesidemus too says. This is also so for Epicurus. Democritus, however, denied that the criterion was any of the appearances, and even that the appearances exist. **107.** Against this criterion of appearances, the dogmatists say that different presentations coming from the same things strike us; for example, from a tower which presents itself as round or square; and if the sceptic does not prefer one to the other, he will be unable to act; but if he gives credence to one or the other, they say, he will no longer be assigning equal force to each appearance. In reply to them, the sceptics say that when various presentations strike them, we say that each one appears; and for this reason, we posit that the appearances appear.

The sceptics say the goal is suspension of judgement, upon which freedom from anxiety follows like a shadow, as Timon and Aenesidemus and their followers put it. 108. For we shall neither choose this nor avoid that in matters which are up to us; as for matters not up to us, but which happen of necessity, like hunger, thirst, and pain, these we cannot avoid, for they cannot be removed by argument. And when the dogmatists say that the sceptic's position is such that he will live a life in which, were he commanded, he would not shrink from cannibalizing his father, the sceptics reply that he will be able to live so that he can suspend judgement about dogmatic questions, but not about matters of everyday life and of observance. So, we can choose and avoid something according to habit and we can follow customs. Some say that the sceptics say that the goal is freedom from passions; others say that they say it is gentleness.

Timon
Diogenes Laertius 9.109-116 [III-23]

109. Our Apollonides of Nicaea says in the first book of his commentary *On the Satires*, dedicated to Tiberius Caesar, that Timon, son of Timarchus, was born in Phlius. Having been orphaned as a youth, he became a dancer, but later rejected this occupation, migrated to Megara to be with Stilpo, and after spending some time with him, returned home and married. Next, he migrated with his wife to Elis to be with Pyrrho, and spent time there until his children were born, the older of whom he named Xanthus; he taught his son medicine and made him heir to his livelihood.

110. He was a highly regarded man, as Sotion says in his eleventh book. Being without means of support, he sailed to the Hellespont and Propontis. At Chalcedon he made his living as a sophist, and his reputation increased. He became prosperous there and sailed for Athens, where he spent his time until his death, except for a small amount of time spent in Thebes. He was acquainted with King Antigonus and Ptolemy Philadelphus,[22] as he himself indicates in his iambics.

Antigonus says he liked drink and if he had time to spare from philosophy he used to write poems; [he wrote] epics, tragedies, satyr-plays (and there were 30 comic dramas, while the tragedies numbered 60), satires,

22. Kings of Macedon and Alexandria respectively.

and lewd pieces. **111.** Moreover, there are prose works of his extant containing up to 20,000 lines, of which Antigonus of Carystus, who also wrote his biography, makes mention. There are three books of *Satires* in which, as befits a sceptic, he pours scorn on everyone and satirizes the dogmatists in the form of a parody. The first of these is narrated in the first person; the second and third are in dialogue form. At least, they seem to be so, for he appears to be questioning Xenophanes of Colophon about each philosopher and Xenophanes is answering him. In the second, he questions him about the older ones, and in the third, about the more modern ones. For this reason, some have titled it *Epilogue.* **112.** The first is concerned with the same matters, except that the work is in the form of a monologue. It begins, "Hurry to me, you busybody sophists."

Antigonus says he died when he was nearly ninety, which is confirmed by Sotion in his eleventh book. I have also heard that he had one eye, which is why he used to call himself "Cyclops." There was another Timon, the misanthrope.

This lover of wisdom was also a great lover of gardens, and minded his own business, as Antigonus also says. At any rate, there is a story that Hieronymus the Peripatetic said of him, "Just as among the Scythians both those fleeing and those attacking shoot arrows, so among philosophers, some catch pupils by pursuing them and some by fleeing them, like Timon."

113. He was quick to grasp a point and sneer at others. He loved writing and was always ready to sketch plots for poets and to collaborate on dramas. He used to work on tragedies with Alexander and Homer.[23] When disturbed by servants or dogs he used to do nothing, eager for his own peace and quiet. They say that Aratus[24] asked him how one could obtain a sound text of Homer, to whom he replied, "You could get it if you happened upon the oldest copies, but not the corrected ones of today." **114.** He customarily used to leave his own works lying around, sometimes half eaten-away, so that when he was reading something to Zopyrus the rhetorician, he would flip through the pages reading whatever turned up, and halfway down the page he would discover the scrap he had been missing all along. That is how indifferent he was. Moreover, he was so easygoing that he would allow a meal to be missed. They say that when he saw Arcesilaus going through the black market district he said, "What are you doing here, where we free men come?" To those who would accept [the evidence of] the senses when testified for by the intellect, he was accustomed continually to quote the line "Birds of a

---

23. Two tragic poets, Alexander the Aetolian and Homer of Byzantium.
24. The astronomical poet.

feather flock together". He was accustomed to tease in this way. He once said to a man who wondered at everything, "Why are you not wondering that we three have four eyes together," since he and his pupil Dioscurides each had one eye, and the other man was normal. **115.** Once when he was asked by Arcesilaus why he had come there from Thebes, he said, "To get a good laugh when I see you [people] arrayed before me." Nevertheless, while attacking Arcesilaus in the *Satires*, he praised him in his work titled *The Funeral Feast for Arcesilaus*.

He had no successor, according to Menodotus, and his school lapsed until Ptolemy of Cyrene revived it. Hippobotus and Sotion, however, say that Dioscurides of Cyprus, Nicolochus of Rhodes, Euphranor of Seleucia, and Praulus of the Troad were his pupils. The last mentioned, according to the history of Phylarchus, was a man of such endurance that he submitted to unjust execution for treason, without saying one word to condemn his fellow-citizens.

116. Eubulus of Alexandria was the pupil of Euphranor; Ptolemy was the pupil of Eubulus; Sarpedon and Heraclides were the pupils of Ptolemy; Aenesidemus of Cnossus, who wrote eight books of *Pyrrhonian Arguments*, was the pupil of Heraclides; Zeuxippus, also of Cnossus, was the pupil of Aenesidemus; Zeuxis the club-footed, was the pupil of Zeuxippus; Antiochus of Laodicea on the Lycus was the pupil of Zeuxis; Menodotus of Nicomedia, an empirical physician and Theiodas of Laodicea were pupils of Antiochus; Herodotus of Tarsus, son of Arieus, was the pupil of Menodotus; Sextus, the empirical physician, who wrote ten books on scepticism and other fine works, was the pupil of Herodotus; Saturninus Cythenas, himself an empirical [physician], was the pupil of Sextus.

Aristocles in Eusebius *Prep. Ev.* 14.18 758cd [III-24]

(758c) It is necessary above all to consider the issue of our knowledge. For if by nature we know nothing, there is no need to consider other things. There were some ancients who uttered this expression, and Aristotle argued against them. Pyrrho of Elis gave a powerful exposition of this view, but left no written treatment of it himself. His student Timon says that he who is going to be happy must look to these three things: (1) first, what things are like; (2) second, what our disposition ought to be with respect to them; (758d) (3) and finally, what will be the result for those who are so disposed. [Timon] says that [Pyrrho] declares that things are equally indifferent and unmeasurable and undecidable, and that for this reason neither our senses nor our opinions tell the truth or lie; and so we ought not to put our trust in them but ought instead to be undogmatic and uncommitted and unswayed, saying of each and every thing that it no more is than is not, or both is and is not, or neither is nor is not. Timon says that the result for those who are in this disposition will first be speechlessness and then freedom from disturbance; Aenesidemus [says they will attain] pleasure. These then are the main points of what they say.

Aenesidemus

Photius *Bibliotheca* 212   [III-25]

169b. I have read: the eight books of *Pyrrhonian Arguments* by Aenesidemus. The whole purpose of the work is to establish securely that nothing can be securely grasped, neither by means of the senses nor even by means of thought. Therefore, neither the Pyrrhonists nor the others know the truth in things; and those philosophizing according to another system, besides being ignorant of other things, are also unaware that they weary themselves and spend their time in continual agonies for nothing; they are ignorant of this very fact, that they have actually grasped nothing of what they believe they have grasped.

As for him who philosophizes according to Pyrrho, besides being happy in other respects, he is wise in knowing above all that nothing has been grasped securely by himself. And as to whatever he does know, he is clever enough to assent no more to the affirmation [of these things] than to their denial.

The entire thrust of the work is as I have stated. Aenesidemus wrote the books and dedicated them to a colleague in the Academy, Lucius Tuberon, a Roman of illustrious ancestry, who held important political offices.

In the argument of the first book he introduces the difference between the Pyrrhonists and the Academics in almost these very words: The Academics are dogmatists, laying down some positions without doubts and rejecting others unqualifiedly. The Pyrrhonists are dubitative and are liberated from every dogma, and no one of them has at all said that all things are ungraspable or that they are graspable, **(170a)** but rather that they are no more like this than like that, or that they are like this at one time and like that at another, or that they are such for one man and not such for another and totally non-existent for someone else; neither all things in common nor some of them are attainable [by our minds], nor are they unattainable, but rather they are no more attainable than unattainable, or at one time attainable and at another time no longer [so] or to one person attainable and to another not. Further, nothing is true or false, plausible or implausible, existing or not; rather, the same thing, so to say, is no more true than false, plausible than implausible, is than is not; or, at one time is like this and at another is like that; or is like this to one person and not like this to another.

Generally, the Pyrrhonist determines nothing, not even this, namely, that he determines nothing. We speak in this way, he says, not having any other way to tell what we think. The Academics, he says, especially the ones now, sometimes agree with Stoic opinions and, to tell the truth, appear to be just Stoics in conflict with Stoics.

Second, they [the Academics] dogmatize about many things. They introduce "virtue" and "imprudence" and postulate such things as good and bad, truth and falsity, plausibility and implausibility, being and non-being, and determine many things with assurance, saying that they only dispute about the graspable presentation. This is why the Pyrrhonists, in determining nothing, remain altogether beyond reproach, although the Academics, he says, are subject to the same critical examination as the other philosophers; the most important point is that those who doubt every thesis both guard their ground and do not conflict with themselves, while the Academics are not aware that they are in conflict with themselves. For when they posit and refute something unqualifiedly and at the same time say that there exist things graspable by all, they introduce an obvious contradiction. For how is it possible that one should know that one thing is true and another false and still doubt and be puzzled and not decisively choose the one and reject the other? If one is ignorant that this is good or bad, or that this is true and that false, that this exists and that does not, one ought to be in total agreement that each of these is ungraspable. On the other hand, if each of these is grasped with the senses or thought, it should be said to be graspable.

At the beginning of his book, Aenesidemus from Aigai [in Macedonia] records these and other such arguments, to describe the difference between Pyrrhonists and Academics. (170b) Immediately after, in the same first book, he gives a sketch of the chief parts of the whole approach of Pyrrhonian arguments.

In the second book he begins with a detailed discussion of that which was previously sketched, and considers separately truths, causes, states, motion, generation and destruction, and their contraries, showing, so he thinks, with close reasoning that there is doubt about all of these and that they are ungraspable.

The third book is a discussion of motion and sense-perception and of their properties; it makes a fuss over the same contradictions and relegates these things too to the [status of the] unattainable and ungraspable.

In the fourth book he speaks about signs, in the sense, for instance,

that appearances are signs of non-evident things, and says that these are
not at all existent, whereas those who think they exist are deceived by a
meaningless positive response. He brings up next the puzzles based on
customs concerning all of nature, the cosmos, and the gods, straining to
show that none of these falls within the class of things graspable.

In the fifth book he proffers the dubitative strategies directed against
causes, alleging that nothing is the cause of anything, saying that causalists
are deceived, and enumerating the modes according to which he thinks
those who have been induced into giving casual explanations have been
led to such a muddle.

The sixth book deals with things good and bad, and also what is worth
choosing and avoiding, and further, things to be preferred and rejected.
He reduces these to absurdity, eliminating, at least so he thinks, the
possibility of our grasping and understanding these.

In the seventh book he takes up arms against the virtues, saying that
those who philosophize about these have feigned empty opinions and
have led themselves astray into thinking that they are in a position to
theorize about these and act accordingly.

The eighth and last book is devoted to the goal of life, in which he
does not allow either happiness or pleasure or prudence or any other
goal held by anyone on the basis of philosophical doctrine; rather, [he
says] that there just is no such thing as a goal which is recognized by
all people.

Later Pyrrhonism: Sextus Empiricus

General Principles

Sextus *PH* 1.1–34   [III-26]

Ch. i On the Main Difference Between Philosophies

1. It is likely that, for those investigating some matter, the result is
either a discovery or the denial that there has been a discovery and an
acknowledgement of the failure to "grasp" [the truth], or else continuation
of the investigation. 2. Perhaps it is for this reason that in philosophical
investigations some said that they had found the truth, some denied that
it was possible for truth to be grasped, and some continue investigating.
3. Those who are called Dogmatists in the narrow sense believe that they
have discovered the truth; for example, the Aristotelians, the Epicureans,

the Stoics and certain others; among those who deny that truth can be grasped are Carneades, Clitomachus and other Academics; those who continue investigating are the Sceptics. **4.** Thus, it is reasonable that there should seem to be chiefly three philosophies: the Dogmatic, the Academic, and the Sceptical. So it will be appropriate for others to discuss the other schools; for the present we will discuss the sceptical approach in outline saying by way of preface that we make no firm assertions that any of what we are about to say is exactly as we say it is, but we [simply] declare our position on each topic as it now appears to us, like a reporter.

Ch. ii On the Argumentative Procedures of Scepticism

5. In sceptical philosophy, the argumentative procedure is in part general and in part specific. And the general part is that in which we set forth the basic features of scepticism, enunciating its fundamental idea, its principles and arguments, its criterion and its goal; further, the modes [of argument leading to] suspension of judgement, how we interpret the sceptical denials and the distinction of scepticism from the associated philosophies. **6.** The specific part is that in which we argue against each part of what is called philosophy. Let us take first the general argumentative procedure beginning our account with the names given to the sceptical approach.

Ch. iii On the Names for Scepticism

7. The sceptical approach is called "investigative" from the activity of investigating and inquiring. Also, it is called "suspensive" from the state produced in the investigator after the investigation. Again, it is called "dubitative" [aporetic], either, as some hold, from the practice of doubting [being in *aporia*] and investigating everything or from being at a loss when it comes to assent or denial. Finally, it is called "Pyrrhonian" from the fact that Pyrrho appears to us to have applied himself to scepticism more wholeheartedly and openly than anyone before him.

Ch. iv What Scepticism Is

8. The sceptical ability is the ability to set in opposition appearances and ideas in any manner whatsoever, the result of which is first that, because of the equal force of the opposed objects and arguments, final suspension of judgement is achieved, and then freedom from disturbance. **9.** We call it an ability not for any elaborate reason but simply in the sense of "being able." By "appearances" we now understand those things which appear to the senses, for which reason we contrast them with ideas. The words "in any manner whatsoever" may be taken with "ability" so that, as we said, the word "ability" is taken simply [i.e., unqualifiedly], or it may be taken with the words "set in opposition appearances and ideas," since we set these in opposition in a variety of ways, viz., appearances to appearances, ideas to ideas, or, interchanging them [appearances to ideas and ideas to appearances]. We use the words "in any manner whatsoever" here to indicate that we encompass all the possible oppositions. Or, in another way, the words "in any manner whatsoever" may be understood to go with "appearances and ideas," so that we need not inquire about how appearances appear or how ideas are thought, but may take them in a simple sense [i.e., unqualifiedly]. **10.** We understand "arguments opposed" not as indicating an unqualified denial and affirmation, but simply as indicating conflicting arguments. We mean by the words "equal force" equality with respect to plausibility and lack of plausibility. That is, that neither of the conflicting arguments stands out as more plausible than the other. "Suspension of judgement" is the repose of intellect owing to which we neither deny nor affirm something. "Freedom from disturbance" is the serenity or calmness of the soul. How freedom from disturbance enters the soul along with suspension of judgement we shall explain in the chapter on the goal [of scepticism].[25]

Ch. v On the Sceptic

11. The Pyrrhonian philosopher is implicitly included in the conception of the sceptical approach, for he is one who partakes of this power.

Ch. vi On the Principles of Scepticism

12. The principle of scepticism in the sense of cause is, we say, the expectation of attaining freedom from disturbance. Men of natural ability are disturbed because of the inconsistency in things, and being doubtful which of the alternatives they should assent to, they came to inquire into what is true and what is false in things in order that from a resolution of their doubts they would attain freedom from disturbance. The main principle of the sceptical system is that for every argument another argument of equal [weight] is opposed. As a result of this we seem to arrive at a cessation of dogmatism.

Ch. vii Does the Sceptic Dogmatize?

13. When we say that the sceptic does not dogmatize it is not in the more common sense of the term "dogma" according to which, as some say, to dogmatize is just to approve of something, for the sceptic assents to the states forced on him as a result of a presentation. For example,

---

25. Ch. xii below.

when he feels hot or cold he would not say, "I seem not to be hot, or not to be cold." When we say that the sceptic does not dogmatize we are using the term "dogma" in the sense according to which, as some say, dogma is the assent to something non-evident investigated by the sciences, for a Pyrrhonist never assents to anything non-evident. **14.** Further, he does not dogmatize even when, in regard to non-evident [propositions], he offers the sceptical utterances "no more this than that" and "I determine nothing" or any of the others concerning which we will later speak. For the one who dogmatizes posits as being the case that about which he is said to dogmatize, whereas the sceptic does not posit these utterances as unconditionally [representing] that which is the case. For he supposes that just as the utterance "all is false" expresses its own falsity as well as that of other propositions, (and similarly for the phrase "nothing is true"), so the phrase "no more this than that" is itself one of the things about which it is said "no more this than that" and for this reason cancels itself along with the other things to which it is applied. We say the same thing for the other sceptical utterances. **15.** Besides, whereas the one who dogmatizes posits as being the case that about which he dogmatizes, the sceptic offers his utterances as implicitly self-cancelling, and so he should not be said to dogmatize in offering them. The most important point of all is that in making these utterances he expresses that which appears to himself and he reports the state he is in, but he does so undogmatically, and he commits himself to nothing about any underlying external things.

Ch. viii Has the Sceptic a System?

16. We take a similar approach when asked "has the sceptic a system?" If by "system" one means "commitment to many dogmas having logical connections with each other and with appearances" and by "dogma" one means "assent to something non-evident", we will say that the sceptic has no system. **17.** But if by "system" one means "a method which follows a rational procedure based on appearances, that rational procedure indicating that it is possible to seem to live rightly" (for "rightly" is interpreted not only as "living according to virtue" but also in a simpler sense), and encompassing the ability to suspend judgement, we will then say that sceptic has a system. For we follow a rational procedure based on appearances, this procedure indicating a life in accord with traditional customs and laws and practices and private states.

Ch. ix Does the Sceptic Have a Physical Doctrine?

18. We say something similar in investigating whether the sceptic should have a physical doctrine. As far as pronouncing with firm confidence regarding any of the matters which have been subject to dogmatic assertions in physical theory, we do not have a physical doctrine. But in the sense of opposing every argument with an equal argument and in the matter of freedom from disturbance, we do touch upon physical doctrine. We proceed similarly in the logical and ethical parts of what is called 'philosophy'.

Ch. x Do the Sceptics Eliminate Appearances?

19. Those who say that the sceptics eliminate appearances seem to me not to have listened to what we have said. For we do not overturn that which, as a result of a state produced by a presentation, leads us involuntarily to assent, as we said previously. But these are just what appearances are. Whenever we investigate the question of whether an object is such as it appears to be, we grant that it appears as such, since we are not investigating the appearance, but rather the claims made about the appearance. And this is different from investigating the appearance itself. **20.** For example, it appears to us that honey sweetens. This we concede, for we have the sensation of sweetness. What we investigate is whether honey is sweet as far as concerns its essence, which is not [a matter of] the appearance, but is something said about the appearance. And even if we use reasoning directly against the appearances, we do not do so with the intention of eliminating them, but rather with the intention of displaying the rashness of the dogmatists. For if such reasoning is so deceptive that it practically snatches away the appearances from under our eyes, ought we not to be suspicious of its use in regard to things non-evident, so that we had best not be so rash as to follow it there?

Ch. xi On the Criterion of Scepticism

21. That we pay attention to appearances is clear from that which is said by us about the criterion of the sceptical approach. The term "criterion" is used in two senses: [1] that which is accepted as a reliable indication of the existence or non-existence of something (concerning which we will speak in our refutation [of the dogmatic positions]); [2] that which is accepted [as a criterion] for action, by attending to which we will do some things and not do others in life. It is the latter which we are now discussing. **22.** We say that the appearance is the criterion of the sceptical approach, in this way referring in effect to the presentation of it, for since it [i.e., the presentation] is located in a feeling or an involuntary state, it is not open to investigation. For this reason, probably no one disputes that an object appears one way or another; the investigation concerns whether it really is such as it appears. **23.** So, attending to appearance we live undogmatically according to the rules of everyday conduct, since we are not able to be completely inactive. It seems that the rules of everyday conduct are divided into four parts: [1] the guidance given by nature; [2] compulsion exercised by our states; [3] traditional laws and customs; [4] the teaching of the crafts. **24.** The guidance of nature is that according to which we can naturally perceive and think. The compulsion exercised by our states is that according to which hunger leads us to food and thirst to drink; traditional laws and customs are those according to which we accept pious living as good and improper living as bad; the teaching of the crafts is that according to which we are not inactive in the crafts we adopt. And we say all these things undogmatically.

Ch. xii What is the Goal of Scepticism?

25. Following these matters, we ought next to explain the goal of the sceptical approach. A goal is that for the sake of which everything is done or thought about, the goal itself not being for the sake of something else; or it is that which is ultimately desired. We say most definitely that the goal of the sceptic is the freedom from disturbance with respect to matters of belief and also moderate states with respect to things that are matters of compulsion. **26.** For the sceptic, having begun to philosophize in order to judge presentations and to try to grasp certain things as true or false so that he could attain freedom from disturbance, tripped up on the equal weight of incompatible [claims]; thereupon, not being able to make a judgement, he suspended judgement. Finding himself in this suspensive state, the freedom from disturbance with respect to beliefs followed fortuitously. **27.** For the one who believes that something is honourable or bad by nature will be disturbed; whenever the things he believes to be honourable are not before him, he believes that he has inflicted upon himself the things that are by nature bad and he goes off after the things which, according to him, are good; and when he possesses them he stumbles into more disturbances because of his irrational and immoderate elation, and fearing that things will soon change he will do everything he can so that he might not lose the things he believes to be good. **28.** On the other hand, the man who determines nothing in regard to things honourable or bad by nature does not flee or go after them excessively. For this reason he has a freedom from disturbance.

In fact, the story about the painter Apelles also applies to the sceptic. They say that when Apelles was painting a horse and wished to depict the horse's froth, he was so unsuccessful that he gave up and flung at the picture the sponge that he used to wipe off his brushes. The mark made by the sponge produced a representation of the horse's froth. **29.** The sceptics hoped to attain a freedom from disturbance by judging the inconsistency of appearances and ideas, and not being able to do this, they suspended judgement. Being in this suspensive state, freedom from disturbance followed fortuitously, as a shadow follows a body. We do not believe, however, that the sceptic is totally without troubles, but rather that he is troubled by things that are matters of compulsion. We agree that he is sometimes cold and sometimes thirsty and that he experiences such things. 30. But even in these cases, whereas ordinary people are distressed by two circumstances—by the states themselves and no less by the belief that the circumstances [under which the states are experienced] are bad by nature—the sceptic, by rejecting the additional belief that each of these is not only bad but bad by nature, will escape with more moderate states. For this reason, we say that the goal of the sceptic is freedom from disturbance in regard to beliefs and moderate states in regard to matters of compulsion. But some of the famous sceptics add to these suspension of judgement in investigations.

Ch. xiii On the General Modes Leading to Suspension of Judgement

31. Since we said that freedom from disturbance follows suspension of judgement about everything, it is appropriate to say next how suspension of judgement comes about in us. Speaking rather generally, suspension of judgement comes about through the opposition of things. We oppose appearances to appearances, or ideas to ideas, or, interchanging them [appearances to ideas or ideas to appearances]. 32. For example, we oppose appearances to appearances when we say, "The same tower that appears round from far away appears square when nearby;" we oppose ideas to ideas when, in reply to someone constructing a proof of providence based on the orderliness of the heavenly bodies, we counter with the fact that frequently good people fare ill and bad people prosper, and from this we infer that providence does not exist; 33. we oppose ideas to appearances just as did Anaxagoras when he opposed the claim that snow is white, saying that snow is frozen water, water is black and, therefore, snow is black. We oppose things according to a different conception when, as in the previous example, we oppose things present to things present and when we oppose things present to things past or future. For example, whenever someone challenges us with an argument which we are not able to refute, 34. we say to him that just as before the founder of your system was born, it was not clear that the argument based on the system was sound, although it existed in nature, so it is possible that the argument opposed to the one made by you exists in nature, although it is not yet clear to us. Therefore, we ought not yet assent to the argument which now seems to us to be the stronger.

Sextus *PH* 1.210–241 [III-27]

Ch. xxix That the Sceptical Approach Differs from Heraclitean Philosophy

210. That it [Heracliteanism] differs from our approach is self-evident. For Heraclitus pronounces dogmatically about many non-evident things, whereas we do not, as has already been said. Aenesidemus and his followers used to say that the sceptical approach is a preliminary to the Heraclitean philosophy because opposite appearances of the same thing lead to [the claim] that the same thing really has opposite attributes, and whereas the sceptic says that there are opposite appearances, the Heracliteans go from this to the claim that the same thing really has opposite attributes. So we say to these people that the statement about opposite appearances is not a dogma of the sceptics, but is something experienced not only by sceptics, but other philosophers and all men as well. 211. At least, no one would dare say that honey is not sweet to healthy people or bitter to the jaundiced. So, the Heracliteans are starting from a basic grasp common to [all] men, just as we do, and probably the rest of the philosophers as well. Therefore, if they [the Heracliteans] got the idea that the same thing has opposite attributes from some sceptical utterance like "all things are ungraspable" or "I determine nothing" or something similar, they would have perhaps inferred their conclusion. But since their starting points are not only our experiences but those of the rest of the philosophers and of daily life, why would someone say that it is our approach that leads to Heraclitean philosophy rather than that of each of the other philosophies or daily life, since we all use common material?

212. Indeed, the sceptical approach not only does not assist in the knowledge of Heraclitean philosophy, but it is a hindrance to it, since the sceptic attacks all the dogmas of Heraclitus as rashly stated, contradicting the [theory of universal] conflagration and contradicting the claim that the same thing has opposite attributes, ridiculing the dogmatic rashness of Heraclitus regarding every dogma, saying repeatedly "I do not grasp" and "I determine nothing" as I said before. This actually conflicts with the Heracliteans. Now it is absurd to say that a conflicting approach is a path to the system with which it conflicts and therefore it is absurd to say that the sceptical approach is a path to the Heraclitean philosophy.

Ch. xxx In What Respect the Sceptical Approach Differs from Democritean Philosophy

213. It is also said that the philosophy of Democritus has some association with scepticism since it seems to employ the same material as we. For from the fact that honey appears sweet to some and bitter to others,

it is said that Democritus reasons that honey itself is neither sweet nor bitter and because of this makes the sceptical utterance "no more this than that." The sceptics and Democriteans, however, employ the utterance "no more this than that" differently. Whereas they deploy the utterance to indicate that [the honey] is neither [sweet nor bitter], we deploy it to indicate our ignorance of whether it is really both or neither of the things it appears to be. **214.** So, we differ in this respect too, a disagreement that becomes perfectly self-evident whenever Democritus says "In reality atoms and void." He says, "in reality" instead of "in truth" and, it is needless to say, I think, that he differs from us when he says that it is in truth that atoms and the void exist, even though he *does* start from the inconsistency of appearances.

Ch. xxxi In What Respect Scepticism Differs from Cyrenaicism

215. Some say that the Cyrenaic approach is the same as scepticism, since that approach says that only our [subjective] states are grasped. But it differs from scepticism, since it says that the goal [of life] is pleasure and the smooth motion of the flesh, whereas we say that the goal is freedom from disturbance, which is opposite to their goal. For a man who asserts definitely that pleasure is the goal experiences disturbances, whether pleasure is or is not present, as I argued in the chapter on the goal of scepticism.[26] Further, whereas we suspend judgement as far as regards the essence of external things, the Cyrenaics pronounce them to have a nature which is ungraspable.

Ch. xxxii In What Respect Scepticism Differs from the Protagorean Approach

216. Now Protagoras wants to say that man is the measure of all things, of what is that it is, and of what is not that it is not. By 'measure' he means the 'criterion'; by 'things' he means 'objects'; so, in effect, he is saying that man is the criterion of all objects, of those that are that they are and of those that are not that they are not. For this reason he posits only what appears to each and thus he introduces relativity. **217.** Therefore, he seems to have some association with the Pyrrhonists. He differs from them, however, and we shall understand the difference, when we have given a reasonably full account of Protagoras' view.

The man says that matter is flowing, that while it is flowing additions are continuously made to replace that which is carried away, and that the senses are rearranged and altered according to ages and the other

26. III-26 (25–30; also 12).

conditions of the body. **218.** He says that the rational principles of all the appearances reside in the matter, so that the matter all by itself is able to be all those things it appears to be to everyone. And men sometimes apprehend different things because of their different dispositions. For one who is in a natural state apprehends those attributes of material things which are able to appear to those in a natural state; and those in an unnatural state apprehend those attributes which are able to appear to those in an unnatural state. **219.** Further, the same reasoning applies to different ages, sleeping or waking, and each type of disposition. Man thus becomes the criterion of things, according to him, for all that appears to man also exists, whereas that which appears to no man does not exist. We see, therefore, that he dogmatizes about flowing matter and about the existence of explanations of all appearances in it, whereas for us, these are non-evident and we suspend judgement about them.

Ch. xxxiii In What Respect Scepticism Differs from the Academic Philosophy

220. Some say that the Academic philosophy is the same as scepticism. Therefore, it is appropriate to discuss this matter next.

According ‹to most› it is thought that there have been three Academies, the oldest one being that of the Plato and his followers, the second or middle being that of the followers of Arcesilaus, the student of Polemo, and the third or New Academy being that of the followers of Carneades and Clitomachus. Some propose a fourth, that of the followers of Philo and Charmidas; some even count a fifth, that of the followers of Antiochus. Let us start with the Old Academy and see how the above-mentioned philosophies differ.

221. Some have said that Plato is dogmatic, others that he is dubitative [aporetic], and others that he is partly one and partly the other. For they say that in the propaideutic dialogues, where Socrates is introduced either as teasing people or as combatting sophists, Plato shows a playful and dubitative character; he shows a dogmatic character when he makes serious pronouncements either through the mouth of Socrates or Timaeus or some such person. **222.** Regarding those who say that he is dogmatic or partly dogmatic and partly dubitative, it would be superfluous to speak now, for they concur in Plato's differences from us. Regarding the question of whether or not Plato is a pure sceptic, we shall consider it more fully in our *Remarks* [Against the Dogmatists].[27] But now let us speak summarily against the followers of Menodotus and Aenesidemus,

---

27. In the five books of *Against the Dogmatists* (= *M* 7–11) Sextus frequently refers to and argues against Platonic doctrines.

for they are the chief proponents of this side of the quarrel. We say that
when Plato pronounces on forms or the existence of providence or the
[claim that] the virtuous life is more worth choosing than the life of vice,
either he assents to their existence—in which case he is dogmatizing, or
he opts for one as more plausible than the other, since he expresses a
preference on the basis of trustworthiness or untrustworthiness—in
which case he steps out of sceptical character. For it is self-evident from
what has been said before that this is alien to our [approach].

223. And even if Plato does make some sceptical utterances when, as
they say, he is writing propaideutics, he will not on account of this
become a sceptic. For whoever dogmatizes about one thing, or at all
prefers one presentation to another on the basis of trustworthiness or
untrustworthiness, or pronounces on something non-evident, assumes
the character of a dogmatist, as Timon makes clear through what he said
about Xenophanes. **224.** For praising him in many respects, so that
he even dedicated his *Satires* to him, he describes him as lamenting
and saying:

> Would that I, through indecision, had hit upon the benefit
> of a well-stocked mind, but a treacherous path deceived me.
> Being old and untutored in total scepticism,
> wherever I turned my mind everything dissolved into one
> and the same. Everything always drawn up in every
> way rested in one self-same nature.

For this reason, at least, he calls him, half-vain, and not perfectly without
vanity, because of which he says:

> Xenophanes, half-vain, derider of deceiving Homer,
> Fashioned a god apart from men self-identical in every way,
> stout, unscathed, thought greater than thought.

He said that he was half-vain, being without vanity in some respect and
'derider of deceiving Homer' since he derided the deceptions in Homer.
225. But Xenophanes held dogmas contrary to the basic grasps of other
men, viz. that everything is one, and that god is naturally [immanent]
in everything, is spherical, impassible, unchangeable and rational. From
this, it is easy to show the difference between Xenophanes and us. Yet,
it is self-evident from what has already been said that should Plato puzzle
over some things he would still not be a sceptic, since in some [dialogues]
he either appears to make pronouncements about the existence of non-

evident things or to express preferences regarding non-evident things on the basis of trustworthiness.

226. Those of the new Academy, even though they hold all things to be ungraspable, probably differ from the sceptics in the very fact of their saying that all things are ungraspable. For they commit themselves to this, whereas the sceptics allow that it is possible for something to be grasped. But they also differ from us clearly in their judgement about things good or bad. For the Academics do not say that something is good or bad in the way that we do, but rather with the conviction that it is more plausible that what they say is good is [so] rather than the opposite, and similarly for what is bad. On the other hand, when we say that something is good or bad, we do not do so with a belief that what we say is plausible, but rather follow a way of life undogmatically so that we should not be inactive. **227.** We say that presentations are equal in plausibility or implausibility as far as concerns the essence; whereas they say that some are plausible and some are not.

And they make distinctions among plausible [presentations]. They regard some as simply plausible; some as plausible and tested; and others as plausible, thoroughly tested and uncontroverted. For example, when one suddenly enters a darkened room wherein is lying a coiled-up rope, it is simply plausible that the presentation coming from this is as if it were that from a snake, **228.** but to the man who has looked carefully and thoroughly tested the circumstances, for example, by ascertaining that it does not move, that its colour is of a certain sort, and so on, it appears to be a rope according to the plausible and tested presentation. An example of an uncontroverted presentation is this. It is said that Heracles brought Alcestis back from Hades when she was dead and showed her to Admetus who received a plausible and thoroughly tested presentation of Alcestis. But since he knew that she was dead, his intellect recoiled from assent and inclined to disbelief. **229.** So those of the new Academy prefer a thoroughly tested and plausible presentation to a simply plausible one and an uncontroverted, thoroughly tested and plausible one to either of the other two.

And even though followers of the Academic philosophy and followers of the sceptical philosophy both say that they are persuaded by certain things, it is self-evident that there is a difference between the two in the respect in which they do this. **230.** For the words "to be persuaded" have different meanings; one of these means not resisting but simply following without considerable inclination or positive response as a boy is said to obey his chaperon; but at the same time the words may also mean assenting with a deliberate intention and something like enthusiasm, on the basis of excessive desire, as the dissolute man is persuaded by someone extolling a luxurious life. Therefore, since the followers of Carneades and Clitomachus say that there are things that are plausible and that they are persuaded by them with considerable inclination, whereas we say that we do so simply yielding without inclination, we would differ from them in this respect.

231. We also differ from the new Academy in matters contributing to the goal [of life]. For while those who say that they order [their lives] by it [i.e., the Academic philosophy] employ plausibility for living, we live our lives undogmatically, following laws and customs and natural states. We could say more about the distinction between the two schools were we not aiming for conciseness.

232. Arcesilaus, on the other hand, who was, as we said, founder and head of the middle Academy, seems to me really to have shared the argumentative procedures of Pyrrho, so that his approach and ours are practically one and the same. For one does not find him committing himself to some things being or not being the case, nor taking sides with respect to the trustworthiness or untrustworthiness of one thing rather than another, but rather to suspend judgement about everything. And he also holds that the goal is suspension of judgement which, as we said, is accompanied by freedom from disturbance. **233.** He says also that suspension of judgement in particular cases is good and assent in particular cases is bad. But whereas we say these things on the basis of appearance and do not commit ourselves, he says them with a view to their nature, meaning that suspension of judgement is in itself a good thing, and assent bad. **234.** If one should trust the things said about him, he appeared on the surface to be a Pyrrhonist, but in fact he was a dogmatist. And since he used to test his associates by means of a dubitative [aporetic] procedure to see if they were clever enough to grasp Platonic dogmas, he seemed to be a dubitative philosopher, but in fact he actually promulgated Platonic dogmas to the clever ones among his associates. It is because of this that Ariston spoke of him as "Plato in front, Pyrrho in back, and Diodorus in the middle," for although he used the dialectical method of Diodorus, he was thoroughly Platonic.

235. The followers of Philo say that things are ungraspable as far as concerns the Stoic criterion, that is, the graspable presentation, but graspable as far as concerns the nature of the things themselves. Further, Antiochus transferred the Stoa into the Academy, as it was said of him that in the Academy he theorizes according to Stoic doctrine; for he tried to prove that Stoic doctrines are contained in Plato. So the difference between the sceptical approach and that of the so-called fourth and fifth Academies is evident.

Ch. xxxiv Whether Medical Empiricism is the Same as Scepticism

236. Since some say that the sceptical philosophy is the same as the empirical system in medicine, it should be understood that insofar as that empiricism commits itself to the ungraspability of non-evident things, it is not the same as scepticism, nor is it appropriate for the sceptic to attach himself to that system. He might, rather, it seems to me, follow the so-called methodical doctrine. **237.** For of the medical systems that alone seems not to be rash by presumptuously saying whether non-evident things are graspable or not. Rather, following appearances, it derives from them what seems to be advantageous, in agreement with the sceptics. For we said previously [23] that the general lifestyle, which the sceptic also uses, is divided into four parts: [1] the guidance given by nature, [2] compulsion exercised by our states, [3] traditional laws and customs, and [4] the teaching of the crafts. **238.** So, just as the sceptic is guided by the compulsion exercised by his states to drink when thirsty and eat when hungry, and similarly for the rest, so the methodical physician is guided by the states [of the patient] to corresponding [remedies], by contraction to dilation; just as someone seeks the refuge in warm sunshine from the contraction caused by extreme cold; or seeks relief from a flux by stopping it up; or as those in a hot bath, being languid and dripping with sweat, proceed to check [the sweat] and so seek refuge in the cold air. It is self-evident that states uncongenial to nature compel one to act to dispel them, seeing that even a dog with a thorn in its paw proceeds to remove it. **239.** Lest I exceed the bounds of a summary sketch by speaking about details, I shall just say that I think that all the things said by the methodical physicians can be categorized under the compulsion exercised by our states, whether they be those according to or contrary to nature, and also that [the methodical and sceptical] approaches have in common the undogmatic and indifferent use of terms. **240.** For just as the sceptic uses the utterances "I determine nothing" and "I grasp nothing" ‹undogmatically›, as we have said, so the methodic physician speaks guilelessly of 'generality' and 'pervade' and related terms. He also uses the word 'indication' undogmatically, for the guidance given by apparent states, according to and contrary to nature, as to what seem to be corresponding [remedies], as for thirst and hunger, and the rest that I mentioned. **241.** For this reason, the approach of the methodics in medicine, on the basis of these and other considerations, should be said to have an affinity to scepticism; at any rate, more than the other medical doctrines, when it is compared with them.

Having discussed this much regarding those who seem to have views comparable to the sceptical approach, let us with these words bring to a close the general account of scepticism and the first book of the *Outlines*.

Sextus *PH* 3.280–281   [III-28]

Ch. xxxii Why the Sceptic Sometimes Purposely Employs Arguments Lacking in Persuasiveness

280. The sceptic, because he loves humanity, wishes to cure dogmatists of their opinions and rashness, with reasoning, so far as possible. So, just as doctors have remedies of different strengths for bodily ailments and for those suffering excessively employs the strong ones and for those suffering mildly the mild ones, so the sceptic puts forth arguments that differ in strength; 281. he employs those which are weighty and able to destroy forcefully the dogmatist's ailment, viz. opinion, in those cases where the disease is caused by excessive rashness, and those which are less weighty in the cases where the ailment, viz. opinion, is superficial and easy to cure and for those who are able to be healed by less weighty persuasions. For this reason, one inspired by scepticism does not hesitate to employ on some occasions arguments that are strongly persuasive, and apparently weaker ones on other occasions. He uses the latter on purpose, since they are frequently sufficient to accomplish his objective.

Sextus *M* 8.479–481   [III-29]

479. Yes, they say, but [the argument] which concludes that there is no demonstration refutes itself by being demonstrative. In response to this we must say that it does not refute itself utterly. For many things are said in a way which implies exceptions; and as we say that Zeus is the father of gods and men with an implied exception of this very point (for he is surely not his own father!), so too when we say that there is no demonstration we say so with an implicit exception for the argument which demonstrates that there is no demonstration. For this alone is a demonstration. 480. And if it refutes itself it is not thereby established that demonstration exists. For there are many things which do to themselves the same thing as they do to other things. For example, just as fire consumes its fuel and then destroys itself along with it, and just as purgative medicines expel fluids from the body and then eliminate themselves as well, in the same way the argument against demonstration is able to wipe itself out after having destroyed all demonstration. 481. And again, just as it is not impossible for someone, after climbing up a ladder to a higher place, to knock down the ladder with his foot after he gets up there, so too it is not unreasonable for the sceptic, after arriving

at the establishment of his point by using the argument which demonstrates that there is is no demonstration as a kind of step-stool, thereupon to destroy this argument itself.

Sextus *PH* 2.204   [III-30]

Ch. xv On Induction

I also think that it is easy to dispense with the method of induction. For since what they [the dogmatists] want is to establish the universal on the basis of particulars by means of induction, either they do so by surveying all of the particulars or by surveying only some of them. But if they do so by surveying only some of them, then the induction is insecure, since it is possible that some of the remaining particulars covered by the induction contradict the universal. But if they do so by surveying all of the particulars, then they are undertaking impossible labours, since the particulars are unlimited in number and indefinite. Consequently, on both of these assumptions I think that it turns out that induction is undermined [as a mode of reasoning].

Sextus *PH* 2.1–12   [III-31]

Ch. i Can the Sceptic Investigate the Claims of the Dogmatists?

1. Since we have embarked on a [critical] investigation of the dogmatists, let us examine, summarily and in outline, each of the parts of what they call philosophy. First, we shall respond to their incessant claim that the sceptic is unable to investigate or form any sort of conception of their dogmatic views. 2. For they say that either the sceptic grasps or does not grasp what the dogmatists say; and if he grasps it, how could he be in doubt about what he says he has grasped? And if he does not grasp it, he will, as a result, not even be able to talk about what he has not grasped. 3. For just as someone who does not know, for example, what the [argument] which turns on [progressive] reduction is or what the theorem via two mode [arguments] is cannot even say anything about them, so he who does not know about each of the claims made by the dogmatists cannot investigate them [critically] on matters he does not know about. For the sceptic is completely unable to investigate the claims made by the dogmatists.

4. Those who say this ought to answer and tell us in what sense they are using the term 'grasp', whether in the sense of simply conceiving without being committed to the existence of the things we are arguing about, or in the sense of also positing the existence of the things we are

discussing. For if they say that in their argument grasping is assenting to a graspable presentation (a graspable presentation being one which comes from an existing thing and is stamped and moulded in accordance with the existing object, and is such that it could not have come from a non-existing object) then they themselves will probably not want to [say that] they cannot investigate things which they have not grasped in this sense. **5.** Thus, for example, when a Stoic makes a critical investigation of the Epicurean who says that substance is divided or that god does not exercise providence over things which happen in the cosmos or that pleasure is a good thing, has [the Stoic] then grasped [these things] or not? And if he has, then by saying that they exist he has utterly abolished Stoicism; but if he has not grasped them, then he is not able to say anything against them.

6. One should make a similar reply to the followers of other systems, when they want to investigate one of the doctrines of those who hold different views. Consequently, they cannot make critical investigations of each other. Or rather, to avoid babbling, virtually their entire dogmatic philosophy will be thrown into confusion and sceptical philosophy will be vigorously promoted if it is granted that one cannot investigate what is not grasped in this sense. **7.** For he who makes a pronouncement and dogmatizes about some non-evident thing either will say that he makes this pronouncement about it after grasping it or after not grasping it. If he does so after not grasping it, he will be untrustworthy. But if he does so after grasping it, either he will say that he grasped it because it struck him immediately, in its own right, and as a clear fact, or that he did so by means of a kind of search and investigation. **8.** But if the non-evident thing is said to have occurred to him in its own right and as a clear fact and that [that is why] it was grasped, in that case it wouldn't even be non-evident but would be equally apparent to all and agreed upon and not a matter of disagreement. But each of the non-evident things has been the subject of an interminable disagreement among the dogmatists; therefore the dogmatist who commits himself to the existence of and pronounces about the non-evident thing would not have grasped it because it occurred to him in its own right and evidently. **9.** But if he does so by means of a kind of search, how (on the present hypothesis) will he be able to investigate it before he grasps it with precision? For since the investigation requires a prior precise grasp of what is to be investigated and investigated in this way, and the grasp of the subject being investigated again itself demands that there should have been an exhaustive prior investigation of this subject, then by the circular mode for producing doubt, the investigation of non-evident things and dogmatizing about them will become impossible for them; if some people want to take the grasping as their starting point, we bring them to see that it must be investigated first and then grasped, but if they want to take the investigation as their starting point, we bring them to see that what is going to be investigated must be grasped before it can be investigated. Consequently, for these reasons they can neither grasp any of the non-evident things nor pronounce about them in such a way as to commit themselves to it. The immediate result of this will, I think, be that the argumentative ingenuity of the dogmatists is abolished and the suspensive philosophy is introduced.

10. But if they say that they do not mean that it is this sort of grasp which ought to precede the investigation, but just a simple conception, then it is not impossible for those who suspend judgement to investigate the existence of non-evident things. For the sceptic is not, in my view, barred from having a conception, since this occurs on the basis of clear appearances which strike him and about which he is passive and also since the conception does not necessarily entail the existence of the things conceived of. For, as they say, we conceive not only existent things but non-existent things as well. Hence the suspensive man remains in the sceptical disposition both when he investigates and when he conceives; for it has been shown that he assents to what strikes him in a passive presentation, in so far as it is apparent to him.

11. But consider whether even here the dogmatists are not barred from investigation. For continued investigation of things is not inconsistent for those who admit that they are ignorant about what things are like in their nature, but it is for those who think that they know them with precision. For the one group is, as they have supposed, already near the end of its investigation, while the other still possesses the key starting point of every investigation, viz. the belief that they have not discovered [the truth].

12. Therefore, we must for the present investigate summarily each part of what they call philosophy; and since there has been a great deal of disagreement among the dogmatists about the parts of philosophy, some saying that there is only one, some two and some three, though it would not be appropriate to prolong our consideration of this now, let us get on with the argument, even-handedly setting out the opinion of those who seem to have dealt with it rather completely.

Sextus *PH* 2.14–21 [III-32]

Ch. iii On the Criterion

14. Let us first say that [the word] 'criterion' is applied both to that with reference to which we make judgements of existence and nonexistence, and to that with attention to which we live. Our present purpose

is to examine the so-called criterion of truth. For we have discussed the other sense of criterion in our discussion of scepticism.

15. The criterion, then, which we are discussing has three senses: general, particular and most particular. In the general sense it is every standard for grasping, in which sense physical [organs] such as vision are called criteria; in the particular sense it is every technical standard for grasping, for example a yardstick and a compass; in the most particular sense it is every technical standard for grasping a non-evident thing, and in this sense things drawn from daily life are not said to be criteria, but only logical apparatus, i.e., what the dogmatists bring to bear on a decision about the truth [are said to be criteria]. 16. So we say that we will first undertake a preliminary discussion of the logical criterion. But the logical criterion too has three senses, that by whom, and that by means of which, and that according to which. An example of 'by whom' is man, of 'by means of which' is either sense-perception or intellect, and of 'that according to which' is the application of the presentation; for it is according to [the presentation] that a man sets himself to judge by means of one of the above-mentioned [criteria].

17. It is, then, perhaps fitting to say this by way of introduction, so that we form a conception of the subject of our discussion. But let us move on to the counter-argument used against those who rashly say that they have grasped the criterion of truth, beginning with the [fact of] disagreement about it.

Ch. iv Does a Criterion of Truth Exist?

18. Some of those who have discussed the criterion have pronounced that it exists, such as the Stoics and certain others; while some have said that it does not, in particular Xeniades of Corinth and Xenophanes of Colophon, who says:[28]

and seeming is wrought upon all things.

But we have suspended judgement as to whether it exists or does not. 19. So, they will say either that this disagreement is decidable or undecidable; and if it is undecidable, they will be immediately granting that one ought to suspend judgement, while if it is decidable, let them tell us by what it will be decided, when we do not even have an agreed upon criterion [to follow], in general do not even know whether it exists but are, rather, investigating [this question]. 20. Moreover, in order to decide about the disagreement which arose concerning the criterion we must

28. B 34.5.

have an agreed upon criterion by means of which we will be able to judge it; and in order to have an agreed upon criterion one must first have decided on the disagreement about the criterion. Thus the argument falls into the mode based on circular reasoning and the discovery of the criterion becomes doubtful, since we do not permit them to adopt their criterion by hypothesis and if they wish to judge the criterion by means of a criterion we drive them into an infinite regress. Moreover, since demonstration requires a criterion which has been demonstrated, and the criterion requires a demonstration which has been judged [to be valid] they are driven into the mode based on circular reasoning.

21. So we think that even these points suffice to show the rashness of the dogmatists in their discussion of the criterion; but it is not out of place to forge on with the theme in order to be able to refute them in various ways. Nevertheless, we do not intend to contest every single one of their particular opinions about the criterion—for the disagreement is unutterably [complicated] and if we do this we too would have to fall into an unmethodical form of argument—but since the criterion we are investigating seems to be threefold (including that by whom, that by means of which and that according to which) let us deal with each of these in turn and establish its ungraspability. For in this manner our discussion will be methodical and at the same time complete. . . .

Sextus *PH* 1.196–208 [III-33]

Ch. xxii On the Utterance 'I Suspend Judgement'

196. We use the utterance 'I suspend judgement' in place of 'I cannot say which of the objects before me I should put my trust in and which not', making clear that things appear equal to us with respect to reliability and unreliability. And we do not commit ourselves to the claim that they are equal, but simply say what appears to us about those things, when they strike us. And the utterance 'suspension of judgement' comes from checking one's intellect [i.e., suspending its judgemental activity] so that it neither posits nor abolishes anything because of the equal strength of the matters under investigation.

Ch. xxiii On the Utterance 'I Determine Nothing'

197. We say this about the utterance 'I determine nothing'. We say that determining is not simply saying something, but that it is making an utterance about a non-apparent thing with assent. In this sense the sceptic will perhaps be found to determine nothing, not even the [principle] 'I determine nothing' itself; for it is not a dogmatic supposition, i.e., assent to something non-evident, but [just] an utterance which reveals

our state [of mind]. So when the sceptic says 'I determine nothing' he is saying this: 'I am now in such a state that I neither posit nor abolish dogmatically any of the matters now under investigation'. He says this simply as an indication of what appears to him concerning the objects before him, and not ⟨dogmatically⟩ making a confident declaration but just explaining what state he is in.

Ch. xxiv On the Utterance 'All Things are Undetermined'

198. And indeterminacy is an intellectual state in accordance with which we neither abolish nor posit any of the matters being dogmatically investigated, i.e., any of the non-evident things. So when the sceptic says 'all things are undetermined' the word 'are' is used in place of 'appear to him'; 'all' does not mean existing things but [only] those of the non-apparent matters being dogmatically investigated which he has discussed; and 'undetermined' means not being more or less trustworthy than their opposites or generally than things with which they are in conflict. 199. And just as he who says '[I] walk'[29] implicitly says 'I walk', so too he who says 'all things are undetermined' signifies along with it (in our view) 'relative to me' or 'as it appears to me'. Thus the statement is like this: 'All of the matters which are dogmatically investigated which I have considered seem to me to be such that none of them is more or less trustworthy than what is in conflict with it.'

Ch. xxv On the Utterance 'All Things are Ungraspable'

200. We are also affected similarly when we say 'all things are ungraspable'. For we give a similar explanation of the word 'all' and we also understand the words 'to me', so that the statement is like this: 'All of the non-apparent matters being dogmatically investigated which I have scrutinized appear to me to be ungraspable'. And this is not the position of someone making a firm commitment that the matters being investigated by the dogmatists are of such a nature as to be ungraspable, but rather [the position] of someone who is declaring his own state; he says that in this state he thinks, 'up until the present time I have not yet grasped any of those matters, because of the equal weight of the opposing [positions]; hence all the arguments advanced to overturn [our position] seem to me to be unrelated to what we actually declare'.

Ch. xxvi On the Utterances 'I Fail to Grasp' and 'I Do Not Grasp'

201. And the utterances 'I fail to grasp' and 'I do not grasp' also reveal a private state [of mind] in which the sceptic avoids, for the present,

---

29. In Greek the verb's ending indicates that the subject is the first person singular.

positing or abolishing any of the non-evident matters being investigated, as is clear from what we have already said about the other [sceptical] utterances.

Ch. xxvii On the Utterance 'To Every Argument an Equal Argument is Opposed'

202. When we say 'to every argument an equal argument is opposed', we mean by 'every' every one examined by us; by 'argument' we intend not the unqualified sense of the word but rather an argument which [purports to] establish something dogmatically, i.e., dealing with something non-evident, and not necessarily an argument composed of premisses and a conclusion but one which [purports to] establish something in any way at all. By 'equal' we mean with respect to trustworthiness or untrustworthiness; and we use 'is opposed' in a general sense, in place of 'conflicts with'; and we also supply the phrase 'as it appears to me'. **203.** So when I say 'to every argument an equal argument is opposed' I implicitly say this: 'to every argument examined by me which establishes something dogmatically it seems to me that there is another and opposing argument which establishes something dogmatically, equal to the first with respect to trustworthiness and untrustworthiness'. Thus the utterance of the statement is not dogmatic but a mere announcement of a state in a human being which is apparent to the person in that state.

204. The utterance 'to every argument an equal argument is opposed' is employed by some sceptics in the following sense. They think that it should be imperatival, like this: 'let us oppose to every argument which establishes something dogmatically an argument which dogmatically investigates [the question], is equal to it in terms of trustworthiness and untrustworthiness, and is in conflict with it'. So their statement is directed at the sceptic but they use the infinitive in place of the imperatival form ('is opposed' in place of 'let us oppose'). **205.** They urge this on the sceptic so that he will not be led astray by the dogmatist and give up his sceptical mode of investigation, and so, because of his rashness, lose that freedom from disturbance which is apparent to them and which they believe is dependent on suspension of judgement about everything, as we said above.[30]

Ch. xxviii Additional Notes on Sceptical Utterances

206. It will be sufficient if we give a rough outline of these utterances, especially since it is possible, on the basis of what we have now said, to deal with the others too. For concerning all the sceptical utterances one

30. III-26 (25–30).

must assume from the outset that we are not unconditionally committing ourselves to their truth, not least in view of the fact that we say that they abolish themselves, since they are included among the things to which they apply; they are like purgative drugs which not only eliminate the [unhealthy] bodily humours but also drive themselves out along with the humours. **207.** And we say too that in positing them we are not in the strict sense of the word revealing the matters for the sake of which we adopt the utterances, but that [we do so] indifferently and, if one likes, in a loose sense of the word. For it is not fitting for a sceptic to quarrel over utterances; moreover, it is helpful to us that even these utterances do not have any unqualified significance but are in fact relative, and relative to the sceptics [themselves]. **208.** Further, one must also recall that we do not make [these utterances] universally about all matters, but [only] about non-evident matters which are investigated dogmatically, and that we say [only] what appears to us, and do not pronounce in such a way as to commit ourselves to the nature of the externally existing objects.

On this basis, I think, every sophistical trick brought to bear on a sceptical utterance can be thwarted.

Sextus *M* 9.1–3   [III-34]

1. We suggested earlier[31] the reason why we examine the physical part of philosophy after the logical part, though it seems to be temporally prior to the other parts. We shall again establish the same manner of investigation here too, not lingering over the details as the followers of Clitomachus and the rest of the Academic chorus have done (for they inappropriately prolonged their counter-argument by plunging into alien subject matter and basing their arguments on a concession to other people's dogmatic views); rather we shall attack the most important and inclusive doctrines; for thus we shall bring the rest as well into doubt. **2.** For in sieges those who undermine the foundation of the wall bring down the towers along with it; similarly, in philosophical enquiries those who defeat the basic hypotheses [which support] their theories have implicitly annulled the grasp of the entire theory. **3.** So some have not implausibly compared those who plunge into detailed investigations to hunters who pursue their quarry on foot, to anglers or to those who try to catch birds with twigs and lime; and also compared those who use the most inclusive doctrines to shake the detailed doctrines too to those who surround [their quarry] with lines, stakes and nets. Hence, just as it is much more craftsmanlike to be able to catch many animals at one swoop

---

31. *M* 7.20–21.

than to labour away on each individual catch, in the same way it is much more elegant to provide one common counter-argument against all [dogmas] than to get entangled in the particulars.

The Modes

Sextus *PH* 1.35–163 (selections) [III-35]

35. In order to acquire a more precise notion of the oppositions, I shall also add the modes by means of which we conclude to suspension of judgement, not committing myself either as to their number or their power. For they may be unsound and there may be more than I am about to relate.

Ch. xiv The Ten Modes

36. The older sceptics traditionally taught ten modes by means of which we seem to conclude to suspension of judgement; they also call them arguments and topics. They are as follows. [1] The first employs the variations among animals; [2] the second employs the differences among men; [3] the third employs the different conditions of the sense organs; [4] the fourth employs circumstances; [5] the fifth employs positions and distances and places; 37. [6] the sixth employs mixtures; [7] the seventh employs the quantities and structures of external objects; [8] the eighth employs relativity; [9] the ninth employs [the fact of] constant or rare occurrences; [10] the tenth employs the practices [of ordinary life], laws, belief in myths and dogmatic suppositions. 38. This order is used merely for exposition.

There are three modes which are more general than these: based on him who judges, on the object judged, and on both. The first four are subordinate to the mode based on him who judges (for that which judges is either an animal or a man or a sense or is in some circumstance); the seventh and the tenth (are referred to) the one based on the object judged; and the fifth, sixth, eighth and ninth are based on [the mode involving] both. 39. Again, these three [superordinate modes] are referred to the relativity mode. So the relativity mode is most general, the three are specific and the ten are subordinate. So much, plausibly enough, for their number. Let us say the following about their power.

40. [1] The first argument, as we said, is that according to which, because of the differences among animals, [all do not] receive the same presentations from the same objects. We infer this from the differences in their modes of generation and from the various constitutions of their bodies. 41. As to their generations, some animals come to be without

sexual intercourse, while some come to be with it. And of those which come to be without sexual intercourse, some come to be from fire (like the tiny animals which appear in furnaces), some from putrefied water (like gnats), some from soured wine (like ants) . . . . **42**. Of those which come to be from sexual intercourse, some (i.e., most) come to be from parents of the same species, some from parents of different species (like mules). Again, generally, some animals are viviparous (like humans) and some oviparous (like birds), while others produce unformed heaps of flesh (like bears). **43**. So it is likely that the dissimilarities in the mode of generation should also produce great differences in their manner of being affected, which would be the source of their incompatibilities, disharmonies and conflicts.

44. Moreover, the differences in the most important parts of their bodies, especially those naturally fitted for discernment and sense-perception, are able to produce the greatest conflict among presentations; at any rate, those with jaundice say that things which appear to us as white are yellow, and those whose eyes are bloodshot see them as red. So since some animals have yellow eyes, some have bloodshot eyes, some have white eyes, and some have eyes of different colours, it is likely, I think, that their grasp of colours is different. . . .

47. And when we press one side of our eye the forms, shapes and sizes of visible things appear long and narrow; so it is likely that to those animals with a slanting and elongated pupil (like goats, cats and the like) objects should be presented differently, not as animals with round pupils suppose them to be. . . .

50. The same argument applies to the other senses. . . . **54**. So it is likely that externally existing objects are observed to be different according to the differing conditions of the animals which receive the presentations.

55. This sort of point can be learned even more clearly from [a consideration of] what seems worth choosing and worth avoiding to animals. Sweet oil, at any rate, seems very pleasant to men, but is unbearable to beetles and bees. And olive oil is beneficial to men, but if sprinkled on wasps and bees it destroys them. And sea water is unpleasant and poisonous for men to drink, but very pleasant and potable for fish. **56**. For washing, pigs prefer the foulest-smelling mud to clear, pure water. Some animals eat grass, others bushes, others graze in forests or eat seeds or flesh or milk; some like rotting food, some like it fresh; some like it raw, some cooked by a chef. And in general, what is pleasant to some is unpleasant, worth avoiding and fatal to others. . . . **58**. It is possible to cite more examples than this, but to avoid seeming pointlessly longwinded, if it is the case that the same things are unpleasant to some animals and pleasant to others, and if what is pleasant or unpleasant depends on presentations, then animals get different presentations from objects.

59. And if the same things appear dissimilar in accordance with the differences among animals, we shall be able to say how the object looks to us, but we shall suspend judgement about how it really is in its nature. For we ourselves shall not be able to decide between our own presentations and those of the other animals, since we are ourselves a party to the disagreement and for this reason shall be in need of someone to make the decision, rather than being able to do so ourselves. **60.** Also, we are not in a position to prefer our own presentations over those which occur in the non-rational animals either with or without a demonstration. For in addition to the fact that demonstration probably does not exist, as we shall suggest, either the so-called demonstration will itself be apparent to us or not. And if it is not apparent, we shall also not receive it with confidence; but if it is apparent to us, then since the investigation is about what appears to animals and the demonstration appears to us who are animals, it too will be investigated [to see] whether it is true in so far as it is apparent. **61.** But it is absurd to try to establish what is under investigation by means of what is under investigation, since the same thing will be trustworthy and untrustworthy, which is impossible; trustworthy in so far as it purports to demonstrate, but untrustworthy in so far as it is [itself to be] demonstrated. Therefore we shall not have a demonstration by means of which we may prefer our own presentations over those which occur in the so-called non-rational animals. So if presentations are different in accordance with the variety among animals, and it is impossible to decide between them, it is necessary to suspend judgement about external objects.

62. As an extra we also compare the so-called non-rational animals and men with respect to their presentations; for after [relating] our effective arguments we do not disapprove of ridiculing these pompous and boastful dogmatists. So our side customarily makes a simple comparison between the many non-rational animals and man. **63.** But since the dogmatists contrive to say that the comparison is unfair, we shall add another extra and ridicule them even more, basing our argument on one animal, the dog for instance, if you like, which is held to be the lowest [animal]. For we shall find in this way too that the animals, which are our topic, are not inferior to us with respect to the trustworthiness of what appears to them.

64. So the dogmatists agree that this animal is superior to us with regard to sense-perception; for it has a keener sense of smell than we do and by means of this can track down animals which it cannot see, and it also has keener vision than we do and a sharper sense of hearing. **65.**

So let us proceed to the faculty of reason. There are two kinds, internal and verbalized. So let us first consider the internal. So, according to the dogmatists who now hold the opinions which are most opposed to us, i.e., the Stoics, it seems to be occupied with the following: the choice of congenial things and the avoidance of uncongenial things, the knowledge of the crafts which contribute to this, the grasp of the virtues which accord with one's own nature, ⟨and⟩ the matters connected to the passions. **66.** So the dog, which it was decided would make a good example for our argument, makes a choice of congenial things and avoids harmful ones, since it pursues food and cringes from a raised whip; but it also has a craft for providing itself with congenial things, viz. hunting. **67.** Nor does it lack virtue, since justice, at least, is concerned with rendering to everyone what he deserves and the dog is not without justice in that he fawns on those who are congenial to it, does good to them and guards them, while it wards off those who are uncongenial and do it wrong. **68.** And if the dog has justice, then since the virtues [all] follow upon each other it also has the other virtues too—which the wise men say that the majority of men lack. And we see that the dog is heroic in warding off attackers, and intelligent; Homer[32] too testifies to this when he has Odysseus recognized only by [his dog] Argos while he went unrecognized by all the members of his household, since the dog was not deceived by the change in his master's physical appearance and had not lost his graspable presentation [of his master], which he seems to have had more [clearly] than the human beings. **69.** And according to Chrysippus, who has a special interest in the non-rational animals, [the dog] also participates in their famous 'dialectic'. At any rate the fellow just mentioned says that [the dog] attends to the fifth indemonstrable with several [disjuncts] when he comes to a three-way intersection; for the dog sniffs at the two roads which the quarry did not go down, and immediately charges off down the third without stopping to sniff it. In effect he says that its reasoning was this: either the quarry went here or here or here; but he did not go here or here; therefore he went here. . . .

73. For now it is not necessary to investigate verbalized reason. For some of the dogmatists dismissed it as an obstacle to the acquisition of virtue, which is why they practiced silence during the [initial] training period. Moreover, suppose for the sake of argument that a man is dumb, no one will [therefore] say that he is non-rational. Passing over these points, it is highly relevant [to note] that animals, which is what we are discussing, also utter human sounds; jays, for example and some others too. **74.** But to let this point go, even if we do not understand the

32. *Odyssey* 17.300.

utterances of the so-called non-rational animals, it is not completely unlikely that they in fact do converse but that we do not understand; for when we hear the utterances of foreigners we do not understand but think that it all sounds the same. 75. And we hear dogs uttering different sounds when they ward people off, when they howl, when they are beaten, and yet another when they are fawning. Generally, if one cared to attend to the point, one would find a great variation of utterances in this and other animals according to their different circumstances; consequently, on this basis it would not be unreasonable to say that the so-called non-rational animals do participate in verbalized reason. 76. And if they fall short of men neither in the accuracy of their perceptions nor in internal reason nor (as a kind of extra) in verbalized reason, they would be no more untrustworthy with respect to presentations than we ourselves. . . .

78. I have made this comparison, as I indicated above, as a kind of extra, after giving what I think is a sufficient demonstration that we are not in a position to prefer our own presentations over those of the non-rational animals. But if it is not the case that the non-rational animals are less trustworthy than we are with respect to judging presentations, and presentations differ with respect to the varieties of animals, then for the above reasons I shall be able to say how each object appears to me but I shall be compelled to suspend judgement regarding its nature.

79. That is what the first mode for suspension of judgement is like; [2] we said that the second was that which employed the differences among men. Suppose for the sake of argument that someone grants that men are more trustworthy than the non-rational animals, we shall find, even as far as concerns the differences among us, that suspension of judgement is introduced. There are said to be two components of which a man is composed, soul and body; and we differ from each other with respect to both of them. For example, in body [we differ] with respect to our shapes and our idiosyncracies. 80. For the body of a Scythian differs from that of an Indian in shape, and, as they say, the difference is produced by the dominance of the humours. But as a result of the differing dominance of humours, our presentations too become different, as was shown in our first argument. Accordingly, there is a great difference among them in respect to both choice and avoidance of external things; for Indians and people in our region enjoy different things, and enjoying different things is an indication that varying presentations are received from the external objects. 81. We differ with respect to idiosyncracies in that some people digest beef more easily than rock-fish, or are more readily afflicted with diarrhoea from drinking Lesbian wine. There was once, they say, an old woman of Attica who ingested thirty measures of

hemlock without being harmed, while Lysis once took four of poppy juice without pain. **82.** And Demophon, Alexander's table-servant, used to shiver when he was in the sun or a bath-house, and got warmed up in the shade. . . .

85. Since there is so much variation in the bodies of men . . . it is likely that men also differ from each other with respect to their souls. For the body [provides] a kind of impression of the soul, as is shown by [the science of] physiognomy. And the greatest demonstration of the great and boundless difference among the intellects of men is the disagreement among the utterances of the dogmatists, especially that concerning what it is fitting to choose and what to avoid. . . .

87. So since choice and avoidance depend on pleasure and displeasure, and pleasure and displeasure depend on sense-perception and presentation, when some people choose and some avoid the same things, it follows that we should reason that they are not moved in the same way by the same things, since [if they were] they would choose or avoid the same things. But if the same things move men differently, as a result of the differences among men, it is reasonable on this basis too to introduce suspension of judgement, since each of us is able to say, perhaps, what each external object appears like relative to each difference [in us], but is not capable of pronouncing on what each thing is in its nature. **88.** For either we shall have confidence in all men or in some. But if in all we shall be undertaking impossibilities and admitting opposing statements. But if in some, let them tell us to whom we are supposed to give assent. For the Platonist will say [we should assent] to Plato, the Epicurean to Epicurus, and the others analogously, and so being in an undecidable conflict they will induce suspension of judgement in us. **89.** He who says that one should assent to the majority is making a childish proposal, since no one can survey all men and calculate what the majority believe. For it is possible that, among some peoples of whom we are not aware, the things which are rare in our experience apply to the majority of men and the things which affect most of us are rare for them . . . So it is also necessary to introduce suspension of judgement because of the differences among men.

90. Since the dogmatists, being a self-satisfied lot, say that one ought to prefer themselves over other men when it comes to making judgements on things, we know that their claim is absurd (for they themselves are a party to the disagreement; and if they decide in favour of themselves and then judge the appearances, they are seizing on the subject under investigation before they make their judgement, by assigning the [task of making] the judgement to themselves). **91.** But still, in order to arrive at suspension of judgement by applying the argument to one man, for example their fantastical wise man, we take up the mode which is third in order.

[3] We say that this mode is based on the differences among the senses. That the senses differ from each other is self-evident. **92.** Pictures, at any rate, seem to the eyes to have recesses and projections, but not to the touch. And honey appears pleasant to the tongue in some cases, but unpleasant to the eyes. So it is impossible to say whether it is, all on its own, pleasant or unpleasant. The same applies to oil. For it pleases the sense of smell but displeases taste. **93.** . . . . Therefore we shall not be able to say what each of these is like in its nature, but it will on each occasion be possible to say how it appears.

94. Many more examples than these could be given, but to avoid delay and in view of the purpose of our treatise the following should be said. Each of the sensibles which appears to us seems to strike us as varied. For example, the apple is smooth, sweet and yellow. So it is non-evident whether on a given occasion it really has just these qualities, or whether it has just one quality and only appears different because of the differing construction of the sense organs, or whether it has more qualities than the ones which appear but some of them do not strike us. . . .

98. But, someone shall say, nature made our sense organs commensurate with the sensibles. What sort of nature [is he talking about], when there is so much undecidable disagreement about its existence? For he who is deciding on this very point, i.e., whether nature exists, is either a layman, in which case he shall not, according to them, be trustworthy; or he is a philosopher, in which case he is a party to the disagreement and himself not a judge but one subject to judgement. **99.** But if it is possible that only those qualities exist in the apple which we seem to grasp, and that there are more than these or again that not even those which strike us [actually] exist, then it shall be non-evident to us what the apple is like. And the same argument applies to the other sensibles. If, however, the senses do not grasp external objects, then neither shall the intellect be able to grasp them, so that by this argument too it seems that we shall conclude to suspension of judgement about external objects.

100. [4] In order to apply the argument also to each sense [by itself] or even to set the [argument from the] senses aside, and still be able to end up with suspension of judgement, let us bring in the fourth mode for it too. This is the one termed 'circumstantial', and we say that the dispositions are circumstances. We say that this mode is seen [to operate] with natural or unnatural states, with being awake or asleep, with ages, with being in motion or rest, with hate or love, with being in need or sated, with being drunk or sober, with predispositions, with boldness or fear, with feeling pleasure or pain. **101.** For example, things strike us differently depending on whether we are in a natural or unnatural state, since madmen and those possessed by the gods seem to hear the voices of daimons, but we do not. Similarly, they often say that they are aware of an aroma of storax or frankincense or some such thing and many other things, when we do not perceive it. And the same water seems to be boiling when poured onto feverish spots, but is [only] lukewarm to us. . . . 102. And if someone should say that a conjunction of certain humours causes uncongenial presentations to come from the objects to those who are in an unnatural state, then one should say that since even the healthy have a blend of humours, these are able to make the external objects, although they are by nature such as they appear to be to those who are *said* to be in an unnatural state, appear different to those who are healthy. 103. For it is a mere whim to give to one set of humours and not to others the power to change external objects, since just as even those who are healthy are in the state natural to the healthy, but unnatural to those who are ill, so too those who are ill are in the state which is unnatural to the healthy but natural to the ill. Consequently, one must have confidence in them too, since they are in a natural state relative to something.

104. Presentations become different because of being asleep or awake, since we do not receive the same presentations when awake that we do while asleep; nor do we receive the same presentations while asleep that we do while awake. Thus the existence or non-existence of the presentations is not unqualified but relative. For it is relative to sleep or to waking. It is likely, then, that we see while sleeping those things which are non-existent in [regard to] waking, but not absolutely non-existent; for they exist in sleep, just as things seen while awake also exist even if they do not exist in sleep. . . .

112. Since there is so much inconsistency in our dispositions, and since men are in different dispositions at different times, perhaps it is easy to say how each of the external objects appears to each man, but no longer [easy] to say what it is [really] like, since the inconsistency is undecidable. For he who is deciding is either in some of the above-mentioned dispositions or he is not in any disposition at all. But to say that he is not in any disposition whatsoever, for example, that is neither healthy nor sick, neither moving nor at rest, nor of any particular age, and that he is free of the other dispositions, is totally implausible. But if he is going to judge the presentations while in some disposition, then he will be a party to the disagreement . . .

114. Further, the inconsistency among such presentations is undecidable in another way. For he who prefers one presentation over another and of one circumstance over another, does so either without judging and without a demonstration or by judging and with a demonstration.

But he cannot do so without these, since he will be unconvincing; nor can he do so with these. For if he is going to judge presentations, he will certainly judge them by means of a criterion. 115. So he will say either that this criterion is true or that it is false. But if he says that it is false, he will be unconvincing. And if he says that it is true, either he will say that the criterion is true without a demonstration or with one, and it will certainly be necessary for the demonstration to be true, since [otherwise] he will be unconvincing. So he will say that the demonstration which is used to confirm the criterion is true; will he say this after judging it or not? 116. For if he does so without judging, he will be untrustworthy, but if he does so after judging, it is obvious that he will say that he made the judgement by means of a criterion, for which criterion we shall seek a demonstration, and then a criterion for that [demonstration]. For the demonstration will always need a criterion to be confirmed, and the criterion [will always need] a demonstration to be shown to be true. And a demonstration cannot be sound without a pre-existing true criterion; neither can a criterion be true without a previously confirmed demonstration. 117. And thus the criterion and the demonstration fall into the mode of circular reasoning, in which both are found to be unconvincing. For each of them awaits the confirmation of the other, and so is just as unconvincing as the other. So if one is not in a position to prefer one presentation over another with a demonstration and a criterion, nor without these things, then the different presentations occasioned by different dispositions will be undecidable; consequently as far as concerns this mode too suspension of judgement is introduced about the nature of external things.

118. [5] The fifth argument is that which depends on positions and distances and places. For because of each of these the same things appear different; for example, the same colonnade appears [to be] tapered when viewed from one end, but quite symmetrical when viewed from the middle, and the same ship appears small and stationary from a distance but from closer it appears large and moving. And the same tower from a distance appears round, but from close up it appears square.

119. These are the effects of distances, and the effects of places are as follows: . . .

120. The effects of positions are these: . . .

121. So since all the appearances are observed from a certain distance or in a certain position, and each of these makes a difference in the presentations, as we suggested, we shall be compelled by this mode too to arrive at suspension of judgement. For he who prefers some of these presentations over others will be undertaking the impossible. 122. For if he makes his pronouncement unqualifiedly and without demonstration

he will not be trustworthy; but if he wants to use a demonstration, either he will say that the demonstration is false and so overturn himself, or if he says that the demonstration is true he will be asked for a demonstration that it is true, and then for another [to confirm] that, since it too must be true; and so on to infinity. But it is impossible to provide an infinite number of proofs. **123.** Therefore, he will not be in a position to prefer one presentation over another with a demonstration. But if one is not able to decide on the above-mentioned presentations either with or without a demonstration, then the conclusion is suspension of judgement, since we are perhaps able to say how each appears in this position or at this distance or in this place but not able to declare how each thing is in its nature, for the above-mentioned reasons.

124. [6] The sixth mode is that based on mixtures, according to which we conclude that since none of the external objects strikes us all on its own but together with something, it is perhaps possible to say how the mixture of the object and that together with which it is observed strikes us, but we could not say how the external object is all on its own. That none of the external objects strikes us all on its own but certainly together with something else, and that because of this it is observed to be different, these points, I think, are self-evident. **125.** At any rate, our colour is seen as different in warm air and in cold, and we could not say what our colour is like in its nature, but rather [we could say] how it is observed when together with each of these. . . .

126. To move on from external mixtures, our eyes have in them both membranes and fluid. So since the visible things are not observed without these, they will not be grasped with accuracy; for we grasp the mixture and for this reason people with jaundice see everything as yellow and those with bloodshot eyes see everything as red. . . . **127.** . . . So because of the mixtures the senses do not grasp with accuracy what the external objects are like.

128. But neither does the intellect, especially since its guides, the senses, make mistakes. And perhaps it too contributes a certain mixture of its own to the announcements made by the senses. For in each of the places in which the dogmatists think the leading part of the soul exists we observe that there are certain underlying humours, whether one wishes to posit that it is in the brain or in the heart or in any other part of the animal. So in this way too we see that, being unable to say anything about the nature of the external objects, we are compelled to suspend judgement.

129. [7] We said that the seventh mode was that which employed the quantities and structures of objects, in a general way meaning by structures the composition [of the things]. It is evident that by this mode too we are compelled to suspend judgement about the nature of things. At any rate, for example, shavings of goat's horn appear white when observed on their own and without being compounded, but when combined to form the horn they are observed to be black. And filings of silver on their own appear as black, but strike us as white when combined into a whole [lump of silver] . . .

134. Thus the argument by quantities and structures throws into confusion the existence of the external objects. That is why it is likely that this mode too would bring us around to suspension of judgement, since we are not able to make an unqualified pronouncement about the nature of the external objects.

135. [8] The eighth mode is that from relativity, according to which we conclude that since everything is relative we shall suspend judgement about what things exist on their own and in nature. And one must realize that here, as in the other modes, we use the word "exist" in place of "appear", in effect saying this: "everything appears to be relative". And this has two senses: first, relative to that which judges (for the external object which is judged appears to be relative to that which judges), and in another sense relative to the things with which it is observed; for example, right and left.

137. And it is possible to conclude by special [arguments] that all things are relative, in the following manner. Do differentiated things differ from relatives or not? If they do not differ, then they themselves are relative; but if they do differ, then, since everything which differs is relative (for they are spoken of relatively to that from which they differ), differentiated things are relative. 138. And according to the dogmatists some existing things are summa genera, some are infimae species, and some are both genera and species; but all these are relative; therefore all things are relative. Again, some existing things are self-evident, some are non-evident (as they say themselves), and the appearances are signifiers while the non-evident things are signified. For according to them the appearances are a glimpse of the non-evident; but signifiers and the signified are relative; therefore all things are relative. 139. In addition to this, some existing things are similar and some are dissimilar and some are equal and some are unequal; but these things are relative; therefore all things are relative. And even he who says that all things are not relative confirms that all things are relative. For by his arguments against us he demonstrates the very claim that ‹not› everything is relative, [but does so] relatively to us and not universally.

140. But when we have established that all things are relative, it is clear that what remains is that we shall not be able to say what each of

the objects is like in its own nature and all by itself, but [only] what it appears to be like in a relative sense. It follows that we must suspend judgement about the nature of things.

141. [9] We shall give the following kind of account of the mode which employs constant or rare occurrences, which we say is ninth in order. The sun is much more astounding than a comet; but since we see the sun constantly and the comet rarely we are so astounded by the comet that we regard it as a divine sign, but are not at all astounded by the sun. If, however, we imagine the sun as appearing rarely and setting rarely, and illuminating everything all at once and suddenly throwing everything into shadows, then we shall see that there is a great deal of astonishment in the thing. . . .

144. Since, therefore, the same things sometimes appear astounding or impressive, and at other times not such, because they occur constantly or rarely, we reason that we shall perhaps be able to say how each of things appears in conjunction with constant or rare occurrence, but we shall not be able to say what each of the external objects is like in itself. So by this mode too we suspend judgement about them.

145. [10] The tenth mode, which has a particular application to ethics, is that which employs the practices [of ordinary life], habits, laws, belief in myths and dogmatic suppositions. A practice [of ordinary life], then, is a choice of [way of] life or of some action which is made by some one person or by many people, for example, by Diogenes or by the Spartans. 146. A law is a written contract between citizens, the violation of which is punished; while a habit or custom (there is no difference) is the shared acceptance by many men of some one thing, the violation of which is not necessarily punished. For example, it is a law that one should not commit adultery, but a custom with us that one should not copulate with a woman in public. 147. Belief in myths is the acceptance of things which never occurred and are made up, a particularly good example of which is the myths told about Cronus. For they convince many people. A dogmatic supposition is the acceptance of something on the basis of analogical reasoning or some demonstration which seems to be effective, for example, that atoms or homoiomeries or minimal parts or something else are the elements of things.

148. We oppose each of these sometimes to itself and sometimes to each of the others. . . .

163. It would have been possible to take many other examples for each of above-mentioned oppositions. But these will suffice for a summary account. But since there is such an inconsistency in things which is shown by this mode too, we shall not be able to say what each object is like in its nature, but we shall be able to say how it appears relative to this

procedure [of ordinary life] or this law or this custom (and so for each of the others). Therefore by this mode too it is necessary for us to suspend judgement about the nature of things.

In this way, then, we wind up at suspension of judgement by means of the ten modes.

Sextus *PH* 1.164–177 [III-36]

Ch. xv The Five Modes

164. The later sceptics offer these five modes of suspension of judgement: the first is based on disagreement; the second is the one forcing an infinite regress; the third is the one based on relativity; the fourth is the hypothetical one; the fifth is the one based on circular reasoning.

165. [1] The mode based on disagreement is that according to which we discover an undecidable dispute occurring for any matter proposed, both in ordinary life and among philosophers, as a result of which we are not able to choose something or to reject it, and so we arrive at suspension of judgement.

166. [2] The mode based on infinite regress is that in which we say that what is offered as confirmation of the matter proposed is itself in need of confirmation, and so on infinitely, so that not having a starting point from which we can begin to establish anything, suspension of judgement follows.

167. [3] The mode based on relativity, as we said previously [1.135–6], is that in which the object appears to be of one sort or another in relation to what is judging it and to the things observed along with it, but as for its nature, we suspend judgement.

168. [4] The mode based on hypothesis is used when the dogmatists, being forced into an infinite regress, take as a starting point that which they do not establish, but rather think deserves to be taken as agreed upon simply and without demonstration.

169. [5] The mode of circular reasoning is introduced whenever that which ought to provide assurance for the thing investigated itself requires confirmation from the thing investigated. Therefore, we are not able to accept either one as establishing the other, and regarding both we suspend judgement.

We shall show briefly in the following way that every thing investigated can be referred to these modes. **170.** That which is proposed is either sensible or intelligible, but whichever it is, it is a subject of disagreement. For some say that only sensibles are true; others say that only intelligibles are true; still others say that some sensibles and some intelligibles are true. Will these say that the disagreement is decidable or not? If they say it is undecidable, we hold that it is necessary to suspend judgement, for, regarding undecidable disagreements, it is not possible to make pronouncements. If they say it is decidable, we ask on what basis it will be decided? 171. For example, in the case of the sensible object (we shall base our argument on this first), is it decided by a sensible or an intelligible? If by a sensible, since we are investigating sensibles, that will require something else for its confirmation. And if that will be another sensible, again, it will require something else for its confirmation, and this will go on to infinity. 172. But if the sensible will need to be decided by an intelligible, since intelligibles are subjects of disagreement, then this will need judgement and confirmation, since it is an intelligible. On what basis will it be confirmed? If by an intelligible, there will occur a similar infinite regress; if by a sensible, since an intelligible was adduced as confirmation of a sensible and the sensible as confirmation of an intelligible, the mode of circular reasoning will be introduced.

173. If, avoiding these [consequences], our interlocutor should take as granted and think proper to assume without demonstration something for the demonstration of the next stages of his argument, the hypothetical mode is introduced and an impasse [*aporia*] ensues. For if the one who lays down the hypothesis is himself trustworthy, we shall always be no less trustworthy when we lay down an opposite hypothesis. And if the one who lays down the hypothesis hypothesizes something true, he casts suspicion on it, since he assumes it according to his hypothesis, but does so without establishing it. If he hypothesizes something false, the foundation for the things to be established is unsound. 174. And if hypothesizing something contributes something towards confirmation, then one might as well hypothesize the conclusion, and not something else on the basis of which the conclusion of the argument is to be established. And if it is absurd to hypothesize that which is investigated, it will also be absurd to hypothesize that upon which it depends.

175. That all sensibles are relative is evident, for they are relative to those sensing them. So, it is clear that whatever sensible thing is proposed to us, it is easy to refer it to the five modes. We reason similarly about the intelligible. For if it would be said that it is a matter of undecidable disagreement, it will be conceded to us that one should suspend judgement regarding it. 176. But if the disagreement will be decidable, if it is decidable by means of an intelligible, we fall into an infinite regress, but if it is decidable by means of a sensible, we fall into circular reasoning. For the sensible is again subject to disagreement, and not being able to decide on the basis of it, because of an infinite regress, it will need an intelligible just as the intelligible is in need of a sensible. 177. For these reasons, one who assumes anything on the basis of an hypothesis will be

again doing something absurd. Further, intelligibles are relative, for they are expressed in relation to the one thinking about them, and if they were by nature of the sort that they are claimed to be, they would not have been the subject of disagreement. Therefore, the intelligible is referred to the five modes, for which reason it is necessary for us to suspend judgement entirely regarding the matter proposed.

These are the five modes offered by the later sceptics. They offer them not as replacing the ten modes, but in order to provide greater variety and to use them along with the ten to refute the rashness of the dogmatists.

Sextus *PH* 1.178–186 [III-37]

Ch. xvi The Two Modes

178. They offer in addition two other modes of suspension of judgement. Since every thing grasped seems to be grasped either by itself or through something else, ⟨when they make us realize that nothing⟩ is grasped ⟨by itself or through something else,⟩ they seem to introduce an impasse [*aporia*] regarding all matters. They say, I believe, that it is clear that nothing is grasped by itself from the disagreement that has occurred among physicists regarding all sensibles and intelligibles, a disagreement that is for us undecidable either by using a sensible or an intelligible criterion, since every one which we might take up has been the subject of disagreement and so is not trustworthy.

179. And this is the reason they do not allow that something is grasped through something else. If that through which something is grasped will itself need to be grasped always through something else, one will fall into circular reasoning or into an infinite regress. But if someone might wish to assume that that through which something is grasped is grasped by itself, it is countered that nothing is grasped by itself, for the reasons given above. And we are at a loss to know how that which is the subject of conflict is able to be grasped either by itself or through something else, when the criterion of truth or of graspability is not apparent and signs, even apart from demonstration, are rejected, as we shall discover in the subsequent discussion. Let what has been said about the modes of suspension of judgement be sufficient for the present.

Ch. xvii The Modes that Overturn the Causalists

180. Just as we offer the modes leading to the suspension of judgement, so some [sceptics] set forth certain modes for particular causal explanations and, by offering up such puzzles, we check the dogmatists because of the special pride they take in these causal explanations. Aenesidemus offered eight modes according to which he thinks he can refute every

dogmatic causal explanation and show that it is pernicious. **181.** [1] The
first of these, he says, is that according to which the whole class of causal
explanations, being wrapped up in the non-apparent, is not supported
by agreed upon testimony from the appearances. [2] Second, is that
according to which it is shown that there is a generous abundance of
[explanations] so that one can causally explain the object of investigation
in many ways, and yet some of them explain it in one way only. **182.** [3]
Third, is that according to which it is shown that for things that have
come about in an orderly way [the causalists] provide explanations which
show no order. [4] Fourth, is that according to which it is shown that
when they grasp how appearances come about, they believe they have
also grasped how things not apparent have come about, whereas though
it is possible that the non-apparent may have come to be in a way similar
to that of the appearances, it is also possible that they did not come about
in a similar way, but in their own peculiar way. **183.** [5] Fifth, is that
according to which it is shown that practically all of them give causal
explanations, according to their own personal hypotheses about the elements, and not according to certain common and agreed upon procedures.
[6] Sixth, is that according to which it is shown that whereas they
frequently admit things indicated by their own personal hypotheses, they
reject things that tend to conflict with them, although they possess equal
plausibility. **184.** [7] Seventh, is that according to which it is shown
that frequently they provide explanations that conflict not only with
experiences but even with their own personal theories. [8] Eighth, is that
according to which when there is similar doubt about things seemingly
apparent and about things being investigated, they frequently base their
teachings on things similarly doubtful [i.e., the appearances] and apply
them to things similarly doubtful [i.e., the things investigated]. **185.** He
also says that it is not impossible that some of those who offer causal
explanations fail in accordance with certain mixed modes derived from
the above.

It is perhaps also the case that the five modes of the suspension of
judgement are sufficient for use against the causalists. For should someone
mention a cause, either it is in harmony with all the philosophical systems
and scepticism and the appearances or not. But it is probably not possible
that it should be in harmony with them, for appearances and non-evident
things have all been subject to disagreement. **186.** If, however, the cause
is not in harmony [with philosophical doctrine, scepticism, and appear-
ances], he who mentions it will be asked for the cause of this [cause],
and if he takes it as an apparent [cause] of an apparent [cause] or, a non-
evident cause of a non-evident [cause], he will fall into an infinite regress;
or, interchanging them, [if the apparent cause is of a non-evident cause

or *vice versa*], he will fall into circular reasoning. But if he makes a stand somewhere, either he will say that the cause is established as far as what was previously said is concerned, in which case he introduces relativity and abolishes the [grounding in] nature [i.e., reality], or he is taking something as an hypothesis, in which case he will be stopped. It is therefore perhaps also possible by means of these modes to confute the rashness of the dogmatists in their causal explanations.

Logic

Sextus *PH* 2.48–79 [III-38]

Ch. vi Concerning the Criterion 'By Means of Which'

48. The disagreements that have arisen among the dogmatists regarding this [criterion] are many, even unlimited. We, however, in view of a systematic treatment, say that since, according to them, man is that 'by whom' matters are judged, a man would have nothing by means of which he will be able to judge (as they themselves agree) unless it is sense-perception and intellect. So, if we shall show that he is not able to judge matters either by means of sense-perception alone or intellect alone or both, we shall have addressed summarily all their particular opinions, for they all seem to make references to these three positions. 49. Let us begin with the senses.

Since, then, some say the senses have "groundless experiences," for nothing they seem to grasp exists, whereas others say that all the things that are thought to stimulate the senses exist, and still others say that some of these exist and some do not, we shall not [be able to] know to whom to give assent. For we can neither decide the disagreement by means of sense-perception, since it is regarding the senses that we are investigating whether they have groundless experiences or whether they truly grasp, nor by means of anything else, since there is no other criterion by means of which one should judge things according to the present hypothesis. 50. Therefore, it will be undecidable and ungraspable whether sense-perception has groundless experiences or grasps something, to which is added the conclusion that, in the judgement about those things, we ought not to attend to sensation alone, regarding which we are not in a position to say if it grasps anything [at all] in the first place.

51. But let us grant for the sake of argument that the senses are capable of grasping. Still, granted this, they will be found to be no less untrustworthy in relation to the judgement of objects external to them. At any rate, the senses are stimulated variously by external objects. For

example, the sense of taste senses the same honey sometimes as sweet and sometimes as bitter; and vision ⟨thinks⟩ that the same color is sometimes red and sometimes white. **52.** Not even smell is self-consistent; at least, someone with a headache says that myrrh is unpleasant, whereas someone without a headache says it is pleasant. And people divinely possessed and frenzied seem to hear voices addressing them, which we do not hear. And the same water seems unpleasant to those with a fever, because of an excess of heat, whereas to others it is lukewarm. **53.** So, whether someone should say that all presentations are true or these are true and those are false, or all are false, is impossible to tell, since we do not have an agreed upon criterion by means of which we might judge that which we are going to decide, nor do we even have supplied to us a true and considered demonstration, because we are still searching for the criterion of truth by means of which it is appropriate for the true demonstration to be decided upon. **54.** For these reasons, he who thinks it appropriate that we should put our trust in those who are in a natural state and not in those in an unnatural state, will be absurd. For he will not be trusted if he says this without demonstration, and he will not have a true and considered demonstration, for the reasons given above.

55. Even if someone should grant that the presentations of those in a natural state are trustworthy and the presentations of those in an unnatural state are not, the judgement of external objects by means of the senses alone will still be found to be impossible. At any rate, even the sight of someone in a natural state sometimes declares the ⟨same⟩ tower sometimes to be round and sometimes square; the taste of those well-fed declares the same food unpleasant that the hungry declare pleasant; hearing similarly apprehends the same sound as loud at night and soft during the day; **56.** the sense of smell of many people regards as a bad smell the same things that tanners regard otherwise; the same sense of touch senses that the antechamber is warm when we are entering the bathhouse and that it is cold when we are leaving. Thus, since even the senses of those in a natural state are in conflict with themselves and the disagreement is undecidable, since we do not have an agreed upon ⟨criterion⟩ by means of which the disagreement can be decided, it is necessary that the same problems follow. Further, it is possible to adduce many other points in support of this conclusion, drawing from what was previously said about the modes leading to the suspension of judgement. Therefore, it probably would not be true that sense-experience alone is able to judge external objects.

57. So, let us proceed to the argument regarding the intellect. Now as for those who think it appropriate that we should attend to the intellect alone in the judgement of matters, first they will not be able to show that the existence of the intellect is graspable. For since Gorgias, in saying that nothing exists, is saying that intellect too does not exist, whereas some have pronounced that it does exist, how will they decide the disagreement? For it is neither by means of intellect, since they will be seizing upon that which is under investigation, nor by means of anything else. For they say that there is nothing else, according to the present hypothesis, by means of which matters are judged. So, whether intellect exists or not is undecidable and ungraspable, to which is added the conclusion that we ought not to attend to the intellect alone in the judgement of these matters, it having not yet been grasped.

58. But let us grant that the intellect is grasped and let us agree to the hypothesis that it exists. I still say that it is not able to judge matters. For if it does not accurately perceive itself, but rather is in disagreement [with itself] about its own being and the manner of its coming to be and of its location, how would it be able to grasp accurately anything else? **59.** And if it is granted that the intellect *is* capable of judging matters, we will not find out how we are to judge matters according to it. For since there is a great difference among intellects, seeing that the intellect of Gorgias is one thing, according to which he says that nothing exists, and the intellect of Heraclitus another, according to which he says that all things exist, and still different is the intellect of those who say that some things exist and others do not, we shall not be in a position to decide regarding the differences among intellects, nor shall we be able to say that it is appropriate to follow the intellect of one man and not that of another. **60.** For should we dare to decide by following one person's intellect, we shall be seizing upon that which is under investigation by assenting to one side of the disagreement. And should we dare to decide by means of some other thing, we shall be false to the assumption that it is by means of intellect alone that one ought to judge matters.

61. Further, we shall be able to show, from what we said of the criterion called 'by whom,' that we are not able to discover which intellect is more clever than the others; and [we shall also be able to show] that if we do discover an intellect more clever than all those that have come into being and exist now, since it is non-evident whether there will be another more clever than this one, one ought not to attend to [the former]; **62.** and that even if we hypothesize an intellect than which there could be none smarter, we shall not assent to him who judges by means of it, being wary that in advancing some false argument he can persuade us of its truth, because of the sharpness of his intellect. Therefore, one ought not to try to judge matters by the intellect alone.

63. The remaining possibility is that we should judge matters by means of both [sense-perception and intellect]. But again this is impossible. For not only do the senses not lead the intellect to grasping, but they are even inimical to it. It is surely the case, at least, that Democritus said that from the fact that honey appears bitter to some person and sweet to another, the honey itself is neither bitter nor sweet, whereas Heraclitus said it was both. The same line of reasoning applies to the other senses and the other sensibles. Thus, the intellect, basing itself on the senses, is compelled to pronounce differing and conflicting things. But this is alien to a graspable criterion.

64. In addition, this should be said. People will judge matters either by means of all the senses and the intellects of everyone or by some. But if someone will say that it is by means of all, he will be endorsing impossibilities, given that there is so much obvious conflict in the senses and in the intellects. Moreover, the argument will be overturned, given the pronouncement of Gorgias' intellect that one ought not to attend either to sense-perception or to intellect. But if they say that it is by means of some, how will they judge that one ought to attend to these senses and this intellect and not to those, not having an agreed upon criterion by means of which they will decide among the differing senses and intellects. **65.** And if they should say that we should judge the differences among the senses and the intellects by means of the intellect and the senses, they are seizing upon that which is under investigation. For we are investigating whether it is possible to judge by means of these.

66. Further, it should be said that someone will judge sense-perceptions and intellects by means of the senses, or the sense-perceptions and intellects by means of the intellects, or the sense-perceptions by means of the senses and intellects by means of the intellects, or the intellects by means of the senses and the sense-perceptions by means of the intellect. If, therefore, they should desire to judge both by means of the senses or the intellect, they are no longer judging by means of the senses *and* the intellect, but only by means of one of these, whichever they should choose. And the aforementioned problems will follow upon them. **67.** If, however, they decide regarding the sense-perceptions by means of the senses and the intellects by means of the intellect, then since sense-perceptions conflict with sense-perceptions and intellects with intellects, whichever of the conflicting sense-perceptions they will use for the judgement of the others, they will be seizing upon the matter under investigation. For they will be taking one side of the disagreement as trustworthy for the decision of those that are equally under investigation with it. **68.** The same argument applies to the intellects. And if they decide regarding the intellects by means of the senses and regarding the senses by means of the intellect, the mode based on circular reasoning is adduced; according to this [mode], in order that the sense-perception should be decided on we shall have to express a prior preference regarding the intellects, and in order that the intellects should be tested, it will be necessary for the senses to be tested first. **69**. Since, therefore, like criteria cannot be decided upon by like, nor can both types [be decided on] by one, nor, interchanging them, can each [be decided on] by the other type, we shall not be in a position to prefer one intellect over another or one sense-perception over another. And for this reason, we shall have nothing by means of which we are able to judge. For if we shall not be able to judge by all the sense-perceptions and all the intellects, we shall not know which ones one ought to judge by and which ones not, and we shall have nothing by means of which we shall judge matters. And so, for these reasons, the criterion 'by means of which' would be unreal.

Ch. vii Concerning the Criterion 'According to Which'

70. Let us consider next the criterion 'according to which' they say matters are to be judged. First, therefore, there is this to say about it, namely, that the presentation is inconceivable. For they say that the presentation is an impression in the leading part of the soul. Since, therefore, the soul and its leading part are *pneuma* or something more subtle than *pneuma*, as they say, someone will not be able to conceive of an impression in it either in terms of depressions and elevations, as we see in the case of wax seals, or in terms of their fantastic 'alteration'. For no one could retain the memory of all theoretical propositions which constitute a craft, since the previously existing [alterations] are wiped out by the subsequent alterations. Even if, however, the presentation were able to be conceived, it would be ungraspable. **71.** For, since it is a state of the leading part of the soul, and its leading part is not grasped, as we have shown, we shall not be able to grasp its state either.

72. Further, even if we were to grant that the presentation is grasped, it will not be possible to judge matters according to it. For the intellect, as they say, does not apply itself to external objects and have them presented to it through itself, but rather by means of sense-perceptions; and the senses do not grasp externally existing objects, but only their own states, if that. And, therefore, the presentations will be of the state of the senses, which differs from the externally existing object. For honey is not the same thing as a sweet sensation, nor is wormwood the same as a bitter sensation, but they differ. **73.** And if this state differs from the externally existing object, the presentation will be not of the externally existing object, but of some other thing different from it. If, therefore, the intellect judges according to the presentation, it judges badly and not according to the external object. So, it is absurd to say that external objects are to be judged according to the presentation.

74. But one cannot even say that the soul grasps the externally existing objects by means of the states of the senses, on the basis of the similarity of these states to the externally existing objects. For on what basis will the intellect know if the states of the senses are similar to the sensibles when it has not encountered the external objects themselves and the senses do not reveal to it the nature of the sensibles but only their own states, as I argued on the basis of the modes leading to suspension of judgement[33] **75.** For just as someone who, not being acquainted with Socrates, and seeing a picture of him, does not know if the picture resembles Socrates, so, the intellect, when it observes the states of the senses, but does not see the external objects, will not know if the states of the senses resemble the external objects. So, it will not be able to judge these according to the presentation on the basis of similarity.

76. But let us grant as a concession that in addition to being conceived and grasped, the presentation admits of having matters judged according to it, even though our reasoning suggested entirely the opposite. And so either we shall have confidence in every presentation ⟨and we shall decide on the basis of it, or on the basis of some [one] presentation. But if we have confidence in every presentation, it is clear that we shall have confidence in the presentation of Xeniades⟩[34] according to which he says that all presentations are untrustworthy, and the argument will be turned around into holding that it is not the case that all presentations are such that we are able to judge matters according to them. **77.** But if we have confidence [only] in some, how shall we decide that it is appropriate to have confidence in these presentations and not those? For if this decision is made without a presentation, they will be granting that the presentation is superfluous for judging, since they will actually be saying that we are able to judge matters apart from it. But if the decision is made with a presentation, how will they grasp the presentation which they are bringing forward for the judgement of the other presentations? **78.** Or again, they will need another presentation for its judgement, and a third for the second, [and so on] to infinity. But it is impossible to make an infinite number of decisions. So, it is impossible to discover what sorts of presentations ought to be used as criteria and what sorts should not. Since, therefore, even if we grant that one ought to judge matters on the basis of presentations, whether having confidence in all as criteria or only in some, the argument is overturned in either case, and the conclusion must be that presentations ought not to be brought forward as criteria for the judgement of matters.

33. III-35 (100 ff.).
34. III-32 (18).

79. What has now been said is sufficient, by way of a summary, regarding the criterion 'according to which,' as it was said, matters are to be judged. It must be understood that we are not proposing to make a pronouncement that the criterion of the truth does not exist; for this [would be] a dogmatic claim. But since the dogmatists seem to establish persuasively that there is some criterion of truth, we ourselves have countered them with apparently persuasive arguments, not that we are committing ourselves to their truth, nor that our arguments are more persuasive than the opposites, but, because of the apparent equal persuasiveness of the arguments, when set besides those of the dogmatists, the conclusion [reached] is suspension of judgement.

Sextus *PH* 2.80–96 [III-39]

Ch. viii Concerning the True [or: that which is true] and Truth

80. Even if we should grant hypothetically that there is some criterion of the truth, it is discovered to be useless and pointless, if we suggest that, as far as concerns what the dogmatists say, the truth is non-existent and the true is non-substantial. 81. We suggest the following. The true is said to differ from the truth in three ways: in substance, in composition, and in power; in substance, since the true is incorporeal (for it is a proposition and a thing said [*lekton*]), whereas truth is a body (for it is knowledge capable of revealing all true things and knowledge is the leading part of the soul in a certain state, just as the hand in a certain state is a fist), and the leading part of the soul is a body, for according to them it is *pneuma*); 82. in composition, since the true is simple, for example, 'I converse' whereas truth is composed of many true cognitions; 83. in power, since truth depends on knowledge but the true does not altogether do so. Therefore, they say that the truth exists only in the virtuous man, whereas the true exists even in the base man, for it is possible for the base man to say something true.

84. These are the things the dogmatists say. But we, with an eye towards our intention in writing this outline, shall now produce arguments regarding only the true, since the truth is included in this refutation, being said to be a complex system of cognitions of true things. Again, since some of our arguments are more general, by means of which we attack the very substantiality of that which is true, whereas some are specific, by means of which we show that the true is not in an utterance or in a meaning or in a thing said [*lekton*] or in a motion of the intellect, we believe that setting out the more general arguments alone is adequate for the present. For just as a wall and superstructure collapse when the foundation is demolished, so when the substantiality of that which is

true is eliminated, the individual arguments contrived by the dogmatists are included.

Ch. ix Does That Which is True Exist in Nature?

85. It being the case that there is disagreement among the dogmatists regarding the true, some saying that something true exists and some saying that there is nothing true, it is not possible to decide the disagreement, since the one who says that something true exists will not be trusted without a demonstration, because of the disagreement. And should he wish to adduce a demonstration, if he agrees that it is a false one, he will not be trusted, but if he claims that it is a true one, he will fall into circular reasoning, and he will be required to provide a demonstration that the truth of the demonstration exists, and another one for that, [and so on] to infinity. But it is impossible to provide an infinite number of demonstrations. So, it is impossible to know that there is something true.

86. Further, the 'something' which they say is the highest genus of all, is either true or false, or neither true nor false, or both true and false. If, therefore, they will say that it is false, they will be agreeing that all things are false. For just as it follows that if animal is animate all particular animals are animate, so if the highest genus of all, the 'something', is false, so it follows that all particular ['somethings'] will be false and none will be true. Connected with this, the conclusion is also drawn that nothing is false. For the propositions 'everything is false' and 'there is something false' will be false, since they are included in everything. If the 'something' is true, everything will be true. Connected with this, the conclusion is also drawn that nothing is true, at least if this existent something itself, i.e., 'nothing is true', is true. **87.** If the 'something' is both false and true, each particular ['something'] will be false and true. From this the conclusion is drawn that nothing is true by nature. For that which has a nature of the sort that is true would certainly not be false. If the 'something' is neither true nor false, it is agreed that all particulars being said to be neither true nor false will not be true. And for this reason, it will be non-evident to us if something is true.

88. In addition to these arguments, either the things that are true are [only] appearances or only non-evident, or some of the things that are true are non-evident and some appearances. As we shall show, none of these are true, and therefore, nothing is true. If, then, the true things are only appearances, either they will say that all appearances are true or some. If they say 'all,' the argument is overturned. For it does appear to someone that nothing is true. If they say 'some,' no one is able to say that these are true and those false, without some means of deciding between the two, but if he employs a criterion, either he will say that this criterion is apparent or non-evident. And it is certainly not non-evident; for just as now the appearances alone are assumed to be true. 89. But if it is apparent, since the question of which appearances are true and which false is what is being investigated, the apparent [criterion] taken up for the judgement of appearances will again be in need of another apparent criterion, and that will be in need of yet another, [and so on] to infinity. But it is impossible to make an infinite number of decisions. So, it is impossible to grasp whether the true things are only appearances.

90. Similarly, one who says that only non-evident things are true will not say that they are all true (for he will not say that 'the number of stars is even' is true and 'the number of stars is odd' is true). If, however, only some are true, by means of what shall we judge that these non-evident things are true and those false? Certainly not by an apparent [criterion]. But if it is a non-evident one, since we are investigating which ones are true and which false, the non-evident criterion will need another non-evident criterion for deciding this, and that one will need another, [and so on] to infinity. Therefore, it is not the case that the true things are only non-evident.

91. The remaining possibility is that of true things some are apparent and some non-evident. But this too is absurd. For either all appearances and all non-evident things are true, or some appearances and some non-evident things. If, then, it is all, again the argument is overturned, since 'there is nothing true' will be granted to be true and it will be said that 'the number of stars is even' and the 'the number of stars is odd' are true. 92. If, however, only some of the appearances and some of the non-evident things are true, how shall we decide that these appearances are true and those not? If it is by means of an apparent [criterion] the argument will be forced into an infinite regress. If it is by means of a non-evident criterion, since the non-evident things are in need of judgement, again by means of what will this non-evident [criterion] be judged? If it is by means of an apparent [criterion], the mode based on circular reasoning is adduced; and if it is by means of a non-evident [criterion], the mode forcing an infinite regress is adduced. 93. And regarding non-evident things, similar things should be said. For he who attempts to judge things by something non-evident is forced into an infinite regress, whereas he who attempts to judge things by something apparent is either always piling on another apparent criterion [to judge the first], [and so on] to infinity, or by shifting to a non-evident [criterion], falls into circular reasoning. It is therefore false to say that of true things some are apparent and some non-evident.

94. If, therefore, neither the appearances nor the non-evident things

alone are true, nor some appearances true and some non-evident things, nothing is true. If nothing is true, and the criterion seems to need that which is true for judgement, the criterion is useless and empty, even if we should grant as a concession that it has some existence. And indeed if we ought to suspend judgement regarding whether there is something true, it follows that those who say that dialectic is the knowledge of false things and true things and that which is neither, are being rash.

95. Since the criterion of truth appears to be doubtful, it is no longer possible to assert anything confidently about that which seems to be clearly evident, as far as concerns what the dogmatists say, nor about things non-evident. For, since the dogmatists believe that they grasp non-evident things from the clearly evident, if we are compelled to suspend judgement regarding that which is called clearly evident, how could we dare to pronounce about non-evident things?

96. Out of our abundant supply, we shall raise further particular objections against non-evident things. And since non-evident things seem to be grasped and confirmed by means of sign and demonstration, we shall suggest briefly that it is appropriate to suspend judgement regarding the sign and the demonstration. Let us begin with sign, for the demonstration seems to be a species of sign.

Sextus *PH* 2.97–133   [III-40]

Ch. x On Sign

97. According to the dogmatists, then, some matters are self-evident and some are non-evident. Of the non-evident ones, some are totally non-evident, some temporarily non-evident, and some naturally non-evident. And they say that self-evident ones are those that come to be known by us, all on their own, for example, that it is day [when it is day]; those that are totally non-evident are those that do not naturally fall within our grasp, as, for example, that the stars are even-numbered; 98. those that are temporarily non-evident are those that have an evident nature that is temporarily made non-evident to us in certain external circumstances, as, for example, the city of Athens is non-evident to me now; those that are by nature non-evident are those that do not have a nature such as [ever] to be evident to us, as, for example, the intelligible pores, for these are never apparent all on their own, but, if at all, they would be thought to be grasped by inference from something else, such as [the presence of] sweat or something similar. 99. Thus, they say that self-evident things are not in need of a sign, for they are grasped all on their own. Nor are the matters that are totally non-evident, since in the first place they are not grasped at all. Those that are occasionally non-

evident and those that are by nature non-evident are grasped by means of signs, and not by the same signs, but the former by means of reminiscent signs and the latter by means of indicative signs.

100. According to them, therefore, some signs are reminiscent and some are indicative. They call a reminiscent sign that which, having been observed together with [the occasionally non-evident thing] that it is a sign of, is, because of its being evident to someone at the time it occurs, a reminder to us of that which it was observed together with, though the latter is now non-evident; for example, as in the case of smoke and fire. **101.** An indicative sign, they say, is that which is not evidently observed together with that which it is a sign of, but, as a result of its own peculiar nature and constitution, signifies that of which it is a sign, as, for example, the motions of the body are signs of the soul. Hence, they define this [kind of] sign thus: "an indicative sign is the antecedent proposition in a sound conditional revelatory of the consequent." **102.** As we said, then, although there are two different signs, we are not arguing against every sign, but only against the indicative sign, on the grounds that it seems to have been concocted by the dogmatists. For the reminiscent sign has been found to be trustworthy by everyday life, since when someone sees smoke, he takes it as a sign of fire, and seeing a scar he says that there has been a wound. Hence, not only are we not in conflict with everyday life, but we are even allied with it, by assenting undogmatically to that which has been made trustworthy by it, while opposing only those which have been especially invented by the dogmatists.

103. It was perhaps appropriate to make these prefatory remarks for the sake of the clarifying that which is being investigated. It remains for us to move on to the refutation, not with the desire to show that the indicative sign does not exist altogether, but with a desire to suggest that the arguments adduced for its existence and non-existence have apparently equal force.

Ch. xi Does an Indicative Sign Exist?

104. Now the sign, at least as far as concerns what the dogmatists say about it, is inconceivable. At any rate, the Stoics, who seem to have described it accurately and who wish to present the conception of the sign, say that a sign is "the antecedent proposition in a sound conditional revelatory of the consequent"; they say that a proposition is a complete *lekton* [thing said] which makes an assertion on its own; and a sound conditional is one that does not begin with a truth and end with a falsity. **105.** For either the conditional begins with a truth and ends with a truth, as in 'if it is day, it is light' or it begins with a falsehood and ends with a falsehood as in 'if the earth is flying, the earth is winged' or it begins with a truth and ends with a falsehood as in 'if the earth exists, the earth is flying.' They say that of these only the one that begins with a truth and ends with a falsehood is unsound, whereas the others are sound. 106. They say that the antecedent is the first clause in the conditional that begins with a truth and ends with a truth. It is revelatory of the consequent, since 'she has milk' seems to reveal that 'she has conceived' in the conditional 'if she has milk, she has conceived.'

107. These are the Stoics' doctrines. We, however, say first that it is non-evident whether a *lekton* [things said] exists. For since the Epicureans say that the thing said does not exist and the Stoics say that it does, either they are making a bare assertion or they have a demonstration. But if it is just a bare assertion, the Epicureans will oppose them with the assertion that the thing said does not exist. If they adduce a demonstration, since the demonstration is composed of propositions which are said, it will not be able to be adduced for the purpose of confirmation that the thing said exists, since it is composed of things said. For how will one who does not grant [the existence of] the thing said allow that a complex of things said exists? 108. So, he who tries to establish the existence of a thing said on the basis of a complex of things said is someone who wants to confirm a matter under investigation by means of the matter under investigation. If, therefore, it is not possible to show either simply or by means of a demonstration that a thing said exists, it is non-evident.

The case is similar for the existence of a proposition. 109. For a proposition is a thing said. And perhaps even if it should be granted for the sake of hypothesis that a thing said exists, the proposition is found to be non-existent, being composed of things said not existing at the same time as each other. For example, take 'if it is day, it is light.' When I say 'it is day' the 'it is light' [part] is not yet in existence and when I say 'it is light' the 'it is day' [part] is no longer in existence. If, therefore, the composite cannot possibly exist without the parts themselves existing at the same time as each other, and [the parts] of which the proposition is composed do not exist at the same time as each other, the proposition will not exist.

110. To pass over this problem, the sound conditional will be found to be ungraspable. Philo says that a sound conditional is one which does not have a true antecedent and a false consequent, for example, 'if it is day, I am conversing' when it is day and I am conversing, whereas Diodorus [Cronus] [says that a sound conditional] is that of which it neither was nor is possible that it should have a true antecedent and a false consequent. According to him, the conditional just mentioned seems

to be false, since it has a true antecedent and a false consequent, if it is day and I am silent; 111. whereas 'if the partless elements of things do not exist, the partless elements of things do exist' is true, for according to him, the false antecedent 'the partless elements of things do not exist' is followed by the true consequent 'the partless elements of things do exist'. Those who introduce the notion of logical connectedness say that a conditional is sound whenever the contradictory of the consequent is in conflict with its antecedent. So, according to them, the above-mentioned conditionals will be unsound, but 'if it is day, it is day' is true [i.e., sound]. 112. Those who judge [the correct answer] by implicit [entailment] say that the conditional is true where the consequent is contained virtually in the antecedent. According to them, 'if it is day, it is day' and all such doubled[35] conditionals will probably be false, for it is impossible for something to be contained [virtually] in itself.

113. So, it would perhaps seem impossible to decide this disagreement. For we shall not be trusted if we express a preference for one of the positions either without a demonstration or with a demonstration. For a demonstration seems to be sound whenever the conclusion follows from the conjunction of its premises as a consequent follows from its antecedent. For example, 'if it is day, it is light; but it is day; therefore, it is light'. 114. But since what we are investigating is how we may judge the following of a consequent from an antecedent, the circular mode is adduced. For, in order that the judgement about the conditional should be demonstrated, the conclusion [must] follow the premises of the dem-onstration, as we said before. And, again, in order that this should be confirmed, one must have already decided about the conditional and [logical] following [or consequence], which is absurd. 115. Therefore, the sound conditional is ungraspable.

But even the antecedent is subject to doubt. For the antecedent, as they say, is the principal [i.e., first] part of the conditional that begins with a truth and ends with a truth. 116. But if the sign reveals the consequent, either that consequent is self-evident or non-evident. If, then, it is self-evident, it will not need something to reveal it, but will be grasped along with it and will not be signified by it, for which reason [the antecedent] is not a *sign* of [the consequent]. If, however, it is non-evident, since there has been an undecided disagreement regarding which of these are true and which false, and, in general, whether any of them are true, it will be non-evident whether the consequent of the conditional is true. With this follows that it is non-evident whether the principal [i.e., first] part [of the conditional] is the antecedent.

35. Reading *diphoroumenon.*

117. To pass over this problem too, [the antecedent sign] is not able to reveal the consequent, at least if the thing signified is relative to the sign and for this reason is grasped along with it. For things relative to each other are grasped along with each other. And just as 'right' is not able to be grasped as 'right' of 'left' before 'left' [is grasped] nor *vice versa*, and similarly in the case of other relatives, so the sign will not be capable of being grasped as being a [sign] of the signified before that which is signified. 118. If, therefore, the sign is not grasped prior to the grasp of that which is signified, there cannot exist something that reveals that which is grasped at the same time as it and not after it.

Therefore, at least as far as concerns the more general claims of those we disagree with, the sign is inconceivable. For they say that it is relative and reveals the thing signified, and that that to which it is relative exists. 119. For this reason, if it is relative, and relative to the thing signified, it ought to be grasped along with the thing signified, just as 'left' with 'right' and 'up' with 'down' and the other relatives. But if it [the sign] reveals that which is signified, it ought to be grasped prior to it, so that, having been understood first, it might lead us to a conception of that which is known on the basis of it. 120. But it is impossible to conceive of a thing, not being able to have previously grasped that which must first necessarily be known. So, it is impossible to conceive of something which is relative and reveals that in relation to which it is conceived. But they say that the sign is relative and reveals that which is signified. So, it is impossible to conceive of the sign.

121. In addition, this should be said. There has been a disagreement among our predecessors, some saying the indicative sign exists, some saying that it does not. The one who says that the indicative sign exists either says it simply and without demonstration, using bare assertion, or else with a demonstration. But if he uses bare assertion, he will not be trusted, but if he should desire to give a demonstration, he will be seizing upon that which is under investigation. 122. For since the demonstration is said to be a kind of sign, and the dispute is precisely whether a sign exists or not, there will be a dispute concerning whether a demonstration exists or not, just as when we investigate, for the sake of a hypothesis, 'does a living thing exist' the existence of man is also investigated, for man is a living thing. But it is absurd to try to demonstrate that which is under investigation by means of that which is equally under investigation or by means of itself. Therefore, someone will not be able to assert definitely that a sign exists by means of a demonstration. 123. If, then, it is not possible either simply or with a demonstration to pronounce definitively about signs, it is impossible for a graspable pronouncement

to be made regarding it. And if the sign is not grasped with precision, it will not be said to be significative of something since it itself [the sign] is not agreed upon. For this reason, there will be no sign. Hence, also according to this line of reasoning, the sign will be non-existent and inconceivable.

124. Further, this should be said. The signs are either only appearances or only non-evident, or some signs are appearances and some non-evident. But neither of these is sound. So, there is no sign.

That not all signs are non-evident is then shown as follows. That which is non-evident does not appear on its own, as the dogmatists say, but becomes known by means of something else. And the sign, then, should it be non-evident, will need another non-evident sign, since there is no apparent sign according to the present hypothesis, and that one will need another, [and so on] to infinity. But it is impossible to get hold of an infinite number of signs. So, it is impossible for the sign to be grasped, if it is non-evident. For this reason, it will be non-evident and, because of its not being grasped, it will not be able to be a sign that signifies.

125. If all signs are appearances, since the sign is relative, and relative to that which is signified, and relatives are grasped together, the things said to be signified, being grasped along with appearances, will themselves be appearances. For just as since we meet 'right' and 'left' together neither 'right' nor 'left' is said to appear more than the other, so, since the sign and the thing signified are grasped together, neither one should be said to appear more than the other. 126. If that which is signified is apparent, it will not be a thing signified, not being in need of something that signifies and reveals it. Hence, just as the elimination of 'right' means there is no 'left' so elimination of thing signified means there can be no sign, if someone should say that signs are only appearances.

127. The remaining possibility is that some signs are appearances and some are non-evident. But in this case the problems [*aporiai*] remain. For, as we have said, the things said to be signified by the apparent signs are appearances and, not needing the sign, will not at all be things signified, and hence, there will be no signs, since they signify nothing. 128. The non-evident signs will need things to reveal them. And if they should be said to be signified by non-evident things, [then] since the argument regresses to infinity, they are found to be ungraspable and so, as we have said, non-existent. If, however, [the signs are signified] by appearances, they will be appearances, being grasped along with the appearances that are their signs, and for this reason too they will not exist. For it is impossible for there to be some thing which is by nature

non-evident but also appears; the argument, however, is about signs that
are hypothesized as non-evident, and yet are found to be appearances,
according to the turning around of the argument.

129. If, therefore, neither all signs are appearances nor all non-evident,
nor are some appearances and some non-evident, and there are no other
alternatives, as they themselves say, the things called signs will not exist.

130. These few, out of the many [available arguments] will be sufficient
for the present purpose of suggesting the non-existence of the indicative
sign. Next, we shall set forth suggestions that a sign exists, so that we
may display the equal force of the opposing arguments.

Either, then, the utterances used against the sign signify something
or nothing. If they are without significance, how could they dislodge the
existence of the sign? If they signify something, a sign exists. **131.** Further,
either the arguments against the sign are demonstrative or not. But if
they are not demonstrative, they will not demonstrate that the sign does
not exist. If they are demonstrative, since the demonstration is a kind of
sign, revealing the conclusion, it will be a sign. Hence, one also propounds
this sort of argument. If a sign exists, a sign exists; and if a sign does
not exist, a sign exists. (For the non-existence of a sign is shown by
demonstration, which is indeed a sign, as has been shown.) But a sign
exists or a sign does not exist. So, a sign exists. **132.** But the following
argument is set against this one. If a sign does not exist, a sign does not
exist; and if a sign is what the dogmatists say it is, a sign does not exist.
For the sign, the subject of the present argument, has been found to be
non-existent according to its conception and as it is said to be relative
and revelatory of that which is signified, as we have shown. **133.** Either
sign exists or it does not; therefore, sign does not exist.

And regarding the utterances about the sign, let the dogmatists themselves reply to us whether they signify something or signify nothing. For
if they signify nothing, the existence of the sign is not confirmed. But
if they signify something, that which is signified will follow, namely, that
a sign exists, which entails that sign does ⟨not⟩ exist, as we have suggested,
on the basis of the reversal of the argument.

These, then, being the plausible arguments brought forth concerning
the existence and non-existence of the sign, we should say that sign no
more exists than not.

Sextus *PH* 2.134–159   [III-41]

Ch. xii On Demonstration

134. It is clear then from these considerations that demonstration too
is not a matter agreed upon. For if we suspend judgement regarding the

sign, and demonstration is a type of sign, it is necessary to suspend judgement regarding demonstration. And indeed we shall find that the arguments regarding the sign can be adapted for use against demonstration, since demonstration is supposed to be relative and revelatory of the conclusion, and practically everything said by us regarding the sign followed from this [line of argument]. **135.** If, however, we must speak specifically regarding demonstration, I shall concisely treat of the argument regarding it, first attempting to provide a little clarification regarding what they say a demonstration is.

Demonstration, as they say, is an argument which, by means of agreed upon premisses, according to conclusive deduction, reveals a non-evident conclusion. What they mean will be made clearer by means of the following. An argument is a complex of premisses and a conclusion. **136.** The premisses of the complex are said to be the propositions taken for the establishment of the conclusion and the conclusion is the proposition established by the premisses. For example, in the argument, 'if it is day, it is light; but it is indeed day; therefore, it is light', the proposition 'therefore, it is light' is the conclusion and the rest are premisses. **137.** Some arguments are conclusive and some are non-conclusive; they are conclusive whenever the conditional which starts from the conjunction of the premisses and ends with the conclusion of the argument is sound. For example, the above argument is conclusive, since, from the conjunction of its premisses 'if it is day, it is light' and 'it is day', 'it is light' follows in this conditional 'it is day, and if it is day, it is light; ⟨therefore,⟩ it is light.' Arguments that do not have this [structure] are non-conclusive.

138. Some conclusive[36] arguments are true and some are not true; they are true whenever not only the conditional formed from the conjunction of the premisses and the conclusion is sound, as we said before, but also the conjunction of the premisses, which is the antecedent of the conditional, is true. A true conjunction is that which has all its conjuncts true, as, for example, in 'it is day, and if it is day, it is light'. **139.** Those which are not like this are not true. For this argument 'if it is night, it is dark; but indeed it is night; therefore, it is dark' when it is day, is conclusive, since the conditional 'it is night and if it is night it is dark; therefore, it is dark' is sound, but the argument is not true. For the antecedent conjunction is false, viz. 'it is night and if it is night it is dark' since it contains the falsehood 'it is night'. For a conjunction which contains a false conjunct is false. Hence, they also say that a true argument is one in which true premisses conclude to a true conclusion.

140. Again, some true arguments are demonstrative and some are non-

---

36. See II-3 (77–78).

demonstrative; the demonstrative ones are those which conclude to a non-evident conclusion by means of self-evident premisses; those that do not have this characteristic are non-demonstrative. For example, the argument 'if it is day, it is light; but it is indeed day; therefore, it is light' is non-demonstrative. For the conclusion 'it is light' is self-evident. But this argument 'if sweat is pouring through the surface [of the skin], there are intelligible [i.e., non-sensible] pores; but sweat is indeed pouring through the surface [of the skin]; therefore, there are intelligible pores' is demonstrative, for the conclusion 'there are intelligible pores' is non-evident.

141. Some of the arguments concluding to a non-evident conclusion are only progressive, leading us to the conclusion by means of the premisses. Some do so both progressively and by revelation. For example, those are [merely] progressive that seem to depend on trustworthiness and memory, for example, 'if some god tells you that this man will become wealthy, this man will become wealthy; but this god (assume I am pointing to Zeus) tells you this man will become wealthy; therefore, this man will become wealthy.' For we assent to the conclusion not so much because the premisses necessitate it as because we trust the pronouncement of the god. **142.** Among the arguments that lead us to the conclusion not only progressively but also by revelation are, for example, 'if sweat is pouring through the surface [of the skin], there are intelligible pores; but indeed the first; therefore, the second.' For the pouring of the sweat is revelatory of the existence of the pores, because it is already understood that moisture is not able to be conducted through a solid body.

143. So, demonstration should be an argument which is both conclusive and true with a non-evident conclusion, revealed by the force of the premisses, and because of this a demonstration is said to be an argument which, based on agreed premisses, according to conclusive deduction, is revelatory of a non-evident conclusion.

So these are the terms in which they customarily clarify the conception of demonstration.

Ch. xiii Does Demonstration Exist?

144. That demonstration does not exist may be inferred from their own words, refuting each of the components of the conception in turn. For example, an argument is composed of propositions, and composites are not able to exist if the parts of it do not coexist with each other, as is self-evident in the case of a bed and similar objects. But the parts of an argument do not coexist with each other. For when we state the first premiss, the second premiss and the conclusion do not yet exist. And when we state the second, the first no longer exists and the conclusion does not yet exist. And when we put forth the conclusion, the premisses no longer exist. Therefore, the parts of the argument do not coexist with each other. For this reason, the argument will seem not to exist.

145. Apart from these considerations, the conclusive argument is ungraspable. For if this argument is judged from the logical consequence of the conditional and the consequence in the conditional is a matter of undecidable disagreement, and is probably ungraspable, as we suggested in the argument regarding the sign, the conclusive argument too will be ungraspable. **146.** At any rate, the dialecticians say that an argument becomes non-conclusive either because of logical disconnectedness or omission, or being asserted in improper form or because of redundancy. For example, there is logical disconnectedness whenever there is no logical consequence between the premisses and between premisses and the conclusion, as in 'if it is day, it is light; but wheat is sold in the marketplace; therefore, Dion is walking'. **147.** [Non-conclusiveness] because of redundancy occurs whenever a premiss is discovered to be redundant for the argument's conclusiveness, as in 'if it is day, it is light; but it is indeed day, and Dion is walking; therefore, it is light'. [Non-conclusiveness] because improper form occurs whenever the argument does not have a conclusive form; for example, 'if it is day, it is light; but indeed it is light; therefore, it is day' is non-conclusive, where the proper syllogisms are, as they say: 'if it is day, it is light; but it is indeed day; therefore, it is light' and 'if it is day, it is light; but it is not light; therefore, it is not day'. **148.** For since the conditional announces plainly that if the antecedent holds the consequent follows, it is [only] reasonable that when the antecedent is admitted the consequent too is inferred; and if the consequent is denied, the antecedent is denied. For if the antecedent held, the consequent would follow. But when the consequent is admitted, the antecedent is not necessarily posited as well. For the conditional did not promise that the antecedent followed on the consequent, but only that the consequent followed on the antecedent.

149. For this reason, therefore, the argument that deduces the conclusion from the conditional and the antecedent is said to be syllogistic; and so is that which deduces the contradictory of the antecedent of the conditional from the [positing of the] conditional and the contradictory of the consequent. The argument, as in the case of the above, that deduces the antecedent from the conditional and its consequent, is non-conclusive, so that even though its premisses are true, it deduces something false [i.e., it is day] when it [i.e., it is light] is said by lamplight at night. For 'if it is day, it is light' is a true conditional, but the additional statement 'but indeed it is light' is true; but the conclusion 'it is day' is false.

150. The argument is improper by omission in which something is left out which is needed for the conclusive deduction of the conclusion. For example, this is a sound argument, as they think, in 'wealth is either good or bad or indifferent; but it is not bad or indifferent; therefore, it is good'; but the following is a bad argument on the grounds of omission: 'wealth is either good or bad; it is not bad; therefore, it is good'. **151.** If, then, I show that on the basis of what they say it is not possible to discern a difference between non-conclusive and conclusive arguments, I have shown that the conclusive argument is ungraspable, so that their limitless treatises on dialectic are superfluous. I show this in the following way.

152. The argument that was said to be non-conclusive because of logical disconnectedness is understood to be so from the fact that there is no logical connection between the premises and between the premises and the conclusion. Since, therefore, the judgement about the conditional ought to precede the understanding of these logical connections and the conditional is undecidable, as I have argued, the non-conclusive argument based on logical disconnectedness will be indiscernible from a [conclusive argument]. **153.** For he who is stating that some argument is non-conclusive because of logical disconnectedness, if he is merely making an assertion, will have contradicting him an assertion opposed to what he previously said; whereas if he demonstrates by means of an argument, he will be told that this argument must first be [shown to be] conclusive, and then he can use it to demonstrate that the argument said to be logically disconnected has premises that are without logical connections. But we shall not know if it is demonstrative, not having an agreed upon means of judging the conditional, by which we can judge if the conclusion is logically connected to the combination of the premises. And, therefore, on this basis we shall not be able to discern the difference between an argument that is improper because of logical disconnectedness and conclusive ones.

154. We shall say the same things to someone who states that some argument is improper because of being asserted in improper form. For he who is trying to establish that a form is improper will not have an agreed upon conclusive argument by means of which he will be able to deduce what he states. **155.** And by means of these criticisms we have implicitly refuted those who attempt to show that arguments are non-conclusive by omission. For if the complete and finished argument is indiscernible [from a non-conclusive argument], the argument defective by omission will also be non-evident. And further, he who desires to show that some argument is defective by omission by means of an argument, since he does not have an agreed upon procedure for judging the conditional by means of which he will be able to judge the logical consequence of the argument he is speaking about, will not be able to say correctly and with judgement that it is defective by omission.

156. Further, the argument said to be improper because of redundancy is indiscernable from demonstrative arguments. For with respect to redundancy, even the arguments touted by the Stoics as 'indemonstrable' will be found to be non-conclusive. And when these [the indemonstrables] are abolished the whole of dialectic is overturned. For these are the ones they say are not in need of demonstration to establish themselves, but seem to demonstrate the conclusiveness of the other arguments. That they are redundant will be clear when we have set out the 'indemonstrable arguments' and thus provided arguments for what we have said.[37]

157. They dream up many indemonstrables, but set forth these five above all others; and the other arguments are thought to be reduced to them. The first is that which concludes from the conditional and the antecedent to the consequent, for example, 'if it is day, it is light; but it is day; therefore, it is light.' The second is that which concludes from the conditional and the contradictory of the consequent to the contradictory of the antecedent, for example, 'if it is day, it is light; but it is not light; therefore, it is not day.' **158.** The third is that which concludes from the denial of a conjunction and one of the conjuncts to the contradictory of the other, for example, 'not: it is day and it is night; but it is day; therefore, it is not night'. The fourth is that which concludes from a disjunction and one of the disjuncts to the contradictory of the other, for example, 'either it is day or it is night; but it is day; therefore, it is not night'. The fifth is that which concludes from a disjunction and the contradictory of one of its disjuncts to the other, for example, 'either it is day or it is night; but it is not night; therefore, it is day'.

159. These then are the touted indemonstrables, all of which seem to be non-conclusive by reason of redundancy. So, for instance, starting with the first, either it is agreed that 'it is light' is logically connected to its antecedent 'it is day' in the conditional 'if it is day, it is light' or it is non-evident. But if it is non-evident, we will not grant that the conditional is agreed upon. But if it is self-evident that, given that 'it is day' it is also necessarily the case that 'it is light', then when we say 'it is day', it is also concluded that 'it is light'; so that the argument 'it is day; therefore it is light' is sufficient and the conditional 'if it is day, it is light' is redundant.

37. II-3 (80–81).

Physics

Sextus *PH* 3.2–12   [III-42]

Ch. iii On God

2. Since, then, most have declared that god is a cause that is most active [in the world], let us examine god, but let us first note that, following [the rules of the everyday conduct of] life, we say undogmatically that gods exist and that we revere them and we say that they are providential. But we speak as follows to counter the rashness of the dogmatists.

We ought to consider the substances of things conceived by us; for example, whether they are bodies or incorporeal. We should also consider the form of things, for no one would be able to conceive a horse not having previously learned what the form of a horse is. Further, one is obliged to conceive of that which is conceived of as existing somewhere. 3. Now since among the dogmatists, some say that god is a body and others that god is incorporeal; some say that god has a human form and others that he has not; some say that he is [located] in a place, others that he is not; some say that he is in the cosmos, others say that he is outside it, how shall we be able to acquire a conception of god when we do not agree about his substance nor about his form nor about his location? Let them first agree and make consistent their thinking so that they can say that god is such and such. After they have outlined his nature to us, *then* let them require us to acquire a conception of god. But so long as they disagree without coming to a decision, we do not know what conception we are to acquire from them on the basis of an agreement.

4. But, they say, conceive of something blessed and indestructible, and believe god to be this. But this is silly. For just as one who does not know Dion is not able to understand his accidents qua Dion, so we who do not know the substance of god, will not be able to learn what his accidents are and [so] to form a conception. 5. Apart from these considerations, let them say to us what something blessed is, whether it is something that acts according to virtue and has providential knowledge concerning those things under his control or whether it is something that is inactive and has no troubles itself nor does it give trouble to anyone [else]. And since they disagree about this without coming to a decision, they have made the words "that which is blessed" inconceivable to us, for which reason god is also inconceivable. 6. But even granted that we have a conception of god, it is necessary to suspend judgement concerning whether he exists or not, at least as far as concerns what the dogmatists say. For the existence of god is not self-evident. And if god impressed his own existence upon us, the dogmatists would have agreed on his

nature and his origin and his location. Their indecisive dispute has made him seem non-evident to us and in need of demonstration. **7.** Now the one who demonstrates the existence of god must do so either by means of something self-evident or something not. Certainly he does not do so by means of something self-evident. For if that which demonstrates the existence of god were self-evident, then, since that which is demonstrated is conceived with reference to that which demonstrates, and is simultaneously understood along with it (as we have already shown),[38] the existence of god will also be self-evident, since it is grasped along with that which demonstrates it and is self-evident. But as we have suggested, it is not self-evident. Nor then is his existence demonstrated by means of something self-evident. **8.** But neither is it demonstrated by means of something that is non-evident. For the non-evident [thing] that is supposed to demonstrate the existence of god is in need of demonstration, but if it is said to be demonstrated by means of something self-evident, it itself will no longer be non-evident, but self-evident. So it is not the case that the non-evident thing which demonstrates the existence of god is demonstrated by means of something self-evident. But neither is it demonstrated by means of something non-evident, for one who says this falls into an infinite regress, always being asked by us for a demonstration of the non-evident propositions adduced as demonstrative of the one previously set forth. Therefore, one is not able to demonstrate the existence of god on the basis of something else. **9.** And if god's existence is neither self-evident on its own nor demonstrable on the basis of something else, the existence of god will be ungraspable.

Further, this too ought to be said. He who says that god exists either holds that god is provident of things in the cosmos or he is not, and if he is provident, then he is so either for everything or [only] for some things. But if he is provident of everything, there would be no bad thing nor any vice in the cosmos. Yet, they say that all things are full of vice. Therefore, god will not be said to be provident of everything. **10.** If, however, he is provident of some things, why these things and not those? For either he wishes and is able to be provident of everything, or he wishes to be provident, but is not able, or he is able but does not wish to be, or he neither wishes nor is able to be provident. But if he wished to be provident and was able, then he would be provident of everything. But he is not provident of everything, for the reasons given above. Therefore, it is not the case that he both wishes to be provident and is able to be. If he wishes to be but is not able, he is weaker than the cause owing to which he is not able to be provident of things of which he is

38. See also *PH* 2.179.

not provident. **11.** But it is counter to the conception of god that he should be weaker than anything. If he is able to be provident about everything, but he does not wish to be, he would be regarded as malign. If he neither wishes nor is able to be provident, he is malign and weak, and to say this about god is the act of impious men. Therefore, god is not provident about things in the cosmos.

If god is provident of nothing and has no work nor any effect, one will not be able to say how one can grasp that god exists, at least if he neither appears all on his own nor is grasped through some of his effects. And for these reasons the existence of god is ungraspable. **12.** From these [arguments] we reason that perhaps those who commit themselves to the claim that god exists are compelled to be impious. For in saying that he is provident of everything, they will say that he is the cause of bad things, whereas in saying that he is provident only of certain things or of nothing either they will be compelled to say that god is malign or that he is weak, and this is self-evidently the act of impious men.

Sextus *M* 9.13–191 (selections)   [III-43]

On Gods

13. The reasoning about gods seems to be most necessary to those who philosophize dogmatically. Therefore, they say that philosophy is the cultivation of wisdom and wisdom is the knowledge of divine and human matters. For this reason, if we show the doubtful nature of the investigation concerning gods, we will have implicitly established that wisdom is not the knowledge of divine and human matters and that philosophy is not the cultivation of wisdom. . . .

Do Gods Exist?

49. Since not everything conceived of partakes of existence, but something can be conceived of though it does not exist, like the hippocentaur and Scylla, it will be necessary to investigate the existence of the gods, after having inquired into the conception of them. For perhaps the sceptic, in comparison with those who philosophize differently, will be found to be in a safer position when he states, following traditional customs and the laws, that the gods exist, and when he does everything pertaining to religious worship and pious practices, but makes no rash statement in the way of a philosophical investigation.

50. Some of these who have investigated the existence of god say that god exists, some say that he does not, and some say that [the evidence does not indicate] one more than the other. **51.** The majority of the dogmatists and the basic grasps of ordinary life hold that [gods] exist, whereas those dubbed 'atheists' hold that god does not exist, for example, Euhemerus, "an old huckster, grinding out unjust books," Diagoras of Melos, Prodicus of Ceos, Theodorus, and very many others. Of these, Euhemerus used to say that those who were taken to be gods were actually certain powerful men and because of this they were deified by the others and thought to be gods; 52. whereas Prodicus said that that which benefits life was supposed to be a god, for example, the sun, moon, rivers, lakes, meadows, crops, and all such things. 53. The dithyramb-writer Diagoras of Melos, as they say, was at first as superstitious as anyone. At least, he began his poem in this way: "Everything is accomplished according to daimons and fortune." But when he suffered an injustice from someone who broke his word to him, and this person did not suffer anything as a result of this, he changed his tune and said that god does not exist. And Critias, one of the tyrants in Athens,[39] seems to be one of the band of atheists, saying that the ancient lawmakers fashioned god as an overseer of the [morally] perfect actions and [moral] errors of men, in order to prevent people from doing injustice to their neighbour in secret, since [if they believed in a god] they would be mindful of the punishment of the gods. . . .

55. Theodorus the atheist is in agreement with these men, and, according to some, so is Protagoras of Abdera; the former, in his book on the gods, provided all sorts of destructive arguments against Greek theological beliefs, while the latter somewhere wrote these exact words,[40] "I am not able to say whether gods exist or what sort of things they are, for there are many things impeding my [understanding]." It was for this reason that the Athenians decreed his death. He fled, and while on board ship, fell overboard and drowned at sea. . . .

58. And Epicurus, according to some, allows a god for the many, but does not allow that a god exists in the nature of things. 59. The sceptics said that, because of the equal force of the opposing arguments, there is no more reason to believe one way rather than the other. And we shall realize this if we give a summary rundown of the arguments advanced on either side.

60. Those then who think it right to hold that gods exist attempt to establish their thesis by four modes: the first is the argument from the agreement among all men; the second is the argument from cosmic design; the third [is a reductio argument which] draws the absurd consequences of denying the divine; the fourth and last is the refutation of opposing arguments.

39. The reign of the Thirty Tyrants in 404 B.C.
40. Fr. I-12 D.-K., cf. II-4.

61. Now arguing on the basis of the common conception, they say that practically all men, Greeks and barbarians, believe that the divine exists, and because of this they agree in making sacrifices and prayers and in erecting shrines for the gods, even though they do this in different ways. So, although they hold in common the belief that something divine exists, they do not have the same basic grasp of its nature. But if this basic grasp were false, they would not all have agreed thus. Therefore, gods exist.

62. Besides, false opinions and *ad hoc* declarations do not stay around for a long time, but last as long as those things for the sake of which they were maintained. For example, men honour kings with sacrifices and with all the other religious observances with which they revere ⟨them⟩ as gods. But they retain these only while the kings are alive and as soon as they have died they abandon them as irreligious and impious. But the conception of the gods, at any rate, has always existed, and persists forever, as is likely since they are testified to by events themselves. **63.** Moreover, even if one ought to ignore the idiosyncratic ideas and ought to have confidence in the most talented and wise men, one can see that the poetic art produces no great or luminous work in which god is not the one who is endowed with power and authority over events, just as he is in the poet Homer's writings about the war between Greeks and barbarians. **64.** One can also see that the majority of natural philosophers are in agreement with the poets. For Pythagoras, Empedocles, the Ionians, Socrates, Plato, Aristotle, the Stoics, and perhaps the philosophers of the Garden (as the very words of Epicurus testify), all allow [the existence of] god. **65.** Therefore, just as if we were investigating some visible object, it would be reasonable to put our confidence in those with the keenest sight, and if some audible object, those with the keenest hearing, so since we are investigating a matter perceived by reason we ought to put our confidence in those with the keenest minds and reasoning ability, such as were these philosophers.

66. But those holding the opposite view are accustomed to reply that all men also have a common conception of the myths about the things in Hades, and that they have the agreement of the poets, and indeed even more so with respect to the things in Hades than with respect to the gods; but we would not say that the myths about Hades are really true. . . .

71. But, [the dogmatist retorts,] whereas the myth contains in itself its own refutation, the supposition regarding gods is not like this nor did it suggest conflict but has appeared to harmonize with [real] events. . . .

74. . . . . This, then, is the argument based on the common conception and agreement in thinking about god. **75.** Let us then examine the argument from the organization of the surrounding cosmos. Now they say that the substance of things [i.e., matter], being in itself immobile and shapeless, requires some cause by which it is moved and shaped. And therefore just as when we see a well-shaped work of bronze we long to know the craftsman, since it is itself constituted of immobile matter, so, seeing the material of the universe moving and endowed with form and organization, we might reasonably inquire into the cause that moves it and shapes it variously. 76. It is not plausible to suppose this to be anything other than a power which pervades in the [same] way that our soul pervades us. So, this power is either self-moving or moved by some other power. And if it is moved by some other power, it will be impossible for the other power to be moved unless it is moved by another, which is absurd. There is, then, some power, self-moving in itself, which would be divine and everlasting. For either it will move itself everlastingly or move itself beginning at some particular time. But it will not move itself beginning at some particular time. For there will not be a cause of its moving itself at some particular time. Therefore, the power that moves matter and leads it in orderly fashion to generations and changes is everlasting. So, this is god.

77. Further, that which generates rational and prudent beings is itself certainly rational and prudent. Indeed, the above-mentioned power is of the nature to produce men, and so it will be rational and prudent, and this is just what a divine nature is. Therefore, gods exist. . . .

88. And Cleanthes argued as follows. If one nature is better than another, there is some nature that is best. If one soul is better than another, there is some soul that is best. And if one animal is better than another, there is some animal that is best. For such [comparisons] are not of a nature to fall into an infinite regress. So, just as nature could not be infinitely increased in greatness, so too neither could soul or animal. 89. But one kind of animal is better than another, as for example, the horse is better than the tortoise and the bull is better than the ass, and the lion better than the bull. And man, in his bodily and psychic disposition, excels and is the best of all the terrestrial animals. Therefore, there is some animal that is best and most excellent.

90. Yet man cannot be the absolutely best animal, considering just the fact that he conducts his whole life in vice—and if not exactly his whole life, then the greatest part of it, for if he ever does get ahead in virtue, he does so late and in the evening of his life. His life is subject to fate and is weak and in need of countless things to assist him in living, such as food, shelter, and other kinds of care for the body, which importune him and exact daily tribute like a cruel tyrant; and if we don't render the body homage by washing, anointing, clothing, and feeding it, it

threatens us with disease and death. So, man is not a perfect animal, but rather imperfect, and far removed from perfection. **91.** But that which is perfect and best would be better than man, fulfilled in every virtue and impervious to all bad things. And this will not differ from god. Therefore, god exists.

101. And Zeno of Citium, taking his inspiration from Xenophon, makes this argument. The thing which emits seed of something rational is also itself rational; but the cosmos emits seed of something rational; therefore the cosmos is something rational. With this its existence is also established. **102.** The plausibility of the argument is manifest. For in every nature and soul the starting point for motion seems to come from the leading part of it, and all the powers which are sent out from the whole to the parts are sent out from the leading part as though from a well-spring, so that every power found in the part is also found in the whole, because it is distributed to [the parts] from the leading part in it. Hence, whatever powers the part has, the whole has too, and preeminently so. **103.** And for this reason, if the cosmos emits seed of a rational animal, [it does not do so as] man does, by emitting a frothy substance, but rather [it does so] in so far as it contains seeds of rational animals. And it includes [them] not in the way we would say that the vine contains grape-pits, i.e., by including them [in a derivative way], but rather because spermatic principles of rational animals are [directly] contained in it. So the sense of the argument is this: the cosmos contains spermatic principles of rational animals. Therefore, the cosmos is rational.

104. And again Zeno says: the rational is better than what is not rational; but nothing is better than the cosmos; therefore, the cosmos is something rational. And [he argues] in the same way for its being intelligent and animate; for the intelligent is better than what is not intelligent and the animate is better than what is not animate; but nothing is better than the cosmos; therefore, the cosmos is intelligent and animate. . . .

108. But Alexinus attacked Zeno thus: what is poetic is better than what is not poetic and what is grammatical is better than what is not grammatical and what possesses theoretical knowledge in the other crafts is better than what is not like that; but no one thing is better than the cosmos; therefore, the cosmos is something poetic and grammatical. **109.** The Stoics respond to this attack by saying that Zeno was referring to what is better in an absolute sense, i.e., the rational [being better] than what is not rational and the intelligent than what is not intelligent and the animate than what is not animate, but that Alexinus was not; **110.** for the poetic is not better than what is not poetic in the absolute sense, nor is the grammatical [better] than what is not grammatical [in this sense]. Consequently, a great difference can be observed in the arguments. Think about it: Archilochus, although he is poetic, is not better than Socrates, who is not; and Aristarchus, although he is a grammarian, is not better than Plato, who is not.

111. In addition to these arguments, the Stoics and those who agree with them try to establish the existence of the gods from the motion of the cosmos. For anyone would agree on the basis of many considerations that the entire cosmos is in motion. **112.** So, it is moved either by nature or intention or by the necessity of a vortex. But it is not reasonable that it should be moved by the necessity of a vortex. For the vortex is either orderly or disorderly. If it is disorderly, it would not be able to move something in an orderly way. And if it moves something in an orderly and harmonious way, it will be something divine and supernatural. **113.** For the universe would not have been able to move something in an orderly way that preserves it if it were not intelligent and divine. And being such, it would no longer be a vortex, for a vortex is something disorderly and lasts for a short time. So, the cosmos would not be moved according to the necessity of a vortex, as Democritus and his followers said. **114.** Nor is it moved by a nature deprived of the power of presentation, since intelligent nature is better than this and such natures are seen to be contained in the cosmos. Therefore, it necessarily has an intelligent nature by which it is moved in an orderly way, which evidently is a god. . . .

123. This, then, is the nature of these arguments. Let us then examine next the kind of absurd consequences that follow for those who reject the divine.

If the gods do not exist, there is no piety—which is one of the virtues. . . . [Here there is a corrupt phrase.] For piety is the knowledge of how to serve gods, and it is not possible for there to be service to non-existent things; therefore, there is no knowledge of such service. Just as it is not possible for there to be knowledge of how to serve non-existent entities like hippocentaurs, so, if the gods do not exist, there will be no knowledge of how to serve them. So, if the gods do not exist, piety is non-existent. But piety exists. Therefore, the existence of gods ought to be declared.

124. Again, if gods do not exist, holiness is non-existent, holiness being a sort of justice in relation to gods. Indeed, holiness exists according to the common conceptions and basic grasps of all men, insofar as something holy exists. Therefore, the divine exists. **125.** But if gods do not exist, wisdom, the knowledge of divine and human things, is abolished. And since there is no [generic] knowledge of human and hippocentaurian things, for one exists and the other doesn't, so there will be no [generic] knowledge of divine and human things, if men exist but gods do not. But it is absurd to say that wisdom does not exist. Therefore, it is absurd to hold that gods do not exist.

126. Further, if justice has been introduced for the sake of the interrelation of men with each other and with gods, if gods do not exist, neither will justice endure. And that is absurd. . . .

133. Zeno offered this sort of argument. One might reasonably honour the gods. ⟨But one might not reasonably honour the non-existent.⟩ Therefore, gods exist. Some counter this argument by saying that one might reasonably honour wise men; but one might not reasonably honour non-existent things; therefore, wise men exist. But this was not acceptable to the Stoics, for according to them, the wise man is hitherto undiscovered. **134.** Opposing this counter-argument, Diogenes of Babylon says that the second premiss of Zeno's argument is implicitly this: one might not reasonably honour things whose nature it is not to exist. For understanding [the premiss] in this way, it is clear that the gods are of such a nature as to exist. **135.** And if so, then they thereby exist. For if once they existed, they exist now, just as, if atoms once existed, they exist now. For such things are indestructible and ungenerated, according to our conception of their bodies. Therefore, the argument will conclude with a consistent logical connection. But wise men, even though they are of such a nature as to exist, do not thereby exist. **136.** Others say that Zeno's first premiss, one might reasonably honour the gods, is ambiguous. For in one sense it means that it may be reasonable for someone to worship gods, but in another sense it means someone may hold them in high regard. The premiss is to be taken in the former sense, in which case it will be false as applied to wise men.

137. Such is the character of the arguments furnished by the Stoics and by the disciples of other systems on behalf of the existence of gods. We should show next that those who teach the non-existence of gods are not inferior to these in persuasiveness, because of the equal force of their arguments.

138. If, then, gods exist, they are living things. And by the same argument the Stoics employed to teach that the cosmos is an animal, one may establish that god is an animal. For that which is an animal is better than that which is not; nothing is better than god; therefore, god is an animal. Supporting this argument is the common conception of men, since ordinary people, poets, and the majority of the best philosophers testify to the fact that god is an animal. So the logical consistency of the argument is secured. **139.** For if gods exist, they are animals. But if they are animals, they have sense-perception, for every animal is conceived of as an animal in virtue of its partaking in sense-perception. But if they perceive, they have bitter and sweet sense-perceptions. For they do not encounter sensibles through some other sense but not also through taste. For this reason, simply to deprive god altogether of this or some other sense is implausible. **140.** For if he has more senses, man will become better than he was, since, as Carneades said, it would be better if, in addition to the five senses, he were to have more to provide him with additional testimony, so that he could grasp more things, rather than to deprive him of the five. It should be declared then that god has the sense of taste and through this grasps tastes. **141.** But if he grasps things through taste, he has sense-perceptions ⟨of bitter⟩ and sweet. And, having such sense-perceptions, he will be pleased by one thing, and displeased by another. And so, being displeased by something, he will also be subject to perturbation and change for the worse. If this is so, he is destructible. So, if gods exist, they are destructible. Therefore, gods do not exist. . . .

148. Further, if something divine exists, either it is limited or unlimited. It could not be unlimited, since it would then be immobile and inanimate. For if that which is unlimited is moved, it goes to one place from another. That which goes from one place to another is in a place, and being in place, it is limited. If, then, something is unlimited, it is immobile. Or, if it is moved, then it is not unlimited. **149.** According to similar reasoning, it is inanimate. For if it is held together by a soul, it is certainly held together by movement from the middle parts to the limits and from the limits to the middle parts. But in the unlimited there is no middle or limits. So, the unlimited is not animate. And for this reason, if the divine is unlimited, it is neither moved nor animate. But the divine is moved and is thought to partake of animation. So, the divine is not unlimited.

150. Nor is it limited. For since the limited is part of the unlimited and the whole is greater than the part, it is clear that the unlimited will be greater than the divine and will dominate the divine nature. But it is absurd to say that there is something greater than god that dominates the divine nature. Therefore, the divine is not limited. But if it is neither unlimited nor limited, and there is no third possibility to conceive of, the divine will be nothing.

151. Further, if the divine is something, it is either a body or incorporeal. But it is not incorporeal, since the incorporeal is inanimate and insensitive and not able to act; neither is it a body, since every body is changeable and destructible, but the divine is indestructible. Therefore, the divine does not exist.

152. But at least if the divine exists it is certainly an animal. And if it is an animal, certainly it is perfectly virtuous and happy (for without virtue happiness cannot exist). But if it is perfectly virtuous, it has all the virtues. But it cannot have all the virtues if it does not have self-control and endurance. But certainly god does not have these virtues if there is not something hard for god to abstain from and hard for him to bear. **153.** For self-control is a disposition that prevents one from trespassing against the deliverances of right reason, or a virtue making us superior to the things that seem hard to abstain from. They say that a man is continent if he restrains himself not from an old woman about to die, but when, having the opportunity to enjoy Lais or Phryne or some such woman, he restrains himself. **154.** And endurance is the knowledge of things which are to be endured and not to be endured, or a virtue making us superior to the things that seem hard to bear. For it is the man who bears being cut and burned who manifests endurance, not the man who is drinking sweet wine. **155.** Therefore, there will be things hard to bear and hard to abstain from for god. For if these did not exist, he will not have these virtues, that is, self-control and endurance. **156.** And if he does not have these virtues, since there is nothing intermediate between virtue and vice, he will have the vices corresponding to these virtues, for example, softness and lack of self-control. For just as one who is not in good health is sick, so one who does not have self-control and endurance has the corresponding vices, which are absurd to attribute to god. **157.** But if there are things hard for god to abstain from and bear, there are things that can change him for the worse, and which can create a disturbance in him. But if this is so, god is subject to disturbance and change for the worse; therefore, he is destructible. So, if god exists, he is destructible. But not the second, so not the first . . . .

162. Further, if god has all the virtues, he has prudence. If he has prudence, ⟨he has⟩ knowledge of things good, bad, and indifferent. If he has knowledge of these, he knows what things good, bad or indifferent are like. **163.** So, since suffering is one of the indifferent things [according to the Stoics], he knows suffering and what its nature is. If so, he has experienced it. Had he not experienced it, he would have no conception of it. Just as a man who was blind from birth and so had no experience of white and black is not able to have a conception of colour, so god would not be able to have a conception of suffering had he not experienced it. **164.** For when we, having often experienced suffering, are not able to understand clearly the peculiar nature of the pain suffered by those who have gout, nor to draw the proper conclusion from their descriptions, nor to get a consistent story from those who have suffered, since they explain it differently (some describe it as a twisting, others as a bending, others as a stabbing), how could god, who is totally free from suffering, be able to have a conception of it?

165. Yes, by Zeus! they say; god has not experienced suffering, but rather only pleasure, and from this he derives a conception of the opposite.

But this is silly. For first, not having experienced suffering, he is powerless to have a conception of pleasure. For it is because of the elimination of everything that is painful that pleasure naturally arises. **166.** Further, granting this, it will once again follow that god is destructible. For if god is subject to such rapture, he will be subject to change for the worse, and is therefore destructible. But if this is not so, neither is the supposition upon which it is based. . . .

182. Such then is the character of these arguments. There are some 'sorites' arguments put forward by Carneades, which his follower Clitomachus recorded as being most serious and effective, and which have this form: if Zeus is a god, Poseidon is a god too:[41]

> We are three brothers, children of Kronos and Rhea,
> Zeus and myself, and thirdly, Hades, lord of the shades,
> All things are divided into three, each with his share of honour.

183. So, if Zeus is a god, Poseidon his brother will be a god; and if Poseidon is a god, Achelous will be a god; and if Achelous, Neilos, and if Neilos, every river, and if every river, the streams would be gods, and if the streams, the mountain run-offs. But the streams are not gods; therefore, neither is Zeus. But if there were gods, Zeus would be a god. Therefore, the gods do not exist. . . .

191. Such are the opposing arguments of dogmatic philosophers to prove that gods exist and to establish that such a thing does not exist. In consequence, the suspension of judgement of the sceptic is introduced, especially so when we add to these arguments the inconsistencies that arise in everyday life about gods. 192. For different people have different and inconsistent suppositions about these matters, so that, because of this conflict, neither are all of them trustworthy nor are some, because of their equal force. This is confirmed by the myth-making of the theologians and poets, for it is full of impiety. . . .

Sextus *PH* 3.13–29 [III-44]

Ch. iv On Cause

13. In order that the dogmatists should not turn to slander against us because of a poverty of substantive counter-arguments, we shall consider in a more general way the efficient cause after first attempting to understand the conception of cause. As far as concerns what is said by the

41. *Iliad* 15.187–9.

dogmatists, it would not be possible for someone to conceive of the cause, if, at any rate, account is taken of their disagreements and strange conceptions of the cause, but also given that they have made its existence undiscoverable because of their disagreement regarding it. **14.** For some say that the cause is a body and some say it is incorporeal. Generally, according to them, the cause would seem to be that because of whose activity the effect comes about, for example, the sun or the sun's heat is the cause of the fact that the wax melts or of the melting of the wax. And even on this they have disagreed, some saying the cause is the cause of nouns, for example, 'the melting'; others saying that the cause is cause of predicates, for example, 'the wax melts'. Therefore, as I just said, generally, the cause would be that because of whose activity the effect comes about.

15. The majority of them think that some of these causes are sustaining, some joint causes, and some auxiliary. Sustaining causes are those whose presence makes the effect present, whose absence brings about the absence of the effect and whose diminution diminishes the effect (thus they say that the binding of the halter is the cause of the strangulation); a joint cause is one which brings to bear a force equal to that of another joint cause for the effect's existence (thus, they say that each of the oxen drawing the plow is a cause of the plow's being drawn); an auxiliary cause is one which brings to bear a little force and so makes easy the existence of the effect, for example, whenever two men are lifting a heavy load with difficulty, when a third comes along, his assistance lightens the load.

16. Some, however, have said that things present are causes of things future, so as to be antecedents, for example, intensive exposure to the sun producing fever. Some reject this, since cause is relative to something [presently] existing, that is, to the effect and is not able to precede it as its cause.

We say the following about these problems.

Ch. v Does Anything Cause Anything?

17. That cause exists is plausible. How else could increase, diminution, generation, destruction, change in general, each of the physical and psychical effects, the disposition of the whole cosmos, and all other things come about, if not according to some cause? If none of these exists by nature, we will say at least that there is a cause of their appearing to us other than as they really are. **18.** Moreover, if cause did not exist then everything would come from everything at random. For example, horses could have come from flies, or elephants from ants; and there would be severe rains and snow in Egyptian Thebes, while in the south there would be no rain, if there were no cause of the storminess in the south and the dryness in the east. **19.** Furthermore, he who says that there is no cause is himself overturned; for if he says that he says this simply and without any cause, he will not be believed, but if he says that he says it because of some cause, then by wanting to abolish the cause he posits ⟨a cause⟩, by giving a cause for there being no cause.

The existence of cause is plausible, then, for these reasons. **20.** That it is also plausible to say that there is no cause of anything will be clear when we have set forth for the present a few of the many arguments used in support of this. For example, it is impossible to conceive of a cause before grasping the effect *as* its effect; for we only understand that one thing is the cause of the effect whenever we grasp the other as the effect. **21.** But we are unable to grasp the effect of the cause as its effect if we do not grasp the cause of the effect as its cause; for we think we understand that something is an effect whenever we grasp the cause of it as its cause. **22.** If, therefore, in order that we may conceive the cause, we have to have previously understood the effect, and in order to understand the effect, as I said, we have to have previously known the cause, the circular mode for producing doubt reveals both [cause and effect] as inconceivable, it being impossible either to conceive of the cause as cause or of the effect as effect. For since each needs confirmation from the other, we will not have a starting point for the conception. Therefore, we will not be able to assert that anything is the cause of anything.

23. In case someone were to admit that the cause is able to be conceived, it would be believed to be ungraspable because of disagreement. For whoever says that something is the cause of something else, either says that he says this simply, being motivated by no reasonable cause, or he will say that he is led to this assent because of some cause. If he says this simply, he will be no more believable than will one who says simply that there is no cause of anything. If he says that there are causes owing to which he believes that something is the cause of something else, he will be attempting to establish what is under investigation with the help of what is under investigation. For when we investigate whether something is the cause of something, he says that the cause exists, since there is a cause of the cause's existence. **24.** Further, since we are investigating the existence of the cause, he will certainly have to provide the cause of the cause of the existence of some cause, and so on, infinitely. But it is impossible to provide infinite causes. Therefore, it is impossible to pronounce definitely that something is the cause of something else.

25. Further, the cause either already is and exists as a cause when it produces the effect, or it is not a cause. Surely, the latter is not the case. If the former is the case, it must have first existed and previously have become a cause and then brought forth the effect which is said to be produced by it, it already being a cause. But since cause and effect are relative, clearly it is not able to pre-exist as cause, nor can the cause, as a cause, produce that of which it is the cause. **26.** If neither being nor not being a cause, can it produce anything, it produces nothing. Therefore, it will not be a cause. For without producing something, the cause cannot be conceived of as a cause.

Hence, some people say the following. The cause must either exist simultaneously with the effect or pre-exist it or exist after the effect occurs. To say that the cause comes to exist after the occurrence of its effect would be ridiculous. **27.** But neither is it able to exist before the effect, for it is said to be conceived of in relation to the effect, and they themselves say that relatives, insofar as they are relative, co-exist and are conceived of in relation to each other. But the cause cannot co-exist with the effect either; for if it is productive of the effect and if it is necessary for that which comes about to be the result of something already existing, the cause must have previously become a cause, and then have produced its effect. Then, if the cause neither exists before its effect nor co-exists with it, nor does ⟨the effect⟩ come about before the cause, it [the cause] has altogether no part in existence.

28. It is perhaps clear on the basis of these arguments that the conception of cause is again overturned. For if the cause, as a relative, cannot be conceived of before its effect, yet in order to be conceived as cause of its effect it must be conceived before its effect, and if it is impossible to conceive of something before that before which it cannot be conceived, then it is impossible to conceive of the cause.

29. From these arguments it remains for us to argue that if the reasons we give for affirming the cause are plausible, and if it is also the case that the reasons we set beside these for holding that it is not appropriate to declare that there is a cause are also plausible, and if it is not possible to prefer one set of reasons to the other, having neither a sign nor a criterion nor a demonstration we can agree upon, as we showed before, then it is necessary to suspend judgement about the existence of the cause, saying that a particular cause no more exists than does not, at least as far as what is said by the dogmatists is concerned.

Sextus *M* 9.218–226   [III-45]

218. . . . . Aenesidemus used the problems about becoming for a superior version of them [the arguments against causality]. **219.** For [on his version] body would not be the cause of body since a body that would be the cause would be either ungenerable, like the atom of Epicurus, or generable, like a man, and either visible, like iron or fire, or invisible, like the atom. But whichever one of these it would be, it would not be able to produce any effect. **220.** For it produces something else [the effect] either while it remains by itself or when it it joined with another thing. But while remaining by itself, it would not be able to produce an effect in something other than itself and its own nature; and when joining with another thing, it would not be able to produce some third thing which was not previously in existence. For neither is one thing able to become two nor are two able to produce a third. **221.** For if one thing were able to become two, each of the things which have become, being one, would produce two, and of the four that have [now] come to be, each of these, being one, would produce two, and similarly for each of the eight that have [now] come to be, and so on to infinity. But it is completely absurd to hold that from one thing an infinite number of things should come to be and therefore it is absurd to hold that from one thing more [than one] should come to be.

222. The same [objections] hold if someone should think that more are produced from less by conjunction. For if one joining with one causes a third thing to be, the third added to the two will produce a fourth, and the fourth added to the three will produce a fifth, and so on to infinity. Therefore, body is not the cause of body.

223. Further, for the same reasons, the non-bodily is not the cause of the non-bodily. For nothing more can come to be from one or from more than one. Furthermore, that which is non-bodily, being an intangible nature, is not able to produce or experience anything. **224.** So, the non-bodily is not able to be productive of the non-bodily. And in this way the opposite is also not possible, namely, that a body be productive of the non-bodily or the non-bodily of a body. For the body does not have in it the nature of the non-bodily nor did the non-bodily contain the nature of the body. Therefore, neither is able to be constituted out of the other. **225.** But just as a horse does not come to be from a plane-tree owing to the fact that the nature of the horse is not in the plane-tree, nor is a man able to come to be from a horse owing to the fact that the nature of man is not in a horse, so the non-bodily will never come to be from a body owing to the fact that the body does not contain the nature of the non-bodily; nor, conversely, will a body ever come to be from the non-bodily. **226.** Yet even if the one does exist in the other, still one will not come to be from the other. For if each has being, it will not come to be from the other, but is already in existence, and since it is already in existence, it will not come to be owing to the fact that coming to be is a process leading to existence. Therefore, neither is a body the cause of the non-bodily nor is the non-bodily the cause of a body, from which it follows that nothing is a cause.

Sextus *PH* 3.63–81   [III-46]

Ch. ix On Motion

63. In addition to what has been previously said, we might turn our attention to the argument regarding motions; this too would make it impossible for the physical doctrine of the dogmatists to be accepted. For it certainly ought to be the case that compounds come about on the basis of some motion of their elements and their efficient principle. If, therefore, we suggest that no type of motion is agreed upon, it will be clear that, even if, for the sake of hypothesis, everything previously mentioned is granted, the so-called physical doctrine of the dogmatists has been elaborated in vain.

Ch. x On Locomotion

64. Now those who seem to have delineated motion more fully say that there exist six types: motion in place, qualitative change, increase, diminution, generation, and destruction. Therefore, we shall turn our attention to each one of the above-mentioned types of motion, beginning with locomotion. This motion, then, according to the dogmatists, is that whereby that which is moved goes from one place to another, either wholly or partly, wholly, as when one walks about, and partly as in the motion of a sphere around its axis, for here the whole stays in the same place, but the parts change places.

65. The chief positions regarding motion have been, I believe, three. Ordinary people and some philosophers suppose that motion exists whereas Parmenides, Melissus, and some others suppose that it does not. The sceptics have said that motion no more is than is not, for judging by appearances, motion seems to exist, but judging by philosophical argument, it does not. Therefore, when we have laid out the opposition between those who suppose motion to exist and those who proclaim that motion is nothing, if we discover that the disagreement is [between arguments with] equal force, we shall be compelled to say, at least so far as these arguments go, that motion no more is than is not. 66. We shall begin with those who say that it exists.

These are supported by the obviousness of the matter. For if, they say, motion does not exist, how does the sun move from east to west, and how does it produce the seasons of the year which arise from its coming close to us and then receding? Or how do ships leave harbours and arrive at other harbours very far away from where they started? And how will he who abolishes motion leave from and return to his house? These considerations are perfectly unopposable. For this reason, when one of the Cynics [Diogenes] had an argument against motion put to him, he did not answer but rather got up and walked around, and so by deed and because of the obviousness of it all, averred that motion can exist.

Thus, these men attempt to put to shame those who hold the opposite position. 67. But those who abolish the existence of motion attempt to use these arguments. If something is moved, either it is moved by itself or by another. But if it is moved by another, since that which moves is active, and that which is active is moved, the mover will be in need of another mover, and the second in need of a third, until infinity, so that motion would be without an origin, which is absurd. Therefore, it is not the case that everything that is moved is moved by another. But neither is it moved by itself. 68. For that which is said to be moved by itself will either be moved causelessly or by some cause. ⟨But⟩ they say that nothing is moved causelessly; and if it is moved by some cause, the cause by which it is moved will become its mover, whereby one falls into an infinite regress, according to the criticism made a short while ago;[42] now, since everything that moves moves either by pushing or pulling or lifting or dragging down, that which moves itself will have to move itself according to one of the above-mentioned ways. 69. But if it moves itself by pushing, it will be behind itself; if it moves itself by pulling it will be in front of itself; if it moves itself by lifting it will be under itself; and if it moves by dragging down, it will be above itself. But it is impossible for something to be above, in front of, under, or behind itself. Therefore, it is impossible for something to be moved by itself. And if something is neither moved by itself nor by something else, then nothing is moved.

70. If someone should take refuge in [the notions of] impulse and choice, one ought to remind him of the disagreement regarding the phrase 'in our power' and that the matter remains undecided, since a criterion of the truth has up until now not been discovered by us.

71. Further, this should be said. If something is moved, either it is moved in the place in which it is or it is moved in the place in which it is not. But it is not moved in the place in which it is. For if it is in a place in which it is, it remains where it is. But it is not moved in the place in which it is not either. For wherever something is not, it cannot there do or suffer anything. Therefore, it is not the case that something is moved. This is the argument of Diodorus Cronos, which has encountered many opposing arguments, only the most powerful of which we shall set

42. III-44 (24).

forth, because of the nature of this treatise, along with what appears to us to be the [proper] judgement on them.

72. Some say then that something can be moved in the place in which it is. At least, spheres revolving around their axes can be moved while remaining in the same place. In response to these, it is necessary to transfer the argument to each of the parts of the sphere, and recalling that as far as the argument goes, it is not moved even according to its parts, to infer that something is not moved in the place in which it is. **73.** We will make the same judgement against those who say that that which is moved has a hold on [or: is in contact with] two places, the one in which it is and the one into which it is carried. For we shall inquire of them when is that which is moved carried from the place in which it is into the other; is it when it is in the first place or when it is in the second? But when it is in the first place, it is not yet passing into the second, for it is still in the first. But when it is not in the first, it is not passing from it. **74.** In addition, the very matter under investigation has been seized upon as settled. For in the place in which it is not, it is not able to act. For certainly someone will not grant that that which he does not concede is moving at all is being carried into some place.

75. Some, however, say this. 'Place' has two senses, one loose, for example, referring to my house, and one strict, for example, the air pressing the surface of my body. Thus, it is said that that which is moved is moved in a place, but not in the strict sense of 'place' but in the loose sense.

Against these, it can be said, subdividing place in the loose sense, that one part of it is just the place in which the aforementioned moving body properly is, i.e., its own place in the strict sense; and the other part is where it is not, that is, the rest of the 'place' in the loose sense. Then we infer that neither can something be moved in the place in which it is nor in the place in which it is not, reasoning that something cannot be moved in the misapplied loose sense of 'place'. For this is just made up of the strict sense plus the place where something is not in the strict sense, and it has been shown that in neither of these can something be moved.

76. Further, this argument should be offered. If something is moved, either it is moved progressively or all at once into a divisible interval. But something cannot be moved either progressively or all at once into the divisible interval, as I shall show. Therefore, it is not the case that something is moved.

That it is not then possible for something to be moved progressively is self-evident. For if bodies and the places and times in which they are said to be moved are divided infinitely, motion will not occur, it being impossible to discover a first point among the infinite [divisions], starting from which that which is said to be moved will move. 77. If the above mentioned [continua] are postulated as having indivisible parts, and each of the things in motion passes through the first spatial indivisible part in an indivisible moment of time with its own first indivisible part, then all things in motion are moved at the same speed, for example, the fastest horse and the tortoise. And this is even more absurd than the previous alternative. Therefore, motion does not occur progressively.

But neither does it occur all at once into a divisible interval. 78. For if, as they say, it is necessary for appearances to testify to non-evident things, then for someone to complete an interval of one stade, it is necessary for him first to complete the first part of the stade, and second, to complete the second part, and so on. So, it is reasonable to suppose all things in motion [actually] move progressively, since, surely if that which is moved were said to proceed all at once through all the parts of the place in which it is said to be moved, it will simultaneously be in all these parts, and if one of these parts through which it moves is cold, and one hot, or perhaps, one dark and one light, so that they colour whatever comes into contact with them, that which is moved will be simultaneously hot and cold, dark and light. But this is absurd. 79. Next, let them tell us how big a place that which is moved has passed through all at once. For if they will say that the quantity is indefinite, they will [thereby] allow that something is moved across the entire earth all at once. If they [want to] avoid the conclusion, let them define for us the extent of the place [through which it moves]. For to attempt to define accurately [the extent of] the place through which that which is moved can pass through all at once so that it could not pass through even a little more is, in addition to being arbitrary, rash, or perhaps even ridiculous; and besides [it] lands us back in the original problem. For everything will move at equal speed, at least if each of them carries out its locomotion in similar fashion through places which are defined. 80. But if they should say that that which moves totally through a small place, but one which is not accurately defined, it will be possible for us, using the sorites argument, always to add a little extent of place to that which is hypothesized. For if they will call a halt at any point while we are making this argument, they will once again fall back on their bluff about an 'accurate definition'. But if they allow the gradual increase, we shall compel them to grant that something can be moved all at once through the extent of the entire earth. So, neither is it the case that the things said to be moved are moved all at once ⟨into⟩ a divisible interval. 81. And if something is moved neither all at once into a divisible place nor progressively, it is not the case that something is moved.

These arguments, then, and even additional ones, are offered by those who abolish locomotion. We, however, are able neither to reject their arguments nor the appearance followed by those who introduce the hypothesis of motion, and so, at least as far as the opposition of appearances and arguments is concerned, we suspend judgement regarding whether motion exists or not.

Sextus *PH* 3.119–150   [III-47]

Ch. xviii On Place

119. 'Place' is used in two senses, a proper sense and a loose sense; the loose sense is broad as in '[the place that is] my city' whereas the proper sense refers to [the place] that exactly contains, by which we are exactly surrounded. We are, then, investigating place understood as that which exactly contains. Some have posited this sense; some have abolished it, and some have suspended judgement regarding it. 120. Of these, the ones who say that it exists take refuge in the fact that it is obvious. For, they say, who will say that place [in the principal sense] does not exist, when he sees its parts: for example, right and left, up and down, before and behind; and when he is in different places at different times; and when he sees that I am now discoursing where my teacher used to discourse; and when he grasps that the natural place of light things is different from that of heavy things; 121. and, moreover, when he is hears that the ancients said, "Surely, Chaos came first into being"[43] (for they say that place is [called] chaos from the fact that it provides space[44] for that which comes to be in it). Moreover, at least if body exists, they say, place will exist. For without place there could be no body. And if there exists the 'by which' and 'from which' there exists the 'in which', which is place. But in each case the first; therefore, in both cases, the second.

122. But those who abolish place do not concede that place has parts, for place is nothing besides its parts, and the attempted inference that place exists, on the assumption that its parts exist, amounts to trying to establish the matter under investigation by means of itself. Similarly, those who say that something comes to be or has come to be in some place are talking foolishly, when [the existence of] place has not at all been conceded. They also seize upon the fact that the existence of body has not been conceded in the first instance, and the 'from which' and 'by which' are shown to be non-existent much as place is. 123. Further, Hesiod is not a worthy judge of philosophical matters. And so having eliminated the considerations on behalf of the establishment of the exis-

---

43. Hesiod *Theogony* 118.
44. There is a word play on *chora* (space) and chaos.

tence of place, they proceed themselves to establish in a variety of ways that place is non-existent, availing themselves of what appear to be the weightiest positions among the dogmatists regarding place, those of the Stoics and Peripatetics, in this way.

124. The Stoics say that void is that which is not occupied by a thing which is, but is such as to be occupied; or an interval empty of a body; or an interval unoccupied by a body; and that place is an interval occupied by a thing which is and coextensive with that which occupies it, calling body a thing which is; space is an interval partly occupied by body and partly not, although some say that space is the place of a large body, as though the difference between place and space were one of magnitude. **125.** It is said, then, that since they say that place is an interval occupied by a body, how do they define 'interval'? Do they mean only the length of the body or the breadth or the depth, or all three dimensions? If they mean only one of these dimensions, then the place is not coextensive with that of which it is the place, and besides, that which surrounds is then part of that which is surrounded, which is altogether absurd. **126.** If, however, ['interval' means] all three dimensions, since neither a void nor any other body having a dimension is assumed to be in that which is called 'place,' but what is said to be in a place is only the body which is composed of the dimensions (for these are length, breadth, depth) and resistance, (which is said to be an accident of the three aforementioned dimensions), then the body itself will be its own place, and the same thing will be surrounding and surrounded, which is absurd. Therefore, there is no dimension of place as an underlying subject. **127.** For this reason, it is not the case that place is something.

Further, this argument is advanced. Since the dimensions for each of the [bodies] said to be in a place are not understood to be duplicated, but rather length, breadth, and depth are each one, are these dimensions of the body alone or of the place alone, or both? If they are only of the place, the body will not have its own length, breadth, and depth, so that the body will not be a body, which is absurd. **128.** If they are of both, since the void has no existence apart from the dimensions, if the dimensions of the void are assumed to exist in the body, and are constituents of the body itself, then the constitutents of the void will be what constitutes the body. For, regarding the existence of resistance, it is not possible to make a definite assertion, as we have suggested previously.[45] But since only the dimensions appear to be in what is called the body, and these [dimensions] are just those of the void and are the same as the void, then the body will be a void, which is absurd. If, however, they are dimensions of the body alone, there will be no dimensions of the place and therefore

45. *PH* 3.45 ff.

place does not exist either. If, then, the dimension of place is discovered in none of the aforementioned modes, it is not the case that place exists.

129. In addition to these arguments it is said that whenever the body enters the void and place comes to be, either the void remains or it withdraws or is destroyed. But if it remains, the same thing will be both void and full; if it withdraws by locomotion, or is destroyed by changing, the void will be a body. But it is absurd either to say that the same thing is void and body or that the void is a body. Therefore, it is absurd to say that it is possible for the void to be occupied by a body and to become place.

130. For these reasons, the void is found to be non-existent, at least if it is not possible for it to be occcupied by a body and to become place. For that which is such as to be occupied by a body was said to be a void. Further, space is overturned along with place and void. For if a large place is space, it is implicated along with place, and if it is what is partly occupied by a body and is partly an empty interval, it is abolished along with both of these.

These things, then, and even more can be said against the Stoics' position regarding place. 131. The Peripatetics say that place is the limit of that which surrounds insofar as it surrounds, so that my place is the surface of the air pressing on my body. But if this is place, the same thing will and will not be. For when the body is about to be in some place, insofar as nothing can be in that which does not exist, it is necessary for the place to exist already, so that the body could come to be in it, and for this reason the place will exist prior to the body's coming to be in it. But insofar as place is made to be the surface of the air that surrounds pressing on what is surrounded, it cannot exist prior to the body's coming to be in it, for which reason it will not then exist. But it is absurd to say that the same thing is and is not. Therefore, it is not the case that place is the limit of that which surrounds insofar as it surrounds.

132. In addition to these arguments, if place is something, it is either generated or ungenerated. But it is not ungenerated. For, they say, it is made by being pressed around the body within it. But neither is it generated. For if it is generated, then the place in which the thing which is in place is said to be is either generated when the body is in place, or when it is not in it. 133. But it is neither the case that the place comes to be when the body is in it (for the place of the body in it already exists), nor when it is not in it, at least if, as they say, place arises when that which surrounds is pressed around that which is surrounded, since it cannot be pressed around that which is not in it. If place is neither generated when the body is in it nor when it is not in it and it is not

possible to conceive of any other alternatives besides these, place is not generated. And if it is neither generated nor ungenerated, it is nothing.

134. These arguments can be stated more generally. If place is something, either it is a body or it is incorporeal. Each of these is doubtful, as we have suggested. Therefore, place is doubtful. Place is thought to be relative to the body whose place it is. But the argument for the existence of the body is doubtful. Therefore, so is the argument for place. The place of each thing is not everlasting, but if we say that it comes to be, it is found to be non-existent, since coming to be does not exist.

135. It is possible to say many other things, but to avoid prolonging our discussion, the moral of the story is that while the arguments confound the sceptics, the obviousness [of the matter] embarrasses them. Therefore, we should not associate ourselves with either side, as far as concerns the things said by the dogmatists, but rather suspend judgement regarding place.

Ch. xix On Time

136. We have the same impression regarding the investigation of time. For as far as appearances are concerned, time seems to be something, but so far as the things said about it, it appears to be non-existent. Some say that time is the interval of the motion of the whole (by 'whole' I mean the cosmos); some say that it is just the motion of the cosmos; 137. Aristotle (or, as some say, Plato) says that it is the number of before and after in motion; Strato (or, as some say, Aristotle) says that it is the measure of motion and rest; Epicurus says, according to Demetrius of Laconia, that it is a property of properties, following along with days, nights, seasons, states, absences of states, motions, and rests. 138. As to its substance, some said that it is a body, for example, Aenesidemus and his followers, for it does not differ from that which is, i.e., from the first body; and some say that it is incorporeal. So, either all these positions are true or all are false or some are true and some are false. It is not possible that all can be true, for most of them are in conflict with each other, nor will it be granted by the dogmatists that all are false. 139. Moreover, if it is granted that it is false that time is body, and that it is false that time is incorporeal, the non-existence of time will immediately be granted, for there is no third possibility. It is not possible to grasp which views are true and which are false, because of the equal force of the arguments of those who disagree and the doubts about the criterion and demonstration. 140. So, for these reasons, we shall be able to assert nothing definite regarding time.

Further, since time does not seem to exist apart from motion, or even without rest, if motion is abolished, and similarly rest, time is abolished.

Some say that the following arguments too are equally effective against time. If time exists, either it is limited or unlimited. **141.** But if it is limited, at what time did it start and at what time will it end? For this reason there was once a time when time was not, that is, prior to its beginning, and there will be a time when there will be no time, after time has ended, which is absurd. So, time is not limited. **142.** If, however, it is unlimited, then since its parts are said to be past, present, and future, the future and the past either exist or do not exist. But if they do not exist and only the present is left, which is infinitesimal, time will be limited and the original problems will follow. If past and future exist, each of these will be present. But it is absurd to say that past and future time are present. Therefore, time is not unlimited. If time is neither unlimited nor limited, time does not exist at all.

143. In addition to these arguments, if time exists either it is divisible or indivisible. But it is not indivisible for it is divided into present, past, and future, as they themselves say. But it is not divisible either. For each divisible thing is measured by some part of itself, the measure being set alongside each part of the things measured, as when a cubit is measured by the length of a finger. But time cannot be measured by some part of itself. For if we say, for the sake of argument, the present measures the past, it will be set alongside the past and so become past, and similarly will become future [in measuring the future]. And if the future measures present and past, it will be present and past, and similarly the past would become present and future, which is absurd. Therefore, time is not divisible either. And if it is neither indivisible nor divisible, it does not exist.

144. Time is said to be tripartite: past, present, and future. Of these, past and future do not exist. For if past and future time exist now, each of them will be present. But the present does not exist either. For if the present exists, either it is indivisible or divisible. But it is not indivisible, since things that change are said to change in the present, but nothing changes in an indivisible time, for example, iron softening, or anything else. So, the present time is not indivisible. **145.** But it is not divisible either. For it could not be divided into present parts, since the present is said to change unnoticed into the past because of the rapid flow of events in the cosmos. Nor could it be divided into past and future, for then it will be non-existent, having one part which is no longer and one part which is not yet. For this reason, the present also cannot be the end of the past and the beginning of the future, since it will then exist and will not exist. It will exist as present, but will not exist, since its parts do not exist. Therefore, it is not divisible either. And if the present is neither divisible nor indivisible, it does not exist. And if neither the present exists nor the past nor the future, time is nothing, for that which is comprised of non-existents is itself non-existent.

147. This argument is also used against time. If time exists either it is generable and destructible or ungenerable and indestructible. But it is not ungenerable and indestructible, at least if the past is said to exist no longer and the future not yet to exist. 148. But it is not generable and destructible either. For things that are generated must come to be from something existing, and things that are destroyed must be destroyed into something existing, according to the hypotheses of the dogmatists themselves. If, therefore, time is destroyed into the past, it is destroyed into something which does not exist; and if it is generated from the future, it is generated from that which does not exist, for neither the past nor future exist. But it is absurd to say that something is generated from that which does not exist or is destroyed into something which does not exist. Therefore, time is neither generable nor destructible. And if it is neither ungenerable and indestructible nor generable and destructible, it does not exist at all.

149. In addition to these arguments, since everything that comes to be seems to be generated in time, if time comes to be, it is generated in time. So, it comes to be either in itself or each comes to be in another time. But if it comes to be in itself, the same thing will exist and will not exist. For since that in which something comes to be ought to exist prior to that which comes to be in it, time, insofar as it comes to be, is not yet, but insofar as it comes to be in itself, is already. 150. So, it does not come to be in itself. But neither does one time come to be in another time. For if the present comes to be in the future, the present will be the future, and if it comes to be in the past, it will be the past. The same points ought to be made about the other times [viz., past and future]. So, one time does not come to be in another time. If time comes to be neither in itself nor each time in another time, then time is not generable. And it has already been shown that it is not ungenerable. So, since it is neither generable nor ungenerable, it does not exist at all, for each thing which exists should be either generable or ungenerable.

Ethics

Sextus *PH* 3.168–197 [III-48]

Ch. xxi On the Ethical Part of Philosophy

168. There remains the ethical part of philosophy, which seems to be concerned with the discernment of things good and bad and indifferent.

In order that we may discuss ethics summarily, we shall investigate the existence of things good, bad, and indifferent, first setting forth the conception of each.

Ch. xxii On Things Good, Bad, and Indifferent

169. The Stoics say that good is 'benefit' or 'not other than benefit' meaning by a 'benefit' virtue and virtuous action, and by 'not other than benefit' the virtuous man and the friend. For 'virtue,' being the leading part of the soul in a certain state, and 'virtuous action', being a certain activity according to virtue, are exactly 'benefit', while the virtuous man and the friend are 'not other than benefit.' 170. For a benefit is a part of the virtuous man, that is, the leading part of his soul. But, they say, the wholes are not the same as their parts, for a man is not his hand, nor are they other than their parts, for they do not exist without the parts. Therefore, they say that wholes are not other than their parts. For this reason, the excellent man, being a whole in relation to his leading part (which they have said is benefit) is not other than benefit.

171. They go on to say that 'good' is spoken of in three ways. In one sense, they say 'good' is that by which something is benefitted, which is the principal sense [of good] and is virtue; in another sense it is that in accordance with which being benefitted is a characteristic result, as virtue and virtuous actions; in the third sense it is that which is such as to benefit, and this is virtue and virtuous action and the excellent man, and the friend, and gods and excellent daimons; so the second meaning of 'good' includes the first and the third includes the second and first. 172. Some say that 'good' is that which is worth choosing for its own sake; others say it is that which contributes to happiness or fulfils it. And happiness is, as the Stoics say, a 'smooth flow of life'.

Now these are the sort of things said about the conception of the good.

Ch. xxii On Things Good, Bad and Indifferent

173. If someone holds that the good is what benefits or what is worth choosing for its own sake or that which is a co-contributor to happiness, he does not offer a definition of 'good,' but rather one of its accidents; and this is pointless. For either the above-mentioned accidents belong to the good alone or also to other things. But if they do belong to other things, they are not unique characteristics of the good, since they are generalized; whereas, if they belong uniquely to the good it is not possible for us to understand from them what the good is. 174. For just as someone who has no conception of a horse does not know what neighing is, nor is able to arrive at a conception of a horse by means of [this] if he has not previously happened upon a neighing horse, so one who is seeking

to know what the good is because he does not know what it is, is not able to know what belongs to it peculiarly and uniquely, so that he might be able to understand through this the good itself. For it is necessary to have learned previously the nature of the good itself, and then to go on to understand the fact that it benefits or that it is worth choosing for its own sake and that it is instrumental to happiness. **175.** That the above-mentioned accidents are not adequate to reveal the conception and the nature of the good, the dogmatists themselves make evident in practice. For perhaps everyone admits that the good benefits, that it is worth choosing for its own sake (which is why the good is called, in a way, wonderful) and that it is instrumental to happiness. But when they are asked what is that to which these accidents belong, they fall into an irreconcilable battle, some saying that it is virtue, others that it is pleasure, others that it is absence of pain, and others something else. But if what good itself is were manifested on the basis of the above-mentioned defini-tions, they would not have quarrelled as if its nature were unknown.

176. In this way, therefore, the seemingly outstanding dogmatists differ regarding the conception of the good. They similarly differ regarding that which is bad, some saying that bad is 'harm or not other than harm'; some saying that it is 'what is worth avoiding for its own sake'; some saying that it is 'what is instrumental to unhappiness'. Therefore, perhaps because they are speaking about certain accidents of bad and not its substance, they fall into the abovementioned doubt.

177. They say that that which is indifferent is spoken of in three ways. In one sense, it is that neither towards which nor away from which an impulse arises, for instance, the question of whether the number of stars or the number of hairs on one's head is even. In another sense it is that towards or away from which an impulse arises, but not more towards this rather than that, for example, two indistinguishable four-drachma coins, whenever one has to choose one of them. For an impulse to choosing one of them does indeed arise, but no more towards this one than that one. In the third sense they say that 'indifferent' is what contributes neither to happiness nor unhappiness, as health or wealth. For that which is sometimes used well and sometimes badly is, they say, indifferent. They say that they discuss especially this sense of 'indifferent' in ethics. **178.** What should be thought about this conception is evident from what we said about things good and bad.

It is thus clear that they have not acquainted us with the conception of each of the above-mentioned, although perhaps in blundering about in non-existent things, they have experienced nothing surprising. For some people argue that nothing is by nature good, bad, or indifferent in the following way.

Ch. xxiii Is Anything Good, Bad, or Indifferent by Nature?

179. Fire, which by nature is hot, appears to everyone as capable of producing heat, and snow, which is by nature cold, appears to everyone as capable of producing cold, and everything which moves something in virtue of its nature moves all people who are in a natural condition in the same way, as they say. But, as we shall suggest, none of the things said to be good move all men as a good. Therefore, there is nothing good by nature. Now they say it is evident that none of the things said to be good moves all men in the same way. 180. For leaving aside ordinary people, some of whom believe that a sound bodily condition is good, others fornication, others gluttony, others drunkenness, others gambling, others greed, and others even worse things, some philosophers themselves, like the Peripatetics, say that there are three kinds of goods, those of the soul, such as the virtues, bodily [goods], such as health and the like, and external [goods], such as friends, wealth and related things. 181. The Stoics themselves also say that there is a triad of goods: those in the soul, such as the virtues; external, such as the virtuous man and the friend; and some that are neither in the soul nor external, such as the virtuous man in relation to himself. But the bodily things said to be good by the Peripatetics, they say are not good. Some [philosophers] have accepted pleasure as good, some say that this is exactly what the bad is, so that one philosopher [Antisthenes] even cried out "I would rather be mad than experience pleasure".

182. If, then, the things that move something in virtue of their nature move all men similarly, and we are not all similarly moved by the things said to be good, there is nothing good by nature. For because of the conflict among the abovementioned positions, it is not possible to have confidence in all or any of them. For he who says that one ought to have confidence in this position and not at all in that one, becomes a partisan in the disagreement, since he is holding a position to which there are opposing positions among the dogmatists and, for this reason, he himself will be in no position to judge the truth of the other positions, but will himself, along with the others, be in need of one who can judge the truth. So, since there is no agreed upon criterion or demonstration, because of the undecided disagreement regarding these matters, he will arrive at the suspension of judgement, and for this reason, will not be able to assert definitely what is good by nature.

183. Further, some say that good is either choosing itself or that which we choose. Choosing, then, is not good according to the proper sense of the term, for we would not be hastening to get that which we choose,

lest we should exclude ourselves from choosing it further. For example, if it were good to exert ourselves to get a drink, we would not hasten to get the drink, for when we enjoy the drink we leave off exerting ourselves to get it. And the situation is similar for hunger and sexual desire and the rest. Therefore, choosing is not worth choosing for its own sake, even if it is not annoying. For he who hungers hastens to partake of food, in order that he might eliminate the annoyance of the hunger, and similarly for sexual desire and drink.

184. But neither is that which is worth choosing the good. For this is either external to us or in us. But if it is external to us, either it produces in us a virtuous motion, a desirable stable state, and a delightful condition, or it does not affect us at all. And if it is not delightful to us, it will neither be good nor will it impel us to choose it nor will it be worth choosing at all. But if there arises in us from something external a pleasant stable state, and an enjoyable condition, the external is not worth choosing for its own sake, but for the disposition in us that arises when it is present. 185. So, that which is worth choosing for its own sake cannot be external to us. But it cannot be in us either. For [in this case] it is said to pertain to the body alone or the soul alone or to both. But if it pertains to the body alone, it escapes our awareness, for acts of awareness are said to be in the soul, whereas they say that the body is considered non-rational in itself. But if it should be said that [the good] also reaches the soul, it would seem to be worth choosing because of a grasp by the soul and a delightful condition. For that which has been judged to be worth choosing is judged by the intellect, according to them, and not by a non-rational body.

186. The remaining alternative is that the good pertains to the soul alone. But this is impossible judging from what the dogmatists say. For the soul is perhaps non-existent. But if it exists, then as far as what they say about it is concerned, it is not grasped, as I argued in the section dealing with the criterion.[46] How would someone be so bold as to say that something comes to be in that which is not grasped? 187. In order that we may pass over these matters, how, then, do they say that the good comes to be in a soul? Indeed, if Epicurus posits pleasure as the goal and says that the soul, like everything else, is composed of atoms, how pleasure can arise in a heap of atoms and assent or judgement that this is worth choosing and good and that is worth avoiding and bad, is impossible to say.

46. *PH* 2.31–33.

Ch. xxiv What is the So-Called Craft of Living?

188. Again, the Stoics say that the goods of the soul are certain crafts, namely, the virtues. They say that a craft is a complex system of grasps practiced together, and that the grasps arise in the leading part of the soul. How, then, there arises in the leading part of the soul which is, according to them, *pneuma*, a deposit of grasps and how an aggregate of so many things becomes a craft, it is not possible to conceive, when each subsequent impression replaces the one before it, since the *pneuma* is fluid and is said to be moved totally with each impression. **189.** And it is perfect nonsense to say that Plato's imaginary construction [of the soul] (I mean the mixture of the undivided and divided substance, and of the nature of difference and sameness[47] or numbers), is capable of receiving the good. Hence, the good cannot be in the soul either. **190.** If, then, the good is not the choosing itself, and if what is worth choosing for its own sake is not an external object, and if it is neither nor bodily nor in the soul, as I have argued, there is altogether nothing good by nature.

For the abovementioned reasons, there is nothing bad by nature either. For things that seem to be bad to some are pursued as good by others, for example, lewdness, injustice, greed, lack of self-control, and the like. Hence, if things [which exist] by nature naturally move all men in the same way, there is nothing by nature bad.

191. Similarly, there is nothing by nature indifferent, because of the disagreement about things indifferent. For example, the Stoics say that of indifferents some are preferred, some rejected, and some neither preferred nor rejected. Things preferred are those having sufficient value, such as health and wealth. Things rejected are those not having sufficient value such as poverty and sickness. Things neither preferred nor rejected are such things as extending or bending the finger. **192.** Some say that none of the things indifferent are by nature preferred or rejected, for each of the things indifferent sometimes appears to be preferred, sometimes rejected, depending on different circumstances. Indeed, if, they say, the wealthy are attacked by a tyrant while the poor are left in peace, everyone would choose to be poor rather than wealthy, so that wealth would become something rejected. **193.** So, since each of the things said to indifferent is said by some to be good and others bad, and everyone would have similarly believed the same thing to be indifferent, if it really were indifferent by nature, there is nothing indifferent by nature.

And so, if someone should say that courage is worth choosing because

47. *Timaeus* 35 ff.

lions seem to be naturally daring and courageous, and bulls, perhaps, and some men and cocks, we say that as far as this is concerned cowardice is by nature among the things worth choosing, since deer and rabbits and many other animals have a natural impulse to it. And the majority of men are observed to be cowardly. For rarely has someone sacrificed himself for his country or has otherwise seemed inspired to do something impetuous; on the contrary, the majority of men seem to avoid all such deeds.

194. Hence, the Epicureans believe that they show that pleasure is by nature worth choosing, for they say that as soon as animals are born, being uncorrupted, they have an impulse to pleasure and avoid pain. **195.** In reply to them one can say that that which is instrumental to the bad could not be by nature good. And, of course, pleasure is instrumental to bad things. For to every pleasure pain is fastened, and pain is, according to them, bad by nature. For example, the drunkard experiences pleasure when he is swilling wine, the gourmand when he is gorging himself, and the fornicator when he is engaged in unbridled sexual encounters. But these activities are instrumental to impoverishment and diseases which are painful and bad, as they say. Therefore, pleasure is not good by nature. **196.** In a related way, that which is instrumental to good things is not by nature bad, and pains produce pleasure. For we acquire knowledge by painfully exerting ourselves and that is also how we acquire wealth and the object of our sexual desire, and painful treatments lead to health. Therefore, painful exertion is not by nature bad. For if pleasure were by nature good and painful exertion bad, everyone would be similarly disposed in regard to them, as we said. But in fact we observe many philosophers choosing painful exertion and endurance, and disdaining pleasure.

197. Similarly, those who say that a life containing virtue is by nature good, are overturned by the fact that some wise men choose a life containing pleasure, so that their claim that this or that is by nature [good] is confuted by the disagreement among themselves.

Sextus *PH* 3.239–249 [III-49]

Ch. xxv Does There Exist a Craft of Living?

239. It is evident from what has been said that there also could not be a craft of living. For if there is such a craft, then it is a craft of contemplating things good and bad and indifferent; and since these are non-existent, the craft of living is non-existent. Moreover, since the dogmatists do not all agree in locating the craft of living in one thing, but some hypothesize one craft, some another, they stand accused of disagreeing, and are held to account by the argument from disagreement, which I expounded previously in what I said about the good. **240.** But even if, for the sake of hypothesis, they were to say that the craft of living is one craft, for example, the notorious craft of "prudence," which is fantasized about by the Stoics, and seems more impressive than the rest, still no less absurd consequences follow. For since prudence is a virtue, and only the wise man has virtue, the Stoics, not being wise men, will not possess the craft of living. **241.** And, in general, since according to them it is not possible that any craft exists, there will not be a craft of living, as far as what they say is concerned.

For example, they say that a craft is a complex of grasps and a grasping is an assent to a graspable presentation. But the graspable presentation is undiscoverable. For not every presentation is graspable, nor is it possible to decide which one from among the presentations is graspable, since we are not able to judge unqualifiedly in the case of every presentation which one is graspable and which one is not. And if we need a graspable presentation to decide what the graspable presentation is, we fall into an infinite regress, since we are asking for another graspable presentation to use in deciding whether a received presentation is graspable. **242.** And, further, the Stoics are not on sure footing in their proposal of the conception of a graspable presentation for the following reasons: on the one hand, they say that the graspable presentation arises from something that exists; on the other hand, by "existing" they mean that which is such as to produce a graspable presentation, and so they stumble into the circular mode for producing an impasse [*aporia*]. If, then, in order for a craft of living to exist there must previously exist a craft, and in order for a craft to exist there must previously exist a grasp, and in order for a grasp to exist, assent to a graspable presentation must be grasped, and the graspable presentation is undiscoverable, the craft of living is undiscoverable.

243. Further, this can be said. Every craft seems to be grasped by means of its peculiar products, but there is no peculiar product of the craft of living. For whatever product someone would say this is, is found to be common to ordinary people also [i.e., those without the craft of living], such as honouring one's parents, paying debts, and all the rest. Therefore, there is no craft of living. For we shall not recognize, as they say, what is a product of prudence from what appears to be something said or done from a prudent disposition by a prudent man. **244.** For the prudent disposition is itself ungraspable, being neither simply apparent by itself nor by its products, these being common to ordinary people. And to say that we grasp that one has the craft of living from the consistency of his actions, is to trumpet human nature and to brag more than to tell the truth for[48]

> The mind of earth-born men is such
> as is the day brought forth by the father of men and gods

245. The remaining possibility is that the craft of living is grasped from those of its products that they write about in books. I shall set forth a few of these as examples of the rest which are many and much alike. Zeno, for example, the head of their school, in his writings concerning the rearing of children, along with many other similar statements, says, "It makes no difference whether you spread the thighs of a beloved youth or one who is unbeloved, a woman or a man, for between beloved youth and unbeloved, women and men, there is no difference, but it befits and is fitting to do the same thing to either." **246.** The same man says, regarding piety towards parents, in the case of Jocasta and Oedipus, that it was not a bad thing for him to have sex with his mother. "If she had been ailing in some other part of her body and he benefitted her by rubbing it with his hands, there would be nothing shameful. So, if he gave her joy by rubbing other parts of her body, and relieved her sorrow, and fathered noble children by her, was that shameful?" Chrysippus agrees with these words. Indeed, in his *Republic* he says, "It seems to me that we should act as many are nowadays accustomed to act blamelessly, so that a mother bears her son's children, a daughter her father's, and a sister her brother's." **247.** In the same works he introduces us to cannibalism. Indeed, he says, "if some part of a living thing is cut off and found to be useful for eating, we should neither bury it nor otherwise dispose of it, but consume it, so that another part might grow from ours." **248.** In his *On Appropriate Actions* he says literally, regarding the burial of one's parents, "When parents die, the simplest burials should be employed, as if the body were nothing to us, like the nails or teeth or hair, the sort of thing which to we give no care or attention. Therefore, should pieces of flesh be useful for eating, men will make use of them, and so too for their own parts, for example, a foot which is severed; it was right to use it and things like it. Should the parts be useless, they should bury or leave them or burn them and let the ashes lie, or throw them away and make no further use of them, like nails or hair." **249.** The philosophers say these and many similar things which they would not dare to carry out unless they were ruled by a Cyclopes or Laestrygones.[49] But if their

48. Homer *Odyssey* 18.136–137.
49. Uncivilized peoples mentioned in the *Odyssey*.

recommendations are totally ineffectual, what they actually do, which is what everybody else does, is not the peculiar product of those who are supposed to have the craft of living. If, then, the crafts ought certainly to be grasped from their peculiar products and there is observed to be no peculiar product of that which is said to be the craft of living, then it is not grasped. Therefore, no one can assert definitely regarding it that such a craft exists.

Sextus *M* 11.96–98   [III-50]

96. But in response to such puzzles some of the Epicureans are accustomed to saying that an animal flees pain and pursues pleasure naturally and without instruction. For when it was just born and was not yet a slave to matters of opinion, just as soon as it was struck by the unfamiliar cold air, "it wept and wailed."[50] And if it has a natural impulse to pleasure and a natural avoidance of painful exertion, then by nature painful exertion is something which it is worth avoiding and pleasure is something naturally worth choosing. 97. Those who respond thus fail to see, first of all, that they are giving even the lowest of animals a share in the good, since they have a great share in pleasure; and next, that painful exertion is not something unqualifiedly worth avoiding. For one painful exertion is alleviated by another, and again the bodies' health, strength and nourishment are produced by painful exertions, while most men acquire crafts and the most accurate forms of knowledge by painful exertion. Consequently, painful exertion is not by nature and unconditionally something worth avoiding. 98. Moreover, even what seems to be pleasant is not by nature and unconditionally worth choosing; at any rate, things which on their first contact put us in a pleasurable disposition are subsequently thought to be unpleasant, though they are the same things; [it is] as though what is pleasant were not like that by nature, but rather affected us differently at different times, in virtue of different circumstances.

Sextus *M* 11.160–166   [III-51]

160. . . . Therefore, he who suspends judgement about everything which is subject to opinion reaps a harvest of the most complete happiness; 161. he is, [to be sure,] disturbed when in the midst of involuntary and non-rational movements—"for he is not born of ancient oak or stone, but comes from the race of men"[51]—but is in a disposition [characterized] by moderation of his states [passions]. 162. Hence, he must despise those

---

50. A quotation from Empedocles, B 112, adapted.

51. Homer *Odyssey* 19.163; the last clause is Sextus' addition.

who think that he is enmeshed in inactivity or inconsistency. **163.** [They think that he will be enmeshed] in inactivity because, since all of life consists in choice and avoidance, he who neither chooses anything nor avoids anything implicitly denies life and would be suspending judgement in the manner of some plant; **164.** and in inconsistency because, if he is ever in a tyrant's power and is compelled to do something unspeakable, either he will not submit to the command but will rather choose voluntary death, or he will avoid the torture chamber by doing what he is ordered to do. And so he will no longer be, in Timon's words, "free of choice and avoidance", but will choose some things and steer clear of others— and that is the act of people who grasp with conviction that there is something which is worth choosing and something worth avoiding.

165. In saying this they do not understand that the sceptic does not live in accordance with a philosophical theory (for he is indeed inactive as far as concerns that) and that he is able to choose some things and avoid others in accordance with unphilosophical observations. **166.** And if he is compelled to do something forbidden, he will perhaps choose one thing and avoid another by [following] the basic grasp which accords with his ancestral customs and habits. And he will bear hardship more easily than the man who bases [his life] on dogmas, since unlike that fellow he has no additional opinions beyond [the hardship itself].

Glossary

We trust the reader to find compound words and negations by looking under the main root. For example, the explanation for the term 'ungraspable' is found by reading the entry on 'grasp'.

abolish (*anairein*):   to show by argument that something is untrue or non-existent; the use of the word does not necessarily indicate that the author regards the argument as successful; also, undermine, deny.

accident (*sumbebekos*):   Accidents can include permanent attributes of a thing; the technical meaning of the term is very broad.

added opinion (*prosdoxazomenon*):   in Epicureanism, the opinion about something which people regularly add to the bare facts as they are observed by the senses.

administered (*dioikeisthai*):   ordered and guided by a rational power.

ailment (*arrostema*):   in Stoicism, a sickness in the soul, a moral and intellectual weakness founded on error.

alive, animate (*empsuchos*):   Etymologically the term means 'having a soul within', 'ensouled'.

alteration (*alloiosis, heteroiosis*):   used particularly for qualitative change.

application (*epibole*):   in Epicureanism, the attention by the mind to perceptual or non-perceptual images; it is the basis of perception, thought and mental concentration. Hence, the term is sometimes used to refer to a view or consideration of something. Application to presentations (*phantastike epibole*) is the attention of the intellect to presentations received through the senses.

approach (*agoge*):   'Approach' is a term used by Pyrrhonian sceptics to indicate their method and technique; it is meant to indicate that the Pyrrhonian sceptic's stance is one which involves no commitments or beliefs. In other contexts the term *agoge* simply indicates a philosophical school, which is also a meaning of the word *hairesis*.

appropriate (acts) (*kathekonta*):   in Stoicism, actions which are reasonable for an agent to perform in view of his nature and the circumstances. An appropriate action can be performed by anyone, but only a wise man can perform a [morally] perfect action, which is a form of appropriate action.

assent (*sunkatathesis*):   agreeing or committing oneself to the truth of a proposition.

atom, atomic (*atomos*):   literally means 'uncuttable'.

avoid (*ekklinein*):   In Stoicism, avoidance refers to something which is rejected or contrary to nature.

bad (*kakon*):   in Stoicism, morally bad.

base (*phaulos*):   in Stoicism, the standard term for foolish and therefore non-virtuous people.

beautiful (*kalon*):   The same term is usually translated 'honourable' (q.v.).

benefit (*opheleia*):   In Stoicism, benefit is narrowly defined in terms of the attainment or preservation of a virtuous state.

canon (*kanon*):   standard of judgement; reference point for decision; criterion.

cause (*aition*):   usually in a narrower sense than that which applies to the four Aristotelian causes (or forms of causal explanation). In Hellenistic thought the term cause indicates the active principle which brings about some other event, object or state of affairs; closer to the familiar modern concept of cause than Aristotle's notion. Often equivalent to Aristotle's efficient cause.

caution (*eulabeia*):   in Stoicism, the rational and correct avoidance of something bad; the virtuous counterpart of fear, which is a passion.

choice (*hairesis*), choose (*hairesthai*):   rational or deliberative desire; in Stoicism, rational desire for the good. Hence, what is to be chosen (*haireteon*); worth choosing (*haireton*).

clarity, clear (fact) (*enargeia, enargema*):   an originally Epicurean term for a presentation (q.v.) obtained directly by the senses or the intellect without interpretive additions. Also, self-evidence.

commit oneself to (*diabebaioo*):   The sceptics believe that the disposition to commit oneself to the truth of anything non-evident is logically unjustifiable. Also, make firm (or definite) assertions. Cf. *bebaioo*.

complete (*teleios*):   also, perfect.

condition (*hexis*):   in Stoicism, a state or alteration of the *pneuma* which constitutes something; hence, a quality or (non-permanent) attribute of something.

condition, stable condition (*katastasis, katastema*):   In Epicureanism katastematic pleasures are those which do not consist in the removal of a pain.

confirm (*bebaioo*):   to provide conclusive confirmation of a theory. A central sceptical strategy is to show that the absence of conclusive confirmation is equivalent to no confirmation at all. Also, establish, affirm, support.

confirmation, what awaits (*to prosmenon*):   in Epicureanism, something which is not completely or permanently non-evident, but which requires further observation under more favourable circumstances in order that the truth about it should become evident.

conflagration (*ekpurosis*):   in Stoic physics, the periodic dissolution of the universe in flames.

congenial, etc. (*oikeios*):   something which is compatible with or promotes the health, well-being, constitution or interests of an animal; opposite: congenial (*allotrios*). Congeniality (*oikeiosis*) is the objective relationship between an animal and things which are congenial to it, not a subjective disposition or attitude.

constitution (*status, sustasis*):   the basic structure and characteristics of a thing which make it what it is.

cosmos, pl. cosmoi (*kosmos*):   world; the organized and structured portion of the universe.

daimon: a supernatural power; the term often includes gods, but is not limited to them.

demonstration (*apodeixis*):   a technical term for a formal argument in syllogistic form which reveals something non-evident.

desire (*epithumia*): irrational striving, one of the four passions in Stoicism. Desire (*orexis*) is also used in a more general sense.

differentiated thing (*to kata diaphoran*): something which exists and can be known all on its own, something non-relative; it is distinct (differentiated) from other things.

disagreement (*diaphonia*): conflict or inconsistency between objects, theories or hypotheses.

discern: see judge.

discover (*heurisko*): to reach a successful outcome in an investigation (*zetesis*).

disease (*nosema*): in Stoicism, a sickness of the soul.

disjunction, disjunctive (*diazeugmenon*): In Stoic logic, the term refers to exclusive disjunction.

disposition (*diathesis*): In Stoicism the term has a special sense: a firm and unchangeable condition (*hexis*).

disposition (*pos echon*): in Stoic category theory, a thing in a certain state.

disvalue (*apaxia*): in Stoicism, negative value; the property of being disadvantageous or contrary to one's health, well-being, moral progress, etc.

dogma (*dogma*): Owing to sceptical attacks, this term has come to be used in a pejorative sense. In a non-polemical context, however, it is simply the content of a belief. Also, doctrine, belief.

doubt (*aporia*): an argument or state of mind which prevents understanding; also, puzzlement, impasse, problem. Hence, dubitative (*aporetike*).

effluence (*aporrhoia*): in Epicureanism, a film of atoms generated by a solid object, which strikes the sensory apparatus and so is responsible for sense-perception and thought.

element (*stoicheion*): one of the basic forms of matter, earth, air, fire, water.

equal force (*isostheneia*): The equal force (or persuasiveness) of opposing arguments is responsible for the Pyrrhonian sceptic's suspension of belief and freedom from dogma.

equilibrium (*arrepsia*): the state of being poised between two equally plausible beliefs; epistemic neutrality; the key to Pyrrhonian peace of mind.

essence (*logos*): *Logos* usually refers to the statement of the essence, but is sometimes used of the essence itself; rational principle.

fact, object (*pragma*): generally, a thing. The term is extended in Stoicism to include *lekta* (things said) and states of affairs.

fate (*heimarmene*): Stoic term for the causal connections in nature.

feeling (*peisis*): in scepticism, a passive state; the closest thing to a sceptical criterion. See also state.

freedom from disturbance (*ataraxia*): In Epicureanism and Scepticism, disturbance (*tarache*) either in the body or in the soul, is the cause of unhappiness. Freedom from it constitutes happiness, the highest human goal.

freedom from passion (*apatheia*): in Stoicism, absence of or freedom from the irrational passions of the soul, viz. pleasure, pain, fear and desire.

fresh (*prosphaton*): in Stoicism, stimulative of irrational contraction or elation.

goal (*telos*): the final aim or purpose of a thing, particularly of a human life. Greek philosophers hold that happiness (q.v.) is the goal of life.

good state [of the soul] (*eupatheia*):   in Stoicism, a virtuous reaction by the soul; good states are joy, caution, and wish, which correspond to the passions pleasure, fear, and desire. The fourth passion, pain, has no rational counterpart since the wise man is not pained (in his soul) by anything which happens in the rational universe.

grasp: A family of terms (nouns and verbs) built on the Greek root which means literal grasping with one's hand. *antilambano* and its congeners are the most general in meaning, and are used by all schools in the Hellenistic period for an intellectual or perceptual awareness of something real. The verb *dialambano* has the sense of distinguishing clearly between things, grasping the distinctions among things. *katalambano* and its congeners (*katalepsis, katalepton, kataleptikon*— graspable) are used specifically in Stoicism to indicate the firm and unshakable grasp of truths or real objects which is the foundation for all other knowledge. A comprehensive grasp (*perilambano, perilepsis*) is, in Epicureanism, a complete grasp of all the aspects or parts of something. There are two distinct categories of things not subject to such a grasp: those which are indefinitely large or complex (though not infinite), and *a fortiori*, the infinite. A basic grasp (*prolepsis*) is, in Epicureanism, a fundamental concept which is virtually a given of experience, being derived (originally unconsciously) from many experiences of the same object. Thus a basic grasp functions importantly as a criterion for Epicurean scientific method.

happiness (*eudaimonia*):   the state of a human being in which it is in the best possible condition relative to its nature; flourishing. It is not a subjective state of personal contentment, but an objective fact about the condition of the human being.

harm (*blapto, blamma*):   in Stoicism, restricted to moral harm, things which hinder the life according to virtue.

honourable (*honestum, kalon*):   in Stoicism, morally good. The Stoic doctrine is that only what is honourable is really good; all other kinds of value are 'good' in the sense of being preferred (q.v.).

hormetic (*hormetikon*):   of or concerned with an impulse (*horme*), as a hormetic condition, the disposition to have a certain impulse.

image (*eidolon*):   in Epicureanism, the effluence emitted by an object which preserves a representation of its shape and features.

impulse (*horme*):   the action of the soul in setting the agent in action, usually to get or avoid something. In a rational agent it is always the result of an act of assent, either conscious or implicit.

inaction (*apraxia*):   the state of not being able to act. The Stoics maintained that if, following the sceptics, one made no judgements, it would be impossible to do anything at all, since actions required assent and judgement. The argument from inaction was held to be a pragmatic refutation of scepticism, since it is manifest that people do act.

indicative (*endeiktikon*):   of signs, revealing to us something not previously perceived.

indifference, indifferent (*adiaphoria, adiaphoron*):   An indifferent thing, in Stoic ethics, is something which does not contribute to happiness or unhappiness;

in another sense it is what makes no difference at all in ethics, absolute indifference.

individual quality (*idios poion*): the particular quality which makes an individual thing exactly what is; thus Socrates is Socrates in virtue of his individual quality, but is a man in virtue of his common quality.

infinite (*apeiron*): having no limit; also translated 'unlimited'.

intellect (*dianoia*): cognitive activity which is not limited to the activities of one or more of the five senses; the faculty which governs this activity.

intercosmos (*metakosmion*): in Epicureanism, the spaces between the various cosmoi in the universe.

internal (*endiathetos*): in Stoicism, internal reason is the (capacity for) thought or mental discourse. Opposite: verbalized reason, i.e., speech.

investigate, investigation (*zeteo, zetesis*): inquiry into something non-evident.

joy (*chara*): In Stoicism this is the rational and morally correct form of pleasure which only the wise man can have.

judge (*krinein*): also, decide; to arrive at a conclusion or a belief by means of a criterion; the Sceptics believe that there is no criterion on the basis of which one is justified in judging one way or another in non-evident matters. Hence, discern (*epikrino*); discern between *diakrinein*; indiscernible (*adiakritos*). Also, prefer (*prokrino*): in Pyrrhonian scepticism, to give credence to one side of an opposition over the other.

knowledge (*episteme*): a cognitive state which cannot be false and which does not change.

lack of self-control (*akrasia*): the inability to control desires deemed undesirable or irrational.

leading part of the soul (*hegemonikon*): in Stoicism, the dominant and controlling part of the soul. In an adult human it is totally rational. All the other parts and functions of the soul operate as ancillary to the leading part of the soul. It is almost the equivalent of the term 'mind' (*nous*).

living and breathing (*empnous*): endowed with soul and breath (*pneuma*).

mode (*tropos*): in scepticism, a dialectical move, or type of argument.

moral choice (*prohairesis*): in the work of the Stoic Epictetus, moral choice is something more than a decision. It is the moral personality of the agent, virtually the same thing as the leading part of the soul (*hegemonikon*). [moral] mistake, [moral] error (*hamartema*): Stoic term for a disposition to act other than according to reason, or the action itself. All actions, except those of wise men, were held by the Stoics to be moral errors.

[moral] progress (*prokope*): in Stoic ethics, development towards a fully rational and virtuous life; someone making moral progress is still considered to be vicious.

[morally] perfect action (*katorthoma*): an appropriate action which is perfect and (by definition) guaranteed to be correct. Only the virtuous wise man can perform such an action, and all of his actions are like this.

natural things (*ta kata phusin*): things which promote or preserve the basic nature of an organism.

nature (*phusis*):   The meaning of the term is just as wide in Hellenistic thought as it is in Greek philosophy generally. It can refer to nature in general, to the specific nature of one object, or to one particular object or kind of object; it might in places also be translated 'entity', as in the Epicurean definition of void as an intangible nature.

no more (this than that) (*ou mallon*):   literally, no more. The slogan of the Pyrrhonian sceptics, which means that things no more seem one way than the opposite way.

non-evident (*adelon*):   not subject to direct observation; unclear; unobservable.

non-[representational] image (*apemphasis*):   Academic term for an impression which is unconvincing or improbable.

opinion (*doxa*):   a cognitive state distinct from a more rigorous form of cognition (knowledge) which does not permit of falsity.

organization (*diakosmesis*):   the basic, rational ordering of the cosmos.

outline [definition] (*hupographe*):   a rough sketch of the meaning of a term, which falls short of the precision of a true definition.

passion (*pathos*):   in Stoic ethics, a vicious state or motion in the soul. The four passions are pleasure, pain, fear, and desire.

perceive (*percipere*):   sometimes used, esp. in Cicero, in the sense of a firm and true perception, i.e., a grasp.

perfect (*teleios*):   also, complete.

pneuma: generally, breath or wind, as it is translated in Epicurean texts. In Stoic texts it is not translated, and designates a special material compound which is fundamental to Stoic physics, being a breathlike compound of fire and air (or the fiery and the airy). God, soul, and conditions (*hexeis*) are all forms of *pneuma*. The specific substance of each thing is determined by its inborn *pneuma*.

predisposition (*euemptosia*):   in Stoic ethics, a tendency to have a passion.

prefer: see judge.

preferred (*proegmenon*):   In Stoicism, an indifferent thing (q.v.) which has value for the life according to nature is said to be preferred.

presentation (*phantasia*):   an intentional state of the soul, ultimately caused by an external object or state of affairs, which by itself indicates both itself and its cause.

principle (*arche*):   the starting point for an argument or theory; may be a definition, axiom, etc. In Stoic physics the two basic principles are god (active) and prime matter (passive).

proposition (*axioma*):   a statement with truth value. In Stoicism, an *axioma* is a form of 'thing said' (q.v.).

providence (*pronoia*):   in Stoicism, equivalent to the rational, causal order of nature.

prudence (*phronesis*):   the highest rational virtue; the flawless use of reason to guide life and so produce happiness.

reason (*logos*):   also, statement, argumentative procedure, argument, theory, rational discourse, account, rational principle. Hence, 'which reason can contemplate' (*logoi theoreton*): not amenable to sense-perception; graspable only by the reason or rational inference. Such things are not necessarily incorporeal, since there are (at least in Epicureanism and Stoicism) material entities which cannot be directly perceived. See also essence.

rejected (*apoproegmenon*): In Stoicism, an indifferent thing (q.v.) which has disvalue for the life according to nature is said to be rejected.

rejection (*apekloge*): in Stoicism, the decision to avoid or flee from something which has disvalue or is contrary to nature.

reminiscent (*hupomnestikon*): of signs, reminding us of something we have already perceived or known.

[representational] image (*emphasis*): an Academic term for an impression which is implicitly plausible.

resistance (*antikope, antikopsis*): physical resistance, which only a body is capable of providing.

right reason (*orthos logos*): a term in ethics indicating correct use of reason in matching up means and ends; in Stoicism, right reason is one of the descriptions of god.

seed (*sperma*): often used in an extended sense for any generative principle.

selection (*ekloge*): in Stoicism, the choice of something which is preferred or according to nature; rational choice of something which is not morally good.

self-control (*enkrateia*): the ability to control desires deemed undesirable or irrational.

self-evident (*prodelos*): something evident which does not depend on something else for its truth or knowability.

self-sufficiency (*autarkeia*): autonomy, the state of not needing anything external; virtue is said to be self-sufficient for happiness by the Stoics, since they hold that the virtuous man is happy no matter what external circumstances he is in. Self-sufficiency in some sense is a goal in most of Greek ethics.

sense-perception (*aisthesis*): occasionally also 'sense', 'sense-organ'.

sensible (*aistheton*): the direct object of one of the five senses.

shame(ful) (*aischron, aischune, aischos*): In Stoic ethics in particular, this term indicates the opposite of what is honourable.

sorites (*sorites*): an argument formed of a complex of linked syllogisms; for an example see C 41, 182–183.

sound (*hugies*): of conditional inferences, one which does not infer from a truth to a falsehood.

spermatic principle (*spermatikos logos*): in Stoicism, the organic bearer of the rational principle of the universe or its contents.

state (*pathos*): also, condition, experience, feeling, modification. See also passion.

state (*polis*): the basic political entity in the Greek world.

subsist (*huphistasthai*): In Stoicism the term indicates the dependent mode of existence which characterizes incorporeals, such as things said.

substance (*hupokeimenon*): also, *hupostasis, ousia*; genuine entity or real thing. In Stoic category theory, it is an underlying primary object and always corporeal.

supervene (*epigignesthai*): to exist or occur as temporally or logically subsequent to something else, on which it is dependent.

suspension of judgement (*epoche*): a mental state or act characterized by an absence of commitment to or belief in dogmatic conclusions.

symmetry (*summetria*): balance and harmony; frequently used by Chrysippus and other Stoics in an extended sense. **sympathy** (*sumpnoia*): in Stoic physics, the state of sharing the same *pneuma* with something, being organically bound up with it.

system (*hairesis*): also doctrine; a connected set of beliefs and theories; also, the school defined by adherence to such a set of beliefs.

testify for/against (*epimarturein, antimarturein*): in Epicureanism, to provide evidence for or against something which is not immediately evident. 'Testify' by itself translates *marturein*.

thing said (*lekton*): the content of propositions and meaningful phrases mediating between the words used and the objects or states of affairs denoted by them.

unaffected, impassible (*apathes*): not subject to change or alteration.

uncongenial (*allotrios*): something which is incompatible with or opposes the health, well-being or interests of an animal; opposite: congenial (*oikeios*).

uncontroverted (*aperispastos*): an Academic term for an impression against which there is no counter-evidence.

undecidable (*anepikritos*): something which cannot be settled because of its intrinsic obscurity or the equally balanced arguments for and against it.

undogmatically (*adoxastos*): free of opinions; without opinions or intellectual commitments; Pyrrhonian sceptics use the term to indicate the manner in which they give provisional approval to views without committing themselves to the truth of claims about what is non-evident (q.v.).

unnatural things (*ta para phusin*): things which impede or oppose the basic nature of an organism.

unqualified substance (*apoios ousia*): prime matter; the passive principle in Stoic physics; material stuff with no qualities; unqualified substance must be shaped by rational principles before it can have qualities; it is prior to the four elements, which are modifications of it.

value (*axia*): in Stoicism, morally significant worth. There are two kinds of value, moral value which is co-extensive with virtue and suffices to produce a happy life, and so-called 'natural' value which contributes to a life according to the specific nature of the species in question. Health has natural value but no moral value.

vice (*kakia*): moral badness.

virtue (*arete*): excellence of soul, in particular moral excellence, but also including intellectual and other excellences. In Stoicism, the only virtuous man (*asteios, spoudaios*) is the wise man.

void (*kenon*): containing nothing; having nothing real corresponding to it. Also, groundless. In Epicurean and Stoic physics, the void is incorporeal.

way of life (*bios*): a broad term for a pattern of activity over an entire life.

wish (*boulesis*): fully rational desire.

yielding (*eixis*): in Epicureanism, the property of the void by which it does not resist an atom; in Stoicism, the concession of the mind [usually an animal's] to some presentation, without rational assent.

Philosophers and
Philosophical Sources

Aenesidemus: *first century* B.C.; former Academic who revived Pyrrhonism.
Aetius: probably first century A.D.; eclectic philosopher and doxographer.
Agrippa: sceptical philosopher active after Aenesidemus and before Sextus.
Alexander of Aphrodisias: late second to early third centuries A.D.; Peripatetic philosopher and scholar.
Anaxagoras of Clazomenae: fifth century B.C.; pluralist philosopher.
Anaxarchus of Abdera: fourth century B.C.; follower of Democritus and teacher of Pyrrho.
Antiochus of Ascalon: ca. 130/120–? B.C.; pupil of Philo of Larissa and initiator of a fully dogmatic and eclectic form of Academic philosophy.
Antipater of Tarsus: second century B.C.; successor to Diogenes of Babylon as head of the Stoic school and teacher of Panaetius.
Antipater of Tyre: first century B.C.; Stoic philosopher.
Aratus of Soli: Stoic poet of the 3rd C. B.C.; author of the *Phaenomena*.
Arcesilaus: 316/315–242/241 B.C.; head of the Academy in the mid third century and originator of its sceptical turn.
Archedemus of Tarsus: Stoic philosopher, probably a pupil of Diogenes of Babylon.
Archelaus: fifth century B.C.; pupil of Anaxagoras and teacher of Socrates.
Aristippus of Cyrene: late fifth century B.C.; acquaintance of Socrates and hedonist. The Cyrenaic school was founded by his grandson of the same name.
Aristocles of Messene: Peripatetic philosopher of the 1st or 2nd C. A.D.
Ariston of Chios: mid third century B.C.; Stoic follower of Zeno of Citium and founder of an independent branch of the Stoic school.
Aristotle: 389–322 B.C.; founder of the Peripatetic school and pupil of Plato.
Augustine of Hippo, Saint: 354–430 A.D.; Christian philosopher and theologian.
Bion: ca. 325–255 B.C.; eclectic philosopher and wandering teacher; he affected a Cynic lifestyle.
Boethus of Sidon: second century B.C.; pupil of Diogenes of Babylon and unorthodox Stoic.
Carneades: 214/213–129/128 B.C.; most famous head of the sceptical Academy.
Charmidas: late second century B.C.; pupil of Carneades.
Chrysippus of Soli: ca. 280–207 B.C.; successor of Cleanthes as head of the Stoic school.
Cicero: 106–43 B.C.; Roman statesman, orator, and philosopher; he considered himself an Academic, but strong eclectic tendencies are evident in his work.

Cleanthes of Assos: 331–232 B.C.; pupil of Zeno and his successor as head of the Stoic school (263–232).

Clitomachus: 187/186–110/109 B.C.; successor to Carneades as head of the Academy.

Colotes of Lampsacus: fourth–third centuries B.C.; pupil and devotee of Epicurus.

Crantor: ca. 335–275 B.C.; pupil of Xenocrates and Academic philosopher.

Crates of Thebes: 365–285 B.C.; Cynic philosopher, follower of Diogenes of Sinope.

Critias: Athenian aristocrat and intellectual of the late 5th C. B.C.

Demetrius of Laconia: Epicurean philosopher active around 100 B.C.

Democritus of Abdera: ca. 470/457–ca. 360 B.C.; along with Leucippus the founder of atomism.

Diagoras of Melos: poet of the late 5th C. B.C., famous for his atheism.

Diodorus Cronus: ca. 300 B.C.; founder of the Megarian dialectical school. Zeno of Citium and Arcesilaus were among his pupils.

Diogenes of Babylon: ca. 240–152 B.C.; pupil of Chrysippus and successor Zeno of Tarsus as head of the Stoic school.

Diogenes of Sinope: ca. 400–ca. 325; founder of the Cynic school.

Diogenes of Tarsus: Epicurean philosopher of uncertain date.

Dionysius of Heraclea: ca. 328–248 B.C.; follower of Zeno of Citium who later converted to hedonism.

Empedocles of Acragas: fifth century B.C.; pluralist philosopher.

Epictetus: 55 A.D. to ca. 135; Stoic philosopher active in Rome as well as Greece.

Epicurus: 341–270 B.C.; founder of the Epicurean school.

Evander: second century B.C.; a head of the sceptical Academy.

Euboulides of Miletus: mid-fourth century B.C. dialectician, with links to the Megarian school.

Galen of Pergamum: second century A.D.; physician and Platonic philosopher.

Gorgias of Leontini: fifth century B.C.; sophist and rhetorician.

Hegesinus: second century B.C.; a head of the sceptical Academy.

Heraclitus of Ephesus: ca. 500 B.C.; Ionian philosopher.

Herillus of Carthage: third century B.C.; pupil of Zeno of Citium and founder of an independent school.

Hieronymus of Rhodes: ca. 290–230 B.C.; trained in the Peripatetic school, he later left to found his own school.

Idomeneus of Lampsacus: c. 325–270 B.C.; a friend of Epicurus with Peripatetic sympathies.

Lacydes: ?–206/205 B.C.; successor to Arcesilaus as head of the sceptical Academy.

Leucippus: fifth century; with Democritus, the co-founder of atomism.

Lucretius: first century B.C.; Roman poet and Epicurean.

Melissus of Samos: mid fifth century B.C.; pupil of Parmenides and naval commander.

Menodotus of Nicomedia: ca. 120 A.D.; Pyrrhonist philosopher and empirical physician.

Metrodorus of Lampsacus: 331/330–278/277; Epicurean philosopher.

Metrodorus of Stratonicea: Academic philosopher; former Epicurean and then student of Carneades.

Nausiphanes: fourth century B.C.; an atomist; student of Pyrrho and teacher of Epicurus.

Numenius of Apamea: second century A.D.; Neopythagorean and Platonist philosopher.

Panaetius: ca. 185–109 B.C.; founder of middle Stoicism.

Parmenides of Elea: early fifth century B.C.; founder of the Eleatic school.

Persaeus of Citium: ca. 306–ca. 243 B.C.; Stoic and pupil of Zeno of Citium.

Philo of Alexandria: ca. 25 B.C.–ca. 50 A.D.; eclectic Jewish philosopher of mostly Platonic leanings.

Philo the Dialectician: a logician of the late fourth and early third centuries B.C., student of Diodorus Cronus.

Philo of Larissa: first century B.C.; successor to Clitomachus as head of the Academy; initiator of the return to a somewhat more dogmatic form of philosophy.

Philodemus: ca. 110–40/35 B.C.; Epicurean philosopher.

Plato: 427–347 B.C.; founder of the Academy and pupil of Socrates.

Plotinus: 204–270 A.D.; founder of Neoplatonism.

Plutarch: 46–after 120 A.D.; Academic philosopher and biographer.

Polemo: ?–270 B.C.; head of the Academy after Xenocrates.

Polyaenus of Lampsacus: died before 271 B.C.; one of Epicurus' earliest followers.

Porphyry: third century A.D.; pupil of Plotinus and Platonic philosopher.

Posidonius: ca. 135–ca. 50 B.C.; middle Stoic, pupil of Panaetius.

Praxiphanes: third century; pupil of Theophrastus.

Proclus: ca. 410–485 A.D.; last head of the Academy.

Prodicus of Ceos: fifth century B.C.; sophist and contemporary of Socrates.

Protagoras of Abdera: ca. 450 B.C.; most famous of the sophists.

Ptolemy of Cyrene: a sceptical philosopher, active ca. 100 B.C.

Pyrrho: 365/360–275/270 B.C.; founder of Greek scepticism.

Pythagoras of Samos: sixth century B.C.; mathematical and religious philosopher.

Pythocles: an early follower of Epicurus.

Seneca: ca. 55 B.C.–37/41 A.D.; Roman politician, playwright, and Stoic philosopher.

Sextus Empiricus: ca. 200 A.D.; physician and sceptic, major source for ancient scepticism.

Simplicius: sixth century A.D.; Peripatetic scholar and philosopher.

Socrates: 469–399 B.C.; the teacher of Plato.

Sphaerus of Borysthenes: ca. 285/265–ca 221 B.C.; pupil of Zeno of Citium and then of Cleanthes.

Stilpo: ca. 380–300 B.C.; third head of the Megarian school.

Stobaeus: late fourth to early fifth centuries A.D.; excerpter and anthologist.

Strato of Lampsacus: head of the Peripatetic school after Theophrastus; died 269 B.C.

Theophrastus: ca. 370–288/285 B.C.; successor to Aristotle as head of the Peripatos; a major philosopher in his own right.

Timon of Phlius: ca. 320–ca. 230 B.C.; poet and philosopher; follower of Pyrrho.

Xenophanes of Colophon: late sixth century B.C.; Ionian philosopher.

Zeno of Citium: 335–263; founder of the Stoic school.

Zeno of Sidon: Stoic pupil of Zeno of Citium and also of Diodorus Cronus.

Zeno of Tarsus: Stoic philosopher and successor to Chrysippus as head of the School in 204 B.C.

Index of
Passages Translated

411

Index

abolish: III-22.90, 92, 94, 104.
accidental properties: see properties.
actions: I-34; II-27.
Aenesidemus: III-22.62, 78, 87, 102, 106, 107; III-23.116; III-24; III-25; III-27.210, 222; III-37.180; III-45.218; III-47.138.
agency: I-34.
Agrippa: III-22.88.
ailment: see disease.
air: I-2.73 (n.9); I-92.3; II-20.136–137; II-23.17–18, 26–27, 42–43; II-71; see also element.
aither: II-20.137, 139; II-23.117.
altruism: I-1.9–10; I-6.44; I-122; I-123; I-157; see also friendship.
ambiguity: II-3.62.
analogy: I-2.40; I-3.102; I-7.32; I-16.49; II-3.52–53; II-10.57; III-35.147; III-37.182.
Anaxagoras: I-1.12; II-85; III-19.44; III-20.100; III-26.33.
Anaxarchus: I-39; III-22.63.
anger: II-95.10b,c; II-119; III-22.66, 68.
Antiochus: II-6.144; II-100.16; III-4.739c,d; III-9.67; III-11.97–98; III-18.162; III-20.98, 102.
Antipater of Tarsus: II-3.54, 55, 57, 60, 68; II-20.139, 140, 142, 148, 150, 157; II-76.2; II-94.84, 92, 121; II-95.6a, 7f; III-3.64; III-4.738c; III-6.
Apollodorus of Seleucia: II-2.39, 41; II-3.54, 64; II-20.135, 142, 150, 157; II-94.84, 102, 118, 121, 125, 129.
appearance: I-2.51, 55; I-18; III-

22.92, 106; III-26.9, 17, 19; III-27.218, 219, 233; III-35.93, 94, 135; III-36.167; III-39.88–94; III-46.78; as criterion: III-22.106–107; III-26.22; and signs: III-25.170b; III-35.138; III-40.124–129; vs. reality: III-22.103, 105, 106; III-35.140, 144; III-37.181, 182; conflicting: III-26.8, 22, 29, 31–33; III-27.210, 214; III-35.118, 121, 129; see also presentation, clear (facts).
application (of the mind to images): I-2.35, 36, 50(n.6), 51, 62, 69, 70, 83; I-5.XXIV; I-7.31; I-71; I-80; I-136; see also reason/intellect/thought, grasp (basic).
approach, sceptical: II-1.42; III-25.170b; III-26; III-27.222, 232, 235, 241.
appropriate act: II-1.171; II-94.88, 93, 107–110; II-95.5b2,b3, 6a, 7b, 8, 11a,m; II-97; II-102.20–22; named by Zeno: II-1.25; II-94.108; see also virtue.
Arcesilaus: I-17.70; II-1.162, 171, 183; III-1; III-2; III-4.736d, 737b–d; III-8.59; III-9.67; III-10.77; III-16; III-17; III-18.150–158; III-19; III-23.114, 115; III-27.220, 232.
Archedemus: II-2.40; II-3.55, 68; II-20.134, 136; II-31; II-94.84, 88; II-95.6a; II-107.1.
Archelaus: I-1.12.
archer (example): II-95.5b5; II-102.22; see also craft (of life).
argument: II-1.20; II-3.43–47, 76–82; II-17; III-41; indemonstrable:

419

95.8a, 11a,d-o; II-102.32; II-
114.1037cd; III-8.59; III-18.157;
see also virtue.
moral progress: II-94.91, 106–
107, 127; II-97; see also virtue.
morally perfect action: II-95.8,
8a, 11a,e,o; II-114.1037cd; III-
18.158; see also virtue, moral
mistake.
motion: I-2.46, 62–63; I-3.88;
I-28; I-37; I-81; I-86; I-89.219,
224; I-96.3; II-25–II-27; III-
22.90, 99, 105; III-25.170b; III-
46; III-47.136, 137, 140; see also
void, atoms.
motivation: see impulse, assent,
criterion (of choice).
myths: I-2.81; I-3.87, 104, 115,
116; II-24.9, 12–16; III-35.145,
147; III-43.66–71.

names, naming: I-2.75–76; I-7.33;
I-102; I-103; see also words.
natural science: see physics.
nature: II-20.148, 149, 156; II-
23.57–58, 81–83, 115; II-25; II-26;
II-71; II-78; II-81; II-94.87–89; II-
95.5b3,b5, 6–6a,e; II-107.5–24; II-
110.14; II-112; III-25.170b; III-
26.23–24; III-35.98; III-48.179,
190–193; see also god, cosmos.
Nausiphanes: I-1.13, 14; III-22.64,
102.
necessity and possibility:
I-4.133, 134; I-6.9, 40; I-17; I-28;
I-34; I-110; I-148 II-76; II-78;
II-83; II-89.5–15; II-90.39, 41–
42; II-91; II-93.5–6; II-107.7;
III-12.1122d; see also fate, cause.
no more (this than that): I-17;
I-29.1109a-e, 1110e; III-22.61,
74–76, 81; III-25.169b, 170a; III-
26.14; III-27.213; III-43.50; III-
44.29; III-46.65; III-50.133.

non-evident (facts): I-2.38–39, 80;
III-4.736d; III-22.91, 103–105;
III-26.13–14, 16, 20; III-27.210,
219, 225, 236–237; III-31.7–9;
III-33.197, 198, 201, 208; III-
35.94; III-39.87; III-40.97–99;
III-41.135, 140–143, 159; and relativity: III-35.138; and criterion:
III-39.88, 90–93, 95; appearance
a sign of: III-25.170b; III-35.138;
III-40.124, 129; III-46.78; lekton
is III-40.107, 116; sign is: III-
40.124–129; god is: III-42.6–9;
see also confirmation (awaiting);
clear (facts), appearance.

old age: I-4.122, 126; I-6.17, 19,
48, 75, 76; II-94.98; II-95.5m,
11q; see also youth, death.
ontology: II-32–II-63.
opinion: I-4.133; I-5.XXIV; I-6.29;
I-7.33–34; I-29.1121e; I-43;
I-68.203, 210–215; I-69; I-70.63;
II-1.23, 177; II-4.41, 42; II-
94.121; II-95.10, 10e, 11m; II-
105; II-119; III-12.1122c,d,f; III-
24; deceptive: I-2.50, 51, 62;
I-5.XV, XXII, XXIX, XXX;
I-6.59; I-34; I-68.209; I-119;
I-135; and the wise man: III-
8.59; III-9.66–67; III-10.77–78;
III-13; III-15; III-18.151–153,
156–157; added opinion (in
scepticism): III-51.166; see also
knowledge, wisdom/wise man.
outline (definition): I-2.35, 36,
68; I-7.33; I-16.45; I-17.76; I-31;
I-67; II-3.60; see grasp (basic),
concept/conception, definition.

pain: in Epicureanism: I-40; I-44;
I-68.203; as bad; I-5.X; I-6.37;
I-21.29–31; I-128; as negative
goal: I-4.128, 131; I-5.XXI;